Marie-Pierre Le Hir
The National Habitus

Culture & Conflict

—

Edited by
Isabel Capeloa Gil and Catherine Nesci

Volume 4

Marie-Pierre Le Hir

The National Habitus

Ways of Feeling French, 1789–1870

DE GRUYTER

ISBN 978-3-11-055923-1
e-ISBN 978-3-11-036306-7
ISSN 2194-7104

Library of Congress Cataloging-in-Publication Data
A CIP catalog record for this book has been applied for at the Library of Congress.

Bibliographic information published by the Deutsche Nationalbibliothek
The Deutsche Nationalbibliothek lists this publication in the Deutsche Nationalbibliografie;
detailed bibliographic data are available on the Internet at http://dnb.dnb.de.

© 2017 Walter de Gruyter GmbH, Berlin/Boston
This volume is text- and page-identical with the hardback published in 2014.
Cover image: Jean-Baptiste Mallet (engraver) and François Marie Beaurain (artist): „L'Amour
de la patrie". Bibliothèque nationale de France, département Estampes et photographie.
Printing and binding: CPI books GmbH, Leck

♾ Printed on acid-free paper
Printed in Germany

www.degruyter.com

Acknowledgments

Year after year, this project evolved as I presented it bit by bit at the Nineteenth-Century French Studies Colloquium. My gratitude goes to friends and colleagues, past and present, who have contributed to making this annual event the vibrant, intellectually stimulating, and collegial gathering it is today. A Fall 2012 sabbatical provided the time needed to write this book, for which I thank to College of Humanities at the University of Arizona. I am particularly indebted to colleagues who generously agreed to read chapters of the manuscript and who provided incisive critiques and helpful advice: Corry Cropper, Isabelle Naginski, Dominique Rincé, Gisèle Séginger, Charles Stivale, and Lynn Wilkerson. Catherine Nesci deserves special thanks for encouraging me to submit the manuscript for publication in the Culture and Conflict series she co-edits with Isabel Capeloa Gil at De Gruyter, for going over the manuscript with a fine tooth-comb, and for her nurturing support in bringing this project to completion. I also wish to thank Stella Diedrich and Angelika Herman for their valuable editorial assistance.

Contents

Introduction

*History can teach us nothing more
than the general picture brought into
view by the force of circumstance but
it cannot admit us to the inner
feelings which, by influencing the will
of a few, have decided the fate of all.*
(Staël 1987a: 4)

I was privileged to grow up in post-World War II Europe at the time when people and political leaders were determined to avoid another devastating war. The reconciliation of the European peoples was on the agenda, nationalism on the wane. Popular singers like Georges Brassens and Boris Vian made fun of the Bastille Day military parade and praised deserters. For young people of my generation, for my friends in France, England, and Germany, national wars were a thing of the past; we grew up confident that we would avoid our parents' mistakes, we protested the War in Vietnam as an aberration. These feelings were widely shared by the young American people I met in Europe, by my husband for instance. When I followed him to the United States in 1979 I was struck by the openness, kindness, and generosity of the American people. While patriotic symbols were more on display than in Europe – American flags adorned our children's classrooms and their school day started with the pledge of allegiance – the Fourth of July celebrations had the benevolent character of a family, community affair and little in common with what I understood as nationalism.

In academe, a similar mind-set led to two decades of scholarship on globalization, post-, and transnationalism to which the outburst of feelings we witnessed in the United States in the first years of the twenty-first century gave lie. Both the surge of patriotism that swept the American nation in 2001 in response to the attack of the World Trade Center of 11 September and the equally passionate wave of scapegoating of foreigners, amplified by France's refusal to join the US in a war against Iraq in 2003, provided striking evidence of the continued resonance and vibrancy of nationalism today. For scholars who had already left behind the realm of the nation these expressions of national love and hate came as shock and a surprise. It is in this discrepancy between theory – the scholarly consensus that has existed since the 1990s on the issue of the demise of the nation-state – and practice – the unexpected, actual assertiveness of the nation-state – that my desire to understand the affective dimension of nationalism is rooted. The purpose of *The National Habitus* is to examine how feelings of national belonging became central to one's sense of identity.

A few years before the turn of the century, Craig Calhoun in *Nationalism* (1997: 26) underscored academics' tendency to underestimate nationalism. From "Kant's dream of perpetual peace" to Marx and Engels' failure to realize "that the very word *'international'* suggests not the absence of nations, but their primacy," and the postmodernist predictions about the demise of the nation-state, it has been common practice "to declare the recent nationalist movements to be merely transitional, or at least among the last the world would see." Pointing to the essential role nationalism has played, and continues to play, in shaping "our entire view of the world – organizing citizenship and passports, the way we look at history, the way we divide literatures and cinemas, the way we compete in the Olympic games [...]" (Calhoun 1997: 1), he showed how nationalism is bound to essentialist notions of stable, integrated identities shaped by a regime of linguistic, racial, and sexual oneness, the most potent in the mix today, he argued, being undoubtedly nationality. Reviewing extant literature on nationalism,[1] he called for studies that would overcome a common methodological hurdle – the division between "constructivists," who view nations as creations or inventions, and "primordialists," who emphasize historical continuity – and also address questions that are germane to my own exploration of the national habitus in nineteenth-century France:

> How does it come to be that people's experience of being at home in the world is often bound up not only by their immediate relations but also with the larger, abstract category of the nation? [...] How can nations that are in fact historical creations come to be seen as 'primordial'? [...] How do nationalist leaders and ideologues claim history and use it in mobilizing people for nationalist projects? (Calhoun 1997: 32)

While much attention has been paid to the emergence of modern nation-states and to the history of nationalism, there is virtually no scholarship on the acquisition of the national habitus, the process by which subjects are transformed into citizens when a state becomes a nation-state. My goal in this book is to retrieve various conceptions of national identity and ways of feeling French that competed against each other in the nineteenth century before a legitimate, republican sense of national identity imposed itself during the Third Republic.

In literary criticism, the adjective 'nationalist' is usually a pejorative term associated with Right-wing French writers such as Maurice Barrès (1862–1923) at

---

1 Calhoun discusses works on nationalism by Elie Kedourie, author of *Nationalism* (1960, 1993); Benedict Anderson's *Imagined Communities* (1982, 1991); Clifford Geertz's *The Interpretation of Culture* (1973); John Hutchinson's *Modern Nationalism* (1994); Ernest Gellner's *Nations and Nationalism* (1983); Eric Hobsbawn's *Nations and Nationalism since 1870* (1990); Liah Greenfeld's *Nationalism* (1992), among many others.

the end of the nineteenth century and Louis-Ferdinand Céline (1894–1961) at the beginning of the twentieth. Cast in that light, nationalism tends to be viewed as a matter of (bad) personal choice and the label therefore restricted to a particular group of individuals, those who share similar 'nationalist' views. In this study, by contrast, nationalism is understood as the cornerstone of all modern Western identities. One of the goals of this book is to illustrate this point in the case of France, to show that the process of nationalization of feelings, thoughts, and habits affected across the board the six nineteenth-century writers on which it centers, irrespective of their social class and political views. Instead of relying on the criteria of language, race, and ethnicity commonly used to examine nationalism, my study draws from the sociological theories of Norbert Elias (1897–1990) and Pierre Bourdieu (1931–2002). Elias's seminal work in *The Germans* provides the criteria that undergird my examination of the national habitus in nineteenth-century literature; Bourdieu's key concepts of field and positions in the field afford its organizing principles.

The use of the term 'habitus' in the title of this book signals a methodological approach grounded in a sociology that sets as one of its goals to explore 'lived experience,' the subjective dimension of life.[2] In contemporary sociology, 'habitus' is most closely associated with Bourdieu's work, but the expression 'national habitus' was coined by Elias. Although one finds numerous references to Elias's work in Bourdieu's, the two sociologists are also seldom compared to one another.[3] The belatedness with which Elias's work on nationalism became available in French translation may partly explain the paucity of critical commentaries on the intellectual affinities between these two thinkers. First published in German by Suhrkamp under the title *Studien über die Deutschen* in 1989, it appeared in English in 1996, under the title *The Germans*, published by the Polity Press, and in French in 2009 only, as *Études sur les Allemands* published by L'Harmattan. Thus, while no mention of Bourdieu is found in Elias's works, except in relatively recent editorial prefaces, Bourdieu's 2012 *Sur l'État*, a collection of the lectures given at the Collège de France between 1989 and 1992, reveals a great deal of interest in Elias's studies on the civilizing process and on his theory of state formation but also the French sociologist's apparent unfamiliarity with Elias's work on nationalism.[4]

---

2 Gerd Schwerhoff, a German historian, points out that "Elias is above all one of the initiators of the so-called history of everyday life, even if he criticized it [...]." My translation from Schwerhoff (1998: 561). On that subject, see Elias's comments in note 6.

3 For an exception, see Déchaux (1993).

4 In 1976, an article by Elias also appeared in *ARSS*, a journal edited by Bourdieu.

Commonalities between these two sociologists are in fact extensive. They include: 1) a relational approach to the social world: the concept of 'interdependence' among social groups plays a central role in Elias's work; and the concept of 'field' understood as a space of tensions and struggles in Bourdieu's; 2) an emphasis on power and competition in the analysis of these relations, so for instance in the analysis of violence and monopoly formation in Elias; or through the concepts of 'capital' and 'symbolic violence' in Bourdieu; 3) their refusal to treat 'society' and 'individual' separately and their focus on the relation between 'social and mental structures' in Elias's case, between 'habitus and field' in Bourdieu's; 4) a common understanding of the nature of this relation, which Bourdieu calls the relation between "the reality that exists in things and the reality that exists in minds," as being one of homology; 5) the central role both grant to history; unlike many contemporary sociologists, they view social relations as historically constituted and treat them as dynamic social processes instead of static structures. Elias uses the terms "sociogenesis" or "psychogenesis" to describe his work,[5] Bourdieu has characterized his as a kind of "genetic structuralism;" 6) last but not least, they share the conviction that everyday language is better suited to express things and states than relations and processes. As a result, they view commonly accepted conceptual terms with a great deal of suspicion and tend to use unusual terms like 'habitus' instead.

In this book, the term 'habitus' signals an agreement with these general principles but also the intent to emphasize one aspect of the social reality that a sociologically grounded critique sets as its goal to explore, namely 'lived experience.' Elias is not as explicit as Bourdieu in his definition of 'habitus' but the term clearly refers to 'everyday life.'[6] In his work, habitus is presented mostly as a censorship device, as a regulator of mental habits and forms of behavior. It is the instance that transforms social constraints into self-constraints. Bourdieu, for his part, views the relation between habitus and field as a back-and-forth: the field conditions habitus but habitus is also what makes the world appear meaningful and worthy of personal investment. On the theoretical level,

---

5 Elias writes that "one cannot [...] clearly recognize the connections between – whatever it is – 'society,' and 'culture', 'state' and 'individual', 'external' and 'internal' steering mechanism—unless one conceptualizes them as something in movement, as aspects of social processes which are themselves processes, indeed as functionally interdependent processes involving varying degrees of harmony and conflict." (Elias 1996: 335)

6 "Currently, it is common practice to use the concept of 'everyday life-world' in observing and investigating such more or less private forms of behaviour and experience. Unfortunately [...] it is a rather useless research tool." (Elias 1996: 67)

habitus signals not only a departure from theories that grant primacy to the subject but also an attempt to reconcile the contradictory accounts on the subject these theories have produced. In Bourdieu's work, habitus is thus both a prisoner of social structures, as in positivist and materialist theories, and a free agent, as in idealist, subjectivist, and rational actor theories, but to a lesser extent. Or more precisely, it is both determined – as a product of a history deposited in certain dispositions – and free, within limits – as the agency that orients practices, that provides a "feel for the game," in accordance with these dispositions. Habitus is the embodied, socially acquired, system of structured and structuring dispositions agents have at their disposal to apprehend the social world and to participate in it. Habitus, in short, encapsulates the significance both Elias and Bourdieu grant in their sociology to practice, to the lived experience of agents. Elias (1996: 45) views, for instance, "the experience of stratification by the participants" as "one of the constituting elements of the structure of stratification" and Bourdieu (1992a: 127) writes in the same vein that "social science [...] must make room for a sociologically grounded phenomenology of the primary experience of the field."

Literature is not the usual kind of material sociologists draw on in their studies. But if one considers that literary texts offer the single most important record of human primary experience, the significance of that aspect of their work for literary studies should be obvious. Commenting on the relative merits of the disciplines of history and literature in the preface of her 1802 novel *Delphine*, Germaine de Staël praised literature for its unique ability to provide access to "inner feelings." This peculiarity makes literary works, such as those of the major nineteenth-century French writers examined in this book, particularly well-suited for serving as primary material in a study of emotions associated with the national habitus. One finds in fact more or less explicit invitations to literary critics to make this kind of interdisciplinary connections in both Elias's and Bourdieu's works. In *The Germans*, for instance, Elias (1996: 47) writes that "if used critically, novels can help reconstruct a past society and its power structure for us;" and Bourdieu goes even further in *The Rules of Art* when he concretely demonstrates how to apply his sociological theory to study literature in his analysis of Flaubert's *Sentimental Education*. But so far, no literary study based in a "sociologically grounded phenomenology" has been devoted to the national habitus.

Norbert Elias's approach to nationalism

Elias's early work, *The Civilizing Process*, first published in 1939, is better known in France and Germany than in the United States. Daniel Gordon (2002: 69), in fact, mocked what he called the French "Eliasomania" and Schwerhoff described a similar phenomenon in Germany where Elias's theory of the civilizing process received belated acclaim among historians.[7] According to him, even the widely publicized controversy that ensued when ethnologist Hans Peter Duerr denounced Elias's theory of the civilizing process as a myth, in *Der Mythos vom Zivilisationsprozeß*, did not seriously endanger its validity in historians' eyes. Centered on the early modern era, Elias's book is not about nationalism, a phenomenon he links, like most contemporary critics, to the modern era. Nonetheless, to the extent that it describes the historical processes leading to the constitution of nation-states and of a national habitus, it deserves be read in connection with his important study on nationalism, *The Germans, Power Struggles and the Development of Habitus in the Nineteenth and Twentieth Centuries*. The first volume of *The Civilizing Process* is devoted to "Changes in the Behaviour of the Secular Upper Classes in the West." It begins with an examination of "the sociogenesis of the concepts of civilization and culture" and traces the development of these concepts over time in an effort to historicize, and thereby de-essentialize them. At stake in his analysis is a notion that is often taken for granted even today, namely that civilization and culture produced radically different brands of nationalism in England and France on the one hand, in Germany on the other. In the second part of the volume, Elias draws from texts written from the Middle Ages to the twentieth century to document changes in social behavior, and in particular increased bodily self-control over time in a wide range of everyday practices including personal hygiene, as well as table and bedroom manners. This "specific transformation of human behavior," he argues, should not be underestimated: it is the very process that gives birth to civility, to "civilization." In the second volume of *The Civilizing Process*, "State formation and civilization," Elias turns to structural social changes that occurred over the same period of time, that is to processes associated with "the dynamics of feudalization" and with the "sociogenesis of the state," a process that eventually led to the state's monopoly in physical violence.[8] Emphasis is placed on France, particularly in the examination of processes leading to absolutism, but the analysis also deals with Great Britain and Germany as points of comparison. How the two processes, the transformation of social behavior on the one hand, and of social structure on the other, relate to one another is the subject of a concluding synopsis in which Elias exposes his "Theory of civilizing processes."

---

[7] "For historians, it is the third fixed star among theories of historical processes." My translation from Schwerhoff (1998: 562). However, Schwerhoff's attempt to debunk Elias's theory is unconvincing as it is limited to a critique of Elias's choice of historical sources.
[8] Bourdieu praises Elias for his analysis of the state as a form of racketeering but criticizes him for not considering the symbolic violence yielded by the state. (Bourdieu 2012: 203–211)

The vision of humanity steadily ridding itself of violent impulses laid out by Elias in *The Civilizing Process* was certainly put to test during his life. The 1933 Nazi take-over led to the closure of the sociology department where he worked with Karl Mannheim at the University of Frankfurt, deprived him of his German identity, and forced him into exile, first to France and then to Great Britain.[9] This devastating experience seems to have given him an intuitive knowledge of the national habitus, as the following lines imply:

> At least for adults, a change of national identity is hardly easier than a change of personality, and the chance of success is hardly any greater. More than just a change of passports is involved. A disturbance of national identity and of the national image embedded in the self-images of people, whether caused by a transformation in the life of a single individual or that of a whole nation, always leads to a reorientation of behaviour and feelings. It requires a reassessment of a person's values and beliefs and a reorganization of their perception of self and others. However much the ability to make such an adjustment may vary from individual to individual, with adults it has definite limits as a rule. An adult Frenchman or German does not easily lose his basic character as such or forget his earlier identity if he becomes an American citizen. (Elias 1996: 356)

Understandably, Elias's primary goal in *The Germans* is to account for "the breakdown of civilization" that so dramatically changed his life, but the book also deserves to be read as a sequel to *The Civilizing Process*. In the first study, he had already shown that the process of state formation, and in particular the progressive fusion of aristocracy and middle class, had occurred at a slower pace in Germany than in France and England. In the second book, he extends his analysis to the modern era, thus bringing into clearer focus the issue of nationalism, which he characterizes as "one of the most powerful, perhaps *the* most powerful, social beliefs of the nineteenth and twentieth centuries" (Elias 1996: 149). But instead of approaching this belief system from an ethical viewpoint, Elias's historical and relational approach underscores the structural changes that allowed it to emerge, thereby also reducing its susceptibility to national biases.[10]

The theory of nationalism embedded in *The Germans* contains the tools used in my examination of the national habitus. According to Elias, the national habitus emerged in connection with a specific historical change, the transformation

---

9 Elias's parents stayed in Germany; his father died in 1940 and his mother was deported to Auschwitz where she died in 1941.

10 Elias argues, for instance, that the difference between nationalism and other belief systems like "conservatism and communism, liberalism and socialism" is that the latter are produced by, and reflect changing power relations within a nation-state. The former, nationalism, originates in a similar change in the balance of power, but among different states. (Elias 1996: 154)

of Western states from estate to class societies, and is the product of a corresponding transformation affecting the "personality structure," that is emotions, thought, ethos, identity, and value system. Its most salient characteristics are presented below.

The national habitus' mental orientation towards the past

In his "Digression on Nationalism" in *The Germans*, Elias (1996: 123) argues that the establishment of nation-states brought along a new conceptual outlook: the "increasing tendency to conceptualize processes as if they were unchanging objects." This "unexpected discovery" originates in his realization that in the eighteenth century the terms 'culture' and 'civilization' "referred to *processes*, while in the twentieth century they represent something almost entirely static" (123). The transformation of dynamic into static concepts is, in his view, paradoxical because it runs counter to processes typically associated with modernity: the increased interdependence in human relations, the multiplication of social networks, and the quickening pace of change. Elias readily grants that the concept of 'civilization' had to do "with national self-image" as early as the eighteenth century. But what strikes him is its "forward-looking" dynamic dimension, the fact that at that time 'civilization' was understood also as a process relating to the development of humanity as a whole:

> The claim that '*la civilisation française est la civilisation humaine*' was, on the one hand, undoubtedly an expression of French nationalism and expansionism. But it expressed at the same time the belief that the French national tradition embodied and represented moral and other values and attainments valid for humanity as a whole. (Elias 1996: 136)

He notes that the Germans did not always think of themselves as a 'culture;' that earlier on, they too shared their contemporaries' dynamic vision of the history of civilization and expressed their faith in human progress. Friedrich Schiller, he points out, did so in his 1789 lecture "What does universal history mean and why do we study it?" Beethoven's Third Symphony provides another example of this dynamic concept of civilization. As Steven Rumph (2004: 1) points out in *Beethoven after Napoleon*, the Eroica "centers around a funeral march evoking patriotic ceremonies from the French Revolution" and even after his disillusion with Napoleon, this "political composer" continued to dedicate "his art to the problems of human freedom, justice, progress, and community."

In the twentieth century, by contrast, concepts like culture and civilization have become reified and static: "People speak of the culture of Australian aborigines as well as of the 'culture' of the Renaissance and of the 'civilization' of neolithic hunters, as well as that of nineteenth century Britain or France."

(Elias, 1996: 125) Elias attributes this conceptual change to two factors: "the fear of revolutionary violence and upheaval" (124); and the social ascent of the middle class. Once the middle class gained political power, once the aspirations of the Enlightenment were fulfilled, concepts that had been associated with human progress simply lost their function and their aura. They stopped being viewed as "auspicious symbol[s] of a better future suffused by the glow of strong positive feelings" (135). As this quote makes clear, these dynamic, "forward-looking" concepts fulfilled an emotional need and that need did not disappear when nation-states came into being. It was filled instead by a new attachment, an attachment to the nation's (largely imaginary) past. Mimicking the aristocracy, the middle class started to bond with imaginary ancestors:

> Just as aristocratic groups had based their pride and their claim to a special value on their family's ancestry, so, as their successors, the leading sections of the industrial middle classes – gradually in conjunction with those of the industrial working classes wherever the latter, too, had reached a ruling position – increasingly based their pride and their claim to a special value either on their nation's ancestry or on seemingly unchanging national achievements, characteristics, and values. (Elias, 1996: 135)

Belief in a better future gave way to "the belief in the unchanging value of national characteristics and traditions" at that point (136). In sum, social change, in the form of a redistribution of power, accounts directly, in Elias's view, for the replacement of a "forward-looking" by a "backward-looking" mental cast. In the national age, immanence (the nation as always already there) takes precedence over process. The transformation of dynamic into static concepts is a manifestation of this change.

The national habitus as a dual, contradictory ethos

As an ethos, the modern national habitus presents itself as the historical product of two incompatible codes of conduct, "aristocratic" on the one hand, and "middle class" on the other. Dating back to an era when physical violence and war were part of daily life, Elias argues, the aristocratic code of conduct is best exemplified by Machiavelli's advice to the prince to be both man and beast, both fox and lion. The salient feature of this code of conduct was, in his words, "the practice of unrestrained pursuit of self-interest in inter-state relations, under the pressure of mutual fears and suspicions, with deception and killing as normal means to one's ends" (Elias, 1996: 138). In estate societies, however, this code applied only to a tiny minority of people, to the ruling princes. The rest of the population, the majority of people, drew their own rules of behavior from the Judeo-Christian tradition. They sought to live a life of virtue and goodness, not of honor and civility. The process of state formation and the rise of the middle class to power that accompanied it are key to understanding how aristocratic and middle class codes of conduct came into contact and eventually merged. To keep the long story told in *The Civilizing process* short, states formed as rulers succeeded in wresting the monopoly of physical violence from an aristocracy that had earned its titles of nobility in war and conquest. Military might and taxation are related processes in Elias's model of the genesis of the state: as the size of the royal armies increased, more money was needed to cover expenses and the source of that money was taxes. But to administer and collect these taxes, rulers turned to members of the middle class, not to the aristocracy. Not only was this kind of activity deemed unsuitable for and by that estate, it would also have been contrary to the central authority's best interests to put this source of power in aristocratic hands. This structural change, the rise of the middle class, occurred all over Western Europe but its timing and its modalities differed greatly from one state to the next. In England and France, "the bourgeois intelligentsia and the leading groups of the middle class were drawn relatively early into the circle of the court society" (Elias 2000: 31), in the seventeenth century in England, in the eighteenth in France.

As long as middle class ascent to high social positions was restricted to individuals, the latter assimilated to the dominant class. But as more and more members of the middle class moved to the top, they no longer had to abandon their values and their culture. As a result, the two traditions often collided. The Enlightenment itself, Elias points out, is evidence of the European middle class' growing social power and self-assurance: by the eighteenth century, bourgeois philosophers all over Europe elevated their own code of behavior based on equality and moral virtues to a universal standard valid for all human beings, turning it into natural law. According to them, aristocratic values were irrelevant, remnants of a past associated with "hypocrisy, deceit, and violence" (Elias 1996: 458). Many aristocrats agreed in theory. But as their mass emigration during the French Revolution would show, their identity was still based in a dynastic and aristocratic "warrior tradition" (161).

At the French court, the division between aristocrats and bourgeois had played a central role in strengthening the absolute monarchy. As the authority called upon to settle conflicts between the two camps, the King was able to use these contradictory forces to his own advantage. But at the same time, contact between the aristocratic and bourgeois elites also had an important unifying effect. By the end of the eighteenth century both groups "spoke the same language, read the same books and had, with particular gradations, the same manners" (Elias 2000: 32). Once the French middle class wrested political power away from the aristocracy through a revolution in 1789, "when the bourgeoisie became the nation," this dominant culture trickled down and became the "national character" (32). Elias notes, for instance, that Robespierre, who is remembered as the most radical of the French revolutionaries, was partial to Old Regime civility in everyday life.

In Germany by contrast, the middle class remained cut off from political power until the end of the nineteenth century.[11] Instead of diminishing, the distance between the two dominant social groups increased during that time, the gap between "the courtly nobility, predominantly French-speaking and 'civilized' on the French model" on the one hand, and a German-speaking, middle class focused on "its own values and accomplishments" became wider (Elias 2000: 9).[12] This insight enables Elias to refute the traditional opposition between 'French civilization' and 'German culture:' this dichotomy is not rooted in two different national traditions, civilization for France on the one hand, and *Kultur* for Germany on the other, as is commonly believed, but rather in an internal division within German society itself. While exclusion from political power led the German middle class to equate 'civility' with aristocratic behavior and to reject it on that count, sharing political power with the aristocracy led the French bourgeoisie to embrace civility as one of its own values. Logically, however, the other values of the aristocratic code of conduct, in particular honor, had no place in the middle class ethical code, and they were indeed often denounced as incompatible with humanist values. Enlightenment philosophers often derided an aristocratic code of conduct they viewed as immoral and contrary to the laws of nature. In France, Voltaire (1694–1778) mocked it in his satires of aristocratic warfare. In England, John Wesley (1703–1791) explicitly condemned it when he criticized Machiavelli for "recommending hypocrisy, treachery, lying, robbery, oppression, adultery, whoredom and murder of all kinds" to the Prince (quoted in Elias 1996: 169). The aristocratic code of conduct did in fact lose much of its appeal in intra-state relations after the French Revolution. The socially distinguishing practice of dueling, for instance, did not survive as long in England as in France, or in France as long as in Germany. In inter-state relations, by con-

11 Germaine de Staël made the same observation as Elias much earlier, noting in *On Germany* that the division between a public life dominated by the aristocracy and the military on the one hand, and the republic of letters on the other, increased the distance between social classes, which was "more pronounced in Germany than anywhere else" and "detrimental to the German spirit." (Staël 1968: I, 57)

12 Among the illustrations of this struggle between two German types – that Bourdieu calls "mondains" and "doctes" – Elias provides this brief quote from *Beyond Good and Evil* in which Friedrich Nietzsche contrasts these two sets of values: "The fact is that we all emancipated from court taste, while Voltaire was its consummation." (Quoted in Elias, 2000: 32)

trast, the aristocratic code of conduct remained the rule not only in France, but everywhere.

The national habitus is thus the product of a structural change: the transformation of estate into class societies was a pre-condition to its development. It is based in contradictory demands: those of "a moral code descended from that of rising sections of the *tiers état*, egalitarian in character and whose highest values is 'man,' the human individual as such;" but at the same time those of "a nationalist code descended from the Machiavellian code of princes and ruling aristocracies, unequal in character, and whose highest value is a collectivity – the state, the country, the nation to which an individual belongs" (Elias 1996: 155). Since this history is common to all Western European nations, the national habitus is a characteristic of all class societies: "The development of a dual and inherently contradictory code of norms is one of the common features of all countries which have undergone the transformation from an aristocratic-dynastic into a more democratic national state." (161)

The contradictory demands of the national habitus are brought to bear mostly in times of international conflict. They are reflected in diverging attitudes towards violence in intra-state relations on the one hand, and inter-state relations on the other. Paradoxically, Elias, writes, "[i]n intra-state affairs, violence between people is tabooed, and, when possible, punished;" but "in inter-state relations, another code holds good. Every larger state is in constant preparation for violence with other states, and when it comes to such violence, those who perpetrate it are extremely highly valued, and in many cases, praised and rewarded" (177). Under normal conditions, in the absence of a national crisis, one is hardly aware of the dispositions associated with the national ethos. But they are nonetheless "all pervasive:" they orient political thinking and action; they make people lean toward one or the other end of the nationalist spectrum; they create "blockages and biases" (157). They are, for that reason, susceptible to instrumentation, to manipulation, by political rulers in particular. They can be brought to the level of consciousness, and even "tempered and modified by informed knowledge and realistic judgment" (157). But knowledge in that area usually comes at a price in the form of "punishment not only from others, but also [...] of guilt feelings, of 'bad conscience" (158).[13]

---

13 One thinks, for instance, of how difficult it was for American liberals to respond to the accusation of being "soft on Terror" during the Iraq war, or for opponents to the war to counter the notion that they did not support the troops.

The national habitus as the self-imposition of constraints

Underlying Elias's analysis of the divergent attitudes towards violence within and between states is the notion that the use of physical violence has decreased considerably over time in "intra-state affairs." In the past, he says, physical violence was seen as a legitimate way of handling personal conflicts: as late as the nineteenth century, it was considered appropriate for fathers to hit their kids, for men to beat women, etc... This kind of violence may still exist today,[14] but instead of being viewed as socially acceptable, it is perceived as shocking by society at large and is punishable by law. The taboo against violence in interpersonal relations is, according to Elias, the product of two related processes: "the self-activated taming of spontaneous violent impulses," that is the transformation of external constraints into self-constraints; and the "monopolization of force" by the state, the fact that in all modern nation-states a clear distinction is made between "legal and illegal violent groups" (Elias 1996: 176). An "unplanned social invention" (174), the state monopoly of physical violence can serve to pacifty a state, but the legal violent groups that control it, i.e., the police and the armed forces, may also try to use it to their own advantage, a risk that is greater in absolutist states than in nation-states where mechanisms ensure the proper use of state violence. Public or private violent behavior is taboo in democratic nation-states but solely refraining from physical violence is not a sufficient condition for participating in politics. The practice of parliamentary politics requires additional forms of self-constraints. In autocratic regimes, a simple personality structure "adapted to a hierarchy of command and obedience" is sufficient because "a symbolic ruling figure bears the responsibility for a nation of subjects" (291). Democracy, by contrast, thrives on the exchange of opinion and does not relegate conflicts "to the category of the extraordinary, abnormal, and irrational" (292); on the contrary, it treats them "as normal, indispensable aspects of social life" (294). Democratic nation-states require a personality structure adjusted to conflict, able to handle disagreement and to submit to majority rule.[15]

Elias (1996: 295) agrees with those who argue that democracy is premised on institutional change, in the form of "a reduction in the power difference between the rulers and the ruled." But he takes issue with the "ahistorical rationalist" notion that the democratization of institutions is automatically followed by "a democratization of attitudes, beliefs, and convictions" (337). Institutions, he

---

14 The decrease of intra-state violence varies considerably from country to country. For statistics on firearm possession and murders, see the 17 December 2012 issue of *The Guardian*.

15 "A 'conflict-free society' may appear to be the pinnacle of rationality, but at the same time it is also a society of 'the silence of the tomb,' of the most extreme emotional coldness and utter boredom – a society without any dynamic." (Elias 1996: 292–293)

claims, are much more responsive to change than habitus. For democratization to occur more than institutional change is needed: habitus must be adjusted to institutional change, and what he calls "an increase in the civilizing self-controls" must take place (75).[16] People accustomed to responding to external constraints must acquire dispositions that will enable them to handle conflict non-violently according to democratic practice. As we will see shortly, they must in fact acquire a new kind of identity and a new belief system. This is why the process of adjusting habitus to structural change, of going from an absolutist to a parliamentary regime, hardly ever occurs in the course of one life. This difficult and lengthy process takes "a chain of several generations" (294).

The national habitus as a form of identity

As late as the eighteenth century, people hardly had a sense of national identity. In France at the time, for instance, provincial aristocrats had more in common with individuals of the same estate in other countries, sharing their civil manners and language, than with individuals of a different estate in their own country who spoke all kinds of dialects and did not behave like them. Prior to the national age, membership in a family, a tribe, or a church, defined one's identity; relations among members of the community were of a personal nature. In these societies, the sense of identity was group-based, and what Elias (1996: 356) calls the "I-experience" and "we-experience" were "hardly separable from one another." The nation-state by comparison is an abstract entity. Its size and the complexity of social relations, the various layers of "human interdependence," make it impossible to have this kind of personal relations with this entity. In nation-states, the "I" and the "we" experiences are therefore "sharply distinguished."[17] As mentioned earlier, the "we-feeling" is particularly responsive to certain triggers, such as the "intensification of fears and threats between nations" (356), but it is always there lurking in the background.

Elias (1996: 151) describes the emotional bond to the nation as "a form self-love:" "the love for one's nation is *never only* a love for persons or groups of whom one says 'you'; it is always the love of a collectivity to which one can refer as 'we.'" The difficulties adults experience when they change nationality, as noted in Elias's own case earlier, underscore the deep-rootedness of the national habitus. The ideal "we-picture" is invested with strong, positive, feelings

---

16 "In this respect, [...] democracy contradicts the laws of classical rationality, which equate order with harmony, that is, with lack of conflict." (Elias 1996: 292)

17 "Under normal circumstances, the experience of oneself as an isolated individual separated from all others, stands sharp and clear in the center of self-consciousness, whilst the perception of relationships experienced as 'we' remains more in the background." (Elias 1996: 356)

that are expressed in a symbolic instead of a personal form. As imaginary as it may be, the nation's past is the source of most of these symbols. Endowed with an "emotional aura," national symbols encapsulate values that need not, and must not, be questioned. The American Declaration of Independence, for example, or Sieyès' pamphlet *What is the Third Estate?* are textual symbols that "lift the image of the nation to highest rank" (455). Countless other examples attest to the emotional investment in these national symbols. But they function differently in intra- and inter-state relations: within the nation-state, they serve to reinforce the common faith in the nation – and to exclude the non-believers. In relation to other states, national sentiment justifies anything, even violence and war, as long as it is presented as being conducted in the best interest of the nation.

The national habitus finds its clearest expression in the feeling of loyalty and duty towards one's country, an attachment viewed by Elias as the internalization of an external constraint: the obligation to defend the nation-state in time of need. In nation-states, the nation's survival ranks higher than the survival of the individual: "One can speak of 'individualism,' prize the 'freedom of the individual' as the highest social value and proclaim the primacy of 'the individual' in relation to 'state', 'nation', or 'society' – in times of national need individual freedom is everywhere curtailed; the survival of individuals is put at the back of the queue, behind that of society" (Elias 1996: 334). The national habitus, in short, combines old characteristics, the fear and suspicion inherited from the old warrior code, and a new one, belief in the nation as absolute value. Ironically perhaps, belief in the nation has turned out to be more effective in war-time than simple obedience to the chiefs.[18]

The national habitus as a secular faith

Elias (1996: 148) locates "the primary impulse for the formation of nationalism as a belief system" in a common fear concerning the nation's preservation and in a common faith, the belief that the nation is worth fighting, and if necessary dying for. This central tenet of the nationalist creed is not new. In antiquity already, one believed that *"Dulce et decorum est pro patria mori."* In ancient times, however, only one class of people was called upon to defend the nation and these people also benefitted from the spoils of war. Soldiers in national armies, on the other hand, are willing to die for free, a relatively recent phenomenon that is linked to

---

18 Thus, the European coalitions fighting the armies of the first French Republic were just as stunned to be beaten by non-professional soldiers as the British redcoats by the American militia during the War of Independence.

the development of conscription. Where does this belief come from? Why are people willing to sacrifice their lives for an abstract idea? Elias responds in the following way: humans are social beings who feel that "without functions for others" their life has no meaning. They therefore believe in whichever social organization gives meaning to their lives. The reason they are willing to die for their belief is that the alternative to fighting is a life without value, "without functions for others" (351). Belief systems are based in a sense of "belongingness and meaning stretching beyond an individual's life-span" (350). They derive their power from an emotional investment in something bigger than life, like the promise of the individual's survival beyond death in the case of religion. The willingness to die for one's beliefs is a common characteristic of all belief systems, religious or national. As with national faith, religious belief has often been and still is being mobilized in "life-and-death struggles" (344) in defense of the faith. Elias notes that historically church and state were in competition as identity carriers, but that nowadays in the West "secular national belief" has become the guarantor of "identity and value" (350, 334).

The deep-rootedness of the national "we-feeling" typically comes from direct inculcation through socialization and education.[19] Once it has been established, it is reinforced by feelings of "enmity towards strangers who do not share in the common national religion and identity" (Elias 1996: 352–53). Even under normal circumstances, when it seems turned off, the national disposition registers "national failures and successes" and invests them with feelings (352). All the more so when it is turned on. If success on the international scene reinforces the sense of national identity, self-esteem, and pride, military defeat, invasion and revolution are conversely associated with "loss of identity" or "loss of self" originating in the feeling "that life is no longer worth living if the older order in which they enjoyed supremacy disappears" (338). The strength of national feelings and their deep-rootedness explain why it is difficult to intervene efficiently in external conflicts.[20] It is all the more unfortunate, Elias adds, in that "in a world of increasingly interdependent industrial

---

19 "Today, the recording, teaching and learning of one's own national history has widely taken the place occupied in simpler societies by the oral transmission of an in many ways secret fund of knowledge – the names and deeds of ancestors, legends, rituals, etc. – which imparts to individuals a feeling of identity and solidarity with a group and a lasting meaning and value in relation to other people." (Elias 1996: 350–51)

20 "An effective intervention to restrain such a process would require an authority which is not wholly identified with either of the two sides, armed with sufficient theoretical knowledge of the nature of such processes to be able to dismiss the idea of the sole guilt of this or that side, and with enough power to be able to work out and effect a relevant strategy." (Elias 1996: 354)

nation-states, military victors are not necessarily the greatest beneficiaries of their victories and the vanquished are not necessarily weakened or led to suffer more than their opponents" (365).

My primary goal in this book is to test the accuracy of Elias's understanding of the national habitus, as described above, by basing my examination of literary texts on a series of questions related to it. If, as Elias claims for instance, the emergence of national habitus corresponds to the abandonment of a forward-looking mental attitude associated with human progress and aspirations valid for humanity as a whole, and its replacement with a backward-looking mental attitude turned towards an imaginary national past, which of these attitude(s) do the texts examined in this book reveal? Is there any evidence in them that the national habitus is the product of a dual contradictory ethos, as Elias contends, and that patriotism and nationalism are closely linked? If the national habitus is the by-product of the civilizing process that started in Renaissance Europe, or more specifically of the extension of this process to the political sphere in the nineteenth century, which kind of clues do these texts offer with regard to violence in the public sphere? If the national habitus is a new form of identity characterized by a sharp sense of individualism and at the same time an identification with the abstract collectivity of the nation, which kinds of 'I' and 'we' feelings emerge from these texts? Finally, if the national habitus is a secular form of faith, how is this faith expressed?

Selecting authors and works: fields and positions

While the criteria used to analyze the national habitus in this study are derived from *The Germans*, my book owes its structure to Bourdieu, and more specifically to his understanding of history as a non-linear process. His concepts of field and positions in the field are used here as a corrective to the vision of history as a unidirectional movement of progress towards civilization that informs Elias's *Civilizing Process*. Whereas according to Elias, for instance, the aristocracy was the nation during the Old Regime and the bourgeoisie became the nation after the French Revolution, Bourdieu's understanding of the field as a site of struggles is particularly well-suited for examining whether it was the case in the first place or whether the meaning of the term 'nation' was still contested in nineteenth-century France. In order to provide a more nuanced analysis than the one proposed by Elias, my study encompasses two historical fields structured around antagonistic positions. The French revolutionary era marks the historical boundaries of the first field in a study that focuses on three writers who experienced the French revolution firsthand as adults. The second encompasses the post-revolutionary era – defined in opposition to the first to the extent that the three other writers included in it were children or not born in 1789.

For each historical field, I selected writers (positions) located as far apart as possible from each other, but whose writings had in common to deal with the nation and patriotism, at least according to Elias's criteria. The selection of an equal number of men and women writers adds an additional dimension to my study: it makes it possible to examine the relation between gender and national habitus.

The revolutionary field

My study of the revolutionary field centers on three writers situated on opposite ends of the literary, social, and political spectrum: Olympe de Gouges, François René de Chateaubriand, and Germaine de Staël. A political writer of the revolutionary era, Gouges tends to better known for her ideas than for her style, as opposed to Chateaubriand and Staël, the most prominent French pre-Romantics. In social and political terms, however, Gouges and Staël represent the bourgeois pole of the revolutionary field, Chateaubriand, its aristocratic counterpart.

Olympe de Gouges (1748–1793)

Opinions on Gouge's social status in pre-revolutionary France have widely differed over time. The few critics who wrote about her in the nineteenth century painted her as an ambitious courtesan turned *femme de lettres*, a marginal figure with a lot of imagination and no real social connections. But the accuracy of this portrait has been challenged, among others by her biographer, Olivier Blanc, who has found evidence to support most of the statements Gouges made about her own life. A native of Montauban, thirty miles north of Toulouse, Olympe Gouze, her real name, grew up in a lower middle class family of artisans (her mother's father was a cloth maker, her mother married a butcher) and she married very young. Althea Arguelles-Ling (2007: 245) writes that "she married a Parisian caterer, Louis-Yves Aubry, who died soon after, leaving her with a son, Pierre." Olivier Blanc (1993b: 7) provides a slightly different account according to which her husband was a low-ranking administrator in her hometown, an "*officier de Bouche de l'intendant de la Généralité de Montauban*," and Gouges's move to Paris occurred after his death.[21] In any case, from the 1770s onward, the young widow lived in Paris where she met Jacques Biétrix de Rozières, a rich navy officer who was to be her companion for many years. Although they were never

---

21 Joan Scott attributes the difficulty of establishing the truth about Gouges' identity to "her refusal of the secondary status that patriarchal law assigned to women" and "her ability to represent herself as an attribute of her imagination." (Scott 1996: 22)

married, the couple was well off financially and connected to Old Regime high society. There was even a member of the royal family in their circle, the Duke of Orléans (1725–1785), the morganatic husband of Charlotte de la Haye de Riou, Marquise de Montesson (1737–1806), a friend of Gouges who shared her literary ambitions.[22] Their social milieu was a *société mélangée* [mixed social environment] of aristocrats and bourgeois intellectuals. Olympe herself claimed to be of mixed social origin, the daughter of a commoner and an aristocrat, the Marquis Jean-Jacques Lefranc de Pompignan (1709–1784), a playwright who wrote a tragedy that made him famous at a young age and who later became a devout man and a well-known "enemy of the Enlightenment" (McMahon: 2001 ch.1), or, as Stendhal saw it, a "wretched poet and Jesuit" (Stendhal 1970: 79). Lefranc de Pompignan is not mentioned by name in Gouges's veiled autobiography, *Madame de Valmont's Memoirs* [*Mémoire de Madame de Valmont*], but critics have had no difficulty identifying him on the basis of her description of him. Moreover, Olympe stuck to the story of her birth, reiterating that her father had been a playwright when, in the early 1790s, she was accused of being Louis XV's illegitimate daughter. One may reasonably assume that her life experience of high society as a crossroad between social classes made her particularly sensitive to antagonisms between aristocrats and bourgeois, that is to the social conflict that eventually led to the French Revolution.

Chapter I, "Olympe de Gouges's Revolutionary Patriotism," centers on works by this militant activist and advocate of human rights that were written shortly before and during the first phase of the French Revolution, the only one Gouges ever experienced since she was guillotined in 1793. My examination of her pre-revolutionary pamphlets and of her quasi autobiographical novel *Madame de Valmont's Memoirs*, published in 1788, underscores the writer's initial ambivalence towards the Revolution. On the one hand, these texts reveal the existence of a pre-revolutionary form of patriotism characterized by a sense of loyalty to king and country and thus an anti-revolutionary political stand. On the other hand, they also highlight the conflict between bourgeois and aristocratic codes of conduct to the extent that the aristocracy's flawed moral values are presented as the source of the kingdom's woes. If the proclamation of the *Declaration of the Rights of Man and of the Citizen* in 1789 encapsulates a victory of bourgeois over aristocratic values, Gouges's insistence that it also apply to women, in her *Declaration of the Rights of Woman and the Woman Citizen* and to slaves, in her play *Black Slavery*, testifies to her embrace of the French Revolution's for-

---

22 On Gouges's relations with the Duke of Orléans, Madame de Montesson, and Fanny de Beauharnais, see Blanc (1993a: 11–12).

ward-looking attitude and to her adherence to its universalist aspirations. Her works also exemplify the dual, contradictory nature of the national habitus, however: if her critique of revolutionary politics, depicted and denounced as a breakdown of civility and as an endorsement of senseless violence, illustrates the non-violent stand for which she is better known, her celebration of revolutionary warfare, in some of her plays, and the anti-foreigner rhetoric of some of her pamphlets also attest to her support of violence in inter-state relations. Throughout her writing career, Gouges's faith in the nation remained steady. She was by all standards an ardent, self-proclaimed patriot, who was willing to die, and did die for her nation. But as we will see her sense of identity as a Frenchwoman evolved nonetheless considerably within a few years under the pressure of events as the "royal patriotism" she initially professed turned into a belief in the republican nation.

François René de Chateaubriand (1768–1848)

Twenty years younger than Olympe de Gouges, François René de Chateaubriand was the last of ten children born to René-Auguste de Chateaubriand (1718–1786) and Apolline de Bédée (1726–1798). This old aristocratic family from Brittany had endured the humiliation of poverty, an experience not uncommon for the Old Regime provincial nobility, but according to Gerald N. Izemberg (1992: 259) "René-Auguste [...] had restored some of the patrimony and prestige of his family through very modern means – investing in ships, privateering, trading in slaves, and fishing cod." By 1771, Count René-Auguste de Chateaubriand was wealthy enough to purchase the medieval castle of Combourg, where, according to his son's autobiographical writings, he sought to revive feudal customs.[23] Chateaubriand spent his youth in relative solitude in Brittany, studying in Dinan and Rennes before joining an ancient, prestigious royal regiment as a low-ranking officer at age seventeen.

Important details for situating Chateaubriand socially are the facts that he was presented to the King in 1787 and that the royal court inspired him "unconquerable dislike" on that occasion (Chateaubriand 1848: IV, 9). Just as relevant are his feelings of alienation in Parisian high society. In *Memoirs from beyond the grave*, he recalled how "odious" Parisian society had seemed to him on his first trip to Paris and how lonely and abandoned he had felt. Between 1788 and 1791, he nonetheless spent time regularly in Paris where his brother Jean-Baptiste, the new Count of Chateaubriand since their father's death in 1786, had married Aline Le Pelletier de Rosanbo, a grand-daughter of Guil-

---

23 On Count de Chateaubriand's efforts to revive feudal customs see Fumaroli (2003: 9).

laume-Chrétien de Lamoignon de Malesherbes (1721–1794).[24] Through them, François-René made the acquaintance of a number of writers and intellectuals. But Malesherbes had a particular influence on the young man's destiny because he was the one who encouraged him to travel. On 8 April 1791, a few days after Mirabeau's death, Chateaubriand left for America, dreaming, as a disciple of Rousseau, of encountering purer beings living in nature's bosom away from civilization. By December of that year, he returned to France a transformed man, determined to become a writer, and full of ideas and images that would, from then on, nourish his literary imagination. That year, he also married Céleste Delavigne-Buisson, a young lady from a merchant family of his hometown of Saint-Malo.

In the summer of 1792, as war could no longer be avoided, Chateaubriand chose sides, selecting the camp Olympe de Gouges was by then accusing of treason. On 15 July, a few days after the *patrie* was declared in danger, he rallied Condé's army, *l'armée des princes*, in Coblenz, and carrying the manuscript of his American travels on the battlefield, fought on the *émigrés'* side until the Republican victories forced the Princes' army to disband. Chateaubriand would later recall how out of place he had felt in Condé's army and how, out of "Armorican patriotism," he had enrolled in the seventh Breton company: "A Breton barbarian in the camp of Princes, I carried Homer, along with my sword; I preferred my country, the tiny impoverished isle of Aaron,[25] to the hundred cities of Crete" (Chateaubriand 1848: IX, 14). Wounded at the siege of Thionville in 1792, physically and morally exhausted, he managed his way to England in May 1793, where he lived mostly miserably for several years.[26] In France, meanwhile, his wife, his mother, and two of his sisters were in jail. His brother Jean-Baptiste, his wife Aline, and Malesherbes, all died on the guillotine in 1794. In London, Chateaubriand devoted much of his time to writing and when his *Essay on Revolutions* appeared in 1797, his life improved considerably: the book, he wrote in his *Memoirs*, "made a stir" and from then on "the émigré nobility sought [him] out in London" (Chateaubriand 1848: XI, 2). Until 1800 when he moved back to France, he continued to work on his American novels, *Atala* and *René*, both part of a literary project devoted to the defense of the Catholic faith, *The Genius of Christianity*. In London, Chateaubriand also resumed his friendship with the poet Louis-

---

24 During his long administrative career, Malesherbes sought to strengthen the monarchy by opening it up to Enlightenment ideas. On this point, see Chartier (1991, Ch.3). He also served as Louis XVI's attorney during the King's trial.

25 Aaron, or Aleth, is a small island off the coast of Saint-Malo.

26 On Chateaubriand's life in England, see Nerozzi (2007).

Marcelin de Fontanes (1757–1821).[27] This moderate reformer was a founding member of the *Institut de France*, the national learned society created in 1795 to replace the royal academies disbanded two years earlier. Following the Directory's Coup d'État of 18 fructidor an V (4 September 1797) against Royalists and Jacobins, Fontanes had to flee to England, but he rose to positions of power during the Consulate. A friend of the future Empress's aunt, the lover of one of Bonaparte's sisters, Fontanes belonged to the First Consul's inner circle and played a crucial role in launching Chateaubriand's literary career in France. It was thanks to his friend and editor of the *Mercure de France* that François-René published the review of Germaine de Staël's *On Literature Considered in its Relation to Social Institutions* [*De la Littérature considérée dans ses rapports avec les institutions sociales*] that brought him out of anonymity. It was thanks to his friend that *The Genius of Christianity* was published with the approval of the government. The timing of the book's publication was perfect: it appeared just when the *Concordat*, the agreement with the Vatican to restore Catholicism as the 'religion of the majority of the French,' was being signed.[28]

In Chapter II, "Identity Lost and Found: Chateaubriand's Culturalist Nationalism," Chateaubriand represents the losing pole of the revolutionary field and the kind of aristocrat Gouges targeted in her critique of the aristocratic ethos. Two works written during his exile in England (1793–1800) in order to make sense of the Revolution, and if possible to reverse its course, are examined here: his *Historical Essay on Revolutions* and *The Genius of Christianity*. These works, I argue, are grounded in a counter-revolutionary discourse that seeks to substitute itself for its revolutionary counterpart: opposing the 'productive' universalism of the Catholic Church to the 'destructive' universalism of the Revolution, Chateaubriand decries individualism as the source of all social ills and contends that the only way to fight this modern disease is to restore a sense of community in post-revolutionary France. As we will see, and as his proclaimed allegiance to Brittany during his enrollment in the Princes' army already indicates, his understanding of the *patrie* is grounded in the concepts of native soil and ancestors.

Germaine de Staël (1776–1817)

Born in Paris on 22 April 1776, Germaine de Staël occupies the highest social position in our revolutionary field and in part for that reason also the most prominent place as a political actor. Jacques-Léon Godechot (1983: 611), however,

---

27 On the friendship between Chateaubriand and Fontanes, see Fumaroli (2003: 137–197).
28 On the publication of the *Genius of Christianity*, see Fumaroli (2003: 367–371); Walsh (1967).

rightly underscores the family's bourgeois origins: Germaine's father, Jacques Necker (1732–1804), was a self-made man who became wealthy as a banker prior to his rise to the highest government positions in France. Her mother, Suzanne Cruchot (1734–1794), worked as a "governess [*demoiselle de compagnie*] for a rich lady from Geneva established in Paris" at the time of her marriage. Although he was a Swiss citizen, Jacques Necker served as France's finance minister and his wife's Parisian salon attracted the remaining cream of the Enlightenment's crop who were still alive. Already as a young child, Germaine would attend her mother's social gatherings, participate in intellectual exchanges, acquire her knowledge of Enlightenment ideals, and enjoy the charms of polite society. She proved, however, resistant to the stern Protestant education Suzanne Necker would have liked to give her and turned to her father, whom she truly idolized, for affection. A great admirer of the English nation and the British Constitution, Necker served as Deputy Director and Director General of Finance for King Louis XVI but his political career was full of ups and downs: he left the government a first time in May 1783, returned, was exiled in April 1787 but recalled a few months later. The same process repeated itself in 1789 until Necker's final resignation in 1790 and his retirement to Coppet on the shores of the lake of Geneva, a chateau that would later be Germaine's home as well.

One of the wealthiest heiresses of her day, Germaine Necker was free to choose a husband herself, provided he was a Protestant. Rumored to have rejected William Pitt (1759–1806), she settled on the Swedish Ambassador to France, the Baron Erik Magnus Staël of Holstein (1749–1803) and their marriage was celebrated at the court of Versailles in the presence of the royal family in 1786. Her first writings date from this period. The *Letters on the Works and Character of J-J Rousseau* (1788) reveal the young woman's knowledge of, and adherence to the principles of the Enlightenment; her correspondence with no less than the King of Sweden her high social status. But there was already sorrow in her life as well: her first child, Gustavine, only lived a few months and her marriage to the Swedish baron did not last. As early as 1788, she was looking for affection elsewhere and found it in the person of a young, good-looking aristocrat: Count Louis de Narbonne-Lara (1755–1813), the presumed father of her two sons, Auguste, born in 1790, and Albert, born in 1792. Thus began Germaine's passionate and often disappointing extracurricular love life.

Politics, and writing about politics, was the other passion of her life. Because she is best known for her opposition to Napoleon it is useful to recall that her interest and participation in French politics began long before she met the future Emperor. As a supporter of enlightened reform, Staël could only welcome the French Revolution. Indeed, she would always remember its early phase as a period full of excitement and joy – although the October 1789 riots she witnessed at

Versailles somewhat tempered her revolutionary enthusiasm. This was the time when her Parisian salon served as a meeting place for moderate revolutionaries, for 'friends of liberty' who favored a constitutional monarchy. Through her salon and her friends, she had considerable political influence. She was able, for instance to have Narbonne appointed minister of War in 1791.[29] She was also powerful enough to engineer, together with her Girondins friends, the fall of the ministry that recalled him a few months later. (Isbell 1997)

As we will see in Chapter III, "Cosmopolitanism and Nationalism in Germaine de Staël's Works," nationalism plays a central role not only in Staël's personal life but also in her works: although born in Paris, she was treated as a foreigner by several French governments, which may in part explain why she thought and wrote so much about nations and nationalism – particularly in *On Literature* (1800) and *On Germany* (1809). But because she famously identified as a European, critics tend to view her as a cosmopolitan thinker, someone who transcends the nationalist mold, a precursor of today's European. Does Staël's case then open up the perspective of a third possible way of relating to the nation? I conclude in the negative in this chapter based on an analysis of her novels, *Delphine* and *Corinne*. The protagonist's attachment to France in *Delphine*, I argue, is grounded in an Old Regime court and salon culture that embodied the French character, *l'esprit français*, for Staël. In *Corinne*, a nostalgic glance is similarly cast at Old Regime cosmopolitanism but the age of the nation has arrived. Corinne's failed attempt to be both Italian and English shows us that it is impossible to maintain fluid identities in the national age, a failure that resonates with Staël's own attempt to hold on to a sense of identity already seen as the remnant of a bygone era by many of her contemporaries. Together with her narrow understanding of the nation as the superior class, this cosmopolitanism made her look like a 'foreigner' in the eyes of the various governments that forced her into exile.

The post-revolutionary field

My post-revolutionary field features three writers who were born shortly before or shortly after the French Revolution and who lived at a time when Romantic patriotic aspirations and sensibilities gave way to a clearer sense of national republican identity, at least among the intellectual elite they belonged to: Stendhal, his friend Prosper Mérimée and George Sand. Although these writers did not experience the Revolution firsthand, at least not as adults, their sense of

---

29 Angelica Goodden describes Narbonne as "a trimmer or turncoat, a man whose moves were dictated by expediency;" he "died in the retreat from Moscow." (Gooden 2008: 36, 240)

identity was shaped by the Revolution's principles, its aspirations and feelings, much more so, according to Stendhal, than their parents' had been. In literary criticism, however, Stendhal, the realist, Mérimée, the ironist, and Sand the idealist, represent opposing literary trends and are, for that reason, seldom compared to one another. The fact that these writers are by no means categorized as 'nationalist,' or their works known for dealing with the topic of the nation, makes their inclusion in a study of the national habitus seem a bit counter-intuitive. But in spite of their authors' divergent literary and political trajectories, these works exhibit an enduring preoccupation with the issue of national identity.

Stendhal (1783 – 1842)

Born in Grenoble three years before the French Revolution, Henri Beyle grew up in a family of notables, part homegrown, part from Provence.[30] Traumatized by the death of his beloved mother when he was only seven years old, little Henri developed rebellious tendencies with religious and political overtones at that early age. He first renounced the cruel God who had taken his mom away and, in a family full of Royalists,[31] found pleasure in shocking his relatives with his republican views. His delight over King Louis XVI's death in 1793, for instance, earned him a reputation of cruelty among his loved ones. Little Henri was a precocious patriot: "On days of republican victory, he walked around carrying a little tricolored flag he had made. *Freedom or death! It is great, it is sweet to die for the patrie.* He wrote these slogans everywhere, their heroic chant soothed him." (Berthier 2010: 61) Calhoun (1997: 47) reminds us that because "the discourse of nationalism [...] promotes categorical identities over relational ones [...] it offers the chilling potential for children to inform on their parents' infractions against the nation". Ten-year-old Henri did not inform on his father, but as Berthier (2010: 58) suggests, his love of the *patrie* was nonetheless a symbolic parricide.

Henri Beyle's life as a young adult was profoundly shaped by the Napoleonic adventure, by the excitement of glorious military campaigns, by the tempo of an era when nothing seemed impossible to a daring young man. The fall of the Empire was thus a devastating event for Stendhal. For the veteran of the Napoleonic wars the humiliation of defeat was unbearable: "Let's not be appalled by the enormous distance between savages and us when half the French do not yet un-

---

30 Philippe Berthier's biography of Stendhal (2010) is used here. Translations are mine.
31 Stendhal's father, Chérubin Beyle, spent time in prison during the Revolution. His grandfather, Dr. Gagnon, helped hide refractory priests during the same period.

derstand the meaning of the word *patrie*," he wrote in December 1814 in his diary. (Quoted in Berthier 1987: 43) The decommissioning of imperial institutions left him without job and income. Having moved to Italy in July 1814, he did not come back to France during the Hundred Days but Napoleon's defeat at Waterloo brought a new show of patriotism: "For the first time in my life, I really feel love for my country." (Quoted in Berthier 1987: 42) Stendhal's life as a writer thus began in Italy where he resided until 1819, with a few trips to France and England during those years. One of his first writings was an homage to the fallen Emperor, *Life of Napoleon*, whose accomplishments he praised when everyone else seemed to be condemning him. The work did not appear in print during Stendhal's life but the books on music, painting, and Italy published during those years are sprinkled with comments on French society and politics as well.[32]

Chapter IV, "Through Stendhal's Eyes: The National Habitus in the Making," investigates the genesis of the national habitus as Stendhal witnessed it and reported on it in a corpus of texts that is less known than his famous novels: *Chronicles for England* [*Chroniques pour l'Angleterre*], an impressive series of book reviews and essays written for British magazines in the 1820s; and *Memoirs of a Tourist* [*Mémoires d'un touriste*], a four volume account of the writer's travels through France in the 1830s. In these works, Stendhal offers a lucid analysis of the socio-political transformation France was undergoing at the time as well as a critique of modern national identity and in particular of the rule of sameness it implies.

Prosper Mérimée (1803–1870)

Prosper Mérimée was born in 1803 in Paris in a bourgeois family more concerned with the fine arts than with politics (Autin 1983: 18).[33] His father Léonor had trained at the Royal Academy of Painting and later taught painting and drawing at the lycée Napoléon (Henri IV), the *Ecole des Beaux Arts*, where the family lived in the 1820s, and art history and chemistry at *Polytechnique* after he became a specialist in the restoration of paintings. His mother Anne-Louise was also a painter, a portraitist who gave private lessons to young ladies at home. Both were fluent in English, a language Prosper learned at an early age; both were well-respected and had many friends in Paris: Count Elie Decazes (1780–

---

32 Stendhal's first publications are in the area of art, music, and literary criticism: *Histoire de la peinture en Italie* (1817); *L'Italie en 1818; Rome Naples et Florence* (1820); *Vie de Haydn, Mozart et Metastate* (1822); *Vie de Rossini* (1823); *Racine et Shakespeare* (1823, 1825). Berthier states that *Rome, Naples et Florence* is "a book haunted by Napoleon," "un anti-*Corinne*" (Berthier 2010: 247–248).

33 Translations from Autin (1983) are mine.

1860), an influential royalist politician close to Louis XVIII who was the family's protector during the Restoration; Emmanuel Viollet-Leduc, a colleague of Leonor and father of the future architect with whom Mérimée would work closely later in life; Viollet-Leduc's brother-in-law, the painter turned art critic Etienne-Jean Delécluze who had his famous *grenier* [attic] in the same house; Philippe Stapfer, a Swiss diplomat who had lived in Paris during the Revolution;[34] and the painter François Gérard whom Napoleon had made a Baron.

By 1829 Mérimée had already written about half of his literary production: a historical novel, *A Chronicle of the Reign of Charles IX* [*Chronique du règne de Charles IX*], and numerous short stories published in the new and prestigious *Revue de Paris*: *Mateo Falcone, Vision of Charles XI, How we Stormed the Fort, Tamango, Frederigo, The Etruscan Vase* and *The Game of Backgammon*.[35] But literature was not making him rich. His parents, who were still supporting him, thought it was about time their nearly thirty-year-old son embarked on a career. Thanks to social connections, Prosper was offered various administrative positions at the beginning of the July Monarchy and stopped writing for a few years. In 1834 he published *Souls of Purgatory*, a short story on Don Juan de Maraña written at a time when he too was enjoying the libertine way of life. The same year he was appointed Inspector general of historical Monuments [*Inspecteur général des Monuments historiques*], a title and position he held until 1853.

Chapter V, "Looking Back: National Past and Culture in Mérimée," centers on another aspect of the construction of modern national identity, the invention of what Anne-Marie Thiesse (1999: 12) calls the "rich legacy of memories." The crucial role Prosper Mérimée played in that regard is explored from different angles. An examination of the first inventory of France's cultural treasures he established as Inspector general of historical Monuments and of writings produced in that capacity underscores the backward-looking attitude that grounds his understanding of culture as a dead and static entity. An analysis of his historical novel, *A Chronicle of the Reign of Charles IX*, foregrounds the theme of national belonging, defined by an attachment to a secular state, while at the same time providing insights into the novelist's attitude towards "civilization." Two Corsican novellas help us define his conception of national identity. Finally, his essay on the Mormons serves to document his reconsideration, later in life, of religious faith as a means of national cohesion and social order.

---

34 According to Autin (1983: 28), Mérimée and Stendhal met at his house. Other frequent visitors included Benjamin Constant (1767–1830); Alexander von Humboldt (1769–1859); and Charles de Bonstetten (1745–1832).

35 These short stories were republished in 1834 in one volume under the title *Mosaic*.

George Sand (1804–1876)

Aurore Dupin, the future George Sand, was born on 1 July 1804, half a year before the beginning of the First Empire. She was a year younger than Mérimée but her political trajectory can viewed as diametrically opposed to his. In her writings, and in particular *Story of my Life*, Sand told of her difficult childhood but she also expressed a great deal of pride in her mixed social background. Her mother, Sophie Delaborde, came from humble working class roots, while her father, Maurice Dupin de Francueil, was the illegitimate grand-son of a French hero, Maurice de Saxe, Marshal of the French army (1696–1750). Elizabeth Harlan has recently argued that Maurice Dupin was not Aurore's biological father and that Sand probably knew it but chose to keep it a secret. This thesis, however, has no bearing on Sand's sense of social identity: whether Maurice was her father or not, Sand lived a life characterized by a dual belonging to the aristocracy and the people.

The Revolution shook her relatives' lives – her mother and her father's mother spent time in the same jail during the Terror – and her parents' love story is reminiscent of Stendhal's *Charterhouse of Parma:* they met in 1800 in Milan, where Maurice, a dashing twenty-two-year old lieutenant in the French army, met General Collin's twenty-seven-year old mistress and stole her heart away from him. Much to his mother's chagrin, Maurice married Sophie hardly a month before their daughter Aurore was born. Their short married life was marked by the Napoleonic wars. In 1808, a pregnant Sophie followed her husband, by then aide-de-camp to Prince Joachim Murat, to Spain, with four-year-old Aurore in tow. In the aftermath of Napoleon's first continental defeat, the family retreated to Marie-Aurore Dupin de Francueil's estate of Nohant in Berry. Aurore's infant brother died shortly after the family returned to France, a trauma followed a few days later by the sudden death of her father in a riding accident.

As mother and grandmother did not get along, they cut a curious deal. In exchange for a small pension, Sophie agreed to stay clear of Aurore's life and to let the aristocratic grand-mother raise the little girl at Nohant, where she lived for the next ten years. Two years in an English-speaking convent in Paris completed the young woman's education at which point she returned to her aging grandmother and helped her run the estate. After Marie-Aurore's death in 1821, Aurore married Baron Casimir Dudevant, with whom she had two children, Maurice and Solange. But her marriage was just as short-lived as her parents': by 1830, George Sand had convinced her husband to let her spend half the year in Paris on her own and by 1836 they were legally separated. In her lifetime, George Sand was well-known for her unconventional lifestyle and her love affairs with famous fellow artists: briefly with Mérimée in 1833; with Alfred de

Musset between 1833 and 1835; with Frédéric Chopin from 1839 to 1847; and with the engraver Alexandre Manceau, from 1850 to his death in 1865. But she was first and foremost a writer. As soon as she arrived in Paris, Aurore earned a living as a journalist and then embarked on a literary career. In 1832, the success of the first novel she signed "George Sand," *Indiana*, brought her fame and a modicum of financial independence, and from then on she never stopped writing. One of the most productive writers of nineteenth-century France, Sand wrote over ninety novels; short stories, plays, and articles by the score; an autobiography; travel journals, and a voluminous correspondence, tens of thousands of letters, many of them addressed to celebrities of the period, actresses like Marie Dorval and Sarah Bernhardt, novelists like Balzac and Flaubert, poets like Musset and Hugo.

In Chapter VI, "National Belonging in George Sand's Novels," the novelist's post-1848 literary production is presented as expression of a political project: her desire to transform France into a true republic. In these novels, the ideals of liberty, equality, and fraternity of the First Republic are praised and presented as the core values of a rejuvenated post-revolutionary French civilization that rejects (what Republicans in those days called "British") materialism and selfishness. Love and marriage between characters of different social backgrounds, between rich and poor, aristocrats and workers, allow society to progress towards greater equality, towards a more perfect national union. Her *Diary of a Traveler during the War* and her letters to Gustave Flaubert (1821–1880) during the Franco-Prussian war confirm her sustained preoccupation with the fate of the nation and attest to a sense of identity deeply grounded in love for the *patrie*. Of all the writers examined in the book, Sand is the most explicit in her understanding of patriotism as a faith, or more precisely as a transfer of faith from church to nation.

National founding myths, because they have the peculiarity of making the past appear as "always already there" (Calhoun 1997: 30), tend to erase the memory of the long struggles that paved the way to the present. Dating the birth of French democracy to the Revolution of 1789 and commemorating it as such, for instance, creates an impression of continuity between past and present that only a study of the twists and turns of history can dissipate. In an article published in *Le Monde Diplomatique* in April 1998, Alain Garrigou, a political science professor at the University of Paris-X-Nanterre, argued that this amnesia is particularly acute in the case of one of the pillars of democracy, universal suffrage:

> All history is contemporary and the history of universal suffrage more so than any other. There lies the main reason for the forgetting of its origins, and, in any case of its promoters: this institution is so grounded in the present that it no longer really has a history. Don't we

make it lose its magic, don't we claim that it hasn't reached the end of its history when we point to its beginnings and study its transformations? (Garrigou 1998)

It is common knowledge that American women did not get the right to vote until the end of World War I, or French women until the end of World War II, and that people of color in the United States had to wait even longer, until 1965. But probably few French and American people realize that 'universal' manhood suffrage is not as old as their founding documents, the French Declaration of the Rights of Man and the Citizen, or the United States Constitution. In France indeed, except for a brief period during the First Republic, from 1792 to 1795, and again during the Consulate and the Empire,[36] the rights to vote and to stand for election were restricted to men and subject to property qualifications until the 1848 Revolution. Similar restrictions applied in the United States until mid-century as well. In both countries, in fact, even acclaimed Republicans like Thomas Jefferson in the United States or George Sand in France were opposed to universal suffrage. Sand believed that the right to vote ought to be linked to education and she opposed universal suffrage on that ground. She was also against women's suffrage and showed little solidarity with the feminists who admired her and had hoped she would run for a seat in the National Assembly in 1848.[37]

The historical exploration of the national habitus proposed in this book proceeds out of a similar intent as Garrigou's examination of 'universal' suffrage: to document the complexity of 'truths' about the nation that are usually taken to be self-evident. Because it is informed by Elias's work on nationalism, this particular "anamnesis of origin" (Bourdieu 2000: 115) takes as its task to mine the writings of the six French revolutionary and post-revolutionary writers introduced above for information on the mental orientation towards future or past that informs them; for any evidence of a conflict between two sets of incompatible values, aristocratic and bourgeois, they might offer; and for clues about attitudes towards violence and war; and, based on this material, to analyze these writers' sense of identity and belief systems, to find out what being French meant for them and how they expressed their feelings of national belonging. It should be clear that, in so doing, my goal is not to pass judgment on them, to add them to the list of so-called 'nationalist' writers, or even less to claim that the works examined here influenced the development of what is commonly understood as French nationalism.[38] As my overview of his theory of nationalism

---

36 Under Napoleon, all men twenty-one-year-old and older had the right to vote but ballots were for or against pre-selected candidates.

37 On Sand's relations with Eugénie Niboyet and Jeanne Deroin, see Harlan (2004: 43–257).

38 On the influence of literature on historical events, see Chartier (1996).

makes clear, Elias views patriotism and nationalism as different points of view on the same phenomenon since "in many cases what one calls 'nationalism' is simply the patriotism of others, what one calls 'patriotism' one's own brand of nationalism" (Elias 1996: 153). Assuming that he is right, that patriotism and nationalism are indeed two sides of the same coin, the central finding of this study should be instead that no one escapes the national habitus' grip, not even writers whose preoccupation with the nation is far from obvious.

Part I: **The Revolutionary Field**

Chapter I
Olympe de Gouges's Revolutionary Patriotism

> *O French People! True French*
> *People, know the depth of my*
> *soul: I am not writing this*
> *letter out of ambition; my verve*
> *is stirred only by the good of*
> *my patrie and the love and*
> *respect I feel for my King.*
> (Gouges 1993b: II, 45)

Written in November 1788, this profession of patriotic faith marks the beginning of Olympe de Gouges's participation in the political debates of the French Revolution. It is the first of many statements in which this unconventional literary and political figure would express her love of France and her willingness to die for her country. Between 1786, when the first volume of *Oeuvres de Madame de Gouges* appeared in print, and 1793, the year she died on the guillotine, there would be many more such proclamations of nationalist feelings. Olympe de Gouges (1748–1793) was a prolific writer who authored over fifty political pamphlets and brochures, a novel, and several plays in the course of her brief literary and political career. Most of them promoted causes that were dear to her heart, from the rights of women to those of slaves, or, in the case of her pamphlets, expressed her deeply felt opinions about revolutionary events and the course of the Revolution. In spite of her gender, she believed that she was destined to play a great political role and did not shy from painting herself as a modern Joan of Arc:

> Yes, Your Majesty, it is a woman who addresses you in this way, a private individual who has only the good of her country in mind; a true French woman who loves and respects her King, and who would sacrifice herself to save the motherland, not like Joan of Arc, sword in hand: fanaticism does not stir up her zeal; it is reason and truth that guide her courage. (Gouges 1993b: I, 84)[1]

Olympe de Gouge's patriotic writings raise an interesting question. According to the dominant critical view, nationalism is first and foremost a modern phenomenon that appeared and flourished in the nineteenth century. But if nationalist feelings were unknown in an estate-society like the one France Gouges grew up in, as Elias for instance claims, how do we account for her patriotism? An an-

---

[1] Unless otherwise indicated translations from Gouges's texts are mine.

swer to this question may be found by examining her political texts against the background of political events between 1788 and 1793. As we will see, Gouges's independent, and even marginal position in the literary and political field, as well as her awareness of the quick pace of revolutionary change offer a unique opportunity to examine the modern national habitus in the making, or more precisely, the passage from Old Regime patriotism ("Vive le roi") to modern nationalism ("Vive la France!").[2]

1.1 Vive le roi! (1788–1791)

Olympe de Gouges's first published work, the epistolary novel *Madame de Valmont's Memoirs* (1788), is of interest to our study because of its focus on the social conflict between aristocrats and bourgeois on the eve on the French Revolution. Historians since Alexis de Tocqueville (1805–1859) have questioned the notions that the French Revolution marked a radical break with the *Ancien Régime* or that it represented the bourgeoisie's political revenge over the aristocracy. On the contrary, these historians have argued, aristocrats and bourgeois, the French social elite of the eighteenth century, shared a common culture. In a passage entitled "How France became the country in which men were most like each other," Tocqueville wrote:

> No doubt it was still possible at the close of the eighteenth century to detect shades of difference in the behavior of the aristocracy and that of the bourgeoisie; for nothing takes longer to acquire than the surface polish which is called good manners. But basically all who ranked above the common herd were of a muchness; they had the same ideas, the same habits, the same tastes, the same kinds of amusements; read the same books and spoke in the same way. (Quoted in Chartier 1991: 13)

Roger Chartier, who quotes these lines in *The Cultural Origins of the French Revolution,* also subscribes to the notion that French bourgeois and aristocrats shared the same ideas, and in particular Enlightenment values, on the eve of the Revolution. The antagonism between the two classes existed but it did not have a cultural origin. It was, rather, the survival of political inequalities in the face of cultural homogeneity among the elite that eventually led to the

---

2 "Unless one asks what changes in the structure of state-societies account for the change from an expression of loyalties and of feelings of solidarity in terms of an attachment to kings and princes – *Vive le Roi* to *Vive la France* – one cannot assess the role which publications of a nationalist intelligentsia have in the nationalization of ethos and sentiment of the great mass of individuals who form these societies." (Elias 1996: 150)

French Revolution: "[c]ommunity of minds made the exhibition of privilege and prerogative both more necessary and more unbearable." (Chartier 1991: 14)

1.1.1 Bourgeois values vs. aristocratic ethos

In *Madame de Valmont's Memoirs*, the issue of the power differential between people who are otherwise cultural equals occupies center stage. Several elements in Madame de Valmont's life story provide evidence of a common culture between aristocrats and bourgeois. She herself comes from a bourgeois family: her maternal grandfather was an attorney [*avocat*] in an unnamed province – Languedoc according to critics who see the novel as an autobiography; but his best friend was a local aristocrat, the Marquis de Flaucourt. As evidence of the mutual friendship that united the two families Madame de Valmont mentions two facts: her grandfather took charge of the education of his friend's first-born son "out of pure friendship;" and her grandmother, after giving birth to a daughter, her own mother, was the wetnurse of his second son. This friendship might appear somewhat lopsided to the modern reader but it accurately describes the bourgeoisie's function in Old Regime France as the provider of services of both intellectual and material nature. In return for these services, the aristocracy granted the bourgeoisie a symbolic social recognition that is also evoked in the novel: the Marquis's first-born son became godfather to Madame de Valmont's mother. Madame de Valmont insists that "all this happened in the name of the friendship that had existed between these two families for so long" (Gouges 1995: 26).

If the love story that develops between the younger Marquis and his goddaughter provides further evidence of a common culture between aristocrats and bourgeois, it also reveals the limits of this social arrangement. Marriage, in this case, was seen as impossible by the parents on both sides and the novel does not say what exactly prevented it. But comments Gouges made in 1789 point to financial concerns more than class prejudice: "Not a day goes by without a destitute noble proposing to a young lady of the Third Estate. The blood of practically every young lady of illustrious house is mixed with that of the Third Estate." (Gouges 1993b: I, 75) Marriage between aristocrats and bourgeois was possible, common, and socially sanctioned, in other words, but only as long as the latter met certain financial requirements. This was no longer the case for Madame de Valmont's family: once "rich and respectable" (Gouges 1995: 15), they had lost their fortune. The young Marquis was thus sent to Paris, where he became a famous playwright, and the young girl married, against her inclination, a man of her own estate.

The story of this star-crossed love affair does not end here, however. When young Flaucourt returned from Paris several years later, his beloved already had several children with her legally wedded husband but since their feelings for each other had not changed, and her husband happened to be away on a long journey, they picked up their relationship where they had been forced to abandon it. The fruit of their love affair was Madame de Valmont. In her letters, Madame de Valmont does not accuse her father of indifference towards her: this "new Amphitryon," she says, "took her illegitimate birth as a courtier, bragged about it, and called [her] 'daughter' in public" (1995: 26). Although her father was wrong to remain "insensitive and deaf to the cries of nature" (26) and to never recognize her legally, he is not the target of her criticism. Nor does she feel entitled to anything from him or from his family.

Instead, the novel draws its central theme from the Enlightenment critique of the aristocracy and the Church. The people Madame de Valmont wants to expose are her father's widow, the woman he married later on and with whom he had a son; and his younger brother, her mother's foster brother, now an Archbishop. Both stand accused of breaking the Marquis de Flaucourt's promise to assist her mother, now old and destitute, and of using religion to justify their indifferent behavior towards her. Madame de Valmont's letters are meant to reveal "the excessive cruelty, fanaticism, and hypocrisy" of her father's legitimate family and in particular their double standards: how dare these "ferocious souls, hardened by fanaticism" paint their inhuman behavior as a duty imposed by religion? "What religion is that?" she asks, "Either I misunderstood its dogma, or it preaches forgiveness and charity" (1995: 15). Madame de Valmont's double indictment of nobility and clergy, in the person of the Marquise and the Archbishop, and her outrage at their broken promise – their refusal to assist a member of their family in times of need after promising they would – illustrates the extent to which the exhibition of privilege and prerogative had indeed become unbearable to the bourgeoisie on the eve of the Revolution: in the story she tells, aristocratic and religious titles have lost any meaning or relevance, they are nothing more than an excuse not to fulfill one's duty to others, to remain "deaf to the cry of blood and humanity" (17). This story of vexed social relations between aristocrats and bourgeois repeats itself a final time in the novel when children of the third generation of both families meet: the young Marquis de Flaucourt is at first delighted to find out he has an older half-sister, Madame de Valmont, and a friendship develops between them for a while. But their relationship sours and ends when Madame de Valmont meddles in his love affairs and tries to bring him back to virtue, an episode that underscores once again the contrast between aristocratic and bourgeois ethos.

Olympe de Gouges returned to the critique of the aristocracy and the church in *The Convent, or the Forced Vows* (1790 – 92). Her play stages the confrontation between the old aristocratic ethos of submission to the rule of social necessity and the bourgeois ideology of free choice through the dilemma of Julie, a young woman forced by her uncle to give up the young man she loves and to take the veil. The Marquis and the Abbess defend these aristocratic values, so for instance when the latter tells poor Julie "to consider it a merit to obey necessity" (Gouges 1991: 61). Here too, history repeats itself since Angélique, Julie's mother, was also the victim of the ethos of "hypocrisy, deceit, and violence" (Elias 1996: 458). But Gouges pushes the critique of the aristocratic code of conduct a bit further in the play than in the novel by equating some of the practices based on it with criminal behavior. As the Marquis, Angélique's brother, disapproved of the husband she had chosen and married against his will, he challenged him to a duel, killed him, and forced his sister to take the veil. In the other camp are the voices of nature, reason, and freedom, the good priest and sister Angélique who make the case for the liberty to marry according to one's own heart and who vow to do everything in their power to spare Julie the miserable destiny the Marquis envisions for her. As opposed to the latter who uses religion for selfish personal ends, the progressive priest believes that "[r]eligion does not demand that people be deaf to the voice of nature" (1991: 50). He also states that everyone has the right to choose his or her place in society.

Two different conceptions of the family confront each other in the novel and the play. On the one hand is the aristocratic family model that the Marquis seeks to perpetuate, a social institution that is based on authority and disregards human rights, a family against nature, in other words. On the other hand, love is the foundation of marriage in the bourgeois family model advocated by the good priest and Angélique. As her defense of Julie also makes clear, maternal love is presented as an instinctual feeling that survives even a long and cruel separation. The happy conclusion of the play reveals Gouges's conviction that the nobility could, and would renounce its old violent ways and endorse liberty. In the last scene, the Marquis acknowledges the crimes his "barbaric prejudices" made him commit and expresses remorse for what he did. As if by magic, his new sensitivity to the 'cry of blood' and the 'voice of nature' transforms his ruthless, unhappy life into instant bliss as his sister, son, and niece open their arms to him. In *L'amour en plus*, Elisabeth Badinter (1980: 137–194) famously argued that maternal love was one of the Enlightenment's social inventions, together with happiness and love. By exploiting the topoi of the 'cry of nature' and 'the voice of blood,' Gouges, and many of her contemporaries who dealt with these themes, were participating in the process of elevation of the bourgeois code of conduct to a universal standard.

In *Mothers of the Nation*, Anne K. Mellor comments on a similar critique of aristocratic mores that appeared in England the same year as Gouges's novel, Hannah More's *Thoughts on the Importance of the Manners of the Great to General Society*:

> Confronted with the decadent practices of the late-eighteenth-century aristocracy – with codes of behavior that licensed libertinism, adultery, gambling, dueling, and fiscal irresponsibility [...] – she [Hannah More] first attacked the highborn members of society, and [...] directly condemned the hypocrisy of the "merely nominal" Christians among the aristocracy. (Mellor 2000: 19)

As Mellor points out, however, More also attributed the British aristocracy's failings to "their excessing dependence on French fashion and behaviors;" and the point of her pamphlet was to urge the aristocracy to "become more British" (20). Mellor rightly underscores the nationalist intent of More's critique, but More's opposition between a British bourgeois ethos and a French aristocratic ethos should be questioned instead of taken at face value, as Mellor apparently does, in my view. Based on the fact that Gouges wrote a similar critique of aristocracy and church the same year as More, it makes more sense to see both works as manifestations of the ascending bourgeoisie's efforts to define the national character according to bourgeois values in both countries, to replace the aristocratic code of conduct with their own bourgeois code of behavior in England as well as in France. In fact, the parallel critique found simultaneously in the two works demonstrates the accuracy of Elias's insights: "Different patriotisms and nationalisms often have a remarkable family-resemblance. They can stoke each other up because, as exclusive belief systems with their stress on the overriding value of a closed society, of a single nation-state, they resemble one another like twins." (Elias 1996: 355)

Just as the attribution of a particular national origin to discourses on the nation should be examined critically, so should the notion that social belonging alone determines the opposition between bourgeois and aristocratic codes of conduct. In Gouges's novel, for instance, the recurrent scenario of aristocratic ingratitude does not apply to all nobles indiscriminately: the Count of ***, a member of the court who serves as intermediary between the author and Madame de Valmont, is just as indignant as she is about the Flaucourts' ill-treatment of her family; furthermore, his knowledge of her illegitimate birth does not prevent him from considering, and treating her as a friend. Overall, it is instead the impression of a common culture among the French elite that prevails in *Madame de Valmont's Memoirs*, as Gouges's "Preface for Ladies" already attests. Although its goal is primarily to urge solidarity among her female readers, her "very dear sisters," the narrator makes a few comments that underscore the uniformity of French culture, at least for those women who ranked above Tocqueville's 'common herd,' or Gouges's 'dregs of society.' In good and bad, in looks and fashion, as well as social intercourse, Gouges writes, it is the court, and particularly women, who set "the tone for appearance, for attitudes, and fashion;" court ladies "are the original of all the copies found in the lower classes" (Gouges 1995: 9). In spite of the social problems diagnosed in the novel, and of their recurrence over the course of three generations, Gouges viewed the vexed relation between aristocracy and bourgeoisie as an aberration more than as a rule, and certainly as a problem that could be solved in a reasonable manner and in the best interest of the nation.

1.1.2 Royal patriotism

Olympe de Gouges made her entry on the political scene in 1788 with a patriotic pamphlet entitled "Letter to the People or Plan for a Patriotic Fund" (Gouges 1993b: 37–45). The trigger for her outburst of patriotic sentiment was the disastrous financial situation of the kingdom, the very problem that led King Louis XVI to call the Estates-General that same year. In this public letter, Gouges advocated a Patriotic Tax, a voluntary contribution to replenish the State's coffers as a means of alleviating France's enormous budget deficit, of rescuing the nation from imminent shipwreck, and of strengthening the monarchy. Her plan was to make "everyone who bears the name of French [...] contribute to the salvation of the State" (1993b: I, 42) irrespective of his or her place in society. But far from pointing to some kind of democratic vision on her part, her reasoning in this pamphlet reveals a strong sense of social hierarchy. Commoners would want to give money, she thought, less out of selflessness than as out of vanity: they would be flattered to see their name next to that of a prince on the roster of contributors (42). Moreover, she further speculated, the social rapprochement of high and low circles of society achieved through common sacrifice would breed patriotism, inflame all hearts with love of the country.

Gouges believed that social change, at least the kind that would breed patriotism and national unity, had to come from the top. The elite had to take the lead: "The state is burdened with debt; it expects its salvation from the elite of the nation." (1993b: I, 77) But apparently it did not comply in this case since we find her appealing for support of her patriotic fund a second time the same year and directly urging the elite to overcome an "awful selfishness" she saw as the source of the kingdom's paralysis. The measures advocated in these "Patriotic Remarks" were also of a more radical nature: a tax on palaces, mansions, sumptuous carriages and works of art, a clever way of forcing those exempt from taxation at the time to open up their wallets, since such luxury items were found most often among members of the aristocracy and the clergy. In response to criticism of her voluntary tax proposal, Gouges repeatedly emphasized its financial and patriotic merits: it addressed the dire financial state of the kingdom in a concrete, pragmatic fashion and working together would bring unity in a divided nation. Taking the lead herself and setting an example of civic responsibility, she announced that she was donating a quarter of her annual income to the State, in the hope that her gesture would encourage others to follow. A while later, she thanked French women for their patriotism, comparing them to the Roman ladies who heroically offered their jewels to save the Republic, thereby also implying that her plan had succeeded. But referring once again to critics who argued that aristocrats would not contribute, she agreed that the latter deserved blame for their lack of civic sentiment. She hoped nonetheless that the desire to escape public infamy would be a sufficient incentive to enroll their support:

> Do not listen to the insidious advice of those a-patriots who claim that this plan cannot be implemented in a Nation that boasts, as her most distinguished members, people who adhere to the strictest aristocratic principles. On the contrary, I maintain, it is the only way to make Aristocrats useful for the public good; as they are not the most numerous [part of the population], the fear and the danger of being marked by infamy, and thereby exposed to the indignation of authentic citizens, will be a more convincing exhortation for them that the dire state crisis is for you. (1993b: I, 121)

Gouges liked to present these voluntary taxation plans as her idea, but they may not have been as original as she claimed they were. As David A. Bell has shown, the monarchy had already introduced similar measures during the Seven Years' War and, on one occasion, in her province of Languedoc.[3] Nonetheless, and irrespective of the outcome of her efforts, her patriotic stand is a testimony to her love of king and country, to her sense of civic duty, and to her desire to contribute to the preservation of her nation's glory: "O France, France! Raise your proud brow again and don't let your neighbors pity you!" (1993b: I, 46).

In Olympe de Gouges's eyes, the stakes in this patriotic struggle were high: the fate of the monarchy, which gave France its identity, depended on its successful outcome. Any other form of government would bring anarchy and chaos. Her positions on a wide-range of political issues during the early phase of the Rev-

---

3 "In 1759 and 1760, with the disastrous state of French finances almost matching the disastrous state of French arms, the crown started encouraging this sort of 'voluntary' activity, including the donation of a 74-gun warship by the Estates of Languedoc, and of at least eight other smaller ships (including one baptized *Citoyen*) by a variety of benefactors." (Bell 2001: 89)

olution testify to her belief in the necessity of preserving the regime. She agreed with those who argued that the King had the right to veto the Estate-General's decisions. Frustrated by the Estates-General's slow progress, she exhorted Nobility, Clergy, and Third Estate to find a quick solution to the nation's problems instead of debating how votes should be counted. She believed, as the title of one of her early political tracts indicates, that "In order to save the Patrie, we have to respect the three Estates" (1993b: I, 82 – 85). In other words, she was opposed to the Third Estate's demand that the assembly's decisions be arrived at through a vote by headcount instead of by estate. Urging nobles and bourgeois to work together as brothers on solving the nation's financial crisis, she characterized the division within the French elite as a family quarrel in her 1788 "Patriotic Remarks." The thought that aristocratic privileges might be abolished did not enter her mind at first and when they were abolished on 4 August 1789, she fretted that their disappearance might diminish France's prestige:

> As for the privileges of the Clergy and the Nobility, it seems to me that, for the glory of France, the support of the State, and the emulation of the people, it was necessary to keep them, up to a certain point; I still believe that the French Monarchy should not be treated like a republic without leadership and order. (Gouges 1993b: I, 125)

Gouges's position on other political issues confirm her conservative stand in the early days of the Revolution. She defended Marie-Antoinette when everyone else was against her, as she recalled in the "Address to the Queen" that serves as a preface to her 1791 *Declaration of the Rights of Women* (1791: 1). Between 1789 and 1791, she made regular appeals for the return of aristocrats who had fled France. She also expressed her admiration for Thomas de Mahy, Marquis de Favras (1744 – 1790), who was sentenced to death and executed in the spring of 1790 for his involvement in a royalist plot meant to put an end the Revolution, going so far as to declare that she "would do today what he did, if [she] believed, as he did, that [her] King's life was in danger." (Gouges 1993b: I, 149) In fact, the character of Mirabeau conveys her deeply felt conviction that France had to remain a monarchy in the concluding sentence of her one-act comedy, *Mirabeau in the Elysian Fields* [1791]: "May France never forget that the only form of government that suits the country is a wisely limited monarchy." (Gouges 1991:130) In light of these various pronouncements, one can safely conclude that she was in favor of the political status-quo, opposed, in other words, to revolutionary innovation in those years.

Her insistence that it was impossible for a disinterested heart like hers to enroll under the banner of either the "aristocratic" or the "democratic" party may therefore seem a bit disingenuous, unless, that is, one realizes that what she meant by "limited monarchy" was an enlightened monarchy. Some of her writings show particularly well that there was no incompatibility in her view between a monarchical form of government and Enlightenment principles – Rousseau and Condorcet are frequently invoked; no inherent contradiction between her defense of human rights, particularly those of women and slaves, and her support of the throne. In the 1790 pamphlet entitled "Response to the American Champion," she defended her play *Black Slavery* in the face of attacks by advocates of the slave trade, taking a stand for human rights, including those of slaves, and in the same breath proclaiming her royal patriotism: "Royalist and true patriot, in life and in death, I show myself such as I am" (Gouges 2009b: 127). Her 1790 letter of "Farewell to the French" also brings this point home: in the signature line, she refers to herself as "The most determined Royalist and the mortal enemy of slavery" (1993b: I, 162).

Her struggle for human rights notwithstanding, her confidence in humanity was at times rather limited: "[H]uman beings are undoubtedly creatures most difficult to define," she wrote in 1788; "superior to all other animals in intelligence, reason, and their ability to enlighten themselves, they are nonetheless more foolish and less human than brutes" (1993b: I, 37). This pessimism colors her observations on the Revolution and explains her doubts about its chances of success: "Were human beings generally good, just, and virtuous, this majestic revolution would make the French happy forever, and serve as a model for the entire universe" (113), she wrote in the summer of 1789, but that was obviously a big 'if.' She understood the significance of the proclamation of the National Constituent Assembly but warned against the dangers of immoderate change in June 1789: "The French monarchy has a foundation that cannot be changed without destroying the State, the throne, and the Citizens' happiness." (91) In that regard, her outlook was past-oriented, and probably tainted by the "rediscovery of the Middle-Ages" (Bell 2001: 134) that was part and parcel of the patriotic propaganda of the second half of the eighteenth century. Gouges endorsed this idyllic vision of Medieval France as both glorious and civil; she praised a chivalric spirit associated in her eyes with an age of "gallantry" defined as the heroic defense of the weaker sex (Gouges 1993b: I, 74, 158).

1.1.3 Manifestations of the aristocratic code of conduct

We just saw Gouges criticize the aristocratic code of conduct as unworthy of an enlightened era in a novel and a play but two controversies in which she was embroiled in the early phase of the Revolution testify to the resilience of the concept of aristocratic honor. The first of them occurred in the context of the debates over slavery and involves the practice of dueling; the second has to do with patriotic honor in the context of the mass emigration of princes following the fall of the Bastille.

The struggles between abolitionists and colonists on the issues of slavery and slave trade took a particularly public and violent turn in December 1789, the month Gouges's abolitionist play *Black Slavery* was performed. Olympe, who intended to donate the proceeds from her work to the State Treasury, announced the upcoming performance of her play in the press on 20 December 1789, noting that the play would be performed in spite of opposition on the part of slave owners in the French island colonies. She used the opportunity to criticize her adversaries for publishing a pamphlet against the *Société des Amis des Noirs* – the French abolitionist society – and for failing to mention the names of the enlightened men who had joined this organization, "M. De la Fayette, M. le duc de la Rochefoucault." An article signed by "an easily identifiable Colonist" appeared a few days later in the press in response to her pamphlet.[4] Of concern here is the aristocratic conception of honor the colonist's letter reveals, starting with an opening sentence that bemoans its disappearance, and continuing with a justification that provoked Gouges's indignation: the alleged refusal of several *Amis des noirs* to handle their disagreement with the colonists over slavery with honor, i.e. by fighting man to man in duels.

As much as the letter documents continued adherence to the aristocratic code of conduct on the part of certain Frenchmen during the Revolution, in this case apparently the colonists, it also seems to point to its growing irrelevance in two ways: first through the refusal of those challenged to a duel by the colonists – "MM. De Pontecoulant, de Crillon, de la Feuillade, et de Lameth" – to respond; and second through the exclusion of certain aristocratic *Amis* – "MM. de Mirabeau, Duport, Clavière, de Villette" – as unworthy of the challenge due to their (alleged) known imperviousness to the point of honor. At the same time, the colonist's letter is itself a renewed challenge to duel since the author not only names offenders and publicizes their disgrace but also adds new insults in an effort to get the hoped-for reaction. Based on the dubious notion that being against slavery is the same thing as endorsing slave rebellions, he charges the Friends of the Blacks with the crime of murder, accusing them of steering the daggers that kill colonists and their families on the plantations. These "cowards, murderers, conspirators, and public enemies" (1993b: I, 131) are therefore challenged to "come out of their caves, drop their cloaks and daggers and pick up

---

4 The colonist's article, originally published in the *Chronique de Paris* in December 1789, can be found in Gouges (1993b: I, 131–132).

their sword" (132), in other words to fight as men of honor ought to. In a final effort to re-awaken the *Amis*' sense of honor, the colonist concludes his letter by insulting their manhood: lacking the courage to speak up and defend their views honorably, they used a woman (Gouges) as their front. The *Amis* chose once again to ignore the colonist's insults but Gouges, who did respond to this letter, proposed a different, more modern definition of honor: having the courage to sign one's writings (Gouges 2009b).

The Friends of the Blacks' refusal to respond to challenges to duel offers itself as evidence of the growing irrelevance of the aristocratic code of conduct. It seems to indicate that a significant number of enlightened French aristocrats, and most of the *Amis* belonged to that social category in 1789,[5] no longer saw honor and the use of physical violence as the proper means of resolving conflicts. But an opposite interpretation is also possible, perhaps even more convincing, namely that honor itself forbade these aristocrats to draw swords with sugar traders who were also merchants of men; that strict adherence to the aristocratic code of conduct compelled them to rebuff attempts on the part of men below their station to gain social recognition by fighting with them as equals. Two testimonies can be invoked in support of the second interpretation, first Germaine de Staël's, who made the continued importance of honor in revolutionary France a central theme of her novel *Delphine* -as we will see in chapter III; and second, William M. Reddy's, who, in *The Invisible Code*, shows that men from the bourgeoisie were still eager to appropriate the socially distinguishing practice of dueling in the 1830s and 1840s and that therefore "honor remained important even as it disappeared from view" (Reddy 1997: 10).

The second issue related to the aristocratic code of conduct is Gouges's position on the mass emigration of aristocrats and princes during the French Revolution, a phenomenon that Elias views as evidence of a pre-national understanding of identity grounded in the aristocratic warrior tradition. The royal elite's exodus was a real puzzle for her at first: when the Count of Artois, the King's youngest brother, left France two days after the fall of the Bastille, she treated his exile as if it were the result of a family quarrel and urged him to stop pouting and come home. In July 1789, she rejected as far-fetched the notion that French princes could ever seek foreign support to bolster their power: "French princes will not hand over their *Patrie*," she exclaimed (1993b: I, 113), a remark that shows that this aspect of the aristocratic code of conduct escaped

---

5 The 1789 membership roster for the Friends of the Blacks Society [Tableau des Membres de la *Société des Amis des noirs*, Année 1789] is available on the website of the *Bibliothèque Nationale de France* through its electronic server *Gallica*.

her. But as her confidence in the royal family faded overtime, her attitude towards *émigrés* changed accordingly: "The fugitives have burdened their *patrie*,
by monopolizing finances they have acted against their own good, they have
fed, strengthened our enemy" (175), she declared in May 1791. But in spite of
her criticism, the goal of the pamphlet that contains the preceding lines was
still to convince *émigrés* to return to France, and in particular Louis-Joseph de
Bourbon, Prince of Condé (1736 – 1818), who had just established a counter-revolutionary army in Coblenz. A month later, when she learned of the King's attempt to flee France and of his subsequent arrest in Varennes, she conveyed
her sadness and growing disillusion with the royal family to her readers, noting
that in a single day the King had gambled and lost the love of his subjects (189).
She also informed Queen Marie-Antoinette in September 1791 that "if foreigners
were to wage war in France," she would no longer see her as an innocent and
"wrongly accused queen," but as "an implacable enemy of France" (1791: 2).
Presciently, she urged her to resist "intrigue, plot, and bloodthirsty designs
[that] would hasten [her] fall" (2). In March 1792, she still believed that war
could be avoided if only the King could convince his brothers to return to France
and make them stop "conspiring against their *patrie*" (1993b: II, 53). Even after
war was declared in April 1792, the idea of a civil war was unfathomable to
her: she envisioned the French camps facing each other on the battlefield, but
yielding to the voice of nature and embracing each other instead of fighting
(1993b: II, 123). History, however, had outrun her understanding.

1.1.4 Attitudes towards foreigners

In spite of her critique of aristocratic emigration Olympe de Gouges was herself
determined to leave France by the spring of 1790. Disappointed by the mixed reception of her play on slavery, exhausted by the controversies surrounding it,
and despairing of the democratic course the Revolution was taking, she asked
the authorities for a passport in return for her services to the nation and announced she was going to England. Jacques Necker, who had served a second
term as Minister of Finance after being dismissed two days before the fall of
the Bastille, was also leaving France for Switzerland in early 1790. In her farewell
letter to the French, Gouges took the coincidence of their double departure as an
opportunity to compare Necker's accomplishments with her own prescriptions
for the good of the nation since the beginning of the Revolution.

  Although Gouges spread the blame liberally for what she viewed as the collapse of France, Necker, in her mind, was largely responsible for it. Personal resentment over his lack of enthusiasm for her patriotic tax may have played a role

in her negative assessment of his tenure, but her unfavorable view of him is tainted with a xenophobia commonly associated with nationalism. Echoing the general public discontent with the once acclaimed minister, she questioned the wisdom of having chosen a foreigner to head the French State in a time of crisis.[6] Necker's personality and ideas, she argued, were utterly unsuited for the job: he had a cold and impassive nature whereas the French were cheerful and kind; he was a "republican by birth" whereas France was attached to her kings (1993b: I, 145). Necker had failed, she claimed, because he had treated the kingdom of France as if it were the small republic of Geneva: disregarding French principles and mores, he had imported foreign solutions to homegrown problems. In stark contrast to her moderate recommendation "not to touch the sacred antique tree of the Monarchy, just to prune its [...] branches" (145), he had overlooked the danger of "turning men away from their ordinary habits" (147) and used radical remedies to try and solve France's problems.He was the one to blame, Gouges stated rather unfairly, for introducing democracy to the kingdom: he had taught France "the first elements of a freedom completely un-suited to the nature of her government" (145); he had intoxicated the French with the ridiculous pipe dream of equality, although he should have known that there is no equality in the natural realm (147). As a result, belief in the erroneous con-cept of social equality had spread, and with it, "a barbarity hitherto foreign" to the French" (149).

For Gouges, in other words, tinkering with the monarchy meant tinkering with the French national character, a topic of great interest since "the second half of the eighteenth century" (Bell 2001: 144). At the time, according to Bell (2001: 148), the French character was defined on the basis of a set of criteria to which enlightened opinion generally subscribed: Montesquieu's climate theo-ry; the belief that the nation's political regime, the absolute monarchy, shaped the French character; and that its salient characteristic was civility, or urbanity as Gouges called it, a mix of "sociability, légèreté, and politeness." In that world-view, 'civility' and 'civilization' were understood as related concepts, both grounded in "a vision of historical progress and cosmopolitan exchange between civilized people" (148). The degree of civility reached by a nation, in other words, served as an indicator of its progress towards civilization, showing "how far it had scaled this chronological ladder" (145). But this vision of humanity steadily progressing towards civilization had as its corollary a restricted definition of the nation: on the one hand, civility embodied the Enlightenment's forward-looking

---

6 Born in Switzerland, Jacques Necker was Germaine de Staël's father, and like Rousseau, a citizen of the Republic of Geneva.

attitude, but on the other hand "French authors generally did not ascribe 'national character' to the entire population of a nation" (144). Civility was a concept that applied to the social elite only, not to the nation at large.

As early as 1789, Gouges deplored what she viewed as a change in the French national character, the coexistence of an older trait, wit, with the new one mentioned in her comments on Necker: cruelty. In her farewell letter to the French, she bemoaned the loss of the nation's "lovely urbanity" (1993b: I, 162) and regretted that "the French nowadays have almost turned English" (160). For the first time in this book, we see the French national character construed in opposition to the British national character and fears expressed about its Anglicization. This will be a recurrent theme throughout our study. In the end, Gouges did not leave for England. Maybe she did not get a passport, maybe her fear of Anglicization made her change her mind about settling in Great Britain; maybe she thought she was needed in France. In any case she stayed in Paris and continued to write pamphlets that, perhaps unbeknownst to her, signal a further deterioration of the French national character, the rise of xenophobia.

Gouges's "Observations on foreigners" was written in July 1791, a few weeks after the King's arrest in Varennes and the National Assembly's decision to keep him on the throne. The pamphlet starts on an enlightened note with a praise of Paris as capital of the civilized world and of France's habitual welcoming attitude towards foreigners:

> Let us be eager to welcome foreigners, let us not allow national prejudices that lead to unfairness keep them apart from society; let us help them forget, through our thoughtfulness and consideration, the charms of their own country; I approve of this conduct and applaud this beautiful maxim of tolerance. (Gouges 1993b: I, 198)

The lines quoted here are in accord with an Old Regime understanding of the French character that was not based in the need to assert the nation's singularity: "The French did not define themselves primarily by 'othering' foreigners or by vilifying them in pre-revolutionary France;" patriotism was not tainted with xenophobia since the French "equated love of the *patrie* simply with concern for the common good" (Bell 2001: 44, 45). This friendly attitude towards foreigners also prevailed in the early days of the Revolution, as the custom of conferring honorary citizenship to foreign nationals – Thomas Paine in France, Condorcet in New Haven – illustrates.

In spite of its warm opening remarks, Gouges's pamphlet does little more than pay lip service to this "beautiful maxim of tolerance," however. It encapsulates instead the changing attitude towards foreign nationals that was taking place in France by 1791. No longer seen as brothers engaged in a universal struggle for humanity's progress, foreigners were now denied political rights, as Gouges noted approvingly:

> When the National Assembly decreed that the quality of Frenchman was a necessary condition for election to public office, it did so out of the conviction that it would not be prudent to entrust the Nation's affairs to a man with no vested interest in managing them well, and whose concern might quite possibly be to do just the opposite. (Gouges 1993b: I, 198)

As positive a step as this measure was in Gouges's opinion, the National Assembly had not gone far enough for her. It should have taken the spirit of the law a bit further and barred foreigners from all circles of political life in France, denied them entry to the halls of government and membership in political clubs. For as it were, she claimed, foreigners were "the ones who proposed and paid for the most incendiary motions, to the indignation of the French" (1993b: I, 199). It was time for France, she argued, to change course and adopt the "healthy distrust" other nations displayed towards foreigners (198).

Gouges's outburst of xenophobia came on the heels of a new outbreak of revolutionary violence. On 17 July 1791 a peaceful petition drive against the King's reinstatement was broken up by force on the *Champ de Mars*, leaving over fifty people dead. Leaders were either arrested or forced into exile (Danton) and hiding (Marat). Gouges deplored the bloodshed but laid the blame for it on the demonstrators and on one of their leaders in particular, a "foreigner," Jean-Paul Marat (1743–1793). In her eyes, all foreigners were potential rebel-rousers and paid agents of hostile, foreign governments ("Pitt and the King of Prussia") sent to foment social unrest and undermine national unity. But she loathed Marat, "the man from Neufchâtel," more than any of them, characterizing him as a "cannibal" (1993b: II, 160) in October 1792 and as a "ferocious Algonquin" (199) in December of that year.

Gouges's negative attitude towards foreigners thus points to the emergence of a new sense of national identity that feeds on the opposition between 'us,' the French, and 'them,' the foreigners. But her feelings of national belonging are not solely based in the hatred of foreigners: the old understanding of the French national character as grounded in civility, a cultural prerogative of the social elite, adds a class dimension to it. From her vantage point, the term "foreigner" thus had a wider extension than it has for us today: it not only referred to people from other countries but also to French people excluded from the circles of civility. Interestingly enough, the French lower class also subscribed to a similar social definition of the term "foreigner," albeit in reverse: those who were culturally different from them, the elite that Gouges viewed as French, were foreigners. From that vantage point, for example, Marat's foreign birth was utterly irrelevant. He was one of them, *l'ami du peuple*, [the friend of the people] and therefore not a foreigner. For Gouges, by contrast, he was a foreigner on two counts, as a member of uncivilized lower class and as a foreign national.

1.1.5 The French Revolution as a breakdown of civility

Although an advocate of human rights, Gouges was by no means a democrat. There were, for her, two categories of people: those capable of rational judgment who deserved "perfect equality," the aristocratic and bourgeois elite; and the rest of the nation. In her view, the educated elite was capable of governing itself and was therefore allowed to address the King and high State officials one on one, as Gouges often did herself, even using the informal *tu* instead of *vous*. This elite also knew how to handle political conflict within the boundaries of established institutions and according to the rules of civil communication. Lack of education and manners, by contrast, automatically excluded the vast majority of the French from 'society' and those people were expected to adhere to the old hierarchy of command and obedience and to refrain from expressing their political views in writing or through demonstrations that led most of the time to violence. With this vision of the lower class as uncivilized and thus violent by nature, it was not difficult for Gouges to predict, as early as April 1788, that the Revolution would take a violent turn:

> Even educated men have a hard time controlling themselves once their heads are exalted: why wouldn't a furious crowd be capable of the worst? Cruel as the French are, they cut throats, set fires, without being moved at all by their barbarity; they sing, laugh, and indulge in extreme debauchery in the midst of all these horrors. (Gouges 1993b: I, 69)

As she constantly watched for signs that would confirm the accuracy of her social analysis, she found them easily, for instance the murder of de Flesselles and Berthier de Sauvigny during the fall of the Bastille in July 1789 (Blanc 1993a: 16), and the burning of castles and the destruction of property by "brigands" during the Great Fear of July 1789 (Gouges 1993b: I, 113).

As a pamphleteer, Gouges's strategy was therefore to preach non-violence to the people and non-provocation of the people to those in power. In June 1789, fear of popular anarchy prompted pleas to the King not to overlook his subjects' misery and to the Estates-General not to tinker with the established social order. In late summer of 1789 she urged a member of the royal family, the Count of Artois, to adopt a conciliatory attitude and abandon his haughty ways instead of fueling the fire (Gouges 1993b: I, 116). In early October 1789, as famished Parisians marched on the King's Palace, she urged the people of Versailles to stay home and remain calm while the King's officers, the Marquis de La Fayette (1758–1834) and the Marquis de Gouvion Saint-Cyr (1764–1830), together with "the good citizens who devote their lives and fortunes to your interests" (128) took care of the problem. Gouges, in short, did not believe at all in the masses' aptitude to organize politically. She systematically denied the 'common herd' the ability to handle conflict non-violently according to the rules of civil, and even less democratic, behavior. In her eyes, popular uprisings were not the people's doings but the outcome of manipulations by ill-intentioned members of the elite.

Gouges's July 1789 "Letter to His Highness the Duke of Orléans" illustrates this point particularly well. She had probably known Louis Philippe II of Orléans (1747–1793) as a child – she being a friend of his father's mistress – and she probably felt entitled to criticize the young Duke's progressive behavior for that reason. Louis XVI had already sent this rebellious aristocrat into exile in England in 1787 for criticizing his fiscal policies, but the Duke had continued to embrace liberal political views. What irked Olympe the most about Philippe was not that he had been the first delegate of the nobility to support the Third Estate's demand for a reform of vote procedures at the Estates-General, a measure she had opposed, but that he encouraged uncensored political expression. "[T]he terrible revolution where the Citizens have taken the liberty to undertake and to say anything" (1993b: I, 97), she believed, was bad enough, the People needed no further encouragement from the nobility. As far as she was concerned, the political meetings the Duke allowed on his property at the Palais Royal only served to foment unrest in the capital city and to undermine the monarchy:

> What is the purpose of these public assemblies? ...What good can one expect from the fomentation at the Palais Royal? Are there any speakers there who, as they dispense instruction to the People, teach them good and useful morals? This hodge-podge, the lack of respect for the place and the sacred persons associated with it, can only further remove the People from their duties and encourage them to undertake who knows what [...]. (Gouges 1993b: I, 99–100)

But Gouges also wondered about the Duke's motives for authorizing these meetings. Unable to conceive that a Prince of Blood could sincerely espouse revolutionary ideas, she accused him of being one of those evil agitators who stirred up the mob and sacrificed law and order to advance their own agenda. The gatherings at the Palais Royal, she said, looked to her like the prelude to a bloody revolution in which Louis Philippe d'Orléans would seize power, like Cromwell in England,[7] eliminate his cousin the King, and replace him on the throne. Time was to prove her wrong: the Duke became Philippe-Egalité during the First Republic and did not try to seize power when the Convention, himself included, sentenced Louis XVI to death. But in 1789, conspiracy was the best explanation Gouges could find to account for this member of the royal family's incomprehensible behavior.

Unlike Philippe-Egalité, Gouges put no more faith in the speakers of the Palais Royal than she did in the "bad" citizens who displayed their uncivil behavior as the unruly audience of the Estates-General's meetings. As one of "the Wise, the Good Citizens who already shudder at so much independence," she was dismayed by so much freedom and so much eagerness to participate in politics on the part of the people: "What are they up to, these delegations of vagabonds that come to the Estates-General each and every hour? Which law authorizes them? Which police allows these public pulpits? And if they are not prohibited, should we not fear the harm that might ensue?" (1993b: I, 100) In her view, the common people were clearly not ready to exercise the kind of self-constraint required by parliamentary politics. Nor did they know how to use their newly won liberty productively. Just about anyone hurried to write and publish, she noted, but do "all these writings bring the necessary peace and order to save France from the frightful upheaval she is headed for?" (112). Her answer to this rhetorical question was a resounding "no." Freedom of the press was dangerous, because it "fired up the minds of the enemies of public rest," and counter-productive, because the wealth of opinions it produced drowned out the voices of those who ought to be heard: it "deprive[d] good citizens of the means of publicizing thoughts that are beneficial to the health of the nation" (112).

As these statements illustrate, Gouges's mode of intervention in the public sphere was more akin to Old Regime practices than to democratic due process. The fact alone that most of her political pamphlets mentioned so far were addressed to prominent members of the royal family reveals a conception of political power based in one-on-one relations and personal influence. The incongruity of this old-fashioned kind of politics in the revolutionary era comes through when she treats collective bodies – the Estates-General or the Constituent Assembly – as individuals, issuing apologies or making deals with them, as if they were individuals.[8] Modern readers are likely to be struck by the overblown sense of self and self-worth these passages convey, but they are also interesting to consid-

---

7 Cromwell was seen as the epitome of treason by Royalists. Lafayette himself was greeted with a "Here comes Cromwell" at court after he failed to stop the women's march to Versailles in October 1789.

8 For examples, see Gouges (1993b: I, 124, 126).

er as evidence of the difficulty to learn how to relate to the abstract national entity. They show that Gouges still felt that it was possible for a private individual like herself to be in touch with the entire nation and to share ideas and feelings with it like with a beloved friend. In a sense, the function of her political writings was to bring this (one-way) relationship to life.

1.1.6 Constructing the nation: the cult of great men

Gouges's contributions to the cult of great men provide another measure of her pre-revolutionary sense of national identity. Long before the French Revolution, great men were the subject of eloquence competitions organized by the *Académie française* and regional academies, of artwork, and collective biographies. According to David A. Bell, the cult of great men went as far back as the Counter-Reformation, but it took unprecedented importance "in the last thirty years of the Old Regime" (Bell 2001: 125).[9] An expression of the process of secularization and nationalization of feelings in pre-revolutionary France, "the cult of great men helped establish the nation itself as the most important reference point in French political culture" (121). By the eighteenth century, only those who had served the nation well and whose endeavors had strengthened it qualified as great, and the cult's traditional function of shaping national collective memory was giving way to "a desire to wipe it clean altogether" (130).

On 2 April 1791, the death of Mirabeau (1749–1791), a man Gouges greatly admired, gave her the opportunity to try her hands at the genre described above. She wrote two *pièces de circonstances*, first a eulogy celebrating the "father of liberty," "*Le Tombeau de Mirabeau*," and then a play, *Mirabeau in the Elysian Fields [Mirabeau aux Champs-Elysées]* that was performed in Paris on 15 April 1791. As the title indicates, the play is set in Elysium but one of its highpoints is the announcement that the great men and women who are assembled there will soon be transferred to the Pantheon, "the superb edifice that will henceforth be known only for its title *To Great Men, a Grateful Nation*" (Gouges1991: 123). Bourdieu (2012: 340), who characterizes the establishment of a Pantheon as "the ultimate state act," remarks that "the Pantheon is [...] the tomb of selected great men that designates men worthy of admiration [...] and at the same time covertly, the principles of selection of great men."[10] But, he adds,

---

9 On the Counter-Reformation, see Maire (1998); on the cult of great men, Bell (2001: 137–139); Ozouf (1984).
10 Translation from Bourdieu (2012) is mine.

"these principles being hidden in the selected products they are all the more self-evident in a subtle way" (340). Since the selection of great people in Gouges's play is entirely her own, it lacks any kind of state-sanctioned legitimacy, except for Mirabeau whose remains had just been transferred to the Pantheon when the play was written. But Gouges meant the principles of selection to operate in the way described by Bourdieu nonetheless: the very act of designating these people as great was to serve as proof that they were worthy of the public's admiration. Whether Gouges succeeded or not is subject to debate. For Althea Arguelles-Ling (2007: 252), the play's didactic effectiveness is not in doubt: this "palimpsest on the French Revolution and the French character," she writes, "contributed to sustaining the national identity through the comments of the great men of the nation." But there are also reasons to doubt that she reached her goal.

By incorporating the celebration of a significant national event that occurred two days after Mirabeau's death, the creation of the Pantheon, or rather the transformation of the Church of *Sainte-Geneviève* into a memorial to great Frenchmen, Gouges paid a double homage to the cult of great men in this play. Her great men form an eclectic bunch that includes philosophers (Rousseau, Voltaire, and Montesquieu); kings, Henri IV, Louis XIV; a foreign statesman who had just died, Benjamin Franklin; and two "shadows" about to be reincarnated by Destiny and sent to France to ease political tensions: Solon, the Athenian statesman, who symbolizes justice; and the Cardinal of Ambroise (1460 – 1510), famous for his charity and concern for the poor, as well as many other secondary characters. In that regard, Gouges's selection of great men is in line with the pre-revolutionary conception of the Pantheon as an assembly of people from all places and all historical periods, meant as a "commemoration without borders" (Ozouf 1984: 144), and reflective of the Enlightenment's forward-looking attitude. But her list is out of sync with revolutionary orthodoxy in that it draws on various historical periods and includes members of both sexes. Rather than limiting entry to the Pantheon to great men associated only with the Revolution as a means of marking the rupture with the past, Gouges brings the Old Regime perspective into play when she combines great men associated with the Enlightenment and the Revolutionary, including Mirabeau, Rousseau, Voltaire, and to a lesser extent Montesquieu, with great 'men' from earlier historical periods, thereby putting a damper on the former's greatness. Equally important, and equally contrary to revolutionary orthodoxy, her selection includes three great seventeenth-century women: Antoinette Deshoulières (1638 – 1694), Marie de Sévigné (1626 – 1696), and Ninon de Lenclos (1620 – 1705). As David A. Bell explains:

> The republican cult of great men implicitly criticized the notion that a nation's treatment of women was a measure of its civilization. [I]t replaced the story of a nation struggling to rise

out of barbarism towards civilization by the story of a nation struggling to restore itself to a pristine condition of republican health, from which it has fallen into dangerous degeneration, in large part because of the reckless freedoms it allowed women. (Bell 2001:124)

Revolutionary greatness, in short, involved qualities that were gendered as male, "independence, steadfastness, virtue, dedication to the common good," to quote from Bell's list, and defined in opposition to the female attributes of "luxury, lucre, and sensual pleasure" (128). Olympe de Gouges spent a great deal of time fighting this revisionist account, particularly in 1791, the year she wrote both *Mirabeau in Elysium* and *The Rights of Woman*. Marie-Claire Vallois states that her *Declaration of the Rights of Women* and Condorcet's *On the Admission of Women to the Rights of the City* "helped to popularize the idea that the word *man* might be problematic," adding that this "terminological dispute would enliven public opinion and be taken up by the Convention again in April 1793 during the drafting of that year's Constitution" (Vallois 2001: 432). Women, like men, Gouges argued, were capable of independent, steadfast, and virtuous behavior; they could and did act as citizens dedicated to the good of their *patrie*, and as such, they too deserved their share of national glory. There is no doubt that Gouges ambitioned this honor for herself: in April 1792, she declared that if she succeeded in saving the *patrie* from the Jacobin dictatorship, she would have earned her place in the Pantheon (Gouges 1993b: II, 115); and in April 1793, a few months before her death, she reminded the French people of her valuable services to the nation in a short and clear statement: "Citizens, [...] I am a woman and I have served the country as a great man." (227)

1.2 Vive la France! (1792–93)

1.2.1 From loving the king to loving the nation

As the examination of Gouges's political writings between 1788 and 1791 shows, her sense of identity was grounded in a pre-revolutionary sensibility in those years, her patriotism closer to the royal patriotism characteristic of Old Regime France than to modern nationalism. In June 1791, she still declared that she was "a Royalist, but a patriotic Royalist" (Gouges 1993b: I, 187). At the same time however she was starting to consider the Republic as a political option for France: "[...] if I saw that the issue was debated with decency and wisdom, if I saw that the spirit of private disinterestedness prevailed, I would perhaps ask for the Republic more than anyone else since I was born with a true republican nature." (1993b: I, 191) Similarly, events that were viewed negatively in texts written at the time they occurred frequently take on positive characteristics when revisited in later texts. In 1789, for instance, the fall of the Bastille was deemed a regrettable instance of popular violence, but by May 1790, less than a year later, it had come to symbolize the end of arbitrary justice (1993b: I, 165). She had experienced Louis XVI's arrest as a moment of national discord in June 1791, due to the division of public opinion on the fate of the King, but in a pamphlet written a few months later, she remembered it as a moment of national unity, as a beautiful day when "fraternity was on the lips of all Citizens" (1993b: II, 120).

A new sense of national pride is also detectable in her efforts to memorialize the revolutionary period. To commemorate the first anniversary of the Revolution, for instance, she composed a song celebrating French unity, and she also decided to write *pièces de circonstances* on teachable moments of the Revolution (Gouges 1993b: I, 170). *Democrats and Aristocrats* [*Les Démocrates et les Aristocrates*], a one act comedy written in the second half of 1790, captures the political atmosphere of the capital one year after the fall of the Bastille through impromptu conversations between people of all walks of life overheard by an officer of the National Guard, M. de Belisle. While giving voice to a wide range of political opinions, Gouges reiterates the views expressed a few months earlier in her "Farewell to the French," namely her refusal to side with either of the two political parties that were, in her opinion, tearing France apart at the time: "aristocrats" wishing for a return to the Old Regime, and "democrats," labeled "incendiary demagogues" in the play (Gouges 1993a: 140).

The terms 'aristocrat' and 'royalist' had different meanings for Gouges. Aristocrats wanted to erase the Revolution and return to the absolute monarchy; Royalists like her embraced the Declaration of the Rights of Man and were in favor of a constitutional monarchy. From her standpoint there was thus no contradiction in calling herself a 'royalist' while at the same time vehemently rejecting the accusation of being an 'aristocrat,' as she did in a tract written in September 1791. She could not be an aristocrat, she told her accusers, because she was in favor of the Constitution passed two days earlier. By March 1792, however, even her royalism was beginning to fade: "I am currently a moderate Royalist and a life-or-death patriot" (1993b: II, 50), she declared – which meant, she further explained, that she loved the King "for the sake of public interest" (51) more than out of personal preference. "The authentic mindset of the French government and the true interest of my country demand a monarchy" (59), she maintained a few weeks later. However, the remnants of her royalism evaporated shortly thereafter when war with Austria broke out in April 1792. Having initially done her utmost to make the case against war, she unequivocally embraced it once she came to believe that it was inevitable; having fought to preserve the monarchy at all costs since 1789, she now sung the praise of the glorious Revolution:

> French people, the universe has its eyes upon you, you have given new laws to the world. Posterity will record this grand monument as a *cause célèbre* and the name of Frenchman will be known in the furthest corners of the globe. The trigger for the Revolution was the struggle for human rights, its greatest patrimony. Rich and poor, all have made liberty and equality triumph. Shudder, tyrants who oppress your own kind, and accept the obvious [...]! The Constitution, founded on reason, justice, and on immutable principles, is protected by public force. (1993b: II, 121)

In October 1792, a month after the proclamation of the First Republic, she had all but forgotten that she had ever been in the counter-revolutionary camp: "I have never wavered in my principles, [...] the Republic suits me best" (1993b: II, 162).

As her political leanings metamorphosed, so did Gouges's understanding of the national community, as the reference to "rich and poor" in the quote above indicates. Whereas her former definition of the 'French people' excluded the lower classes – dismissed in many of her political pamphlets as lacking the *caractère français* and therefore deemed incapable of participating in civil society and in political life – by April 1792, she had reached the conclusion that "the true nobles are those the nobility calls commoners" (1993b: II, 85) because "true nobility resides in constant adherence to reason, nature, and the interests of society" (86). In the play *Dumouriez's Entrance in Brussells* [*L'entrée de Dumouriez à Bruxelles ou les vivandiers*], for instance, she has a folk-woman declare that the nobles who "have never been touched by virtue and have never known true honor" are "bold enough to think that the common people have none [of these virtues]" (1991: 199). Her unexpected support of universal suffrage (1993b: II, 87) strikingly underscores this new understanding of the 'French people.'

The reason for Gouges's change of heart on those issues had much to do with the fact that constitutional monarchists like her were now in power, either as ministers or members of the Assembly. From their vantage point the King had now become the problem. Conflicts between the executive and the legislative branch of government started in the Fall of 1791 when the King vetoed two decrees dear to Gouges that had been passed by the Assembly, one of them demanding the return of *émigrés*, the other, the priests' civic oath. In the spring of 1792, war became the reason for a new standoff. As support for a declaration of war against Austria and Prussia grew strong in the Girondist party, the King chose to dismiss a war minister who favored it – Louis de Narbonne, Germaine de Staël's lover at the time.

1.2.2 "L'esprit français"

On 22 March 1792, Gouges published a brochure entitled *"L'esprit français"* ["The French mindset"] and sent it to the Legislative Assembly and two political clubs, the Jacobins and the Feuillants. Dedicated to the King and addressed to him, it criticized his actions on a number of issues, his veto of the legislative decree demanding the *émigrés'* return, as well as his dismissal of Narbonne – she urged him to dismiss counter-revolutionary ministers instead. Although initially opposed to war herself, Gouges (1993b: II, 59) wondered about the King's intentions in this regard and warned of aristocratic plots to re-establish the absolute monarchy. The Constitution, she said, was a great achievement but the executive branch still needed improvement. She bemoaned "the growing disorder, the poor choices made by public administrators, new excesses as terrible as the old ones, and a noticeable fluctuation in opinions" (59), signs, she thought, that the French were not yet ready for liberty. They needed help, and particularly protection and safety: they would "never be worthy of liberty as long as liberty lacked the support of a public force capable of applying the law and maintaining order in society" (59).[11]

It is hard to nail down the precise meaning of *"l'esprit français"* as it appears in the pamphlet by the same name. Some character traits identified as defective are those usually associated with the court, namely lack of common sense and inability to plan ahead and take action. The problem with *émigrés*, for instance, could have been avoided, Gouges claimed, "[i]f we had cut off supplies" and "intercepted every communication related to their odious plots," but unfortunately she added, *"l'esprit français* does not look that far ahead" (1993b: II, 58). But the unreflected enthusiasm that embraces change too fast, the downside of the famous French *légèreté* praised elsewhere, is clearly a failing associated with the people, not the court:

> Did you [French people] really know yourself enough to aspire to perfect equality and total liberty? Should you not have mistrusted the light character nature gave you? Did you know when you rose up and cut off a few heads that you triumphantly paraded on pikes, that your friendly nature, instantly transformed into a somber and ferocious one, would lead you to commit all kinds of crimes? Had you let the law speak with all its force, you would have regained your natural kindness. (Gouges 1993b: II, 60)

---

11 The reference to 'public force' may be an allusion to a legislative measure proposing the establishment of a base of twenty thousand federates near Paris, a decree vetoed by the King.

In Gouges's opinion, the regeneration of the French character required self-examination, the identification and correction of shortcomings, but it could be achieved by balancing new positive traits (common sense oriented toward action) and old ones, such as urbanity, "the only component of the French character that can bring us back [to putting] society's interest [first]" (1993b: II, 62). In his 1792 *Projet d'Education nationale*, Jean-Paul Rabaut Saint-Etienne had argued that reshaping the French character "demanded a second 'revolution in minds and hearts,' parallel to the one accomplished in government and society," a revolution that would "use every means available: 'the senses, the imagination, memory, reasoning, all the faculties that man possesses'" (Rabaut quoted in Bell 2001: 2). Gouges agreed with him, but she was less optimistic than he was on the people's ability to actually change without a prior knowledge of their "instincts" (1993b: II, 69). In a pamphlet published a month later, "French common sense," she stated that her goal in "The French mindset" had been to highlight the gap between rational understanding and the ability to act according to it:

> I wanted to show my fellow citizens that, given the degree of Enlightenment reached by the French, it was easy to draft a Constitution worthy of all, assuming they were all reasonable and virtuous; but also, that it would always be difficult to implement it if the shortcomings of some and the vices of others stood in the way. (Gouges 1993b: II, 79)

Admitting that she had herself often lacked common sense – when she had let a royalist bias smother her republican dispositions for instance – she aptly summarized the two main hurdles she saw to the regeneration of the French character: the people's natural propensity towards violence (1993b: I, 75) and the difficulty "to uproot one's aristocratic biases and fanaticism, even with the help of a sane philosophy" (75, 84) – thus bringing into focus the issue of the durability of habitus.

Given the subtitle of the pamphlet in which the preceding thoughts are consigned, "Apology of the true nobles dedicated to the Jacobins," it is tempting to dismiss Gouges's act of contrition – in her own words a "metamorphosis inspired by common sense" (1993b: II, 74) – as political maneuvering. Because her political views were close to those of the Feuillants, the future Girondins, because she shared their disappointment with the King's unwillingness to cooperate fully with the moderate Assembly, she may have been appealing to the Jacobins to join forces with the stronger political faction in an effort to twist the King's arm. There is some merit to this argument but also two caveats. First, Gouges, unlike Brissot and the Feuillants, "opposed the plan for war like M. Robespierre" (88) – at least initially – and was thereby genuinely closer to the Jacobins on that issue. Second, she denied being affiliated with any political party. In fact, she made a point of telling her readers that the views she expressed were hers and hers alone. As proof of her intellectual independence and integrity, she often reminded them that she self-financed her publications – the plays, pamphlets, the posters she had pasted on walls all over Paris – and in her "Political Will" she expressed satisfaction for having "sacrificed her own fortune" (135) for the sake of free expression. Towards professional journalists, by contrast, she felt only scorn: as opposed to a freelancer, a disinterested citizen like herself, this "literary vermin" (101) operated for profit and, by serving as the tool of political factions, was a counter-productive force that fomented division instead of national unity (81). "Man [...] has the right to express his opinions," she wrote (135), but only "as long as they do not disturb public order." In her view, journalists did just that, hence her conviction "that men would be more robust and less extravagant if there were no physicians and no journalists, for physicians wear out the body, and journalists alienate the mind" (82).

As opposed to these forces of division and decay, Gouges wanted to be a force of cohesion. By reaching out to the Jacobins in April 1792, she hoped to bring the two rival factions closer to each other and thereby to prevent further public unrest. Her refusal to side with one or the other party was based on her appreciation that both of them were destructive and that taking side could only lead to senseless violence. She acknowledged that the fear of violence had always been a major concern on her part and found it regrettable that blood had been shed during the Revolution. But when addressing the Jacobins, she also felt compelled to state that her advocacy of non-violence was in no way a stain on her revolutionary credentials. On the contrary, the very reason she wrote to them, she said, was to make sure that they would work with the opposition and implement the new constitution, "this splendid, recently launched vessel kept from leaving harbor by mariners fighting over its destination" (1993b: II, 83).

Gouges's lack of faith in party politics, as expressed by her conviction that taking sides could only lead to violence, exemplifies an important point Elias makes, namely that people raised in a society based on a hierarchy of command and obedience have a hard time envisioning "strife [as] limited to non-violent forms of struggle fought out primarily in the form of discussion or word duels, the resolution of which depends on all participants adhering to certain rules" (Elias 2000: 292). In light of the bloody course the Revolution had taken, her mistrust in the ability of word duels alone to bring about revolutionary change was justified. But Elias's insight raises the general question of whether it can ever be otherwise. Can revolutions occur without bloodshed? Can people who were raised in a non-democratic society and are suddenly charged with inventing the rules of democratic exchange be expected to succeed immediately? Olympe certainly harbored hope that they could. When even the 20 April 1792 declaration of war against Austria failed to bring Jacobins and Feuillants together, she expressed outrage at their refusal to put the nation first (1993b: II, 111). Abandoning her conciliatory tone, she lashed out at revolutionaries and counter-revolutionaries alike with unprecedented verbal violence:

> These monsters differ in character, as you can imagine: one plots and lights the fires of civil war and aims at putting France under the yoke of the old regime; the other preaches anarchy and associates with brigands who want to divide properties, who will spare no one if they gain power and will kill each other after slaughtering three quarters of the Citizens. (Gouges 1993b: II, 112)

Bruised but not defeated, she continued her struggle for the preservation and implementation of the new constitution on her own, warning the French that civil war would most certainly lead to the restoration of the despotic absolute monarchy and promising for her part to remain faithful to the motto of the Revolution of "*Patrie*, Liberty, and Equality" (1993b: II, 123). In May 1792, she penned a series of "Letters to the Queen, the army generals, the friends of the Constitution and French women citizens" in a renewed effort to muster support for the constitutional monarchy. She requested and obtained funding from the Queen to allow destitute women to participate in the Bastille Day celebrations, the first time women were ever allowed to participate in state-sanctioned ceremonies.[12]

In June 1792, she asked the mayor of Paris to forbid a march from the Faubourg Saint-Antoine to the Tuileries but the demonstration took place. Parisians forced their way into the royal palace and symbolically crowned the King with the red cap. More convinced than ever that the Republic was impossible in France in the current political climate she penned a new leaflet, "National Pact," in which she asked all representatives to take the oath to "abjure the two-chamber system and the Republic" (138) and she sent it to the Legislative Assembly on the fifth of July. The same month she once again exhorted the French to non-violence, appealing to their sense of moral responsibility: "[W]hat would Nations of the future say if in the century of the Enlightenment, Humanity, and sound Philosophy, the French were to tarnish their reputation

---

12 Gouges did not meet with the Queen but with the Princess of Lamballe – a future victim of the September massacres. This court visit was the inspiration for a play, *La France sauvée ou le tyran détrôné* – of which only the first two acts were completed (Gouges 1993a: 183–209). Ironically, the Queen's anti-revolutionary rhetoric in the play was used as evidence of Gouges' own counter-revolutionary activities at her trial. See Blanc (1993b); Vanpée (1999).

with crimes that could only be committed in the days of utmost and vile barbarity?" (144)

But the Revolution was rapidly taking the violent course Olympe had hoped it would avoid. On 11 July, the *patrie* was declared in danger; on 25 July, the Brunswick manifesto, seeking to preserve the monarchy by threatening the French with invasion if anything happened to the royal family, produced the opposite effect. On 10 August, the revolutionary *sans-culottes* invaded the royal palace and proclaimed the National Convention; a few days later, the royal family was incarcerated. The popular violence Gouges had predicted and dreaded was unleashed by Marat, leading to the gruesome murder of over fourteen hundred people between 2 and 7 September. After the proclamation of the Republic on 22 September, Gouges condemned these massacres as senseless and contrary to human rights and justice; at the same time, she accused those who had toppled the monarchy of anti-patriotism (1993b: II, 152–154).

Supporting the weak against the strong, as she had always done, she said, she now leaned towards the moderate wing of the *Gironde*. In November 1792, she sent the mayor of Paris, Pétion,[13] a brochure denouncing Maximilien Robespierre as public enemy number one. Presenting him as a hypocrite, she attributed his involvement in politics to personal ambition instead of patriotism, accused him of seeking the dictatorship, called him the "disgrace" of the Revolution, and offered to commit suicide with him so as to rid France of his nefarious influence (1993b: II, 167–168). A few days later, on 5 November, she resumed her attacks in a pamphlet entitled "Prognosis on Maximilien Robespierre by an amphibious animal," in which she alleged that murder was Robespierre's preferred political weapon and that he had in mind to get rid in that fashion of "Pétion, Roland, Vergniaud, Condorcet, Louvet, Brissot, Lasource, Guadet, Gensonné, Hérault-Séchelle, in a word all the torch-bearers of the republic and of patriotism" (171). Predicting doom and gloom if Robespierre had his way, she urged France, "now a Republican nation" not to become "a murderous nation" (172). As far as she was concerned, the Jacobins' reign of Terror had already begun.

---

13 A deputy of the Third Estate from Chartres at the Estates-General, Jérôme Pétion de Villeneuve (1756–1794) played an important role during the Revolution: as president of the criminal tribunal, he was part of the escort that brought the King back to Paris in September 1791 and after his election as Mayor of Paris in November 1791, one of the first to call for the King's overthrow. A member of the *Gironde* and for a time Robespierre's rival, he fell out of favor with his party as the Jacobins gained control of the government. He lost his position in December 1792, survived the June 1793 attacks that sent other members of his party into hiding or to the scaffold, and committed suicide a year later.

In criticizing so openly the party in power, Gouges realized she was putting herself in danger, as she acknowledged in December 1792: "Mr. Bourdon blames the Jacobin club for not paying more attention to me and swears that I am Louis XV's daughter so as to better sharpen the knives that are meant to murder me" (1993b: II, 175). Threats, however, did not dissuade her from speaking up for justice. She even invoked the rule of law for her worst enemies, not only Louis XVI (173), whom she openly called a traitor by then, but also Robespierre and Marat (175): all of them had the right to a fair trial and to a fair sentence. Contemptuous of women's official exclusion from the professions, she went as far as to offer to serve as public defender for Louis Capet, because, she later wrote, no one seemed willing to defend him (192–193). In an effort to save the King's life, however, Gouges was ready to bend the rules herself, or to invent new ones. Given her professed attachment to the rule of law, it is curious to see her still search for ways to keep the King alive after he was duly sentenced to death. She declared in one breath that she too was voting "for the tyrant's death" (201) and at the same time she urged lawmakers to commute his sentence. She also argued that a guilty verdict against Louis XVI could not be carried out without prior approval of all "eighty three *départements* and of the armed forces" (193), a remark indicative of her growing impatience with the disproportionate power exercised by Paris over the rest of France. In light of women's exclusion from political clubs since 1789, however, she could sincerely deny having any formal affiliation with the Girondists (239), but she clearly shared their federalist views. In fact, she was still promoting them in the pamphlet that broke the camel's back and got her arrested (246–247).

Gouges's position can certainly be accounted for by her belief in human rights and her horror of violence. But it also originates in the exacerbation of her patriotic feelings under the pressure of war. Executing the King would irremediably tarnish France's glory, turn her *patrie* into another England, since "By executing Charles I, the British disgraced themselves in the eyes of posterity." (193) In Gouges's political writings, Cromwell, the King's murderer, is the figure that grounds the opposition between a civilized France and an uncivilized England. Until Louis XVI was sent to the guillotine, it was still possible to hope that regicide would not taint France's civilizing credentials: "The British sent their king to the scaffold, but they were not Republicans." (1993b: II, 172) After January 1793, however, the contrast between the two countries could no longer be maintained on that ground. Furious, Gouges took to calling anyone who, like Philippe-Egalité, followed England's example and voted in favor of Louis XVI's death a "Cromwellian." The *Montagnard*s became "the Cromwell faction," she wrote that Robespierre's reason had been "seduced by Cromwell" (166); argued that "The Cromwell faction" wanted to reduce the French people "to the most cruel slavery" (227); and that "these vile *Cromwelliens*" also wanted to murder "those who voted to exile Louis Capet" (230).

1.2.3 War: the catalyst of national sentiment

Gouges, we recall, initially opposed war against Austria and Prussia. Philippe Contamine (1986: I, 34) notes that Voltaire in his *Dictionnaire philosophique* had described the concept of "just war as 'contradictory and impossible'" and contrasted "'the natural religion that condemns all wars'" with "'the artificial religion' in which each of the murderers' commander has the flags blessed.'" Gouges viewed things the same way. In her opinion, war belonged to the past, to earlier stages of civilization, to the "centuries of ignorance," and, like all forms of physical violence, it simply had no place in "the most enlightened age," it belonged to "the Dark Ages" (Gouges 2009a: 93). As David A. Bell has shown, her view was widely shared in the early phase of the Revolution, when peace, not war, was on the agenda:

> [T]he French revolutionaries initially did little to revive the concept of wars of nations. These were the years of the Constituent's Assembly Declaration of Peace to the World and frequent proclamations about the brotherhood of peoples. Such gestures, themselves predicated on the concept of France as the pole of civilization and the world's schoolmaster, expressed the hope that in the brave new world of 1789 there would be no more barbarians, and all peoples would embrace the new gospel emanating from Paris. (Bell 2001: 99–100)

Even shortly before France declared war to Austria, Gouges was still holding on to this progressive vision of humanity's progress towards peace and happiness: "Nations, recognize your rights, but do not abuse them [...]. And you French people, who were the first to display the banner of independence, may your gentle laws spread across the universe and pave the road to universal felicity." (Gouges 1993b: II, 74) Like Friedrich Schiller's 1789 essay, "What does universal history mean and why do we study it?," this message to the "Peoples of Europe" is characteristic of the forward-looking mental orientation of enlightened thought.[14]

When war became imminent, however, Gouges stopped preaching peace. Instead, she encouraged her fellow citizens to fight the enemy with bravery and the generals "to fight and die for freedom," so as to "inflame the hearts of all our young soldiers" (1993b: II, 133). Her justification for war at that point was that

---

14 For a commentary on Schiller's essay, see Elias (1996: 124).

the French were being attacked, forced to react, to engage in a defensive war (121, 123). Whether they were actually capable of winning it was an entirely different matter. Behind the patriotic rhetoric, doubt and uncertainty pervade the political pamphlets she wrote in those months. Was the King really on the side of France? (1993b: II, 134). Would the citizen-soldiers really obey their leaders? (135). As these nagging doubts illustrate, Gouges had a second, more pragmatic reason to oppose the war: she did not think the French could win. How could they possibly do so when the professionals of war, the French princes and aristocrats, had joined the ranks of the enemy and turned their weapons against France? "How will we endure a campaign? We can only fear the effects of the smallest attack" (58), she worried. During the summer of 1792, news from the battlefield only confirmed her worst fears: in July, her friend François Gouvion was killed in battle and in August and early September, the French lost at Longwy and Verdun.

The victories at Valmy, in September, and Jemmapes, in November, therefore came as a truly unexpected and welcome surprise. At the same time, they transformed the advocate for peace into an advocate for war. With victory, the nature of war changed in Olympe's mind: the defensive war became a war for the liberation of the oppressed nations of Europe, a war conducted in the name of human rights. In her letter to general Dumouriez, the republican soldiers are described as "noble defenders of human rights." Similarly, her play *Dumouriez's Entrance in Brussells,* written within weeks of the battle Jemmapes,[15] makes it abundantly clear that the initial incompatibility between war and Enlightenment no longer held by that time for her. On the contrary, the French army's achievements on the battlefield are taken as further evidence of humanity's march towards universal happiness. Jemmapes, then, was not, in Gouges's eyes just a French victory, but a victory for all nations that aspired to liberty.

At the beginning of the play, for instance, a Belgian City Councilor named Balza states that "the Brabant people do not see the French as enemies, but as liberators" (Gouges 1991: 159), as "a free people, fighting tyranny alone, defending the cause of all Peoples and giving them back their rights as Nations" (160). A German woman, married to a Frenchman, both of them *vivandiers* [sutlers], echoes the Belgian's message: "May all the French you lead, break the tyrants' scepters and establish, equality, union among nations, and the fatherly love of our ancestors throughout the universe. Such is my burning wish for all

---

15 The battle of Jemmapes took place on 6 November; Gouges submitted her play to the Theater of the Republic on 23 November for immediate performance. See Thiele-Knobloch (1991: 18).

of Europe and for universal happiness." (188) Dumouriez, the play's hero, agrees: "Time has come for the universal revolution." (239)

The celebration of humanity's march towards liberty, thanks to war, does not preclude the manifestation of feelings of national pride, however. In the play itself, patriotic, revolutionary songs serve as transition from one act to the next: "La Carmagnole (II);" "The Marseillaise (III); "Ça ira (IV)."[16] In her homage to the great man she has just added to her Pantheon, Gouges characterized Dumouriez as a philosopher-soldier and her play has a similar dual function: on the one hand to inspire love of humanity everywhere -"to instill hatred of tyrants and love of liberty in all nations;" and to express her love of France – "to document my country's glory" (1993b: II, 214). As a result, the citizen-soldiers in her play appear doubly disinterested, willing to sacrifice their lives for nationals and non-nationals alike. In act IV, Lucas and Suzette sing a song that makes this very point:

On doit vivre pour son prochain	[One must live for each other
C'est la devise de la France	T'is the motto of France
Affranchir le genre humain	Liberate all of mankind
Par un grand pacte d'alliance	Through a great pact of alliance
Rendre aux hommes les saintes lois	Return to men the holy laws
De la nature souveraine.	Of sovereign nature]
	(Gouges 1991: 210).

Gouges gives a feminist twist to her play by incorporating two young women soldiers, the Freling sisters, into Dumouriez's army. Like the men, and even more so, the Frelings distinguish themselves on the battlefield and inspire other women to join the troops and share in the glory. But contrary to what one might expect, Gouges's homage to revolutionary women warriors is not the product of her imagination, as Patrice Higonnet points out:

About one hundred women are thought to have joined the army under false identities. Collot d'Herbois, a radical and populist Jacobin, hailed one of them as a hero – an intrepid warrior – who though female by sex was male by spirit. It was also suggested here and there that women form entire battalions in the National Guard. [...] The prestige of militarized and sacrificial involvement was such that dozens of women cross-dressed to take part in revolutionary soldiering. [...] Many decades later, Napoleon III honored one such survivor with the cross of the Legion of Honor. (Higonnet 1998: 93; 133 – 134)

---

16 Also included in act V is a song celebrating the joys of family life: "Où peut-on être mieux qu'au sein de sa famille?" ["Which better place to be than home?"] – a song that became the unofficial French anthem during the Restauration.

Gouges may well have ambitioned this glorious career herself. But, as she had stated in an earlier text, there was more than one way of serving the *patrie*. Her play was *her* contribution to the war effort: "If the writings of our great philosophers led to the French Revolution, a woman's play may produce similar results in Belgium and in of all other Nations in need of regeneration." (Gouges 1993b: II, 215)

This regeneration, however, was to be achieved without the assistance of organized religion, or more exactly against it. As early as 1788, Gouges had proposed the secularization of indigent relief and good works, arguing that priests would have more time to mind their own spiritual business that way (1993b: I, 51). In *Dumouriez's Entrance in Brussells,* she had a character, City Councilor Balza, call members of the clergy "men useless to society" (1991: 221) and another, Grisbourdon de Molinard, a chaplain in the Austrian army, provide living proof of this assertion.[17] When mentioned at all in Gouges's writings, the Church is presented as a social, not as a spiritual institution, and criticized for its defects. Among the few religious characters found in her texts, only one, the priest in *The Convent,* is given positive features. Perhaps more surprising given her involvement in national festivals, references to the "Supreme Being" are also scarce. The Supreme Being itself, it seems, had sided with the Revolution against organized religion, and, "tired at last of the crimes that defiled the altars," had "directed the Revolution to thwart hypocrisy and purify the cult" (1993b: II, 79). A testimony to the secular nature of Gouges's frame of reference, this absence of religion in her writings is worth keeping in mind.

As all drama committed to a social or political agenda, Gouges's revolutionary plays had an ephemeral existence until they were rescued from oblivion in the twentieth century. Marvin Carlson portrayed their author as "an eccentric old lady who possessed an uncanny ability for writing unsuccessful plays on apparently foolproof subjects" (Carlson 1996: 89). Granted, she turned out to be wrong twice in her choice of heroes: Mirabeau was removed from the Pantheon as early as 1794 and Dumouriez's posthumous fame is that of a traitor. But the selection of great men was a risky business and she was no more wrong than all other citizens who embraced the Republican cult of great men in those days. After all, as David A. Bell (2001: 138), echoing Mona Ozouf, states, there was no way of predicting which political figures would survive the ever changing course of the French Revolution. Gouges herself expressed great pride in her *Dumouriez,* characterizing it as a play "à la Shakespeare" (1993b: II, 212) – which

---

17 The scene was deemed too radical by the director of *Théâtre de la République* who, to Gouges's indignation, had it cut when the play was performed. (Gouges 1993b: II, 206)

shows that she did not indiscriminately reject all things British. Yet if her *drame* was meant to inspire universal brotherhood, the value of human life is elsewhere presented as a variable of nationality, a French soldier as worth more than a Swiss guard, for instance (108). Besides, her love of foreigners did not extend to those residing in France. On the contrary, her position on this issue only hardened with time:

> And would it not be extremely useful if the *départements* and municipalities were to banish all brigands from society; if all these disreputable men, foreigners in France, were regrouped and sent back to their countries' borders! I made such a proposal in the *Bonheur primitif de l'homme* in 1788 already. We are filling our prisons with foreigners. Let us send them back to their own countries to vomit the venom they were trying to poison us with. (Gouges 1993b: II, 73)

As shocking as Gouges's xenophobic rhetoric may be, her case was far from unique: it was the norm more than the exception to view all foreigners as potential spies or traitors in the context of war.[18] The war's implacable logic, you're either with us or against us, had turned noble *émigrés* from France into foreigners and helped unmask European rulers' hypocrisy. In December 1792, gloating after the French victories of Valmy and Jemmapes, Gouges lectured the "Don Quixote of the North," King Frederic William II of Prussia, and expressed her disappointment in him for she "had always thought that mind and philosophy were more natural in [his] house than the empty and arbitrary power of kings" (1993b: I, 195). The opposition between "mind and philosophy" on the one hand and "the empty arbitrary power of kings" on the other, shows that she had come to view bourgeois Enlightenment and monarchy as incompatible. At the same time, a new vision of commoners emerged, that of a virtuous, instead of an uncivilized people, a valorization counterbalanced by a further dive of the aristocracy in her opinion.[19]

Conclusion

From the time she began to write, Gouges's identity was grounded in her sense of national belonging. She was proud of being a French woman and never shied

---

18 Bell writes that "in 1793–94, as the war against the allied powers grew desperate, the ruling Convention changed tack. It enacted a series of repressive measures against foreigners living in France [...] and its leading members again began to claim that the English had willfully set themselves outside the universal (and France-centered) human community." (Bell 2001: 100)
19 Gouges (1993b: I, 67) even started to tap the myth of aristocratic sexual depravity.

from saying so: "O French people! O, my Nation! Should I regret to have been born among you? No, this thought shall not enter my soul." (1993b: I, 80) All along her career, she peppered her writings with statements expressing her feelings of loyalty and her sense of duty towards her *patrie*: "I have served my country with loyalty, with courage, and if I dare say so, with all the abnegation of a truly civic mind." (1993b: II, 250) Like a true nationalist, she was willing, indeed eager to sacrifice her life for France: "How beautiful it is to serve the Nation's cause! How beautiful it is to die for it!" (151)

But as we saw, her patriotism evolved nonetheless from an attachment to the monarchy to an attachment to the republican nation. From its initial formulation – "I am a royalist patriot" – her profession of faith became: "I am a frank and a loyal republican." As she herself acknowledged, this transformation came about as the result of insight: convinced at first that it was the monarchy that defined and guaranteed the preservation of the national community, she came to realize that she had been "blinded by prejudice," or more precisely that for the very people who had embodied France in her eyes, the King and the royal family, this national community did not exist. Unlike her, they did not swear allegiance to France but to a transnational, aristocratic community. This 'betrayal' led her to view the republic as a viable alternative to the constitutional monarchy. She relentlessly preached non-violence and denounced the evils of "civil war" but when her unrelenting efforts to unite the French failed, she embraced the Republic and contributed to the revolutionary war propaganda through her patriotic pamphlets and plays. She had learned to view the First Republic's war as a step towards the liberation of the peoples of Europe.

For Olympe de Gouges, the *patrie* was an object of a sacred, secular devotion. The figures or symbols expressing some kind of transcendence in her work are non-religious and virtually all associated with the nation – the figure of Destiny, the Pantheon in *Mirabeau in Elysium* – but above all words revered as sacred: *Nation, Patrie, Liberté, Egalité, Fraternité*. To say that she put her faith in the nation is an understatement. Jacques-Pierre Brissot (de Warville), a Girondist leader, wrote that "her patriotism and love of liberty made her even more famous than her beauty and her works;" that "the glory and the independence of the Nation were her most ardent wishes;" that "all her writings and actions were inspired by these feelings" (quoted in Blanc 1993b: 18). Gouges's sense of identity was indeed grounded in her attachment to France, a national community she had a hard time conceiving as an abstract entity, so emotional was her relation, so strong her faith in it, so deep her conviction that it was worth dying for it: "I have no regrets, I fear nothing, I ask for nothing, I've made all the sacrifices a brave man is capable of in order to defend such a glorious cause, and all I can do now is sacrifice my life. I will lose it without effort if it is for my country." (Gouges 1993b: I, 119) Nothing better illustrates her burning love of France than these words in her "Political Will:" "I bequeath my heart to the *patrie*." (1993b: II, 240)

Chapter II
Identity Lost and Found:
Chateaubriand's Culturalist Nationalism

And you, o, my fellow citizens!
You who are governing this
country still so dear to my
heart, think about it: is there is
a single nation worthy of
democracy in all of Europe? Make
France happy again and
restore the monarchy, as will
inevitably happen.
(Chateaubriand 1978: 269)[1]

Written in 1793, the year of Olympe de Gouges's death, these lines from the *Historical, Political, and Moral Essay on Revolutions, Ancient and Modern* (1797) aptly capture Chateaubriand's early endeavors as a political writer: to cast the French Revolution as an unfortunate, but not unique accident in the course of humanity's history, and to return the nation to the presumably happier times of altar and throne. Chateaubriand's and Gouges's writings on French identity stem from very different approaches. A lived chronicle of the Revolution, her political pamphlets document her reactions to political change while at the same time testifying to her own evolving sense of identity. Written mostly in exile, the *Essay on Revolutions* offers a wide-ranging critique of eighteenth-century France and of the Revolution. Conceived by an author who has reintegrated the national community, *The Genius of Christianity* lays out Chateaubriand's plan for the regeneration of post-revolutionary France. If, as Marc Fumaroli contends in *Chateaubriand, Poésie et Terreur*, the former is "the point of departure of an immense labor aimed of reconstituting a French identity that proved elusive in a France that had become too fleeting" (Fumaroli 2003: 36), the latter has as its object to describe the nation's foundations and to affirm the Christian identity of France. As different as they may appear at first, these two works also deserve to be examined jointly, not only because, as Maurice Regard notes, they bring to light different facets of the same thought, but also because, as Dominique

---

1 Only the first part of the *Essay on Revolutions* is translated in the 1815 edition, which is still the only one available in English. Quotes from the second part are from Chateaubriand (1978) and translations mine, as are quotes from secondary sources in French.

Rincé points out in his study on Chateaubriand's early works (1977: 39), the issue of identity is central to both of them.

Today, *The Essay on Revolutions* and *The Genius of Christianity*[2] are no longer widely read, with the exception of *René* and *Atala*, two novels that were originally part of *The Genius of Christianity*. At the turn of the nineteenth century, by contrast, they enjoyed tremendous success undoubtedly because of the beauty of their prose and the originality of their style, but also, as Chateaubriand acknowledged, due to the serendipitous timing of their publication. Napoleon Bonaparte, during the early part of his rule, approved of their anti-revolutionary and religious message. Eager to turn the revolutionary page and to establish his authority over all political factions, the First Consul initially encouraged the development of a counter-revolutionary press in tune with his own authoritarian vision of French society and government. Because he saw religion and the patriarchal family as excellent means of social control, he let royalist writers like Chateaubriand and his friends at the *Mercure de France* and the *Journal des Débats* spread this message in the press and in their works. In the preface of a new edition of *The Genius of Christianity,* Chateaubriand wrote that his work appeared at a time when Napoleon Bonaparte "wishing to establish his power on society's foremost foundation had just concluded an agreement with the court in Rome and did not seek to prevent the publication of a work that suited his own designs" (1978: 460). With this agreement, the Concordat of 1802, France not only resumed ties with the Holy Seat that had been severed during the Revolution, it also enjoyed, according to Darrin McMahon (2001: 125) "a revival of religion." Three years later, the *Civil Code* enshrined the principle of the father's authority over his family into law.

Following the publication of *The Genius of Christianity* Chateaubriand was initially on good terms with the First Consul. In 1803, he was sent to Rome with Cardinal Fiesch, Bonaparte's uncle, as part of the French legation to the Vatican. Having fallen out of favor with the ambassador almost immediately, he was called back to Paris and nominated to a new ministerial position in Valais, Switzerland. But he never went. On 21 March 1804 news broke out that the Louis Antoine de Bourbon, Duke of Enghien, had been executed.[3] In *Memoirs from beyond the Grave*, Chateaubriand later wrote that this murder had marked

---

2 The two works appear together Maurice Regard's 1978 edition.

3 The Duke of Enghien had lived in exile since 1789 and fought with his grandfather, the Prince of Condé, who was the French commander of the counter-revolutionary army. He resided in Baden in 1804 when Napoleon, who believed he was conspiring against him – which turned out to be false – had him kidnapped and brought to France. The Duke was charged with treason, found guilty by a military court, and executed immediately.

the end of his participation in Napoleon's government; that as soon as he had heard the news, he had resigned his position. Marcel Rouff (1929: 127–128) questions this account, however, stating that Chateaubriand has already made up his mind not to go to Valais for personal reasons prior to the Duke's death. The relations between the writer and the Emperor, he argues (156–159), went well until 1808 when Chateaubriand's cousin Armand, who was an agent of the Princes, was caught, sentenced to death, and executed. François-René then published a letter in the *Mercure de France,* a newspaper he had purchased from Fontanes a year earlier, in which he compared Napoleon and Nero. At that point, the newspaper was shut down and Chateaubriand exiled out of Paris by order of the Emperor.

The break was predictable. On virtually every issue that did not pertain to the restoration of social order in France, Napoleon and the Royalists were at odds. Even when they agreed, they did so for different reasons. Napoleon acted on the basis of pragmatic considerations and had no intention of returning the Catholic Church to its former position of power and glory. As Michèle Sacquin (1998: 7) notes, unlike "the 1787 edict of Toleration that did not cut at all into the Catholic monopoly," the Concordat officially recognized "the plurality of cults."[4] In fact, by serving as a model of church-state relations for minority religions as well as the Catholic Church, the Concordat embodied a spirit of tolerance that true believers and Royalists had long interpreted as a sign of religious indifference. For them, religion was much more than a tool in the hands of men: it was the truth God had revealed to the world,[5] just as "the paternal authority set forth in the Bible" (McMahon 2001: 40) was the foundation of an immutable social order and of divine kingship. Napoleon's signature legislative achievement, the *Civil Code,* had nothing in common with this theocratic worldview. On the contrary, it reaffirmed instead the *philosophes'* principles and the Revolution's conquests. The patriarchal family model it adopted was the expression of Republican biases against aristocratic women's alleged negative political influence in Old Regime France, the goal being to keep unruly women like Germaine de Staël in their place. On the one hand, the *Civil Code* turned gender inequality into law, but on the other hand, it stood as a continuation of the Revolution to the extent that, as Claudie Bernard points out, it "undermined the

---

4 Sacquin adds that the 1802 concordat dealt only with reformed (Protestant) cults; that the Jews had to wait till 1808.

5 "At a time when many chastened republicans, such notable fellow travelers of the philosophes as Madame de Staël and Benjamin Constant, and of course, Napoleon himself, were acknowledging the instrumental importance of religion with precious little faith and more than a touch of Voltairean cynicism, the distinction was critical." (McMahon 2001: 129)

vertical and horitzontal bonds or 'chains' which had cemented feudal society and [...] foremost among them, of family – family as extended kinship and some- times household, embedded in a patriarchal structure" (2005: 260). But far from destroying the family, as the anti-revolutionaries accused them of having done, the Jacobins and Napoleon, she argues, redefined the family as a nuclear family in accordance with their conception of the individual, "less as hierarchical entity than as an aggregate of discrete persons" (261). It is to this new sort of family that they applied "the trinitary slogan, Liberty (hence the abolition of paternal power, on offspring of legal age, hence the instauration of divorce), Equality (hence the equal division of inheritance among the offspring), and Fraternity (hence the val- orization of domestic affection)" (Bernard 2005: 261).[6] To the extent that imperial legislation adopted this conception of the family and of the "consentual nation" (Bernard 2005: 259), the Emperor was on the side of modernity, or at least what is commonly understood as modernity: the victory of the forces of reason and jus- tice against those of superstition and privilege.

This vision of modernity emerging triumphantly from the French Revolution has been challenged recently by historians and critics who make a case for view- ing the anti-Enlightenment and the Counter-Revolution as another facet of mod- ernity instead of the last remnant of a bygone era. Darrin McMahon, for instance, characterizes the counter-Enlightenment as "a distinctly new ideological cul- ture" (2001: 15). The enemies of the Enlightenment's goal, he argues, was not "to recover privileges lost or to restore a world that had been" but instead "to remake society in keeping with an ideal image" (2001: 75). Gérard Gengembre (1989: 38) similarly views the Counter-Revolution as a new beginning instead of a throwback to the past when he locates the origins of the French Right that blossomed in the late nineteenth century in that very counter-revolutionary movement. Their insights are important because they cast a new light on mod- ernity: instead of figuring a historical turning point, modernity thereby appears as the stake of an ongoing struggle between competing visions of man, society, government, and nation. McMahon's and Gengembre's observations are also ger- mane to this study of the national habitus in Chateaubriand's works because both view Napoleonic France as the birthplace of the French Right and Chateau- briand as a major contributor to its ideology:

---

6 Transitioning from extended to nuclear family takes time. Le Bras and Todd (1981: 30) showed that "communitarian" or "authoritarian" family models still existed in some rural areas of France in the 1970s although by then "[T]he entire country, in a single movement, [wa]s evolving towards a crushing domination of the nuclear family."

> Although historians have largely ignored the fact, the turn of the century was a critical moment in the coalescence of what Chateaubriand termed 'conservative doctrines.' In the first half of Napoleon's reign and under his aegis, anti-philosophes consolidated their political vision of the Right, refining a set of principles on which enemies of the Revolution would trade for years to come. (McMahon 200: 123)

The first part of this chapter discusses the aristocratic understanding of self and nation and makes the case for classifying Chateaubriand in the anti-Enlightenment, anti-revolutionary camp on the basis of his critique of both movements in *The Essay on Revolutions*. Our examination of *The Genius of Christianity* in the second part of the chapter highlights the consistency of his thought by foregrounding themes that are common to both works, and in particular the central role Christianity plays in Chateaubriand's understanding of identity, government, and nation.

2.1 *The Historical, Political, and Moral Essay on Revolutions*

2.1.1 The aristocratic sense of self and national identity

The *Historical, Political, and Moral Essay on Revolutions, Ancients and Modern* opens with a question that hardly seems to bear on the serious topic announced by this title: "Who am I?" (Chateaubriand 1978: 41).[7] Chateaubriand's project thus appears paradoxical from the start: the book presents itself as a history and, its title suggests, a history similar to abbé Raynal's famous *Philosophical and political History of European Establishments and Commerce in the Two Indies* (1770). But it is also meant as an autobiography since the very first line not only signals the author's intent to embark on an identity quest but also points to a deep sense of loss originating in the disappearance, at this particular historical juncture, of identity markers that had previously been taken for granted. Béatrice Didier (1975: 1006) sheds light on the nature of this identity crisis when she compares the conception of the self that informed Old Regime memoirs with the sense of identity found in modern autobiographical writings: "[t]he emblematic value of the NAME that compels the aristocratic memorialist of the Old Regime to assert the adequacy of his self and his name leads to an 'extensive' understanding of the individual," she writes. In the case of the autobiographer, by contrast, "[t]he name becomes closure. In order to exit anonymity, a door must be forced;

---

7 As the first two pages of *The Essay* are also omitted in the 1815 English edition, translations are mine.

collective discourse must acknowledge the individual as founding value" (1006). The four answers Chateaubriand gives to his own question – French, emigrant, unfortunate, dying – situate him somewhere in-between, with the loss of the former self acknowledged, but no clear idea yet emerging on how to replace it. And yet, as Jean-Marie Roulin (1994: 129) notes in a comment that underscores the crucial importance national belonging plays in the writer's identity quest, national identity ("French") is the only one of these four identity markers that is presented as "an indisputable evidence" and as a "positive identification" (131).

During the Old Regime, when French society was divided in estates, the social hierarchy molded every subject's sense of identity. In his biographical notice on Chateaubriand in *The Genius of Christianity*, Charles White describes the viscount's aristocratic pedigree in the following way: "His family, on the paternal side, one of the most ancient in Brittany, descended in direct line, by the barons of Chateaubriand, from Thierri, grandson of Alain III, who was the sovereign of the Armorican peninsula." (White 1856: 23) The aristocratic understanding of the self as bearer and protector of an illustrious name described above by Didier went hand in hand with the aristocratic sense of national belonging. As opposed to Gouges, who viewed the monarchy as the nation's embodiment, aristocratic opponents of a strong central state claimed to be the nation, as Bell explains: the *parlements*, who represented them, "did not simply speak for the nation, they were the nation" (Bell 2001: 60). When the provincial aristocracy talked of the "rights of the nation," it had in mind "positive rights defined by French law" that "belonged not to the nation as a whole [...] but to the institutional descendants of the ancient assemblies" (59–60). This characterization fits the Chateaubriand family. In his introduction to the *Essay on Revolutions*, Maurice Regard (1978: 1378) notes that Chateaubriand's aristocratic father was "vehemently opposed to taxation and a fierce opponent of the court," an hostility grounded in part in Brittany's history of relative autonomy and perhaps best exemplified by the exclusively Breton membership of Club of the Jacobins when it was founded in 1789. It is fair to say that the Chateaubriands belonged to the aristocratic camp that opposed the monarchy's central power and that had used the concept of nation "to claim [its] historical rights through the *parlements* against the crown" (Bell 2001: 59).

Whether François-René himself belonged to that camp and espoused his father's values, however, is subject to debate. Gerald Izemberg (1992: 259) argues that "the coherence of Chateaubriand's views with those of his father [...] is far from perfect" and Fumaroli makes contradictory statements on that point. On the one hand, he states that Chateaubriand "never felt any nostalgia for [...] the social hierarchies and privileges his father and brother were so strongly attached to" (Fumaroli 2003: 71); on the other hand, he also notes that the aristocratic code of conduct was bred in François-René's bones: "In reality, his father and mother, without seeming to, and pretending to look down on it, had silently and mimetically transmitted the tao of aristocratic conduct to him: to be everything for all people, while belonging only to yourself" (Fumaroli 2003: 395). The two viewpoints, however, are not mutually exclusive. Chateaubriand had initially no reason to be attached to privileges he would never enjoy since he was not the first-born son and therefore not destined to become a Count himself. But everything else in his life attests to his adherence to the values of the estate he was born in and in particular to the aristocratic motto of civility on the outside and fierce independence on the inside that, from a bourgeois vantage point, was just hypocrisy and deceit. Nemoianu (2006: 10) has it right when he succinctly paints Chateaubriand as "a product of the 'old regime,' by origin as well as by existential and ideological choice."

The sense of social hierarchy was a constitutive element of this aristocratic habitus. Commenting on the experience of emigration in the *Essay*, Chateaubriand noted that the moral and physical pain of enduring exile was much greater for an aristocrat like him than for commoners. Being used to working, the latter would find it normal to fulfill their basic needs in that manner. But as needs and habits differed from estate to estate, to ask an aristocrat to work for a living was to "understand nothing about the human heart:"

> We do not support adversity by such or such principle, but according to our education, taste, character, and above all, our genius. One person [...] will scarcely perceive the change in his condition; while another, of a superior order, will regard it as the greatest of evils to be obliged to renounce the faculties of his soul [...]. Such a man would rather die of hunger than procure the necessaries of life. It is, therefore, not so easy to associate happiness and the satisfaction of our mere wants [...]. (1815: 312–313)

These lines contain a pertinent insight regarding the durability of habitus, which is to say the difficulty of transforming an aristocrat into a commoner at will. But they also define aristocratic identity as a difference in essence between those at the top and those at the bottom of the social ladder. Examining Chateaubriand's *Historical Studies* [*Etudes historiques*] [1831], Jean-Paul Clément highlights this facet of the aristocratic sense of self as expression of an innate superiority over others when he quotes from a passage in which one of its social manifestations is identified: the "'inequality in social consideration" that gave "'any little country squire [...] the privilege of insult or scornful behavior towards bourgeois, including the refusal to cross swords with them'" (Chateaubriand quoted in Clément 2006: 69). According to White (1856: 24), Chateaubriand made use of that privilege himself in 1789 when "he attended the session of states of Brittany, and took the sword in order to repulse the mob that besieged the hall of this assembly." It was precisely this estate-based understanding of identity that the French Revolution had sought to eradicate when it defined the individual in neutral, abstract terms.

Man, endowed with natural rights, and his political counterpart, the citizen, were at the core of Enlightenment philosophy and of revolutionary and Napoleonic law. As Gengembre (1989: 149) has shown, however, this conception of the individual was anathema in the anti-Enlightenment camp: human beings, as God's creatures, belonged to the place divine Providence had assigned them to. Man was thus necessarily a "relational, determined, concrete, social being that [was] part of a community from which it receive[d] its properties" (150). The *philosophes'* understanding of the individual as an abstract entity was contrary to this divine scheme and so was the notion that man had rights: God had given him only duties. For the anti-Enlightenment, these preposterous constructs, the individual and his rights, were nothing more than the product of the *philosophes'* misguided faith in reason and the manifestation of their rebellion against God. But Gengembre also cogently argues (1989: 114) that those who based their struggle against the Revolution on these ideological positions had, at first at least, to deny any actual efficacy to concepts and principles they dismissed as nonsense. Blind to the transformative processes that were occurring before their eyes, they paid particularly scant attention to the new nation born of the will of the people the Revolution had produced: they held on to traditional conceptions of the *patrie*; questioned the sincerity of popular patriotic sentiment; and refused to see it for the new driving historical force it was (1989: 38).

Chateaubriand was one of those counter-revolutionaries who made the "main and fatal error [...] to underestimate the power of nationalism" (Gengembre 1989: 38). According to the *Essay on Revolutions*, there was no national spirit, no real enthusiasm among the French population for the cause of the Revolution, no willingness to die for the *patrie*. The soldiers of the Republic, he maintained, were not moved by the desire to fight and die for their country; they were not even willing participants in these wars. They only fought as the result of manipulation and despair.[8] Far from being a sign of personal disinterest, their alleged sense of self-sacrifice was just the opposite: the expectation of benefitting directly not from the spoils of war, but from the spoils of the reign of Terror. In

---

8 "The citizen suddenly awoke in the night by reports of cannon and roll of the drum, to receive an order for his immediate departure to the army. He was thunderstruck and knew not whether he was awake; he hesitated and looked around him. There he espied the ghastly heads and hideous trunks of those unfortunates wretches, who had perhaps refused to march at the first summons, only that they might take a last farewell of their families." (Chateaubriand 1815: 47)

fact, according to him, the Jacobins had reached their goal by sending aristocrats to the guillotine or by drowning them:

> Thus the Jacobins attained four leading points at once towards the establishment of their republic: they destroyed the inequality of rank; levelled the fortunes of individuals, augmented the finances by the confiscation of every person's property who was condemned, and attached the army to their interest by buoying it up with the hope that it would some-day possess these estates. (1815: 50–51)

In light of such denial of patriotic feelings on the part of the French revolutionaries, one may be surprised to find a transcription of *L'Hymne des Marseillais*, today's French national anthem, in Chateaubriand's *Essay*, together with a relatively positive appreciation – "it is not devoid of merit" (1815: 85) – and the prediction that "this republican ode will be preserved because it formed an epoch in our revolution" as the hymn that "led many [...] Frenchmen to victory" (86). But the objective nature of these comments suffices to convey Chateaubriand's personal detachment from the ideas and feelings associated with this hymn. As far as he was concerned, the future national anthem was void of any emotional aura.

The actual function of his remarks on the *Marseillaise* is to introduce the topic of war in general and of warfare old and new in particular. The prospect of perpetual peace heralded by the Jacobins, their forward-looking vision of a world finally rid of war, did not sit well with the aristocracy. Like Joseph de Maistre (1753–1821), who probably inspired Chateaubriand since his *Considerations on France* appeared a year earlier than *The Essay on Revolutions*, Chateaubriand maintains the inevitability of war: "in every age, men have been mere machines urged to slaughter by words" (1815: 86).[9] The revolutionary wars, in fact, provide him with ammunition to buttress his pro-war argument: the Jacobins had claimed they wanted peace, he points out, but they had made war instead. Without going as far as de Maistre, who claimed that war was the "divine law of the world"[10] in his *St Petersburg Dialogues* [1821], Chateaubriand presents war as a necessity for an obvious reason: it is through war only that the aristocracy's existence and hence its social superiority can be legitimized. The republican victories, however, seriously challenged this self-serving claim. In the *Essay*, Chateaubriand therefore endeavors to transform these victories into defeats. There are proper and improper ways of conducting war, he argues, the honorable aristo-

---

9 The reference to war is clear in French: "dans tous les âges, les hommes ont été des machines qu'on a fait s'égorger avec des mots" (1976 : 116). We've restored it by translating "qu'on a fait s'égorger avec des mots" by "urged into slaughter" instead of "urged into action."
10 My translation from de Maistre in McClelland (1970: 33).

cratic fashion and the dishonorable Republican manner. The republican armies, these "troops of savages, instigated by other savages emerg[ing] from their caverns" (1815: 285) did not understand or subscribe to the doctrine of fairness that was part and parcel of the aristocratic warrior ethos. They attacked armies half or a third of their size and timed these attacks to be as speedy and as destructive as possible, with "[t]he telegraph convey[ing] flying orders" (50) and soldiers and artillery crisscrossing France by "travelling post" for maximum destructive effects (49).[11] The Republic's military victories were thus not true victories. The result of heartless calculations, they stood instead as a testimony to the Jacobins' cruelty, to their willingness to shed the blood on a grand scale for small gains. "When the blood of men is reckoned as nothing," he quipped, "it is easy to make conquests" (49).

Compared to the self-interested, unpatriotic, and cruel military recruits of the First Republic, the aristocratic *émigrés* who left France for Austria or Prussia during the Revolution and fought against the revolutionary armies, fare well in the *Essay*. From the critique of lower class recruits, one may already infer that they possessed the opposite qualities of disinterestedness, patriotism, and humanity. Indeed, the few comments on the French character found in the *Essay* paint a picture of them that corresponds to the aristocratic ethos of civility and honor. On the eve of the Revolution, the French, meaning the aristocracy, were gentle people guided by civility, but they also transformed into warriors when needed (1815: 57–58). Countering their detractors' depiction as "villains, the refuse and disgrace of their country," Chateaubriand presents them as "virtuous and brave, the flower and honor of the French nation" (283). Bristling at the thought of being called a traitor, he insists that he acted with honor in fighting in the Princes' army. He also denies anyone, and particularly the Republic, the right to judge him "for allegedly deserting" (1978: 292). On the contrary, he later maintains in a passage of the *Genius of Christianity* that provides the best illustration of his narrow understanding of the nation as restricted to the aristocratic warrior class, this was the only honorable thing to do since "the *patrie* was no longer to be found at home, but in a camp on the Rhine."[12] Like "the Jewish nation expelled from the land of Gessen," he writes, the French nation encamped on the border also had God on its side: it was spurred on by "the spirit of salvation," as opposed to the armies of the Republic which acted in "the spirit of destruction" (1856: 418). Chateaubriand understands that his account faces a

---

11 The "technological" advances presented as "dishonorable" in the context of the revolutionary wars are seen positively in the context of a cosmopolitan Europe (1815: 242).
12 My translation from Chateaubriand (1978: 832) departs from (1856: 418): "The country no longer resided in the homes of her children."

major objection. If God sided with Princes and *émigrés*, why did they lose the war? But he has an explanation ready. Divine Providence intervened: "God beheld the inequities of courts and said to the foreign soldier, 'I will break the sword in thy hand, and thou shall not destroy the people of Saint-Louis.'" (1856: 419)

2.1.2 Christianity: the foundation of French identity

The preceding lines speak volumes to the centrality of religion in Chateaubriand's thought. But they come from *The Genius of Christianity* and critics typically tend to see an evolution on the issue of religion from the *Essay on Revolutions* to that work. Joseph F. Byrnes (2005: 70), for instance, contrasts Chateaubriand's embrace of a "fundamental theism/deism" and attendant condemnation of "the organized – that is, authoritarian – religions of history" in *The Essay* with his full embrace of Catholicism in *The Genius*.[13] Fumaroli goes much further: on the basis of a note reproduced in the *Pléiade* edition of the *Essay on Revolutions* (Chateaubriand 1978: 1575), in which Chateaubriand wrote that "there may be a God," he contrasts "Chateaubriand's violent and atheist anti-clericalism" in the *Essay on Revolutions* with his "firm Christian convictions" in the *Genius of Christianity* (Fumaroli 2003: 364). Granted, Chateaubriand dared ask which religion could possibly replace Christianity in *The Essay*. In the chapter devoted to this question, chapter LV of the second book, he even entertained the notion that people might reach universal happiness without religion one day. These questions were certainly bold for a true believer and must have seemed even bolder with hindsight once the monarchy was restored in France. But, as is shown below, Christianity plays a central role in both works nonetheless. The topic is simply broached from different angles: *The Genius of Christianity* expounds "the spirit and beauty of the Christian religion"- the book's subtitle – as proofs of God's existence; *The Essay* highlights the perfection of God's plan by denouncing the vanity of human efforts to deviate from it through revolutions.

Quoting Rousseau, Chateaubriand enunciates the postulate that "explains all the work," Jean-Jacques's *L'Emile* as well as the *Essay on Revolutions:* "'Everything is right when it leaves the hands of the Creator; everything degenerates in the hands of man.'" (1815: 366) In the *Essay,* Chateaubriand seeks to prove the excellence of God's design for men, societies, governments and nations by show-

---

13 Byrnes nonetheless concedes that "[d]epending on how you look, you can see a break or continuity between the *Essai* and the *Génie*" (2005: 74).

ing how, throughout history, disaster ensued each time men dared tinker with God's plans. Christianity is presented in an affirmative fashion in *The Essay:* it is the mother of all virtues, the source of morality for the people, the foundation of personal and national identity; and the pillar of society and government. Christianity's universal appeal and its superiority over all other religions stem from its beneficial civilizing influence. Islam, for instance, Chateaubriand contends, may have perfected "utilitarian discipline" and mastered the art of warfare – albeit not on its own but "with the help of Christian renegades" – but it has produced no civilization (1978: 429). Christianity, by contrast, has done so because Christ, by revealing God's designs to men, not only offered humanity a universal model of moral conduct but also exemplified Christian virtues during his own life on earth: friendship, with his disciples; love and respect for one's parents, when he entrusted his mother to John; tolerance, when he forgave the adulterous woman; pity for misfortune, love of the innocent and the poor, the spirit of equality, when he treated slaves as brothers, and last but not least, spiritual strength and compassion "in the midst of the torments of the cross" (384–385).

Chateaubriand posits as a general rule that religion defines the national character. God saw to it that Christianity developed in Europe. He made Western countries Catholic nations. For him, therefore, the national character is a function of these nations' ability to embody Christian virtues. Among them, France is the one that best embodies the Christian virtue of charity: "The French nation [...] is the most charitable of all [European nations], and the most sensitive to a fellow creature's distress because it is beyond contradiction the least fond of gold." (1815: 308–309) The idealism that marks France as a superior nation has as its counterpart the materialism characteristic of nations that imperfectly adhere to Christian precepts. When England moved away from the Catholic faith during the Reformation, for instance, its national character changed accordingly. As opposed to generous, charitable France, it became a heartless, materialist nation where love of gold ranks above love of men. Chateaubriand has "proofs" of the accuracy of his claim to offer: reviewing various nations' reactions to "the sight of distress," a veiled reference to his own experiences in exile, he contrasts the Catholic countries' "sensibility" (Italy) and "nobility" (Spain) with Protestant Holland's "brutality" and England's "sovereign contempt" for the unfortunate.[14] "In fact," he notes in conclusion, "I do not know two nations more completely opposed to each other with regard to genius, manners, virtues and vices, than

---

14 It is worth noting that his praise of Germany's "hospitality" extends to the lower classes in the *Essay.* In the *Genius of Christianity* the German upper-class is presented as "corrupt."

the English and French [...]" (308–309).[15] It is important to pause and note the key-role these considerations play in Chateaubriand's argument because they reveal the purely rhetorical nature of a question he raised at the end of the *Essay*, a question that critics tend to take seriously: whether France could ever have a different religion than Catholicism. The answer is already provided here, however: of course not! Of course Protestantism would not be suitable in France (1978: 418). Why would France want a different religion when the one she has proclaims her superiority as a nation? (1978: 428–429).

As mentioned previously, *The Essay* foregrounds the negative effects of human interference with the designs of Divine Providence, or at least what Chateaubriand believes them to be. That the Reformation marked such a departure from God's plan makes no doubt in his mind. In England, it opened a spigot of religious skepticism that proved impossible to close and therefore led to the proliferation of religious sects. Persecuted in their country, these religious minorities found refuge in America where, according to Chateaubriand, they ended up providing striking evidence of a further deterioration of Christian virtues and of the national character: "men burn their brethren in New England, for the love of God;" others "in Pennsylvania profess to let their throats be cut without resistance;" some "in Maryland [...] covered with crosses, armed with conjuring books," advocate "universal toleration;" and another group in Virginia is strangely made up of "black slaves and learned persecutors in long robes" (1815: 119). Imagining the Native Americans' reactions to these sects, Chateaubriand intimates that they must have formed a poor opinion of Western religion. Futhermore, he goes on, they could not possibly have fathomed "that all these people came from the same country," that they "belonged to the same nation" (120). As far as he was concerned, the history of England vividly showed that tinkering with the national religion led to a loss of morality and of national cohesion.

According to Chateaubriand, the national religion determines not only the national character but also the form of the national government. This principle has as its corollary that "[e]ach time the religion of a state is altered, its political constitution necessarily changes as well" (1978: 381). Deviating from it, either by modifying one's religion, as in the case of Reformation, or more radically by adopting a foreign religion as one's own always has political consequences: "When men begin to be sceptics in religion, they begin also to have political

---

15 Preempting the justified accusation of ungratefulness towards a nation that welcomed him during the Revolution, Chateaubriand writes that "though the individuals that constitute that nation are greedy of wealth, they are equally generous as a nation." (Chateaubriand 1815: 309)

doubts. Whoever ventures to search into the ground of faith is not long before he inquires into the principles of the government under which he lives." (1815: 380) When the Romans adopted foreign Gods, their own faith weakened and religious doubt set in, eventually bringing down not only their polytheist religion, but also the "Roman colossus" itself (1978: 383). The Reformation led to the introduction of the constitutional monarchy in England, which in turn had disastrous unforeseen consequences: "An incendiary spark, lighted up during the reign of Charles the First, fell in America, when the Puritans emigrated thither in 1637, spread itself in 1765, and repassed the ocean to ravage Europe of 1789" (1815: 119). Similarly, by weakening their countrymen's faith through their writings, Greek philosophers in antiquity and French philosophers in the eighteenth century weakened their national religion, thereby opening the door to the overthrow of their political institutions (1978: 376–377). Following England's example, France replaced the divine monarchy with a constitutional monarchy a century and a half later. "I need not remark," Chateaubriand concludes, "that religion and politics are [...] closely related" (1978: 376).

According to the *Essay on Revolutions*, when a nation loses its faith, this process does not only affect the national character and national institutions, it also leads to a general moral and social degeneration: "Religion is needed [...] or else society perishes." (1978: 429) Once incredulity sets in, vice replaces Christian virtue in the national fabric. In France, disregard for the King's sacredness led the abolition of the divine monarchy; the reign of immorality heralded by the constitutional monarchy culminated in a Republic that offered the most striking proof that French society was morally rotten to the core: regicide. Chateaubriand, unlike Gouges who had come to view the King as a "citizen," held on to his belief in the King's sacredness. Characterizing 21 January 1793, the date of Louis XVI's execution, as a day of "everlasting affliction for France," he contrasts the virtuous King, who approached death with "serenity" because "his conscience was pure and religion opened to him the heavens" (1815: 336) to the degenerate commoners who governed the country, and in particular "the gloomy Robespierre, brooding over crimes and great only in not possessing a single good quality" (344). Louis XVI's execution takes on the character of a new revelation in *The Essay*. Just like Jesus's crucifixion marked his moment of triumph instead of his demise, Louis XVI, "this other Christ" (1978: 324), proved the truth of his divine filiation through his firm and dignified behavior throughout his ordeal. Just the like Roman centurion guarding Christ was touched by him, so too was Sanson, the executioner, who viewed the King's unshakable faith as the source of his exceptionally calm and regal behavior on the guillotine. Ironically, Chateaubriand comments, it was left to this man to "this hand that dared touch my King's head, and make this sacred head roll before presenting it to a fright struck people" (322), to thus witness and proclaim "one of the greatest triumphs religion ever knew" (334).

The establishment of any political regime that rejects the principle of the King's sacredness is premised on a social revolution that does away with the aristocracy in the sense Chateaubriand vests in it, a revolution symbolically and practically founded on regicide. In the second part of his *Essay on Revolutions*, chapter XVI "Trial and Sentencing of Charles I, King of England," is devoted to a comparison between the British and the French regicides. In England's case the blame for the regicide is placed on the Chamber of Commons and in particular on "Colonel Harrison, who was the son of a butcher and the most furious demagogue in England" (1815: 329); in France's case on the Jacobins in general, and on Robespierre in particular, as the quote above indicates. In both cases, the forces of virtue are associated with the martyred King and the aristocracy, the forces of evil with commoners willing to kill their King, but then incapable of taking the reins of government.

In the *Essay*, Chateaubriand does not refrain from mentioning that the Catholic identity of France was already seriously compromised before the Revolution. The decline of Christianity that started during the Crusades in Europe, he explains, continued later on as a result of the bad behavior of the Roman Court and of struggles within the Catholic Church during the Renaissance. In France, the absolute monarchy also contributed directly to the decreased influence of the Church. Louis XIV, Chateaubriand maintains, already acted against the spirit of Christianity but the Regent who succeeded him, the Duke of Orléans, did much worse. Famous for his immorality, he committed the unforgivable mistake of allowing the implantation of a "philosophic sect" that set out to destroy religion and morals in France (1815: 388–392). In his eyes, however, the most egregious illustration of the absolute monarchy's moral decline was France's violation of "the sacred right of nations," her decision to side with American colonists in rebellion against their king:

> France, seduced by a philosophical jargon, by the interests which she expected to deduce from it, and by the narrow passion of humbling her ancient rival, without any provocation on the part of England, violated, in the name of the human race, the sacred right of nations. She first furnished the Americans with arms against their legitimate sovereign, and then openly declared in their favor (1815: 122).[16] I realize that defending the cause of liberty may be seen as in humanity's best interest according to the subtleties of logic; but I also know that every time the law of all or nothing is applied to the *patrie* there is absolutely no vice that can't be justified. The American Revolution is the immediate cause of the

---

16 The rest of the quote is my translation from Chateaubriand (1978: 149) as this passage is omitted in the 1815 English edition.

French Revolution. France, deserted, drowned in blood, covered in ruins, her King led to the scaffold, her ministers exiled or murdered, are proof that eternal justice, without which all would perish [...] has formidable ways of avenging itself.

For her "duplicity [...] towards England" (1815: 122), for renouncing her aristocratic code of honor, France deserved to be punished and divine providence saw to it that it happened. In Chateaubriand's eyes, the French Revolution was God's retribution for France's dishonorable conduct towards the Crown of England.[17]

In stark contrast with the degraded image of nobility so strikingly reflected in the dishonorable actions of the corrupt court of Versailles, Chateaubriand held up the ideal of Christian virtue exemplified by the purer, freer, more authentic ethos of the provincial aristocracy. The aristocratic belief in perfectibility noted by McMahon and Gengembre originates in the discrepancy between the provincial nobility's ideal (and idealized) vision of a France actually adhering to its values, and the inauthentic France exemplified by the courtiers' shortcomings in matters of liberty, religion and mores. Just like *the philosophes*, Chateaubriand believed in a better France, albeit not the same one.

2.1.3 Against the Enlightenment and the French Revolution

As with the issue of religion, critics tend to see an evolution in Chateaubriand's attitude towards the Enlightenment. Fumaroli (2003: 98), for instance, contrasts Chateaubriand's pro-*philosophes* position in *The Essay* with his harsh condemnation of the Enlightenment in the *Genius*, "a thesis," Guy Berger (2002: 93) notes, "accredited by Chateaubriand himself in commentaries on his works." The case for a pro-Enlightenment stand in the *Essay* hinges on two points: the numerous references to the *philosophes*, and in particular to Jean-Jacques Rousseau; and what appears to be Chateaubriand's endorsement of an idea particularly dear to them, perfectibility. In support of the second point, Berger (2002: 96) quotes three statements from *The Essay* that seem at first to unambiguously demonstrate Chateaubriand's adherence to the concept of perfectibility: 1) "Mankind will one day arrive at a purity of government of and morals, now unknown."

---

17 Chateaubriand also condemns the Americans who failed to support a King who had supported them: "Americans, your idol La Fayette was a villain, and the Frenchmen, once the objects of your eulogium, who shed their blood in your battles, are wretches whom you now despise, and to whom you would perhaps refuse an asylum. The august father of your liberty too – did not one of you pass sentence on him? – Have you not sworn friendship for, and entered into alliance with his assassins?" (Chateaubriand 1815: 123)

(Chateaubriand 1815: 44) 2) "Nations will reach such a degree of knowledge and morals that they will no longer need religion."[18] 3) "Having accumulated an enormous well of knowledge, nations will all become enlightened and unite under one government, in a state of permanent happiness."[19] The problem with these statements, however, is that they are edited and taken out of context. The first quote refers to "the famous system of perfection" of the Jacobins, not of Chateaubriand; the second is a hypothesis, phrased as a question, not a statement.[20] The third quote is actually the first of the two predictions Chateaubriand makes about the future of humanity: either the world will enjoy happiness, or nations "will return to a state of barbarity," a proposition, he adds, that seems more likely to him than the first "if the future is to be appraised on the basis of the past" (1978: 430). But another scenario is presented as just as possible, and in final analysis, as more probable: France, corrupted by the Revolution and in need of moral regeneration, will embrace her Catholic identity again. Berger himself (2002: 107), even after twisting the stick in the other direction and playing the devil's advocate, ends up with the following conclusion: far from endorsing Enlightenment thought, Chateaubriand was actually intent on "denounc[ing] and refut[ing]" it in *The Essay*.

Basing the evidence for Chateaubriand's endorsement of the Enlightenment on the idea of perfectibility is also a flawed argument because his belief in perfectibility, the notion that man, society, government, and the national character must be perfected, does not stem from an agreement with the *philosophes* but from a critique of the court nobility. If the *philosophes*' works were read and appreciated by the provincial aristocracy, it was precisely because they criticized the absolute monarchy. Maurice Regard (1978: 1377) tells us that Chateaubriand's father was an avid "reader of Enlightenment philosophy with a particular predilection for Abbé Raynal," an outspoken critic of the absolute monarchy, and so was his son. But reading these works was by no means the same thing as endorsing Enlightenment philosophy, as Roger Chartier (1991: 83–84) points out when he cautions against "linking philosophical books and revolutionary thought." Fumaroli's comment (2003: 53) on the elder Chateaubriand's "naïve feudal interpretation" of Raynal's pamphlet against despotism is a good indication that familiarity with the *philosophes*' works did not preclude readings that went against their spirit. In *The Essay on Revolution*, his son (1815: 390) similary expressed as-

---

18 My translation from Berger (2002: 96).
19 My translation from Berger (2002: 96).
20 "Other possibility: Wouldn't it be possible that nations reach such a degree of knowledge and morals that they will no longer need religion?" My translation from Chateaubriand (1978: 429).

tonishment that the revolutionaries had misinterpreted Rousseau's *Social Contract* and taken "it as their guide, for no work more condemn[ed] them" in his eyes. Prior to the Revolution, a common critique of the monarchy's shortcomings could allow the aristocracy and the enlightened bourgeoisie to overlook differences between them. In its aftermath, however, the latter could only take center stage.

One of Chateaubriand's key arguments against the Enlightenment in *the Essay* is that the *philosophes*' ideas do not stand the test of experience. If, according to him, the French Revolution offered the most vivid illustration of the accuracy of this observation, his voyage to America taught him the same lesson:

> On the faith of books and the reports of interested persons, we were, on this side of the Atlantic, enthusiasts at the very mention of the Americans. Our journals spoke only of the Romans at Boston and the tyrants at London. For my own part, I was fired by the same ardour, and on arriving at Philadelphia, full of my Reynal [sic], I intreated as a favor to be shewn one of the famous Quakers, the virtuous descendants of William Penn. What was my surprise on being told that if I wished to be duped, I had only to walk into the shop of a *friend*; and that if I had any curiosity to know how far the spirit of interest and mercantile immorality would extend, I might easily see two Quakers, the one trying to buy some article from the other, and each trying to impose on his *friend!* (1815: 120)

Chateaubriand may fail to demonstrate the Quakers' alleged immorality – if only because his 'proof' is based on hearsay – but his point is clear: the abstract knowledge dispensed in books is an inadequate rendering of reality. Instead of telling the truth, books tell lies. In light of the disillusion caused by the comparison between bookish knowledge and a life experience that made these "chimerical ideas" dissipate daily "one after the other" (1815: 120), it is difficult to maintain, as Regard does (1978: 1377) that the *Essay* is a work deeply imbued with a spirit of the Enlightenment. Granted, Chateaubriand wrote that it would be "much better for mankind to return to nature and to flee naked to the woods" than to try to live according to the principle of the people's sovereignty (1978: 279). But it is not man that he finds attractive in the New World. It is nature, the virgin and magnificent nature that reveals the beauty of God's creation. The 'desert' fulfills a spiritual aspiration that goes beyond the human need for community; it instills a sense of the sacred in humans; it is their direct link to the Divine: "The feeling of God originates in the mysteries of nature." (1978: 378–79)

Similarly, the six pages of the *Essay on Revolutions* devoted to a commentary of Jean-Jacques Rousseau's *L'Emile* are an homage to the religious thinker who revered God's creation, "knew the baseness of our institutions, and wept for his fellow man" (1815: 93), not to the revolutionary who, together with "Mably and Raynal sounded the republican trumpet" (379). The Rousseau Chateaubriand admired and contrasted with Voltaire's "Philosophic Sect" (388) was a Christian who believed that "[t]here is a God who avenges guilt and remunerates virtue" (390); a religious thinker whose greatest merit was to have shown "that our best books, and most upright institutions had never yet exhibited the creature of God, [...], the unsophisticated man of nature" (372). As Virgil Nemoianu (2006: 12) rightly points out, "Chateaubriand descends from Rousseau [...] but only in the sense in which Marx descends from Hegel: as an acceptance and reversal at the same time." It is not Rousseau's concept of civilization as "open and all-inclusive, ready to welcome any 'civilized' person" and "stretching across different countries" (Bell 2001: 41) that informs Chateaubriand's *Essay*, but rather, the pessimistic vision of social degeneration conveyed in the famous opening sentence of *L'Emile*.[21] On that account, Chateaubriand was still willing to grant a place in paradise to the writer he had adored in his youth, but with hindsight, how dismal did Rousseau's achievements seem compared to those of noble Malhesherbes, the King's defense attorney at his trial! (333). Compromise with the Enlightenment was longer possible in the wake of the sobering experiences of America, emigration, and the Revolution.

In order to attack the *philosophes* in *The Essay*, Chateaubriand had at his disposal an arsenal of anti-Enlightenment intellectual weapons that had been piling up during the eighteenth century and, according to Jonathan Israel (2001; 2006), much earlier. McMahon (2001: Ch.1) has provided the best analysis so far of the anti-*philosophes'* militant struggle against the Enlightenment's alleged atheism, materialism, and utilitarian ethics, prescriptions that, according to the enemies of the *philosophes*, could only lead to the corruption of morals, the destruction of society, and in the end, the demise of the monarchy. These unsettling developments, they had argued in vain before 1789, could be prevented only if religion reclaimed the central place it had once occupied in France as the organizing principle of society and government; if the traditional alliance between altar and throne was repaired and strengthened; if traditions, customs, and *préjugés* triumphed over the pernicious philosophy of natural rights and the spirit of free inquiry.

Borrowing these arguments, Chateaubriand provides an unambiguous and overwhelmingly negative assessment of the Enlightenment in *The Essay*. He categorically rejects the notion that the *philosophes'* works were grounded in moral values, and even less in moral values valid for humanity as a whole: the French Enlightenment is simply equated with destruction, vice and moral decay (1815:

---

21 On Rousseau's influence on Chateaubriand, see Dédéyan (1973); Fumaroli (2003: 97–136).

358). Diderot was an advocate of "pure atheism;" Voltaire, who "understood nothing about metaphysics," is presented as the epitome of French frivolity, "laughing, making pretty verses, and distilling immorality" (359). The real purpose of his so-called struggle for religious tolerance was to eradicate religion and the "philosophic sect" he led was particularly active in spreading atheism (392) and "destroy[ing] morals in France" (399) during Louis XV's reign: "It was a rage against what they called *l'Infâme*, or Christian Religion, which they had resolved to exterminate." (389) All these people were materialists and hypocrites to boot who railed against corruption, luxury, and despotism while at the same time practicing all these vices (374). They lacked not only religious faith but also the ability to believe in anything, even in what they wrote and published: "Men are so vain and weak that the love of notoriety often induces them to make assertions which do not accord with their convictions." (359) Last but not least, these "famous philosophers," who believed that "there was more happiness among the mob of the Parisian suburbs than the court-mob at Versailles" (255) encouraged the people to rebel. Chateaubriand was so convinced that the Enlightenment philosophers were wrong on all counts, he found so little to praise in their works that he wrongly predicted that they would have no lasting influence (357).

In the *Essay*, Chateaubriand contends that the *philosophes'* campaign against Christianity in France had had a domino effect: "The spirit of this sect [was] destruction" (1815: 358) and it destroyed everything in its path: the people's sense of identity, the fabric of society, France's national character and its political institutions. Incredulity reduced the number of faithful among the French and weakened the social institutions that had previously given sense and meaning to human life, the Church in the first place, but also the family. The cities were hit harder than the countryside, but according to him, the Enlightenment's myth of happiness on earth had a real negative social impact: "'Why create unfortunate beings? said some. 'Why beget beggars?' exclaimed others?" (1815: 252) Beneath this kind of philosophizing, Chateaubriand claims, was self-love plain and simple, "the refusal to sacrifice the comforts of life, in order to educate a large family" (252). These arguments were rationalizations in his eyes, but as they offered convenient excuses for refusing to marry and have children, they had led to the destruction of the family. People, once they had broken free of the web of concrete social relations that had traditionally defined human beings and given them a sense of identity, no longer felt any obligations to others, not even their parents: "The man, who no longer found his happiness in the union of a family and revolted at the tender name of father, accustomed himself to form a felicity independent of others." (253) In Chateaubriand's eyes therefore, individualism was first and foremost a moral disease: selfishness (*égoïsme*) was at the root of the family's disintegration and the loss of identity resulting from the atomization of the self was a cause of further moral decay. Individualism also had disastrous consequences for society at large: the severing of family and community bonds produced a depraved society narrowly focused on selfish interests, on material needs, and immediate pleasures.

Individualism also changed the national character for the worst as the traditional Christian virtues in which it had been grounded, charity and generosity, were suddenly replaced by "a hardened egotism, which destroyed virtue to its very root" (1815: 253). Moreover, by cutting themselves loose from their traditional moorings, the French lost not only the settings that had traditionally given them a measure of happiness on earth, but also their hope for a better life beyond: "In this situation, finding himself alone amidst the universe, being devoured by an empty and solitary heart which had never felt another heart beat against it, can we be astonished that the Frenchman was ready to embrace the first phantom which a new universe opened to him?" (253) Unhappy, bereft of a sense of social and spiritual identity, the French were ready to hang on to the first pipe dream that came along.

Chateaubriand's claim that the Enlightenment bore no aspirations fulfilling moral or emotional needs, that "knowledge[22] does not impart virtue" (1815: 243), is grounded in a dichotomy that pits religion and morals on the one hand against abstract knowledge on the other. On the basis of this rigid separation between heart and reason, all beliefs and projects associated with the Enlightenment can then be discarded for lack of a solid foundation. Viewing, as he did, "the Revolution as the realization of philosophy" (McMahon 2001: 56) Chateaubriand also claimed, therefore, that the Jacobins were atheists who could not grasp the religious nature of the French national character any more than their predecessors, the *philosophes*.[23] Lacking true roots in France, they preferred foreign nations, they were "rather inhabitants of Rome and Athens than of their own country" (1815: 54) – foreigners in short. Compelled to borrow their ideas from elsewhere, the Jacobins turned to the history of antiquity in search of suitable

---

22 Anti-revolutionary sentiment was at a high point in 1815 when this English translation of the *Essay on Revolution* appeared. The editor noted in the preface that the work had acquired "additional weight at the moment that all the nations of Europe, forgetting their ancient animosities, are arming the flower of their youth, and preparing to snatch the sceptre of usurpation from the hands of the most odious of tyrants, who 'Cover'd with Bourbon blood, and stern in arms Call'd upright Henry a mere rabble king.'" (vii-viii) It is thus perhaps no coincidence that "*les lumières*," a term that unambiguously connotes the Enlightenment, is translated systematically as "knowledge."

23 On the Jacobins, see chapters XIII and XIV in the *Essay* (1815: 39–62).

models for their own revolution. Convinced that revolutions had brought about change in the past, they set out to export these foreign systems, they tried to do in France "what Lycurgus did in Lacedæmon" (40). Their Revolution was a foreign import, the result of efforts "to bring back the manners of antiquity into modern Europe" (54). But this project, he claimed, had been doomed from the start because it was based in erroneous rationalist assumptions on the nature of society and men. The Jacobins wrongly believed that society could be remade from scratch by implementing a knowledge system made of "speculative views and abstract doctrines." By disregarding the religious, moral nature of France, they left out the key component needed to affect change: the heart. The Revolution had to fail because "[i]f the heart cannot attain perfection, if morality remains corrupt in spite of knowledge, adieu to a universal republic, adieu to the fraternity of nations, a general peace, and the brilliant phantom of durable happiness on earth" (244). And what a failure it had been!

Examining the Revolution's record, Chateaubriand states that the Jacobins, "these fanatics of antiquity," (1815: 28) overthrew the monarchy only to plunge their country into chaos and disarray. They tried "to annihilate commerce" and "extirpate letters" (41). In their enthusiasm for Greece, they borrowed everything from the Greeks, their "gymnasia, public festivals and clubs" (41), even the names of their political parties. In that regard, the Revolution had been nothing but a farce, a grotesque pastiche of the past:

> [A] new race of men [...] sounded the resurrection of Sparta and Athens. At the same time, the cry of liberty was heard. Old Jupiter, suddenly awaken from a slumber of fifteen centuries in the dust of Olympus, was astonished to find himself at St. Genevieve. The head of the the Parisian Clown was covered with the cap of the Lacedæmonian citizen. All corrupted, all vicious as he was, the grand virtues of the Lacedæmoninan were forced upon the little Frenchman, and he was constrained to play the character of Pantaloon in the eyes of Europe, attired in this masquerade dress of Harlequin. (254–255)

The materialist, libertine *philosophes* had already been poor imitators of the Greeks, who were "frugal, had only contempt for any kind of pleasure, and embodied all moral virtues in their character" (1978: 371). But the Jacobins had failed even more splendidly: though they "undoubtedly fixed on Lycurgus as their model," they had not even been able to copy it faithfully and had "set out on a principle totally opposed to his" (1815: 43). Painting the Jacobins as shadowy figures of darkness and as conspirators, Chateaubriand let it out that this principle was "a great mystery" reserved for the initiated. But having learned the truth about the Jacobins's mysterious system from a Jacobin himself, Chamfort, he was ready to "unmask the idol:" "The grand basis of their doctrine was the famous system of perfection: [...] that mankind will one day arrive at a purity of government and morals, now unknown." (43–44)

The Jacobins' system may have been a secret, Chateaubriand continued, but its disastrous outcomes were well-known. In fact, if the Revolution had had any merit at all, it was to have demonstrated what the ideals of the Enlightenment actually meant in practice. The French Revolution was first and foremost an outbreak of unprecedented violence that rendered its slogans – the grand words of justice, general will, and philanthropy – meaningless. Clearly, France had gained very little and instead lost a great deal socially and politically by exchanging the absolute monarchy's despotism for the republican amorality and violence:

> Here a despotic minister gags me, plunges me in a jail where I stay for twenty years without knowing why. I escape from the Bastille and, full of indignation, rush to democracy where a man-eater awaits me at the guillotine. The Republican, constantly at risk of being robbed, torn apart by an angry mob, rejoices about his happiness; the [King's] subject, calm slave, praises his master's good meals and caresses. O, natural man, only you make me proud of being a man. (1978: 439–440)

The Revolution had revealed the republican ideals for the lies they were and unmasked the so-called republican virtues as vices. Liberty may have existed in the state of nature (1978: 440), but in society it was an illusion, and in fact a prison by another name (437). Equality had produced social chaos, theft, murder, violence, far greater evils than the absence of liberty under a despotic regime. As for fraternity, all it had meant for aristocrats was an endless persecution that had nothing to do with political opinions, only with envy and greed since "if you bore a name known to have been noble, this was enough to make it certain that you would be persecuted, burnt, or hung at the lamp-iron" (1815: 284).[24]

Chateaubriand chose biblical imagery reminiscent of the exodus from Egypt to convey a sense of the trauma aristocrats had experienced during the Terror: their "hotels marked with red or black, the signals of intended fire or murder," (1815: 286) their cries for mercy answered with "insults and growing rage," and their despair forcing them into exile (1978: 291–292). As far as he was concerned, what we call "social cleansing" today was already part of the Jacobin program for regenerating the French nation, "of the total subversion" they "wished to effect in the manners of the nation, by assassinating the men of property, transferring estates, changing the customs, usages, and even worship of the country" (1815: 40); or perhaps even worse, by forcing "the wives of emigrants, and the girls belonging to their families [...] to marry such persons as they called *citizens*"

---

24 On Chateaubriand and the French Revolution, see Bertrand Aureau (2001).

(42). According to this depiction, revolutionary violence took on hitherto unknown proportions and targeted primarily aristocrats, but historian Robert Darnton (1996: 25) argues that "by twentieth century standards," the Terror "was not very devastating:"

> It took about 17,000 lives. There were fewer than twenty-five executions in half the departments of France, none at all in six of them. Seventy one percent of the executions took place in regions where civil war was raging; three quarters of the guillotined were rebels captured with arms in hands; and 85 % percent were commoners – a statistic that is hard to digest for those who interpret the Revolution as class war directed by bourgeois against aristocrats. Under the Terror, the word 'aristocrat' could applied to almost anyone deemed to be an enemy of the people. (25–26)

For Chateaubriand, however, the measures the revolutionaries had taken, had been so radical, so relentless their efforts to change France to its core, that the country had become unrecognizable in all the commotion:

> The unfortunate confounded people no longer knew where they were, nor whether they existed. They sought in vain for their ancient customs – these had vanished. They saw a foreign nation in strange attire, wandering through the public streets [...] and in this land of prodigies they had fears of losing themselves even in the midst of the streets, the names of which they no longer knew. (1815: 51–52)

The Revolution was such a horrendous event, in fact, that even the *philosophes* who had laid the groundwork for it, would have been horrified by it: "Voltaire [...] would never have forgotten his office of gentleman in waiting to the King," and presumably therefore never have accepted the fall of the monarchy (1815: 369). Rousseau "given his detestation of bloodshed would have been a decided anti-revolutionist" (369).

The French Republic was bound to be the reign of vice because it was the rule of the "dregs" of society, of immoral people who governed through violence and intimidation – "pushing back the honest folk" (1815: 369) – and electoral corruption. The same way the Jacobin leaders had destroyed French society, they had also searched "for a legal reason to destroy" France by "handing over the republic to these men without morals," or so it seemed at least (1978: 436). Chateaubriand even questioned the notion that the one-chamber system adopted by the First Republic had been an expression of the revolutionaries' desire to see the entire nation represented. As far as he was concerned, it was an institution that was not only foreign and thus incompatible with the national character,[25] but also void of any character at all.[26] Class hatred is as manifest in the contempt expressed for revolutionary leaders in Chateaubriand's *Essay* as it was in Gouges's revolutionary pamphlets. Marat was such a "monster" (88), he says, that even if historical truth demands that he be remembered for his crimes, apologies must accompany the mention of his name. The Revolutions in England and France vividly showed that when the most uncivilized elements of the nation seize political power, they prove incapable of governing. From Chateaubriand's vantage point, Fumaroli adds, the First Republic also had the disadvantage of retaining the flaws of the absolute monarchy, and in particular the centralization of institutions and administration that granted unequal power to Paris and to the rest of France (2003: 56). Any form of government that would include "violence, centralization, and social leveling" (111) was unacceptable to him.

As with his assessment of the Enlightenment, in short, Chateaubriand appropriated the anti-Enlightenment camp's line of reasoning described by McMahon (2001: Ch.2–3) in his judgment on the Revolution. According to this view, the French Revolution was in part the result of absolute monarchy's failure to heed the anti-*philosophes*' justified warnings regarding the dangers it faced, and as mentioned earlier, Chateaubriand placed some of the blame for the Revolution on the King and the nobility for failing to control the flow of new ideas. But the Revolution's ultimate failure, however, was God's retribution for the French Republic's misdeeds: "Thus was the unhappy nation bandied about by the hands of this powerful faction, suddenly transported into another world, stunned by the cries of victims, and the acclamations of victory resounding from all the frontiers, when God, casting a look towards France, caused these monsters to sink into nothingness." (1815: 53) To say, therefore, that Chateaubriand's assessment of the Revolution is entirely negative is an understatement. *The Essay on Revolutions* is more than a critique of the Enlightenment. It marks a decisive step in the development of counter-revolutionary propaganda.

On the face of it, Chateaubriand's assessment of the Enlightenment and the Revolution in *The Essay on Revolutions* is patently biased and unfair. His central argument is premised on the questionable equation of virtue and religion and, based on that hypothesis, vice easily fits into the non-Christian camp, or the

---

25 Chateaubriand does not say that the one-chamber system was 'foreign' but, having been in Philadelphia he might have known that the state of Pennsylvania had adopted this system of representation earlier than the Convention.

26 "What then was their constitution? I am incapable of defining it – a chaos, which had every form without having any; an indigested mass in which all principles were confounded [...]." (1815: 114).

camp that is supposedly non-Christian. Philip Knee (2010: 148) criticizes Chateaubriand "for failing to solve any of the explanatory dualities he reviews (ancient vs. modern, nature vs. culture, religion vs. Enlightenment)." But Chateaubriand did not want to solve them. He needed all the dichotomies derived from his initial premise that non-believers are necessarily immoral – generosity vs. selfishness; heart vs. reason; idealism vs. materialism, etc – to contrast good and evil. He also had to overlook central aspects of Enlightenment thought to construct them, to disregard the fact, for instance, that the Enlightenment was not just about ideas, but also about feelings; that Diderot did not only contribute to the *Encyclopédie*, but also made the sentiment of empathy, evidenced by the ability to shed tears, the cornerstone of his dramaturgy.[27] He had to forget that pre-revolutionary French society was not divided between virtuous aristocrats and vicious bourgeois philosophers and that the philosophy of the Enlightenment was not "an ideology exclusive to a conquering bourgeoisie in confrontation with the aristocracy" (Chartier 1991: 14). Moreover, as he himself noted when it suited his arguments, the *philosophes* did not advocate revolution or social violence, nor were they necessarily all atheists. Besides, wasn't blaming Enlightenment philosophy for the French Revolution a convenient way of excusing his own social order's share of responsibility in it, of disregarding the fact, for instance, that in the 1789 *Cahiers de doléances* prepared for the Estates-General, "eighty two percent of the parishes stated complaints against the institution of seigneury" (Chartier 1991: 148)?

Chateaubriand also deserves criticism for his double-standards. The *philosophes*, he claimed, had missed the most important lesson history has to teach, namely that history repeats itself, that "[o]ne already finds in the history of Ancient Greece, and in almost exactly the same form, nearly all the so-called innovations of the French Revolution" (1978: 433). To make that point, however, he had to devote a huge amount of space to classical history, to do, in other words, what he accused his enemies of doing, namely to live in the world of classical antiquity himself. It apparently didn't occur to him that his dismissal of the 'philosophic sect' as a bunch of foreigners could be applied to him as well. In order to turn familiarity with antiquity into an attack on the Enlightenment he also had to distort the facts – since classical education was the standard education in eighteenth century France. He apparently saw no contradiction between his discursive denunciation of a classical education presented as specific to the Enlightenment and the factual demonstration to the contrary his book offered

---

27 In *Memoirs from beyond the Grave*, Chateaubriand recalled attending a private performance of Diderot's *Père de famille* and the bewilderment it caused him as a young man.

through his own mastery of the history and letters of Ancient Greece and Rome. He criticized the revolutionaries for their attempt to learn from the Greeks and the Romans but his own effort to demonstrate that "there is nothing new in history" (433) was also a way of learning from the past.

Overall, his judgment of the Revolution is also skewed because the primary goal of the Revolution was not to imitate the past but to build a better present. He tries to play fair by acknowledging the enormity of the challenges the Jacobins had faced – of not only turning a corrupt into a virtuous Republican people, but of doing so while at the same time confronting political crises and fighting a war (1815: 45). He is also willing to mention a few positive points, the "disciplined armies," "the creation of a navy," the "great discoveries that were made in natural science" (53), but the First Republic's real achievements (laws on education and public assistance, copyright, the abolition of slavery, etc...) are not mentioned. It is clear that for him these were paltry, incidental results that weighed little against the repeated massacres and the destruction the Jacobins had caused. From the caricature of the Jacobins as conspirators or bloodthirsty monsters to the open condemnation of the First Republic, the *Essay* demonstrates that Chateaubriand was against the Revolution. In terms of "boundaries of time" (Bell 2001: 41), or mental orientation toward past or future, it is not the Enlightenment's forward-looking vision of civilization that informs the *Essay*. It is instead a cyclical conception of time that is directly related to the work's central message and purpose: because history is on a loop, because it repeats itself, the past can never serve as a source of innovation. Not only that, but innovation itself is the enemy: "One of the greatest evils afflicting Europe right now" is "its taste for innovation" (1978: 433).

As opposed to the Jacobins, who (allegedly), once they had destroyed everything, were incapable of "rebuild[ing] an edifice proper for the French to reside in" (1815: 255), Chateaubriand did not only want to criticize the Enlightenment and the Revolution in the *Essay*, he also had in mind to propose a counter-model that would reconcile heart and knowledge and prevent future revolutions. His program can be deducted from Emmanuelle Rebardy's observation (1997: 495) that "revolutionary excess has only two causes [...], a deep ignorance of French identity and the absence of religion in the reconfigured society." The Jacobins' overconfidence in the power of reason and abstract knowledge, he claimed, had only produced enthusiasm for falsehoods. The real knowledge imparted in *The Essay*, that there is nothing new under the sun, would make the French Revolution appear for what it was: a repeat of the past, not the dawn of a new era it was billed to be. More importantly, since "[e]nthusiasm proceeds from ignorance," by "cur[ing] the latter," i.e. by setting people straight on the vanity of believing in innovation, the former, enthusiasm, the deleterious passion for change, would disappear for "the knowledge of things is an opium, a soothing cure for exaltation" (1978: 433).

Chateaubriand does not comment on the socio-political implications of the arguments he puts forth in *The Essay* in its original version, but remarks on England added in a note for a new edition shed some light on this point. In England, he argues, aristocrats drew a lesson from their Revolution. They regained power and, provided they succeeded in "never being passed by the classes below, they w[ould] retain all the rights a natural superiority ascribes to them" (1978: 367), they would be able to prevent future revolutions. The central role business plays in British social life – "everyone is either customer or owner" – he figured, would help them achieve that goal because people are quick to mobilize in the defense of their interests: "When proletarians or workers rise up, property owners get their weapons; a few rebels are killed and everything is over." (367) One may infer from these comments that Chateaubriand's hope was to see his country follow in England's footsteps. In France, however, business was not the means that would allow aristocrats to regain "all the rights a natural superiority ascribes to them," religion was. Several chapters towards the end of *The Essay* strongly suggest that Chateaubriand had this objective in mind as early as 1797. Insofar as they are devoted to the refutation of various objections formulated by the *philosophes* against Christianity, they prepared the ground for Chateaubriand's *exposé* on the value and beauty of Christianity in his next work.

2.2 *The Genius of Christianity,*
or The Beauties of the Christian Religion

2.2.1 Chateaubriand's case for Christianity's modernity

The Genius of Christianity begins with an unexpected critique of anti-Enlightenment writers.[28] This move not only signals Chateaubriand's departure from his predecessors' defensive position, as well as his own in *The Essay*, it also marks a milestone in the construction of a new, Catholic identity for France and the French. Underscoring the anti-Enlightenment's failure to stop the propagation of the *philosophes*' ideas, Chateaubriand argues that "those who undertook the vindication of Christianity" (1856: 48) committed two major errors: they had the wrong message and they addressed the wrong crowd. What the "defend-

---

[28] Translations are from Charles I. White's 1856 edition of *The Genius of Christianity* except when otherwise indicated.

ers of the Christians" had done was to rely on an old apologetic tradition that consisted in proving "that religion is excellent because it comes from God" (48). This strategy had made sense in earlier times, he states, but it no longer did when religion was under attack and God's existence questioned. In the post-revolutionary era, this kind of apologetics was of interest only to a very restricted circle, "possibly to a few sincere Christians who [we]re already convinced" (49). Dialog with the "sophists" (48) who propagated pro-Enlightenment and pro-revolutionary views was also a waste of time: being moved by self-interest and vanity, these people had no real interest in the truth and always argued in bad faith. In fact, they wrote just about anything as long as it brought them out of anonymity. What had to be done instead, and what Chateaubriand therefore proposed to do in his new work, was to go about it the other way around: to prove "that religion comes from God because it is excellent" (48).

In the introduction to *The Genius of Christianity*, Chateaubriand boldly proclaimed that the days of blind faith in religious authority were over: "We no longer live in those times when you might say, 'Believe without inquiring.' People *will* inquire in spite of us, and our timid silence, in heightening the triumph of the infidel, will diminish the number of believers." (1856: 49) If religion was to survive, he contended, arguments in its defense had to provide satisfactory answers to those who had been "seduced" by ideas the philosophes had billed as their own when they actually bore the stamp of Christianity's genius. For Christianity was modernity. If people who had believed the *philosophes'* lies were presented with convincing evidence that Christianity was not the "barbaric" religion the Enlightenment had painted, they would embrace it again. The task at hand was thus to show that the Christian religion had not sought to "encourage bloodshed" or "enslave mankind," as the philosophes and the Republicans claimed. In order to dispel this error, Christianity's civilizing influence on mankind throughout the ages had to be recalled; it had to be shown that it had always been the religion "the most humane, the most favorable to liberty, [....] and peace" (48), and not a religion that preached unhappiness on earth. The notion that Christianity had sought "to retard the program of the human understanding" and been "an enemy of the arts and sciences" could similarly be refuted by enumerating the precious contributions it had made in these areas. In fact, by subjecting Christianity "to the test of the fullest and severest scrutiny of reason," his book itself would continue the long Christian tradition "of reason and refinement" (49). Finally, and this was its true beauty, Christianity spoke not only to the mind, but also to the heart. To make the French embrace it again, it would thus be necessary to speak to their soul, to "summon all the charms of the imagination and all the interests of the heart to the assistance of that religion" (49).

In nearly eight hundred pages methodically organized in six books, Chateaubriand thus set out to present Christianity's "dogmas, tenets" and "poetics" (I and II); to discuss Christianity's influence on "the fine arts, literature, the sciences, philosophy, history" and "eloquence" (III and IV); to highlight the "Harmonies of the Christian religion with the scenes of nature and the passions of the human heart;" and to remind his readers of the beauties of "Worship," of religious sites and symbols ("churches, ornaments, singing, prayers; tombs") and of the "services rendered to mankind by the clergy and by the Christian religion." *The Genius of Christianity* foregrounds the sea-change this religion, born within a fundamentally cruel world, brought along as it slowly civilized it through a gentle ethics based on love and respect for God and for fellow human beings. Just as God by "*fiat* had once produced the beautiful arrangement of the physical world," the coming of Jesus Christ had brought order and peace on earth: "the human soul was a chaos; the Word spoke and order instantly pervaded the intellectual world" (1856: 94). God had revealed himself to "the human heart" in the mysteries of the animal kingdom and in "the sublime scenes of nature" (172) – the immensity of the ocean, the "solemn roar of the Falls of Niagara" in the "stillness of the night [...] among the solitary forests" (173), for instance.

Chateaubriand acknowledges that faith is not specific to Christianity. At all times in the course of humanity, he says, belief has moved human beings to greatness – Alexander to the conquest of the world, the Romans, of the universe, and Christopher Columbus to the discovery of a new world (1856: 95). Faith is such a "formidable power," he points out, that "[t]here is nothing a man who is under the influence of a profound conviction [...] is not capable of performing" (96). Without morals, however, this power can be harnessed for evil as well as for good. Historically, Christianity's crucial role was to show that "the most eminent virtues, when separated from God [...] border on the greatest vices" (96). The superiority of the Christian faith over other religions originates, he argues, in the clear line it draws between good and evil; its most precious gift to humanity had been to redefine ethics by effecting a radical permutation of vice and virtue. Prior to the "proclamation of the gospels," for instance, "humility was considered as meanness and pride as magnanimity," but afterwards, the former became "the chief of virtues," and the latter "the first of vices" (269). Born with Christianity, ethics is inseparable from it. Christianity "makes the mysteries of the Divinity and the mysteries of the human heart go hand-in-hand" (232). According to Chateaubriand, morality rests on the promise of a "future state" (190), as "the respect of man for tombs" reveals. The prospect of immortality, of reward and punishment incites Christians to virtuous behavior (202). Man has "within his own hear" a conscience, "a tribunal, where he sits in judgment on himself till the Supreme Arbiter shall confirm the sentence" (187), but also "a second conscience" established by Jesus Christ "for the hardened culprit who should be so unfortunate as to have lost the natural one" (189).

Because of its moral nature, Chateaubriand writes, Christianity is an invitation "to dive [...] into the secrets of passions" (1856: 232). The antique poetry of polytheist societies may have equaled Christian literature with regard to the "marvelous" and "supernatural things" but it was incapable of depicting the "inward conflicts of the soul" and was thus void of moral drama (233). Christian writers and artists, by contrast, excel in that area because of their concern for "the picture of the internal man" (233). Every great work of art, every great work of literature was produced by the genius of artists under the spell of this exquisite religion, from "Newton and Bossuet," to "Pascal and Racine" (49). Even Voltaire, who "disclaim[ed] against religion," was "inspired by Christianity" when wrote his "finest pages," his historical writings (431). For every "improvement from agriculture to the abstract sciences – from the hospitals for the reception of the unfortunate to the temples reared by Michael Angelo and embellished by Raphael" (49), Chateaubriand maintains, the modern world is "indebted" to Christianity. All ameliorations in the human condition are due to the "divine [...] morality" and the beneficial influence on morals and mores exerted by a Christian religion that encourages "the virtuous passions" and "imparts energy to those ideas" (49).

The same way religion and morals are inseparable in *The Genius of Christianity*, so too are religion and government: "[...] the doctrine which commands the belief in a God who will reward and punish is the main pillar of both of morals and civil government" (1856: 96). Christianity is not only the source of morality for the people but also the main support of society and government: "without religion, morals and society perish" (1978: 430). Historically, Christianity provided society with a stable structure by creating lasting social institutions like the family, the church, and the army. It made the family strong by granting everyone a role in it and by defining the respective roles of husband and wife (1856: 269), father (233–242) and mother (247–250), son (250–252) and daughter (253–256). By preaching reward and punishment after death, by teaching to "submit one's reason to the direction of another" (95–96), religion brought order and happiness to the family. As opposed to "the infidel wife [who] seldom has any idea of her *duties*," "the religious woman" knows her place. As a result, her "days are replete with joy;" because she "is respected, beloved by her husband, her children, her household" (199, 200).

Christianity brought order to society at large as well by establishing institutions that the warrior and the priest best embody. In *The Genius of Christianity* the noble medieval knight is the epitome of faith: "In the language of ancient chivalry, *to pledge one's faith* was synonymous with all the prodigies of honor.

Roland, Duguesclin, Bayard were faithful knights [...] who plighted their faith and homage to their God, their lady, and their country." (1856: 96)[29] The age of chivalry, when the knights of Malta, of the Teutonic Order, of Calatrava and Saint Jago of the Sword fought for Christianity, was the age of "disinterestedness" and "true virtue" (617). The faith that moved medieval knights to "greatness" is viewed and presented as the mother of all virtues in *The Genius of Christianity* (95–96): of friendship, that of the medieval brothers in arms; and of patriotism – as the parting of knights pledged to different lords supposedly shows. Unlike the "ferocious warriors of antiquity," medieval knights were "ingenuous," "disinterested," and "humane" (618). Chateaubriand views love as a Christian invention (242), but he believes that courteous love had "but a secondary claim upon their [the knights'] hearts;" that "each succored his friend in preference to his lady" (617). Olympe de Gouges was drawn to the Middle Ages by the civilizing role women had played in chivalric France. The source of Chateaubriand's attraction to the period is his identification with the knights' masculine ethos of freedom and power.

Last but not least, Chateaubriand explains, Christianity contributed to humanity's salvation and well-being through the good works of its religious orders. Its missionaries saved "so many souls still languished in the darkness of idolatry" (1856: 557) that "we are indebted [to them] for the attachment to the French name still cherished by the savages in the forests of America" (561). The religious orders invented hospitals, nursing, education; the clergy "brought the wilds of Europe under cultivation" (647), built roads, bridges, created towns, and were instrumental in the development of manufactures and commerce (651–653), of civil and criminal law (653–657), and of politics and government (658–664). All the Enlightenment and the French Revolution had done by contrast was to destroy, to bring the most civilized nation on earth back to barbarity.

In two chapters devoted to the writing of history, Chateaubriand explains "why the French have no historical works, but only memoirs" (1856: 425–228). This genre, he argues, is better suited for the Frenchman as it leaves him "at full liberty to follow the bent of his genius" which is "his observation of details" and his impulse "to stage himself" (425). Memoirs are also deemed better than histories because they conform "to the nature of man, in which the purest truth contains always some mixture of error," something "general theories" are incapable of rendering (426). In the next chapter, however, Chateaubriand makes a case for the "Excellence of modern history," a modern French history that

---

29 De Maistre also used the figure of the knight to make his case for the sublimity of war in the seventh of *St Petersburg Dialogues*. See McClelland (1970: 48–59).

would deal with the origins of France ("the establishment of the Franks in Gaul") and center on the Middle Ages ("Charlemagne, the crusades, chivalry, the battle of Bouvines") (428). The point of this modern history would be to underscore the different ways in which Christianity has imprinted its character on European nations, but particularly on their societies:

> The grand point to be seized in modern history is the change produced by Christianity in social order. By erecting morals on a new basis, it has modified the character of nations, and created in Europe a race of men totally different from the ancients in opinions, government, customs, manners, arts and sciences. (428)

More clearly than in the *Essay*, Chateaubriand asserts in these pages that the national character is determined by the nation's relative success in implementing Christian morals. Among the Germans, he claims, only the lower class succeeded, the higher classes remained "corrupt" – a remark that may be an attempt to explain the Princes' defeat in the revolutionary wars. The Batavians (or Dutch), who strayed from Christianity's true ethics during the Reformation, became materialists, "laborious" and "cold" (429); "Italy with her hundred princes and magnificent recollections forms a strong contrast to obscure and republican Switzerland" (429); and Spain, with its pure but dormant Christians morals, is destined to greatness: when Europe succumbs to corruption, it will rise again (429). England's imperfections stem from her double origin, from "a mixture of German and French blood" (429). The French are more "brilliant" than their English cousins, their religion most "pompous" (429). The distinctive characteristic of England is its "public spirit;" that of France its "national honor" (429). France is blessed among the nations: its "good qualities are rather the gifs of divine favor than the effects of a political education" (429). France has a divine origin: "Like the demi-gods, we are more nearly allied to heaven than to earth" (429).

But religion's primary function, Chateaubriand contends, is to help humans face their existential angst and to overcome death: "Since we must sooner or later quit this mortal life, Providence has placed beyond that fatal boundary a charm which attracts us, in order to diminish our horror of the grave." (1856: 187) For him that "charm" is the universal wish for happiness. But contrary to the Enlightenment philosophers who viewed the pursuit of happiness as a noble human aspiration and a right, Chateaubriand claims that pursuing happiness on earth is futile: happiness being what remains to be desired when all other desires are fulfilled, the pursuit of happiness has no object on earth (184). Materialists and atheists who define happiness narrowly – as feeling good or possessing things – can therefore only miss the essential point in his view: the constant aspiration humans have for something else than what is available to them is God's gift, his sign to them that life exists beyond the grave, and therefore also his way of helping them overcome the fear of death. Chateaubriand affirms the universal character of the desire for happiness in a discussion on the common people's aspirations. "[T]he vulgar," he argues, though perhaps less receptive to "that mysterious restlessness" because they "drown the thirst of felicity in the sweat of their brow," are no "strangers to that thirst of happiness which extends beyond this life" (186–87). Once we understand God's designs, once we realize that "the desire of happiness has been placed in this world, and its object in the other" (187), he explains, it is easier to accept our condition on earth, and in particular social injustice, "the seeming injustice in the distribution of wealth" that is "the most violent temptation not to believe" (Chateaubriand 1978: 1324).

As Chateaubriand's defense of Christianity reveals, his central thesis did not change much from the *Essay* to the *Genius:* his argument remains that religion is necessary for morals, governments, societies, and nations. Critics who argue otherwise, who contrast the un-Christian *Essay on Revolutions* with the Christian *Genius of Christianity*, base their assessment on two chapters of Chateaubriand's *Memoirs from Beyond the Grave* written in 1822 in which the writer explained the personal circumstances that had led him to write a book on Christianity.[30] The second of these chapters deals with the writing of *Le Génie du Christianisme*, but the first one, entitled "The death of my mother; Return to Religion," is the most important because in it Chateaubriand explains why he wrote this book. The inclusion in that chapter of a letter his sister wrote to him in July 1798 underscores the key role that letter played in his decision: it conveyed his mother's disapproval, and his sister's, of the *Essay on Revolutions*, a book that had appeared a year earlier. This letter, according to him, had unfortunately only reached him after his mother's and his sister's deaths. But the impression these "two voices from the tomb" had made on him had been such that he had instantly regained his faith: "I became a Christian. I did not yield, I must admit, to great supernatural enlightenment: my conviction came from the heart; I wept and I believed."

This short, but powerful narrative of conversion has usually been left unchallenged by critics but Charles Byrnes (2005: 72–73) has recently questioned the sudden character of Chateaubriand's conversion. On the basis of a closer examination of the chronology of events mentioned in that passage, he was able to show that Chateaubriand knew of his mother's death a month after it occurred, and not much later, as he claimed, and that he had already started working on

---

30 All quotes from *Memoirs from beyond the Grave* in this section are from book XI, chapter 4 and 5 in Chateaubriand (1848).

The Genius before his sister passed away, not after. Having thus shown that the poet "arranged events to dramatic effect" in his *Memoirs*, Byrnes proposes a counter-narrative of *"gradual"* conversion (72) while at the same time attributing the composition of *The Genius* to "mixed motivation," not just to grief and mourning. If the nature of Chateaubriand's conversion takes on a different character in Byrnes' account, the conversion itself is left unchallenged. It retains the essential function of grounding the opposition between the "theist-deist" *Essay* and the Christian *Genius*.

Chateaubriand's contention that he "became a Christian," however, deserves the same scrutiny as his chronology of events. We need to ask why, for instance, if he was not a Christian when he wrote the *Essay*, he defends the Christian nature of that work in the same passage of *Memoirs from beyond the Grave* in which he tells of his conversion; why, in the same chapter, he rejects the accusation that it was "an impious work;" and why he characterizes it instead as "a book of doubt and sorrow" illuminated by "a ray of the Christian light that shone on my cradle." In his defense, he could also have pointed out that the "skepticism" of the *Essay* belonged to a well-established Christian philosophical tradition in France, that René Descartes and Blaise Pascal had discussed God's existence in their works much earlier without being charged with incredulity. But he did not do so because the actual reason for his mother's and sister's disapproval of the *Essay* did not pertain to the nature of the book, but to the act of writing itself.

Chateaubriand did not omit or hide this fact in his *Memoirs:* his sister words are reproduced, her hope that her letter will "induce [him] to renounce writing" is clearly stated. He similarly indicates that he understood the nature of her wish: "Why did I not follow my sister's advice! Why did I go on writing?" He even explains that for his sister, Julie de Farcy, who "had grown to hate literature, because she regarded it as one of her life's temptations," writing proceeded from vanity, from a desire for fame and glory apparently contrary to the Christian spirit of humility. Still in the same passage, Chateaubriand directly addressed the dilemma he faced: "Fontanes urged me to work, to become illustrious; my sister pressed me to renounce writing: one proposed glory, the other oblivion." And yet, in spite of all these clues, critical attention has remained focused on Chateaubriand's narrative on conversion instead of on his real moral dilemma. The beauty of the simple line devoted to his conversion ("I wept and I believed") certainly accounts for the faith critics have placed in a narrative that testifies to Chateaubriand's ability to enchant readers: with these few words, he effectively modeled the effect *The Genius of Christianity* was meant to have on them. At a personal level, the conversion narrative deflects attention from his relatives' real criticism and provides Chateaubriand with the means of having his cake and eating it too. It enables him to justify his choice of glory through writing over his relatives' objections while at the same time making himself look like the repentant son who has fulfilled his relatives' wishes, a dutiful son "building a mausoleum to his mother" and "expiating the effect of [his] first work by a religious work."

In light of these half-truths, it may not be inappropriate to question the sincerity of Chateaubriand's conversion. Stendhal, who called Chateaubriand "the great hypocrite of France" (Stendhal 1988: 36), did not hesitate to do so, describing him as "a man who had found out the art of touching and pleasing while supporting lies and absurdities of the most extravagant kind, and which, it is plain to see, he does not himself believe a word" (Stendhal 1985: 196). So did Marcel Rouff in his biography of the *enchanteur*, the great charmer, in a passage in which he contrasted what Chateaubriand wrote about religion and what he said in private to his friends on that topic in salon conversations.[31] As example of the latter, Rouff quotes historian Jean de Sismondi (1773–1842), who, in an entry dated 25 March 1813 of his diary, recalled an evening at the home of their common friend Claire de Duras (1777–1828) where the topic of religion had been discussed. Sismondi then provides the following account of Chateaubriand's attitude towards religion: "however attached to the religion that once existed in his country he may be, he also feels very strongly that the religious rites [...] have been reduced to naught; he finds it necessary, for others and for himself, to believe; he makes it a rule of conduct for himself, but then he does not follow it." (Quoted in Rouff 1929: 110) Judging by his personal life – his abandonment of his wife for over ten years and his constant marital infidelities – Chateaubriand also had a hard time believing what he wrote about family values. In both areas, his conflicted attitude may have had a lot to do with his politics.

2.2.2 Chateaubriand's politics

As the brief overview of *The Genius of Christianity* in the preceding section reveals, Chateaubriand appropriates the Enlightenment's key concepts of progress and perfectibility and gives them a Christian twist or origin in that essay. Christianity, he maintains, already valued equality, liberty, and brotherhood; it was

---

31 "If pen in hand, the writer was the champion of a Christian religion he viewed as irreparably linked to the cause of the state [...], orally, in salon conversations, he did not shy from proclaiming the rationalism of his mind and from predicting a sinister future to the religion he was officially championing." (Rouff 1929: 109)

the Catholic Church, not the Convention that abolished slavery;[32] unlike the *phil-osophes*, Christianity had defined happiness the way it should be. Overall, his general strategy of appropriation consists in severing the link between *le siècle des Lumières* and its intellectual products and in associating them instead with the seventeenth century. In this revisionist account, centuries of Christian virtue culminate in Louis XIV's reign, making it the apogee of civilization. The *Genius of Christianity*, Chateaubriand would later claim, had been an ode to the monarchy: the glance it had cast towards a past "[f]ull of memories of our antique mores, of glory, of the monuments of our Kings" had paved "the road of the future" (1978: 460).

But the monarchy he embraced was clearly the "old monarchy," not the absolute monarchy. In *The Genius of Christianity*, the priest and the warrior embody Christian institutions but apparently not the King. The monarchy is also conspicuously absent from the long list of Christian religious and military institutions that rendered innumerable services to humanity. Moreover, Chateaubriand makes it very clear that the greatness France achieved in the seventeenth century was conquered against monarchical constraints; that if "[i]n no age, in no other country [...] was greater freedom of thought enjoyed than in France during the time of the monarchy," it was not thanks to the monarchy but because "the Frenchman [...] always indemnified himself by the independence of his opinion for the constraint imposed upon him by monarchical forms" (1856: 427). Far from being an eighteenth century invention, liberty was the prerogative of an aristocracy that "never bowed with abject servility to the yoke" (427). Far from being a new revolutionary value, brotherhood, the "sacred friendship [...] confirmed by the most awful oaths" (617) was already the defining characteristic of relations among knights.

Being himself a knight, a *chevalier*, Chateaubriand never departed from his sentimental attachment to France's medieval past: "The mere word of *chivalry*, the mere expression *an illustrious knight*, imply something wonderful in themselves, which no details or explanation can surpass" (1856: 608), he wrote in *The Genius of Christianity*. In 1806–1807, he went all the way to the Middle East on the tracks of the Crusaders in search of images for *The Martyrs* (1809) and wrote about his pilgrimage in *Itinerary from Paris to Jerusalem* (1811). "This voyage," Rouff comments (1929: 147) "had haunted him ever since the day when, as a child, [...] he had heard an abbot mention the battlefield in Pal-

---

32 "Men, unworthy of the name of Christians slaughtered the people of the New World, and the Court of Rome fulminated its bulls to prevent these atrocities. Slavery was authorized by law, and the Church acknowledged no slaves among her children." (1856: 660)

estine where his ancestor had picked up the family motto." Years later, his emotional investment in aristocratic lineage was still shining light and bright when he wrote that "[e]ver since attempts were made to prove that nobility is nothing, [he had] felt that it [was] worth something."[33] Chateaubriand's evocation of the chivalry conjures up the vision of a stable society that enjoyed liberty and brotherhood without ever "abusing governments and shaking the foundations of duty" (427–428).

Of course, this idealized depiction of the chivalry makes short shrift of the fact that warriors of all ages kill people but, as discussed earlier, Chateaubriand had good reasons to present war as unavoidable. He also seems to forget that the French aristocracy did shake "the foundations of duty" when it rebelled against royal authority during the *Fronde* in the seventeenth century. But more problematic from a post-revolutionary vantage point is his praise of a knightly brotherhood so sacred that it instantly dissolved in the face of war.[34] A breach of this sacred friendship is called treason in the post-revolutionary era. It is also the worst expression of hypocrisy and deceit, not a proof of "disinterestedness" that justified "the glorious title of *irreproachable*" (1856: 618). But Chateaubriand ploughs ahead because his glance towards the past is primarily meant to pave the road for a new political future, that of his class and his own. The evocation of this perfect world is a re-statement of aristocratic claims, an update of the strategy the aristocracy had used to claim its rights as a nation in Old Regime France.[35] Pointing to this glorious chivalric past is a way of justifying the "rights a natural superiority ascribes" the current knights (1978: 367). As Colin Smethurst (2009: 149–150) notes, Chateaubriand sees that the Revolution handed down aristocratic values to the people – "honor, glory, duty, fidelity to oath" – and he does not like it. He wants to restitute these values to the caste that, he claims, founded them, "to re-dedicate them and attach them to the idea of royalist patriotism." The title of Smethurst's article captures well Chateaubriand's goals in *The Genius of Christianity*: to place "history at the service of political discourse."

History has a double function in this political discourse: to restitute values to the aristocracy and to replace those thereby taken away from the French people. As Smethurst further notes, history looks more like the stuff of legends than

---

33 My translation from Chateaubriand (1973: I, 62–63).

34 "One circumstance, however, was capable of dissolving these ties, and that was the enmity of their native countries. Two brothers-in-arms of different nations ceased to be united whenever these nations were at warfare." (1856: 617)

35 For a discussion of the "rediscovery of the Middle Ages and medieval chivalry" in pre-revolutionary France, see Bell (2001: 134).

like real history in *The Genius*. Chateaubriand waxes emotional about the knight who "delivered princesses detained in caverns, punished miscreants, succored orphans and widows, and defended himself against the treachery of dwarfs and the strength of giants" (1856: 613). The line between vice and virtue is easily drawn in these medieval tales. The knights know right from wrong, they condemn ladies of ill-repute through "a mark of infamy left on the gate" and they praise of "pious and virtuous female(s)" through words of commendation (613). In that regard, *The Genius of Christianity* looks like a moral tale meant to teach commoners how to look up to the superior class and to embrace virtue and reject vice. In fact, these naive, undeveloped characters, the unimaginative plot lines, the clear separation between good and evil are the very characteristics of the "classical" melodrama that appeared on the Parisian stages around 1800, shortly before the *Genius of Christianity* was published. The father of the genre, René Charles Guilbert de Pixérécourt, was another provincial aristocrat who hated the French Revolution just as much as Chateaubriand (Le Hir 1992).

Although he claimed otherwise, Chateaubriand must have been aware that his ideas would not be well received by the French population at large. The key argument in his case for the excellence of Christianity, the inseparability of ethics and religion, was contested by secular thinkers and in particular by the *Idéologues* during the Consulate. In strength at the *Institute of France*, the *Idéologues* saw themselves as the *philosophes*' heirs but held more radical positions than their predecessors on the issue of religion. Their leader, Destutt de Tracy, for instance, considered Voltaire's claim "that morality was divine, that it came from the hand of the Great Being" as "a false assertion" (Byrnes 2005: 78–89). In *The Genius of Christianity*, the *Idéologues* are described as "[t]hese men who pretend that atheism is not destructive of either happiness or virtue and that there is no condition in which it is not as profitable to be an infidel as a pious Christian" (1856: 197). Chateaubriand's attitude towards these atheists ranges from pretend indifference and contempt to an anger and aggressiveness manifest in his burning desire to prove them wrong: to deny God's existence, he tells them, is to reject the notion that there is a "difference between good and evil," and thus to believe that "the world belongs to those who possess the greatest strength and the most address" (196). But as it is premised on the very postulate atheists reject, the inseparability of morals and religion, his argument falls flat. Ad-hominem attacks consequently follow: it is through the discrepancy between their words and actions that the "hypocrites of incredulity" demonstrate that there is no morality without religion. These people "would call you brother while cutting your throat;" they have "the words morality and humanity [...] continually on their lips," but they "are trebly culpable, for to the vices of the atheist they add the intolerance of the sectary and the self-love of the author" (196–

197). Chateaubriand tries to deal his enemies a final blow by turning one of their idols against them: Rousseau himself extolled the superiority of religion over philosophy in *L'Emile* in a passage that therefore finds its way into *The Genius of Christianity*:

> 'It [..] remains to be seen whether philosophy, at its ease and upon the throne, would be capable of controlling the love of glory, the selfishness, the ambition, the little passions of men, and whether it would practice that engaging humanity which, with pen in hand, it so highly recommends. ACCORDING TO PRINCIPLES, PHILOSOPHY CAN DO NO GOOD WHICH RELIGION WOULD NOT FAR SURPASS; AND RELIGION DOES MUCH THAT PHILOS-OPHY CANNOT ACCOMPLISH.' (1856: 683–684)

For Chateaubriand, it is clear that what religion can do that philosophy cannot is to prevent revolutionary violence and stop the "throat cutters." In that regard, the atheists' greatest vice is less to undermine Chateaubriand's case for the excellence of Christianity than to shake the foundation of the social order it produced. This apology of Christianity thereby takes on an undeniable practical socio-political dimension. Religion is a useful means of controlling those who are most receptive to the lure of violence, the people of the lower classes:

> It is high time to be alarmed at the state in which we have been living for some years. Think of the generation now springing up in our towns and provinces; of all those children, who, born during the revolution, have never heard anything of God, nor of the immortality of their souls, nor of the punishments and rewards that await them in a future life: think what may one day become of such a generation if a remedy be not speedily applied to the evil. The most alarming symptoms already manifest themselves: we see the age of innocence sullied with many crimes. (1856: 682)

Religion was cast aside during the French Revolution, but, Chateaubriand argues, it is needed as the efficient means of social control it is: "Let philosophy, which, after all, cannot penetrate among the poor, be content to dwell in the mansions of the rich, and leave the people in general to the care of religion." (682) As long as the poor and the wretched hang on to the dream that their lot may change after death, they won't rebel on earth. With regard to Chateaubriand's politics, in short, the message is the same in the *Genius* and in the *Essay*.

Chateaubriand insisted that *The Genius of Christianity* had a wide-ranging impact when it was first published in 1802. According to him, "newspapers, pamphlets, and books" mentioned it, and writers started copying his style. More importantly, he thought, a nation still traumatized by the French Revolution had embraced Christianity following its publication: "The faithful thought they were saved by the publication of a book that corresponded so well to their inner feelings: there was a need for faith, a voracious hunger for religious consolation that originated in the deprivation of these very consolations endured for so many years." (Chateaubriand 1978: 460) But as we know, René had a way of embellishing the truth when it suited him. It is thus difficult to gauge whether *The Genius of Christianity* actually led to conversions and thereby accomplished its stated purpose. Gengembre (1989: 94) seems to think it did not when he contends that the book belongs to the traditional genre of "apologetics for high society usage." "Apologetics" is correct, and the book's nature and scope would certainly seem to support the notion of a restricted readership, an audience targeted to direct the flow of ideas, to spread the Christian message. Henry H. Walsh questions the notion that *The Genius of Christianity* actually led to a resurgence of religious sentiment in France. For him, the book had more to do with another kind of faith.

2.2.3 Grounding identity in faith and soil

In the *Essay on Revolutions*, Chateaubriand had stuck to the dominant counter-revolutionary discourse that placed no credibility in revolutionary patriotic sentiment. Gengembre (1989: 38), who highlights the non-nationalist character of the early counter-revolutionary movement, wonders how nationalism ended up playing such a key role in the Right's discourse and contributing "so forcefully to [its] popularization [...] a century later." Like patriotism, individualism was also a discredited concept in anti-Enlightenment discourse and, as we saw, Chateaubriand had criticized it as well in the *Essay*. In *The Genius of Christianity*, by contrast, not only does the noun 'individual' appear here and there in it,[36] the concept itself is acknowledged and given a new meaning. The abstract individual born of the recognition of its natural and political rights during the Revolution becomes under his pen a human individual torn by inner conflicts that reveals its dual nature as God's creature and as son of Adam. *The Genius of Christianity*, Gengembre argues, thereby "opens a door to the spiritualist reaction: the re-psychologization of the now unavoidable individual. If the individual triumphs, let's recuperate it by linking its interiority to God" (1989: 118), so goes the counter-revolutionary line of thought. According to him, this recasting of the individual is the crucial linchpin that allowed nationalism to become a central tenet of the French Right down the road. The question on which the last part of this chapter centers is thus this: how far did Chateaubriand himself succeed in opening this door in *The*

---

36 About England he writes: "Autant les individus qui le composent..." (1978: 311).

Genius of Christianity? How else did he contribute to making nationalism acceptable in counter-revolutionary discourse?

So far, we saw Chateaubriand refute the idea of revolutionary patriotism in *The Essay on Revolutions* and seek to identify "the national character [...] with its large and brilliant aristocracy of the sword" (Fumaroli 2003: 76) in *The Genius of Christianity*. The lengthy description of the age of knights is meant to underscore the Catholic origin of the French nation, or more specifically, of the French aristocratic nation – given Chateaubriand's objection to separating military and religious chivalry (1856: 600). But as Thiesse (1999: 50 – 51) notes, this understanding of the nation was contested during the Revolution: Sieyès in his famous revolutionary pamphlet, *What is the Third Estate?*, presented the aristocracy as Frankish, and therefore foreign, and the Gauls as the nation's real ancestors. In an earlier section of *The Genius of Christianity*, Chateaubriand attributed a different meaning than 'aristocratic nation' to the term *patrie: patrie* in that context simply meant "native soil," and patriotism was defined as the bond that instinctively attaches us to that native soil: "Love of one's native country is the pre-eminent instinct with which man is endowed, the most beautiful and the most moral of all." (1856: 177) Seen in that light, it is interesting to consider that Chateaubriand's recourse to the rhetoric of roots and soil might have been a response to Sieyès's exclusionary politics.[37]

In the *Essay on Revolutions*, Chateaubriand had already defined patriotism as the instinct that binds man to the place he was born, and ideally should die, because the roots his ancestors planted for him are there: "After having wandered over the globe, man, by an affecting species of instinct, likes to return and die in the land that gave him birth, and to sit for a moment on the borders of his grave under the same trees which overshadowed his cradle." (1815: 32) This idea was left undeveloped, however, because the point of the passage in which it was inserted was to underscore the devastation caused by revolutionary change and the traveler's grief at finding a country he had left in "flourishing prosperity [...] on his return, deserted, or torn by political convulsions" (33). Thus placed under the sign of loss, "love of our country" was just a diffuse "sensation of tenderness and melancholy" (32). In the chapter of *The Genius of Christianity* entitled *"L'instinct de la patrie"* ["Love of our Native Country"], by contrast, man's instinctive love for his *patrie* is recast as a proof of God's existence.

---

37 Commenting on this passage of Sieyès's pamphlet, Le Bras and Todd (1981: 110) argue that the "audacious abbott proposed a revolution of ethnological character [...]: to rid France of its Germanic element in the name of the democratic ideal."

Olympe de Gouges used Montesquieu's climate theory to account for a given nation's character. Chateaubriand borrows this Enlightenment idea, the notion that there is a relation between climate and nation, but adjusts it to his defense of Christianity. The proof that God exists is that he gave human beings this instinctual attachment to their native soil whatever the climate may be:

> If this law were not maintained [...] all mankind would crowd together into the temperate zones, leaving the rest of the earth a desert. We may easily conceive that great evils would result from this collection of the human family on one point of the globe. To prevent these calamities, Providence has, as it were, fixed the feet of each individual to his native soil by an invisible magnet, so that neither the ices of Greenland nor the burning sand of Africa are destitute of inhabitants. (1856: 177)

At one point, when positing a law of reversed opposites to determine the strength of this attachment, Chateaubriand briefly extends this restricted sense of *patrie:* "[T]he more sterile the soil is, the more rude the climate, of a country, or what amounts to the same thing, *the more severe the persecution we have suffered there*, the more strongly we are attached to it." [Emphasis mine] (1856: 177) In that sentence, the highlighted words are clearly a reference to France, but overall the understanding of *patrie* as "native soil" dominates in this chapter. In fact, it immediately returns when the following explanation for the variability of patriotic feelings noted above is provided: "The reason of this phenomenon is that the profusion of too fertile a soil destroys, by enriching us, the simplicity of the natural ties arising from our wants." (177)

Echoing Rousseau, Chateaubriand constructs a theory of degeneration of feelings, instead of morals, as he evokes a primitive state of nature characterized by the simplicity of man's relation to his environment. In the original state of nature, love for one's "native soil" was strong because the relation to nature was direct, unmediated, and necessary. It is still true that "[t]he heart is naturally fond of contracting itself," but in the state of civilization, only "persons of delicate sensibility – such the unfortunate generally are – prefer to live in retirement" (1856: 179). As society developed, as man "enriched" himself and intermediaries were placed between him and nature, the relation grew weaker. The same principle applies in the realm of human relations because the attachment that binds human beings to their native soil and to their local community are closely related in Chateaubriand's mind. Love of the native country and love of the family go hand in hand: "When we cease to love our parents and our relations because they are no longer necessary to us, we actually cease to love our country." (177) We note that in this scenario, love is no longer presented as a gift of God, but as a function of human necessity, "of the natural ties arising from our wants," in the state of nature as well as in state of society – as the reference to "parents and relations" indicates. Conversely, love of one's country is such a powerful instinct that it survives the severing of the physical ties to the native soil. In fact, "[i]t is when at a distance from our country that we feel the full force of the instinct by which we are attached to it" (181), that we become homesick, a disease cured only by coming home. If love of one's country is thus conceptualized here as a one-on-one relation to nature, or, in the case of society, as a direct relationship between persons, home is the locus of the emotional investment, not the abstract nation. In both cases, love of the *patrie* is conceivable only as a form of close, personal attachment.

The symbols associated with the *patrie*, and endowed with a strong emotional aura, are thus also personal, not impersonal, ones. They are visual memories of places and people that recall home away from it and, as such, the expression of the "powerful ties which bind us to the place of our nativity" (1856: 182). For the "Scotch Highlander," these symbols are the recollection of "his beloved mountains," of "his flock, his torrents, and his clouds;" of the taste of "barley bread" and "goat's milk"; of the "ballads that were sung by his forefathers" (178). More commonly, the symbols of the *patrie* are human faces, "the smile of a mother, of a father, of a sister," an "old preceptor" or a faithful servant. They can also be auditive memories associated with familiar animals, "a dog that barked in the night in the fields" (183), or of birds that Chateaubriand views a "the true emblem of the Christian" (148): the "nightingale that returned every year to the orchard" (183) because it shares the human instinctual attachment to the native soil and thus reinforces it; "the nest of the swallow over the window" (183) because it recalls the "Great Creator's [...] divine beneficence, which imparts industry to the weak and foresight to the thoughtless" (150).

The counterpart of the spatial restriction Chateaubriand imposes on the term *patrie* is its temporal expansion: the "religious man who loves his country [...] gives the hand to his forefathers and to his children; he is planted in his native soil, like the oak which sees its aged roots below striking deep into the earth, while at its top young shoots are aspiring to heaven" (1856: 455–456). Symbols meant to convey this sense of transcendence have the peculiarity of linking earth to heaven: "the village clock that appeared above the trees, the churchyard yew, or the Gothic tomb" (183). The tree actually combines the spatial and temporal dimensions of the symbol if we agree with Roy Groen (2013: 134) that "for Chateaubriand, death is not opposed to life but part of it," and that the image of the tree is meant to express this idea in his work. All these symbols, all "these simple things," Chateaubriand concludes, "demonstrate the more clearly the reality of a Providence, as they could not possibly be the source of patriotism, or of the great virtues which it begets, unless by the appointment of the Almighty himself" (182–183). Both the sense of space, of native soil, and the sense of time, of family roots, that are combined in the concept of patriotism, of love of the *patrie*, are

God's imprint on the human heart. The "religious man" must therefore be more receptive to patriotism than the secular man: because "his mind is simple," love of *patrie* is "the habit of his heart" (455).

Chateaubriand faced the problem of having to reconcile his particularist understanding of the *patrie* with the universalist religion he embraced and which he saw as the source of patriotic attachment in the first place. Walsh, who devotes a chapter of his book on the Concordat to this issue (1967: 62–75), considers Chateaubriand's attempt to reconcile the "inherent antagonism" between "the universal ethics of the Church" and the "exclusive ethics of the nation" (5) in the *Genius of Christianity* as a failure. For him, the book fulfilled the political mission of reconciling Church and State in 1802 but Chateaubriand did more in the end to "popularize uncritical nationalistic fervor than to deepen religious faith" (75). This assessment may seem odd however in light of Chateaubriand's claim that Christianity was instrumental in curbing patriotic fervor. Patriotism, he wrote, had "led to the commission of crimes among the ancients, because it was carried out to excess," but Christianity, by preaching that all men were brothers and ordering them "to cherish the whole family of Adam," had tempered the violence of these patriotic feelings; it had "invested patriotism with its true character" by balancing out "the first claim to our attachment" our countrymen have and the Christian imperative "above all things to be just" (1856: 180). These remarks reveal Chateaubriand's Old Regime conception of patriotism since what he describes here corresponds to what David A. Bell (2001: 60) characterizes as the "pre-political impulse that allowed humans to avoid killing each other and to act for the common good," an instinct that was seen as "the product of *amour de la patrie*" until the mid-eighteenth century. The notion that religion puts a rein on human passions could conversely be used to demonstrate that its absence has the reverse effect, in other words to point to atheism as the cause of excessive patriotic zeal, and in particular of the crimes committed during the French Revolution when "[t]he spirit of God having withdrawn from the people, no force was left except that of original sin, which resumed its empire as in the days of Cain and his race" (1856: 418).

In another respect, however, Walsh has a point: for if Chateaubriand argues against patriotic fervor in the lines quoted above, he embraces it when it is inspired by religious enthusiasm. "Christian religion," he argues, "is itself a species of passion, with its transports, its ardors, its sights, its joys, its tears, its love of society and of solitude" (1856: 291). The *philosophes* denounced it as "fanaticism" (291) because they did not understand "the divine enthusiasm which animates the apostle of the gospel" any more than "[i]dolatrous nations" (557) do. In addition to the religious passion that had moved martyrs and missionaries to die for the "hope of possessing God" (292), fanatic faith inspired the religious chivalry to conduct just wars: the Teutonic knights to "bring the savages into subjection" and to "oblige them to [...] attend to agricultural pursuit" (606); the military orders of Spain to vanquish the Moors, who were "an invincible obstacle to civilization and the welfare of mankind" (606). It was the power of religion that had led to the institution of the chivalry, to "associations of men who swore in the name of God to spill the last drop of blood for their country" (607). Rousseau himself, Chateaubriand added, had acknowledged the greatness of this fanatic faith in a passage of *L'Emile:*

> 'Fanaticism, though sanguinary and cruel, is nevertheless a great and powerful passion, which exalts the heart of man, which inspires him with a contempt of death, which gives him prodigious energy, and which only requires to be judiciously directed in order to produce the most sublime virtues.' (291)

Chateaubriand's position on patriotic fervor is clearly contradictory: the knights are praised but revolutionaries condemned for doing the same thing; enthusiasm is deemed "divine" when it "animate[s] the apostle of the gospel" (557), i. e. missionaries and knights, but it is labeled "senseless violence" when it moves the people. By judging faith and commitment to a cause positively or negatively depending on their religious or secular nature, Chateaubriand reveals the relativist character of his ethics. He also denies any transcendence to all other forms of belief when he presents religious faith as the only means of conquering matter and death, when he appropriates belief for religion alone. What atheists lack in his view is precisely the ability to feel: "Without religion, the heart is insensible and dead to beauty; for beauty is not a thing that exists out of us; it is in the heart of man that all the charms of nature reside." (402) Voltaire, whose most beautiful pages were inspired by religious feelings in spite of him, he claims, "would have gained by being a Christian. [...] His works would have acquired that moral tint without which nothing is perfect" (455). Because religion alone has the ability to graft morals onto belief, because religion alone provides a sense of transcendence, Chateaubriand claims, secular forms of belief cannot exist. Those who do not believe in God cannot believe that the survival of the community is more valuable than their own and act selflessly. For the "soldier who marches forth to battle" death means losing everything if he is an atheist – "to perish forever" – and gaining everything – "an endless life" – if he is Christian (197). Dying for one's country makes sense if the reward is eternal life, but it does not if the reward is mere fame. For Chateaubriand, in fact, it was the very sense of belonging to a community stretching beyond one's life that was lost during the French Revolution (418). If the two opposed understandings of patriotism, one geared towards peace and one towards war, can co-exist in Chateaubriand's mind, it is because they apply to different categories of people. The humble express their instinctual attachment to their country primarily through their fidelity to soil and roots; the aristocracy demonstrates its patriotism by shedding blood for the *patrie*. In Chateaubriand's view, dying for France had to remain an aristocratic prerogative.

Conclusion

Written within a period of a few years, Chateaubriand's *Historical Essay* and *Genius of Christianity* foreground the issue of national identity from the perspective of a provincial aristocracy that still viewed itself as the embodiment of the nation in 1789. Its insistence on retaining its rights and privileges was one of the major causes of the French Revolution and yet it refused to acknowledge its responsibility in it. Chateaubriand mourns this old understanding of the nation in the *Historical Essay* and, taking revolutionary excess as proof of the Revolution's fundamental evil, attributes the Revolution to other causes than the one just mentioned. According to him, the absolute monarchy's corruption had allowed the advent of "the philosophic sect." Far from being enlightened, as they claimed, these *philosophes* had no understanding of France, no stakes in the nation. Living as they did in books, spending their life in classical antiquity, they favored "foreign" ideas and models utterly unsuited for the French.

The *Historical Essay* amply demonstrates the conformity of Chateaubriand's ideas with those of the anti-philosophic and anti-revolutionary camp. For him, the Enlightenment's abstractions led to the breakdown of the age-old bond between religion and morals, religion and politics, and as a result to the disintegration of the family, the birth of individualism, or rather selfishness, and the disapperance of the aristocratic values of honor and civility. France, for instance, had broken the aristocratic code of conduct by siding with American rebels instead of lending its support to the British Crown. The French Revolution was divine retribution for that sin. But if the absolute monarchy was bad enough, the Republic was far worse. The attempt to implement the grand, but empty principles of liberty and equality had only proven the falsehood of the *philosophes*' *esprit de système* and brought murder and chaos to the country.

The *Genius of Christianity* proposes remedies to the national ills diagnosed in the *Historical Essay*. The way to restore morals and to bring social peace to France, Chateaubriand argues, is to place the nation once again under Christianity's civilizing influence, since, unlike enlightened philosophy, religion breeds morals. With regard to national identity, two different ways of bonding with the nation are proposed depending on one's station in life. Given its knightly origin, *amour de la patrie* means shedding blood for the nation when war breaks out and patriotism in that case is conceived as an aristocratic privilege. The concept of "instinct de la *patrie*," briefly introduced in the *Essay* and further developed in *Genius of Christianity*, applies to the rest of society. Chateaubriand presents it as a gift of God to mankind meant to moderate man's instinctual love for his country, to dampen his zeal and enthusiasm. In that sense, the meaning of the expression "*amour de la patrie*" is the same in the *Genius of Christianity* and in the *Essay*: it remains associated with the "native soil" and with "ancestors." The symbols conveying this form of *amour de son pays* are of a personal nature (cradle, tree, grave) and have nothing in common with the national symbols expressing love and devotion for the abstract national entity.

It is interesting to compare Chateaubriand's reflections on national differences, seen by him as a reflection of nations' deviations from religious orthodoxy, to the account proposed by Hervé Le Bras and Emmanuel Todd (1981: 81). For these two anthropologists, France's traditional embrace of Catholicism must be viewed as an expression of its predicament as an extremely diverse country, ethnically as well as linguistically. In sixteenth-century Europe, they explain, relative ethnic and linguistic homogeneity allowed "feelings of national belonging" to hatch out in some countries, and these countries, breaking with Catholic universalism, created national churches and adopted their vernaculars as national languages. France, a nation "without a definite anthropological identity," was by contrast condemned to view "Catholicism, which is indifferent to the national idea, as a better agent of integration" (79). "France's ideological history," they argue, "is an unending sequel of ruses against particularist, ethnocentric, racist conceptions" (80) that have historically threatened the kingdom's unity and later the nation's: "The glorious episode of the Revolution, is just one such moment in the history of France, it is preceded by other ideological choices of the universalist sort." (81) Catholic universalism, however, precisely because "it is indifferent to the national idea," could only lose ground once it found itself in competition with the more powerful agents of national integration put in place during the Revolution, and even more so when combined, as in Chateaubriand's essays, with a particularist understanding of the nation.

The French national model tends to be contrasted with others because of its universalist aspirations. Alyssa Goldstein Sepinwall, for instance, subtitles her 2005 book on Abbé Grégoire, "the making of modern universalism;" and Joan Wallach Scott her work on *Parité*, "the crisis of French universalism." This universalism's modernity and Frenchness are said to originate in the French Revolution understood as both a historical turning point in the history of mankind and as the producer of rights and principles valid for humanity as a whole. The nation is no longer embodied by the King but conceived as expression of the will of the people; subjects become citizens, individuals endowed with rights; differences among individuals are erased and commonalities empha-sized; the relation between the individual and the nation-state becomes the pri-mary identity marker. In the *Essay on Revolutions* and the *Genius on Christianity*, by contrast, roots, religious traditions, local culture, in short, ground Chateau-briand's conception of the *patrie*. This culturalist understanding of the nation unsettles the traditional association between universalism and France. It also blurs the neat line typically used to contrast French universalism to the German culturalism of Herder and Fichte.[38] But all things considered, it is not surprising that this culturalist understanding of the nation would also be found in France. The concept of "nation-state" emerged as a corrective to the concept of the "state," that is to a political order emanating from a strong central power initially embodied in France by the absolute monarchy. Chateaubriand, the religious no-bleman of provincial origin, the enemy of the absolute monarchy, had good rea-sons to reject this centralized understanding of the state and to propose a nation-al model grounded in the local instead. But as this centralized state survived the French Revolution and was imposed on the 'sister republics' of the Napoleonic empire, including Germany, German nationalists produced a similar culturalist concept of the nation in their fight against foreign occupation and France's uni-versalist pretentions.

Chateaubriand's critique of the Enlightenment and the Revolution has as its main target their radical questioning of a world order he presents as created by God. His determinism is a direct response to the Revolution's voluntarism and a negation of all the precepts that are derived from it. To their forward-looking vi-sion of new beginnings, he opposes a backward-looking glance at the history of Christianity. To the revolutionary conception of the nation grounded in principles and rights valid for humanity as a whole, he opposes a particularist understand-ing of the nation that interprets national differences as a function of their respec-tive relative success in adhering to Christian precepts. To the revolutionary con-ception of the nation as expression of the will of the people, he opposes an organic conception of the nation as a community rooted in its soil and connected to ancestors through blood. To the revolutionary conception of society as the sum of equally free individuals, he opposes a hierarchical understanding of society that is a reflection of the well-ordered world created by God, in which each has a place and corresponding duties, the higher class, the aristocracy, to fight for God and country, the lower class to labor, love its native soil, and stay on it. To the revolutionary sense of national belonging that subordinates the will

---

38 Izemberg (1992) and Prickett (2009) also examine the relation between Chateaubriand and these German thinkers.

of all individuals to the will of the nation, he restitutes patriotism proper to the aristocratic elite and grants the meek a milder form of patriotism, their instinctual attachment to their place of birth.

Chateaubriand's ideas consistently remained the views of a minority of the French during most of the nineteenth century. Stendhal did not envision that they would survive at all when he wrote, in 1826, that "twenty-four years ago, M. de Chateaubriand, with his eloquent rhetorical flourishes, succeeded in giving an exaggerated picture of the mild spirit of that religion which sentences a man to nine months' imprisonment for merely passing over the miracles in silence" (Stendhal 1991a: 432). But they resurfaced nonetheless and by the end of the nineteenth-century found their way into the writings of many writers who prepared the ground for the conservative nationalist movement that blossomed between the last decade of the nineteenth century and World War II before culminating in Pétain's France. Hyppolite Taine (1828–1893), for instance, shared Chateaubriand's elitist belief in the existence of a "superior class" or rather a "rational elite making judgments for an irrational mass" (MClelland 1970: 22), and later, Charles Maurras (1868–1952) would still call for the restoration of the monarchy. Like Chateaubriand, Maurice Barrès (1862–1923) opposed his nationalist relativist ethics to the universalism of reason: during the Dreyfus affair, he saw it as a necessity to suspend any individual sense of justice for the sake of national honor, in other words to sacrifice the truth and condemn an innocent for the glory of France and its army. His refusal to accept "the Dreyfusard testimony of Emile Zola" (McClelland 1970: 160) is also characteristic of the nationalist movement's position against positive truth and scientific evidence. For him as for Chateaubriand, being French was to have French ancestors buried in French soil. The concept of the unavoidability of war in *The Genius of Christianity*, defended by Joseph de Maistre who claimed that war was "divine," was picked up by conservative nationalists like Barrès and Georges Sorel (1847–1922) who also found war "ennobling." For them the butchery of World War I was morally cleansing for the nation and to participate in it a religious duty. Even Chateaubriand's use of religion to draw the line between 'us,' the French, and 'them,' the foreigners, resurfaced at the end of the century, only this time the enemy was no longer the atheist, but the Jew.

Chapter III
Cosmopolitanism and Nationalism in Germaine de Staël's Works

> *Exile cut the roots that bound*
> *me to Paris and I became*
> *European.*
> (Staël 2000: xi)

Two different conceptions of *amour de la patrie* have been examined thus far: Olympe de Gouge's patriotism, which privileges the individual's relation to the abstract entity of the nation-state, expresses this bond through emotions and symbols commonly shared and understood, and corresponds to the modern conception of national identity; and Chateaubriand's nationalism, which refers to the bond to ancestors and native soil, and offers a French version of the culturalist approach to the nation usually associated with German nationalism. But was nationalism, in this or that guise, inescapable at the turn of the nineteenth century? If there was any resistance to this trend, Germaine de Staël could be expected to be the voice of that opposition given her intellectual trajectory. She undoubtedly played a crucial role in shaping modern nationalism as the first modern thinker to argue, in *On Literature* (1800), and again, in *On Germany* (1809), that each nation ought to have its own language, culture, and literature. But by the end of her life, Staël viewed herself as a European, as a transnational figure, as the lines quoted in the epigraph above indicate. It is also the way critics tend to view her, as "more European than French" (Godechot 1983: 30); "a cosmopolitan by nature" (Gautier 1921: 142);[1] "a great European," the subtitle of Sabine Appel's biography (2006). Kathleen Kete (2012: 69, 70) goes a step further when she argues that, at Coppet, Staël succeeded in creating a kind of anti-nationalist "social space" that "functioned on the principle of acceptance of difference, of tolerance of the other, and in the belief that there was something to learn from others, that one could take from others 'without chauvinism,'" a model, she adds, that stood in crass contrast to the Napoleonic Empire's "homogenizing project."

In *The Birth of European Romanticism*, John C. Isbell (1994: 3) rightly contrasts Staël's key role in the development of European Romanticism[2] to the "routine indifference" with which her work is met, particularly in France. This indifference, I

---

1 Translation from Gautier (1921), Godechot (1983), and Minart (2003) are mine.
2 Mueller-Vollmer (1991) similarly argues that *On Germany* played a key role in the creation of a national literature in the United States.

believe, has much to do with the issue of national belonging. Was Madame de Staël even French? Simone Balayé (2006) thought the question was important enough to discuss it in a fairly recent publication. For unlike Gouges and Chateaubriand, Staël was often perceived and treated as a foreigner in France during her life and from a legal standpoint she may in fact not have been French. In his history of French nationality entitled *Qu'est-ce qu'un Français? Histoire de la nationalité française depuis la Révolution* Patrick Weil points out that the concept of nationality was of little concern during the Old Regime and that it remained on the backburner in the early days of the Revolution as well. The Constitution of 1790, which defined citizenship but not nationality, created a new social division among the French, between active and passive citizens, propertied men on the one hand, and women and the poor on the other, but between 1790 and 1794, citizenship and nationality were linked and acquired automatically by foreigners "simply by residing in France" (Weil 2004: 16). The residency requirement was even waived for foreigners who had made significant contributions to the enlightenment of mankind and were granted honorific citizenship on that account.

The sheer number of laws and decrees seeking to define and refine the relationship between citizenship and nationality during the revolutionary era testifies to a growing concern with these issues, however. War in 1792, for instance, put a strain on the initial revolutionary openness toward foreigners when new decrees were passed that subjected them to a registration requirement and sent those from countries at war with France to jail 'until peace.' As we saw in the first chapter, war also aroused feelings of xenophobia. Foreigners were still able to acquire citizenship automatically through residency, however, at least until 1795 when a declaration of intent and a residency requirement of seven years at first, and then, in 1799, of ten years, were added. But in 1804, the *Code Civil* turned these previous laws upside down in two major ways: first, by separating citizenship, defined by the Constitution; and nationality defined by the *Code Civil*; and second, by grounding nationality in filiation instead of place of birth or place of residency, by substituting *jus sanguinis* to the Old Regime's *jus soli*. From then on, anyone who was born of a French father, in France or anywhere in the world, was French.

All these changes affected Germaine de Staël personally. Born in Paris in 1766, she was French according to the old *jus soli*, and theoretically at least, remained French after marrying a Swede – since foreign residents were considered French in the early years of the Revolution.[3] One may safely assume, however,

---

3 Kete writes that "Miss Necker's choice of the Baron of Staël-Holstein as a husband had much

that Staël did not have to think about her nationality too much at the time. As a well-connected member of a privileged intellectual, political, financial, and diplomatic elite, she was free to come and go as she wished. After the proclamation of the Republic in 1792 she had little trouble, for instance, leaving France for Switzerland and a little later for England when many of her aristocratic friends faced real danger. At that point, she herself was also leaving on her own accord to mark her opposition to the new regime – since according to Isbell she "did not accept the Republic until she met Ribbing at the end of 1793" (Isbell 1997: 211). She stayed away from France during the Jacobin Republic but when she returned to France after the fall of Robespierre, she was ordered out of Paris or the country several times between 1795 and 1803. By then she was seen and treated as a foreigner by the French authorities.

Between 1798 and 1802, Staël nonetheless managed to reclaim her place in a Parisian high society that was her natural habitat, the place where she felt she belonged. High society meant politics for her: "'True pleasure for me can be found only in love, Paris, or power,'" she once told her father (quoted in Kete 2012: 48).As Kete convincingly argues, her answer to women's exclusion from politics was to adopt "the persona of genius" so as to create "a space for herself as a political being" (48). To a large extent, Staël fulfilled her dream: she had it all from December 1791 to March 1792 when her lover, Louis de Narbonne, was minister of war, but she also lost it all the same year. She tried again and again, and succeeded, through the men in her life – "Talleyrand, Ribbing, Constant and others" (Isbell 1997: 214) – to exert political power.

Whether or not she truly "wished to assume with Napoleon the burdens of future rule" (Kete 2012: 48), as many critics have maintained, is possible, but nothing came of it. She did, however, play a role in French politics during the Consulate through Benjamin Constant. When Bonaparte took power through a coup d'état on 9 November 1799 (18 Brumaire, An VIII), she successfully lobbied Sieyès, one of the three consuls, to appoint Benjamin Constant (1767–1830) to the Tribunat, a post he occupied from December 1799 to January 1802. But less than a month after his appointment, Constant's first speech in that chamber aroused Bonaparte's anger, a feeling that was also directed at Staël whom the First Consul rightly suspected of leading the opposition to him behind the scene. In the spring of 1800, Bonaparte reportedly went on the attack, criticizing Staël's way of life and her treatment of her husband, whom, he claimed, she had abandoned in utter poverty in spite of her wealth – the Baron was actually a

---

to do with the fact that he was "established in Paris" and that her marriage contract stipulated that he "would never insist that Madame de Staël be forced to live in Sweden" (Kete 2012: 49).

gambler. Bonaparte is also rumored to have orchestrated violent attacks in the press after the publication of *On Literature* in April 1800, a book he saw as a personal attack on his government. A month later, Staël left for Coppet where she began writing *Delphine*.

Between 1800 and 1802, as Bonaparte was consolidating his grip on power, Staël hoped he would fail. As mentioned earlier, one of the reasons for her opposition to him may have been unreciprocated love on his part, but as Godechot (1983: 18) points out, their ideas also widely differed: she detested military dictatorship, which he considered the best means of government. Much to her dismay, Bonaparte's popularity continued to grow in France, as peace treaties with Austria and even England were signed. With even France's traditional enemy now enamored with him, Staël worried that no one seemed to care about liberty anymore. Few protested for instance, when, in January 1802, he eliminated the most vocal advocates of freedom on the Tribunat, twenty of Staël's friends, Benjamin Constant included. Then in April 1802, the Concordat re-established Catholicism as 'the religion of the majority of the French people,' an act, according to Paul Gautier (1921: 74–75), that "Mme de Staël never forgave Bonaparte because it destroyed her most cherished hope," to see Protestantism become the official religion of France. Staël was indignant: adding insult to injury, Bonaparte had called the British "heretics" in a public letter to the French.[4]

Although it should have been increasingly obvious to her that her "sentiments were not those of France" (Gautier 1921: 59), that the majority of the French people did not share her political views, Staël was not ready to concede defeat. In the spring of 1802, she took part in a plot to overthrow Bonaparte and replace him with another general, Bernadotte. Fouché's police did its work, however, and the plot was broken up. The First Consul, who knew about her role in it, chose to avoid publicity and did not have Staël arrested. A little while later, in May 1802, she left Paris to visit her father, accompanied this time by her husband – who died on the way to Coppet. That same month, Bonaparte's term as First Consul was prolonged for ten more years and in August 1802 a plebiscite made him Consul for Life.

These events did not stop Staël and her friends from continuing to express their opposition to Bonaparte. Gautier (1921: 84) mentions the pamphlet by Camille Jordan (1771–1821) that criticized his new elevation, "True Meaning of the National Vote on the Consulate for Life," and notes that Napoleon knew who was behind this call to rebellion, but did not act. Then, a few months

---

4 "We Protestants, are a bit upset to see the British labeled as heretics," she wrote to a friend. Quoted in Gautier (1921: 77).

later, in August 1802, Jacques Necker's *Last Views on Politics and Finance* [*Dernières vues de politique et de finances*] appeared in Paris, a book that contained the same critique of military despotism as *On Literature* and was thought by some people to have the same author. Like Staël, Necker expressed the wish for a better constitution and the hope that Bonaparte would act for the good of the nation by stepping aside after a few years. In *L'individu effacé, ou le paradoxe du libéralisme français*, Lucien Jaume underscores Staël's and Bonaparte's different understandings of liberty. For the latter and the *Idéologues*, the government guaranteed the citizens' liberty, their rights to own and enjoy property, to practice their religion, and to live in security (Jaume 1997: 33). For Staël, individual liberty came first: "the *liberal* idea dictate[d] heads of states' conduct: they could not impose to the people, what the people would not adopt, as a law, for themselves." (61) Staël's conception of liberalism was already not the dominant one during the Consulate and, as Jaume further notes, her "liberalism of the subject" (25) was never to become a tenet of French liberalism. What the "friends of liberty" failed to realize was how out of synch they were with French public opinion: Bonaparte was popular, Necker was not, at least according to Gautier (1921: 99) who bases his assessment on the negative press reactions to his book. And by that time, the Consul for Life's power was strong enough to put an end to Staël's opposition. He did not positively forbid this *intrigante*, this trouble-maker, to return to Paris the following winter. He let her know instead that it would be best if she chose to stay in Coppet. She did. She was not, however, altogether gone that winter. Her novel *Delphine*, a semi-autobiographical *roman à clef*, appeared in Paris in December 1802 and enjoyed considerable success.

3.1 *Delphine*, an ambiguous critique of the aristocratic ethos

"History can teach us nothing more than the general picture brought into view by the force of circumstance," Staël wrote in the preface of *Delphine*, "but it cannot admit us to the inner feelings which, by influencing the will of a few, have decided the fate of all" (Staël 1995: 4). Making the case for literature's *raison d'être*, Staël compares it to history, thus establishing a distinction between the two disciplines at a time when it was not commonly made, and arguing that literature has the ability to explain what history cannot, the *impressions intimes* [inner feelings] that make people act in certain ways and thereby also influence others. The novelistic form chosen to convey these inner feelings may seem a bit old fashioned: *Delphine* is an epistolary novel, nearly five hundred pages long, more reminiscent of *La Princesse de Clèves* than of Chateaubriand's *Atala*. But its originality is twofold: it is set during the French Revolution, covering the period from 12 April 1790, date of the first letter, to October 1792, in other words, shortly after the proclamation of the First Republic – a period that corresponds to the height of Staël's love story with Louis de Narbonne. Like all of Staël's works, it also serves as a commentary on French politics.

Delphine deals with a topic Staël had already examined in *Current Circumstances*,[5] the relation between "friends of liberty" and "moderate Royalists," but from a different vantage point: it is the literary, subjectivist, counterpart of the historical, objectivist, account written four years earlier. Through the characters of Delphine, the friend of liberty, and Léonce, the moderate Royalist, the novel brings to life the emotions of those who tried to make this difficult relationship work and it also offers a psychological account of the tensions that led to its failure. In the political context in which it appeared, the novel also functions as a renewed appeal to moderate Royalists, people like Chateaubriand and Fontanes, as yet one more effort on Staël's part to rally them to her cause. By recalling their failure to support liberty in the early phase of the Revolution and, by hinting, through both endings of the novels, to the disasters that ensued, Staël warns of the dangers ahead, should they persist in their support of Bonaparte.[6]

Delphine also seeks to convince moderate Royalists that they are wrong on moral and religious issues. In a chapter on "Religions" in *Current Circumstances*, Staël had argued that it was appropriate for a nation to adopt a new religion following a radical change in political institutions, such as a passage from the absolute monarchy to the republic for instance (1979: 222–241), and as Higonnet notes (1998: 67), she "toyed with the idea of staging a conversion of the French to Protestantism." Her book did not appear in print at the time, but Chateaubriand's defense of Catholicism in the *Genius of Christianity* may well have been a response to similar proposals. In the preface of *Delphine*, in any case, Staël showed her willingness to engage in a dialog with Chateaubriand directly: "It has been said that religious opinions of the day contributed the most to the splendor of seventeenth-century literature and that no work of imagination could achieve distinction without the same beliefs. A work that even its adversaries should admire for its original, extraordinary, brilliant imagination, *The Genius of Christianity*, has strongly supported that literary system." (Staël 1995: 6–7)

---

5 Staël wrote *On the Current Circumstances which can end the Revolution* [*Des Circonstances actuelles qui peuvent terminer la révolution*] in 1798, but the book remained unpublished until 1979.

6 Staël's narrative implies that the aristocracy did not participate in Revolution, an account that contradicts historical evidence. On the nobility's participation in the early phase of the revolution, see Wick (1996); Tackett (1996).

Her reference to "seventeenth-century literature" reveals her awareness of the stakes of the battle being waged by Chateaubriand: she understands the Royalists' attempt to upstage the Enlightenment. On the face of it, she seems to concede that Christianity may have had a positive influence on literature, but her praise soon turns into sarcasm[7] and substantive critique. If Chateaubriand intended to disprove the thesis of the perfectibility of the human mind by opposing heart and reason, he failed, she claims. She sees Chateaubriand's "effort to establish a kind of opposition between reason and imagination" as absurd and dismisses it by saying that there are now "many people incapable of imagination [who] give reason short shrift from the start in the hope that this proof of zeal will always count in their favor" (Staël 1995: 7). She also takes him to task for suggesting that Christianity deeply influenced French classical literature but for failing to mention the Reformation which she credits for having introduced liberty in France and elsewhere in Europe. Staël was apparently anxious to see how her objections, in *Delphine,* to Chateaubriand's main thesis in *The Genius of Christianity* would be received. Acording to Gautier (1921: 115), "she wrote to friends that she would postpone her return to Paris until the effects of her attacks against Catholicism and divorce were known." But Staël's most relevant target of criticism for a study of the national habitus in *Delphine* is her refutation of the claim that Christianity informs the aristocratic ethos. Through the character of Léonce, who is repeatedly presented as totally insensitive to religious feelings, Staël demolishes Chateaubriand's pious image of the Christian knight and replaces it with a more accurate picture of the brilliant, flashy, but also selfishly ruthless aristocrat.

Delphine is divided in six parts organized around three kinds of settings: the world of Parisian salons (I and II); the country estate in close distance from Paris (III and IV); and exile and war – although Delphine's exile is motivated by personal, rather than political reasons (V and VI). The novel's social settings highlight the dominant theme in the novel, the contrast between bourgeois and aristocratic codes of conduct. The Parisian salon is ruled by the aristocratic ethos; bourgeois happiness reigns in the countryside and Delphine's flight into exile signals the failure to bridge these two worlds. About the same amount of time is spent in each of these places: eight months in Paris, from April to November 1790; an entire year in Bellerive, from December 1790 to December 1791; and nearly a year, from December 1791 to September 1792, for the exile period.

---

7 "[...] since Christianity goes back eighteen centuries and our masterpieces in literature only two, I thought that the progress of the human mind in general ought to count for something in an examination of the differences between the literature of the ancient and that of modern writers." (Staël 1995: 7)

3.1.1 The aristocratic ethos of the Parisian salon

In spite of obvious differences, *Delphine* prefigures the plot of the realist novel: a young person leaves the province for Paris in the hope of love and glory only to be crushed by society. Of course, Delphine d'Albémar is a young woman, not a man, and she does not arrive in Paris alone from her home town of Montpellier. She is accompanied by relatives, Sophie de Vernon and her beautiful and dutiful daughter, Matilde. Similarly, Delphine's ambition is not to make a fortune: the young widow is already wealthy – a sign of her bourgeois origins – and extremely generous with her money. Thanks to her fortune, she and her relatives have established residence in the most prestigious neighborhood in Paris, on the *Champs-Elysées* close to the aristocratic *faubourg Saint-Germain*. Finally, Delphine does not have to struggle to make it in Paris: she masters the rules of "good society" and immediately becomes the toast of the capital's salons.[8]

But her story is nonetheless a tale of lost illusions. In Paris, Delphine meets Léonce de Mondoville and the two young people fall in love in spite of numerous obstacles: Léonce is her cousin Matilde's fiancé; Delphine's extreme generosity with her cousin – the gift of a property with a "twenty throusand *livres*" income – has made this marriage possible; and last but not least, Delphine and Léonce are said to have incompatible characters. Delphine's bourgeois ethos makes her trust in the goodness of the human heart, believe that kindness, generosity, pity for the unfortunate, and self-sacrifice are moral values that lift the human spirit and should always guide human action. Léonce does not share these moral and religious values. As he acknowledges in a letter to his tutor, Barton, his actions in life are guided by a strict adherence to the aristocratic code of conduct, which he defines in a positive way as "the prejudices of [his] ancestors."[9] Delphine's description of the aristocratic code of conduct by contrast, highlights the negatives. For Léonce, she states, imagination ("the example and memory of ancient Spanish ways") and identification with imagined ancestors and medieval ideas ("the knightly and military ideas that have fascinated you since childhood") re-

---

8 "Mastery of 'good society's' subtle strategies for dealing with people, which members begin to learn from childhood onwards, is among other things a symbol of the membership of an especially prestigious group, and through the practice of these strategies the need for continual reaffirmation of individual self-esteem is met. It strengthens solidarity with their own group, and the feeling of being better people, superior to others." (Elias 1996: 72–73)

9 "Although I received an enlightened upbringing, thanks to you, the most powerful motives for all the acts of my life are nonetheless a sort of military instinct, prejudices if you will, but the prejudices of my ancestors, perfectly suited to the pride and impetuosity of my soul." (Staël 1995: 45–46)

place "the delicate principles of religion and morality" (Staël 1995: 219). As evidence of his lack of religion and morals, she cites his adherence to a degraded "cult [...] of honor" that makes him react to appearances instead of substance. Léonce, according to her, has such an "almost superstitious respect for public opinion" that he would rather die than suffer "the world's praise or blame" (220). If he had any real moral sense, she contends, he would not take public opinion so seriously; he would try to distinguish between rumors and facts before acting.

In her depiction of Léonce, Staël thus unmasks Chateaubriand's religious rhetoric for what it is: a new strategy, a recasting and repackaging of aristocratic claims to social superiority instead of the continuation of an authentic religious aristocratic tradition. At the same time, she also underscores the unavoidable influence the Enlightenment had on the French aristocracy by giving Léonce an enlightened tutor. Confronted with bourgeois values in Parisian salons, she implies, the aristocracy had a chance to improve, and to a certain extent it did. Léonce falls in love with Delphine precisely because he is seduced by the bourgeois values she embodies: her "beguiling blend of genius and candor, gentleness and strength;" her "great enthusiasm" when "she speaks of virtue," her genuine good heart that "breathes what is good like pure air" (Staël 1995: 58). It is also his initial ability to recognize Delphine's genius, to distinguish between true feelings and pretense that makes him a "moderate Royalist," someone who can be brought to adhere to these values himself. Strangely, however, Delphine is the one who will make concessions all along. One of her first faux-pas is to publicly proclaim her "love of liberty," a mistake she immediately regrets as she fears that it will make her look like "a madwoman" in the eyes of "Mme de Mondoville whose hate for the Revolution in France is curiously excessive" (59). Then when Léonce begs her to stop talking politics,[10] she readily complies. Moreover, her good heart, her generosity with her friends, Thérèse d'Ervins, M. de Serbellane, repeatedly get her into trouble in the censoring eyes of her entourage. Although her love for Léonce is pure, she must, as a result, constantly contend with society's gossip about her alleged relationships with other men.[11] Still, she and Léonce overcome these first obstacles, and, convinced that their strong love can bridge all differences between them, decide to get married.

---

10 "Why, lovely Delphine, why do you defend opinions that arouse such hateful passions, and for which the people of your class have such great antipathy, perhaps rightly." (1995: 60)

11 Léonce mistakenly thinks that Delphine is having an affair with M. De Serballane when it is her friend Thérèse d'Ervins (modeled on Madame Récamier) who actually is. Madame de Vernon, who knows the truth, encourages this erroneous belief out of self-interest.

Enter Sophie de Vernon, the character Staël created to bring to life the female side of the aristocratic code of conduct in this novel.[12] A savvy socialite,
a cunning manipulator, Sophie pulls the plot's strings in the first two chapters
and the immoral tale she spins is meant to contrast bourgeois and aristocratic
ways, to once again underscore the superiority of Delphine's bourgeois morality
over Sophie's aristocratic immorality. Delphine thinks that Sophie is her friend,
she is captivated by her charm, but Sophie is not who Delphine thinks she is. For
Sophie, women have two options in a world dominated by men: to submit and
become prudes like her daughter Matilde, or to rebel and cultivate the art of dissimulation. Sophie, as she admits in her deathbed confession, has chosen the
latter. She derives "no other pleasure than from the art of hiding [her] tastes
and inclinations, and [she has] fashioned this art into a principle" (Staël 1998:
171). Delphine gives, Sophie takes. But Sophie even lacks a sense of gratitude,
a moral failing that the rules of proper social behavior usually keep hidden
since "there is nothing more indelicate than rebukes for services rendered"
(156). Delphine, for her part, views ingratitude as "the harshest [...] of all
human vices" because it points to an "extreme coldness of soul and forgetfulness
of the past" (155). She believes that kindness to others is the key to happiness;
Sophie, that "[w]e do nothing in life except for selfish motives or for pleasure"
(157).[13] Thanks to Sophie, Staël can turn the tables on the anti-Enlightenment
discourse and accuse the aristocracy of being materialist and selfish. Sophie
loves luxury, wealth, she has gambled her husband's fortune away and now
needs her daughter to marry Léonce to settle a debt she owes his mother. In
order to reach her goal, she has no second thoughts about damaging Delphine's
reputation, no hesitation transforming false rumors into outright lies, and no regret destroying her friend's happiness. In short, Sophie de Vernon's misdeeds
testify to the aristocracy's capital crimes: duplicity, hypocrisy, ruthlessness, a
lack of empathy and feelings for fellow human beings, flaws that can be all accounted for by an inconsiderate attachment to oneself, to one's place in society,
to one's rank.

Instead of helping Delphine marry Léonce, as she promised she would, Sophie succeeds in convincing him to marry her daughter by using some of her habitual weapons, in this case character manipulation – Léonce is "enamored of
reputation almost as much as of Delphine" (Staël 1995: 70) – and by plainly de-
ceiving him. In the dark about Sophie's treachery and Léonce's change of mind,

---

12 Sophie de Vernon's visit to court indicates her high social standing: "Mme de Vernon went to
the Tuileries to pay court to the queen; she asked me to accompany her." (Staël 1995: 76)
13 Staël justifies Sophie's behavior to a certain extent when she has her character assert that it
is "the only defense left to women against the injustices of their masters" (Staël 1995: 171).

Delphine learns at the last minute that her cousin Matilde is about to wed the man of her dreams. On the symbolic date of 14 July 1790, as thousands of French people gather on the *Champ de Mars* to celebrate the first anniversary of the Revolution, Delphine, alone, hidden behind a column in the church, watches heartbroken and dumbfounded her dream of perfect happiness disappear.

Sophie wins the first round but in the moral contest winner loses in the end. That at least, is the still optimistic morality found at the end of the first two chapters. On the one hand, Delphine's inability to hate people, even Sophie, is cast as yet another proof of her moral superiority; on the other hand, her virtues also triumph over the dark and powerful forces of dissimulation when a dying Sophie admits that Delphine is the only person she ever loved, that she always admired her as a being "at one superior and natural, simple in manner, and generous in sacrifice, steadfast and passionate, witty like the cleverest, trusting like the best, in a word, so kind and tender a being [...]" (Staël 1995: 176). At the end of her life, Sophie suddenly realizes that she has led an empty, superficial life; that she has "misconstrued the road" to her own happiness. Even if the lesson is learned too late, she now knows that love has the power to change people, to put them 'on the road to happiness.'

In the first two chapters, the world of the Parisian salons seems completely unchanged by the French Revolution. We hear distant echoes of peasant revolts[14] but Parisian high society is presented as uninterested and uninvolved in revolutionary politics. In the social world in which Delphine and Léonce evolve, it is not even proper to mention the Revolution. Old Regime mores are still the norm, conversation still revolves around social gossip, not politics; honor still reigns supreme; dueling is still seen as the standard way of solving conflicts.[15] The date of 14 July 1790 is important in *Delphine* but not as a commemoration of the first anniversary of the Revolution. With no mention of the *Fête de la Fédération*, it is emptied of its symbolic aura and acquires a private instead of a public dimension as well as a reverse meaning: disunion instead of national unity.

3.1.2 Bourgeois life in the countryside

Parts III and IV of the novel are set mostly at and around Delphine's country estate of Bellerive, a few hours' ride from Paris, where the novel's heroine finds ref-

---

14 M. de Serbellane is said to have saved M. d'Ervins from a peasant revolt in June 1789.
15 Even women, like Mme De Marset and Madame de Tesin, abide by this code of honor. They are the ones, for instance, who push an unwilling M. D'Orsan to duel with M. De Mondoville who, they feel, has insulted them. See Staël (1995: 328).

uge after the wedding of Léonce and Matilde. The aristocratic conception of marriage exemplified by this loveless, duty and honor bound contractual union is set in sharp contrast with the bourgeois family model illustrated by Delphine's neighbors, Henri and Elise de Lebensei. The couple's marital bliss rekindles Delphine's belief in love as the path to true happiness and her faith in its power to overcome social hurdles. In spite of their religious differences – she is a Catholic; he is a Protestant – in spite of her divorce from her first husband, Henri and Elise have refused to bow to social conventions and built a happy family. On the one hand, Staël thereby suggests that interfaith marriages constitute an excellent means of healing social divisions. On the other hand, she also underscores the severity of religious biases in France at the time when she presents Elise's family's refusal to socialize with her and her husband as her only source of suffering. Perhaps less consciously, she also points to bigotry on the Protestant side in her depiction of Henri's rather intolerant attitude towards Catholicism, not only in his critique on the Church's position on "the indissolubility of marriage," but also in his characterization of Catholicism as a religion bent on "impos[ing] pain on man in a thousand forms as the most effective means of moral and religious training" (Staël 1995: 305). In that regard, Higonnet's characterization of Delphine as "a quasi-Protestant modernizer" (Higonnet 1998: 93) seems accurate. Lebensei extols the merits of his faith at length in a passage that serves as a counterpoint to Chateaubriand's thesis of its alleged degeneration:

> The protestant faith, closer to the true spirit of the Gospel than Catholicism, does not use suffering to scare or to chain the mind. As a result, mores are purer, crimes less heinous, laws more humane in Protestant countries [...]; whereas in all countries where Catholicism is vigorous, [...] political institutions and private mores are affected by the errors of a religion that considers constraint and suffering as the best ways of perfecting humanity. (Staël 1995: 398)

The Belmont family offers another example of bourgeois happiness built on love and family values. He is blind, he lost his fortune, but she married him out of love and they too lead a happy live centered on their children's well-being and education. Upon witnessing "so happy a union" (Staël 1995: 231), Léonce vividly regrets what he has forfeited by marrying the aristocratic way. But when M. de Belmont proclaims that "Happiness is found through marriage alone" (231), he also understands that the blind man's praise of bourgeois marriage doubles as a condemnation of his irregular relationship with Delphine.

For Léonce and Delphine have resumed their relationship after finding out how he was tricked into marrying Matilde. At his request, she left Parisian high society to live in seclusion in Bellerive where he comes to visit daily. Delphine's sense of morality precluding sex, the two lovers spend hours reading and conversing. From her vantage point, this interaction has an educational purpose. She would like to bring Léonce to see the world her way, to convince him that "religious ideas give morality better support than the cult of honor and public opinion" (222); that moral conviction, not custom should guide his actions. But Léonce is a recalcitrant student and it is through his exchange on religion with Delphine that Staël best illustrates the point she made in the introduction of the novel, namely that religion has nothing to do with the aristocratic code of conduct; that aristocratic behavior is based on honor, not on religion.

Léonce thus continues to believe that "honor, like religion, has its conscience," that "to blush with shame in one's eyes is more unbearable than all the remorse prompted by the fear or hope of a life to come" (Staël 1995: 222). For this "inheritor of illustrious blood," the fear of dishonor in the eyes of public opinion is stronger than any other passion, and like the Cid, he views the world as "a struggle between love and honor" (440). Although he realizes that his adherence to honor ruined his personal life, his aristocratic ethos continues to guide him in public matters. He deems his personal opinion irrelevant on important issues, such as the nobility's privileges or war, and simply does what his caste deems honorable:

> I concede that for myself, I would not make it a point of honor to maintain the privileges of the nobility; but for me it is enough that some of the older gentry have decided this is the way things should be, to find intolerable the idea of being thought a democrat. Even if I were right a thousand times over when I explained my position, I do not even want an explanation to be necessary in anything related to my respect for my ancestors and the duties they have handed me down. (Staël 1995:244)

What Léonce enunciates in clear terms is his rejection of individualism. This abdication of will, this submission of the individual to the group, is at the core of the ideological conflict between the Enlightenment and anti-Enlightenment camps. Delphine is therefore at a loss to counter this kind of arguments. She tries to appeal to Léonce's manhood, to tell him that "If [she] were a man, it would be as impossible for [her] not to love liberty as to close up [her] heart to generosity, to friendship, to all the truest and purest feelings" (244), but no true dialog is possible with someone who will always choose the opinion of his group over his own. Such 'friends' can also only make unreliable allies.

Delphine and Léonce also have different conceptions of patriotism. They argue about it when he declares that, should it come to a civil war in France, he would fight on the side of the nobility. Delphine views his patriotism as old fashioned, as rooted in "the opinions of [his] mother and the great lords of Spain," and as class-based, as a "defense of the nobility" (Staël 1995: 244). As opposed to him, she praises "the generous enthusiasm" (244) that makes people willing to fight for "the dignity and the independence of the entire nation" (245). But in this case as well, the two lovers remain at loggerheads. The prospect of having to join the aristocratic camp in case of war precludes a friendship between Léonce and Henri de Lebensei, who shares Delphine understanding of patriotism. On 20 April 1791, Léonce writes to Delphine that he "would rather not be associated with M. de Lebensei" because "in a civil war" they "would surely serve" in opposite camps (243). In the end, he does befriend the Lebenseis but it takes him a while to overcome his prejudice and socialize with a divorced woman.

Henri is Delphine's male bourgeois counterpart in the novel. He is said to be modeled on Constant but is clearly modeled on Staël as well. Not surprisingly, the critique of the aristocratic ethos emanates largely from these two characters. Like Delphine, Henri believes that "the heart's affections may not be offered up to men's opinions, but to virtue alone;" that "between God and love" there is "no intermediary but conscience" (1995: 116). Like her, he is virtuous, unbiased, independent-minded and he loves liberty; with her, he shares the "generous enthusiasm that sweeps you off as do all noble and proud passions" (244) and the dream of transforming society on the basis of these value – even if what they mean by 'society' is 'high society' alone.[16] As Delphine points out, Henri is also "Léonce's mirror opposite:" "under a cold, often stern manner," he harbors "more openness to pity than anyone" (115). Léonce, by constrast, has an ebullient character that often leads him to misjudge people or act unfairly.

Staël agrees with Chateaubriand that religion influences morals but she strongly disagrees with the notion Catholicism is the most ethical religion. For her, unlike him, the Reformation brought clear religious and moral improvements and she compares England to France to make that point. To his decadent image of Great Britain, she opposes the portrait of two men who, though French, have achieved moral perfection thanks to England's beneficial influence. Like Delphine and other reasonable characters in the novel, Henri already has the advantage of being a good kind of French since he comes from Montpellier, a city with a large concentration of Protestants. But he has also improved through travel abroad: he is British through his education at Cambridge, his religion, and his excellent manners. Barton, the other virtuous man in the novel, has also adopted an unpretentious British look: simple brown dress, "hair unpowered," and the straightforward manners of that nation which give him a "respectable cast of fea-

---

16 Goodden rightly points out that Delphine "conducts herself in a spirit of moral liberalism that may be related to the Revolutionary principles of freedom, equality, and fraternity, but is rarely able to connect them with any larger sphere than that of private life." (Goodden 2008: 158)

tures" and an "impressive appearance" (Staël 1995: 34). In fact, he has assimilated British ways so well that "you think him English or American, rather than French" (34). By contrast, Léonce, who is French through his father and Spanish through his mother, has a double handicap. The reader is invited to perceive his flaws through Delphine's eyes and to adopt her value judgment on the respective merits of French and British national traits:

> Have you noticed how easy it is to recognize a Frenchman's rank in society at a single glance? The moment he has cause to fear being thought inferior, his pretensions and anxieties almost always betray him whereas the customary calm dignity of Englishmen and Americans preclude such ready judgment or ranking. (Staël 1995: 34)

Because he is obsessed with rank, the Frenchman is always insecure; because he does not think about rank, the Englishman is self-assured. In Léonce's case, by contrast, national hybridity only serves to intensify flaws.

Charity may be France's cardinal virtue, as Chateaubriand claimed, but those who illustrate it best are Protestants in the novel. Henri acts generously and selflessly, serving his political enemies as much as his friends. Thanks to his contacts in the Constituent Assembly, he is able to intervene twice on behalf of Delphine's aristocratic friends, first in April 1791, when M. de Marset "is threatened with the loss of his regiment for expressing an opinion said to be against the revolution" (Staël 1995: 241); and then in August 1791, when M. de Valorbe is about to be arrested for having helped the King flee to Varennes. More lucid than Delphine on matters of aristocratic ingratitude, Henri makes it clear in a letter to her that he does not expect anything in return for his good deeds. On the contrary, he feels quite certain that they will be forgotten since "as a general rule, one must not count on their [the aristocrats] remembering what one has done on their behalf" (242). He is correct, of course, in his assumption that no good deed will go unpunished. Instead of thanking him for what he did for her nephew, Mme de Marset slanders Delphine for associating with Lebensei, and Mme d'Artemas warns her that her "relationship with M. de Lebensei makes [her] more enemies than [her] love for Léonce" (251). Here again, Staël unmasks Chateaubriand's claim regarding the aristocracy's adherence to Christian virtues as a falsehood.

Unlike these aristocrats, Henri is concerned with the happiness of his friends. A proponent of progressive social values, he encourages Léonce and Delphine to take advantage of the new law on divorce and marry.[17] Delphine rejects that idea – "Léonce's consent [to divorce] would be as painful to me as his refus-

---

17 Divorce became legal in France in September 1792 just when the novel ends.

al" (Staël 1995: 309) – not because she objects to divorce as a matter of principle, but because of the "deep despair" it would cause her devout Catholic cousin Matilde (310). The divorce project never gets past that initial stage anyway: when Matilde finally discovers that her husband has spent all his evenings with Delphine during their first year of marriage, she informs her that she is expecting a child and demands that she never see Léonce again. In spite of the pain it causes her, Delphine agrees. She has a second good reason to leave: to escape a suitor's unwelcome advances.[18]

3.1.3 Exile and war

Nation and nationalism play a more prominent role in the last part of the novel as the prospect of war turns into reality. In the fragments of the diary reproduced at the beginning of part V and dated December 1791, Delphine consigns her regrets of leaving France in heart-felt patriotic terms: "France, Land of my fathers and of his [Léonce's]; delightful country I was never meant to leave. France! Whose name alone so deeply moves all those who from childhood on have breathed your sweet air and gazed on your serene skies!" (Staël 1995: 351) Her sense of national identity is expressed through references to personal roots and memories and the beauty of this attachment conveyed in images that evoke sweetness and serenity. Her feelings of love are also clearly directed towards the country as a whole, France, rather than a particular place in France, as with Chateaubriand. Staël soon returns to the issue of patriotism but first completes her critique of Catholicism by addressing a topic dear to the *philosophes*, and to Gouges: monastic vows and monastic institutions.

The abolition of monastic vows in February 1790 in France, i. e. before the start of the novel, and the maintenance of their prohibition in spite of the Concordat, probably explain Staël's postponement of the discussion of this religious issue until the heroine arrives in foreign lands. In the last part of the novel in any case, two female characters, Thérèse d'Ervins and Delphine d'Albémar become nuns. Brought to despair by the loss of Léonce, pursued by Valorbe, Delphine

---

18 Valorbe, who has been pressuring Delphine to marry him, was insulted by Léonce. Valorbe forfeited reparation, however, because Léonce convinced him to leave Paris immediately or else be arrested. As they were alone when Léonce's words were once again prompter than his judgment, no one would know. But there was a witness, of course, and when officers in Valorbe's regiment found out that he had given up on a duel, they refused to serve a man without honor. Valorbe then fought to defend his honor and was wounded. When news of these events made its way to Paris, Delphine was held responsible for Valorbe's misfortunes.

decides to withdraw from the world and to live as a boarder in a convent in Switzerland. In the *Abbaye du Paradis*, she befriends the abbess, Madame de Ternan – who turns out to be Léonce's aunt – and she soon falls under the charm of this aristocrat, as cold, as manipulative, but as charming as Sophie de Vernon. In part out of selfishness – she likes Delphine's company and her good manners – in part at the request of her sister, Léonce's mother, Mme de Ternan easily convinces an emotionally fragile Delphine to take permanent vows. The ceremony that takes place in June 1792 is central to the love plot: it sounds the death knell of the relationship between Léonce and Delphine.

Delphine is thus about to become a nun when France declares war on Austria in April 1792 but Léonce is still very much on her mind. Apart from the love plot, which seems to face a hopeless future at that point, much of the novel's suspense is provided by the issue of Léonce's patriotism: will he be loyal to France or to his estate? Elise de Lebensei confirms that Delphine's concerns in that regard are well-founded: "A few words Léonce let slip make me fear that he may one day cede to the impetus given French noblemen to leave France and bear arms against their country [...]. M. de Lebensei is fighting that idea with all the strength of his reason." (Staël 1995: 357). Then Delphine learns from Mme de Ternan that Léonce, in spite of Henri's efforts, is still "strongly attracted to the idea of fighting in the war that threatens France" (373). Concerned that he might join the Princes' army, as he had told her he would, she begs Henri "to keep Léonce from leaving France and joining the party which intends to go to war at the side of the foreign army" (373). Henri complies and in a very long patriotic letter exhorts Léonce not to give in to the French nobility's impulse to leave France and bear arms against the country, not to believe those nobles who "say that it is shameful for people of their class not to join them [the *émigrés*] in a war to restore royal authority and their own personal rights" (374). That fight is over, Henri claims in a statement that clearly locates the origin of liberty in the Reformation rather than the Enlightenment: "[T]he hope of liberty can arise only from the principles of the revolution; and to align oneself with the party trying to overthrow it is to risk lending one's support to events that would snuff out all the ideas enlightened minds have labored to assemble *for the past four centuries*." [my emphasis] (37) Henri reminds the young aristocrat that "a man's most sacred duty is never to summon foreign armies into the land of his fathers" and that "national independence is the first of treasures" (375). Allegiance to a transnational, aristocratic caste, both Lebensei and Delphine point out, precludes allegiance to the nation. In *Delphine*, this aristocratic defection is cast in moral terms, as an ideological divide between good aristocrats, those who like Léonce stayed in France in 1789 and will hopefully always refuse to bear arms against their country, and bad ones, those who left. But as the novel's ending tells us, the distinction between patriotic and non-patriotic nobles holds even less in the novel than in real life. In fact, Staël herself acknowledged in *Considerations on the French Revolution* [1818] that the first aristocrats to leave France were not the last, that "[t]he earliest emigrants obliged the nobles who had remained in France to follow them" (Staël 2008: 286). In other words, the so-called patriotic nobles shared the same values as the non-patriotic aristocrats, all of them "enjoined this sacrifice in the name of a kind of honor connected with the *esprit du corps*" (286).

In the original ending, Léonce meets with Delphine in Baden after his wife's death to begin a new life with her, but once again, his sense of honor gets in the way. He cannot marry a nun who has broken her vows. Heartbroken, he leaves Delphine to join the émigré army in September 1792, and, before he has time to enroll, gets caught in a cross fire between royalist and republican troops at Verdun – which actually fell to the Prussians on 2 September. Having shot on French republican soldiers to protect a cousin in uniform, Mme de Ternan's son, he is arrested, imprisoned in Chaumont where Delphine catches up with him. Delphine regards him as innocent – it was an accident, he was just acting out of generosity for a relative, she claims – and does her best to free him. The scene at the courthouse where she fights for her lover's life reveals the other side of her exceptional character. Her arrogance in demanding special treatment, her willingness to break the rules of due process, her attempt to corrupt the judge, her disregard of the risks she is exposing him to, her embrace of emotional blackmail, all her maneuvers illustrate that when it comes to getting what she wants, to her own self-interest, she can be just as ruthless as Sophie. But of course, it is not the way this scene is meant to be read. It is supposed to illustrate the heroine's courage, her determination in the face of danger, her exceptional character. Yet it uncovers two things instead. First, her pre-modern way of seeing the world, her conviction that justice can be administered at an interpersonal level, that a sentence can be overturned by appealing to a powerful individual, and therefore also that certain individuals are above the law; and second the contradiction between her patriotic discourse on war – her exhortations to Léonce not to bear arms against *la patrie* – and her inability to see that Léonce is guilty precisely because he shot at fellow citizens in wartime. In short, this episode illustrates particularly well the internal contradictions attached to what Jaumes (1997: 25) praises as "Staël's liberalism of the subject."

In the second ending, the two lovers settle on the estate of Mondoville in Western France. They are about to be married when Léonce incurs popular blame for wanting to marry an ex-nun. Delphine dies of sorrow before they are married; Léonce joins the counter-Revolution in the *Vendée* in the wake of the September massacres and gets killed immediately. In both endings, in short, Léonce takes side against the Republic; in both cases, Léonce, who should have learned to act and feel as a true patriot instead of an aristocrat under his lover's and Lebensei's positive influence, fails the patriotic test. In the end, his attachment to the aristocratic ethos is so strong, so bred in the bone, that it smothers any attempt on his part to develop opinions of his own, to act as a modern individual and as a French citizen.

Delphine raises a series of perplexing questions for the reader. If the aristocratic and bourgeois codes of conduct are as incompatible as the novel shows them to be, why do its bourgeois protagonists so desperately attempt to reconcile them? Why does Delphine fall in love with Léonce in the first place? Why do moderate revolutionaries like Delphine and Lebensei stake their political hopes on an alliance with such unreliable allies as aristocrats like Léonce? The logical answer to this question is that there is no viable alternative in their eyes. The social elite in *Delphine* may be comprised of aristocrats and bourgeois who disagree on moral and political issues but who share the same way of life, the same polite manners and language, the same refined behavior. In their eyes, or for that matter the author's, they are the civilized world as opposed to the uncivilized world of the Parisian street. As fraught with disappointment and rejection as this relationship may be, the aristocracy exercises a boundless fascination on them.

Delphine may criticize the world of Parisian salons as petty, shallow, and mean-spirited in her letters, she may underscore how much it contradicts the bourgeois code of honesty and truthfulness she subscribes to, she may hope to see it change for the better, but it is still the world as she knows it, and leaving it is exile. For all her progressive talk, she is no less immune to appearance and reputation than the other members of high society she criticizes. She rejects Léonce's sexual advances on moral grounds – she fears that he would despise her later – but also on social grounds: she does not want to ruin her reputation. She makes her own the maxim by Suzanne Necker that adorns the novel's cover: "A man must be able to brave public opinion, a woman to submit to it." When she breaks the rules of proper behavior, it is by default, innocently. She would never openly rebel against them. When undeserved criticism of her actions threatens to tarnish her reputation, she is in agony. For all her claims of independence and progressiveness, she is in fact quite conventional and reluctant to change. As soon as she meets Léonce, she agrees to silence her ideas, to stop talking about liberty, for the sake of Léonce's prejudices and those of her aristocratic friends. When the opportunity to take her destiny into her own hands presents itself, she rejects offhand Henri de Lebensei's reasonable recommendation that the two young lovers take advantage on the new law on divorce approved by the Constituent Assembly and marry. Her desire not to hurt Matilde may inform her decision, but so does perhaps the fear of having to endure Elise de Lebensei's fate, permanent exclusion from high society. Delphine is generous but her generosity is often misguided, directed towards undeserving people like Sophie de Vernon or M. De Valorbe, or spontaneous when it should be based on serious reflection, so for instance when she adopts Isore, Thérèse d'Ervins's daughter, but then promptly abandons her to become a nun. She is not as reasonable as she claims to be and time and time again demonstrates her inability to distinguish between friends and foes and to reconcile ends and means. Her hope of changing Léonce is so strong and so misguided that she is the one who changes in the end. In the name of love, she sacrifices her peace of mind, her reputation, her freedom, and last but not least her health and her life.

For Germaine de Staël as for Delphine, the Parisian salon was home, her real *patrie*. Leaving it was worse than dying, she wrote in *Ten Years of Exile*.[19] Although she herself did not heed her mother's maxim, many scenes in *Delphine* come from experience. Léonce, for instance, represents an aristocratic type of men that Staël always felt attracted to in her personal life. In her biography of Staël, Sabine Appel (2006: 69) characterizes him as "cosmopolitan and playful, easygoing, a little flippant, with some debts but ravishing looks and seductive manners, his life full of sensual pleasures, his mind anxiously turned to the outside world for effects." Staël loved the aristocracy. The irresistible charm she attributes to Sophie de Vernon is actually borrowed from Charles Maurice de Talleyrand (1754–1838), a former lover on whom the character is based.[20] Just like Delphine, who learns so little from her experience with Sophie that she falls under the spell of Madame de Ternan, Staël indirectly depicts Talleyrand as a villain in *Delphine*, but years later, in *Considerations on the French Revolution*, celebrates him as "the most agreeable man whom the old government produced;" as a man who, "amidst popular dissensions [...] brought to them the manners of a court;" and whose "graces which ought to be suspected by the spirit of democracy have often seduced men of coarse dispositions, who felt themselves captivated without knowing how" (Staël 2008: 559). Talleyrand was indeed the consummate Machiavellian aristocrat, a man of great charm and great intelligence but so ruthless in his self-loyalty that, with the exception of the First Republic, he managed to occupy high offices in virtually every political regime from the Estates-General to the Restoration.[21] In life as in the novel, these

---

19 "Albertine Necker de Saussure confirms that the claims of sociability always appear stronger to her cousin than the need to write." (Goodden 2008: 16)
20 Talleyrand retaliated by saying that Staël had painted both of them as women in *Delphine*.
21 "Talleyrand had been betraying Napoleon since 1808 to the benefit of Alexander I, with whom he secretly corresponded." (Godechot 1983: 667)

aristocrats were a source of powerful attraction for bourgeois: they wanted to be like them, to be liked by them. Jacques Godechot writes that although Staël "accepted the abolition of privileges," she "regretted the disappearance of titles of nobility" (Godechot 1983: 29). He also reminds us that her father, Necker, had fought hard to retain the latter in September 1790 and that "[h]is daughter approved him. She wished for the reconstitution of some kind of nobility" (1983: 29). As early as 1798, less than ten years after the Revolution, he adds, she proposed a French version of the House of Lords that Napoleon actually implemented when he created the Senate.

Based on such an irrational attitude of love and hate towards the aristocracy, the high bourgeoisie's stand on the nation and on war is also bound to be fraught with contradictions. On the one hand, Delphine is opposed to waging war against fellow citizens, on the other she defends someone who did. Staël's stand in real life was no different: on the one hand, she criticized the nobles' departure into exile at the beginning of the Revolution because it had destroyed her dream of social union and paved the way for the fall of the monarchy; on the other hand she personally helped aristocratic friends escape, as Lebensei does in the novel. And yet, years later, she still stood by her critique of the aristocratic ethos as anti-national: "The nobles of France unfortunately consider themselves rather as the countrymen of the nobles of all countries than as the fellow citizens of Frenchmen." (Staël 2008: 287) She still criticized aristocratic *émigrés* for their lack of patriotism, even to the point of shaming them in the following lines:

> When they found themselves in the midst of foreign uniforms, when they heard those German dialects, no sound of which recalled to them the recollections of their past life, is it possible that they could still think themselves devoid of blame? Did they not see the whole of France arrayed to defend herself on the opposite bank? Did they not experience unspeakable distress on recognizing the national music, on hearing the accents of their native province, in that camp which they were obliged to call hostile? (Staël 2008: 289)

Staël's position on the civil war in *Vendée* denotes a similar inconsistency. On the one hand, she represents, as Suzanne Guerlac (2005: 43) succinctly puts it, a French national tradition that "derives the idea of the nation from the concept of national sovereignty as it emerged during the French Revolution [...] in opposition to the rule of the king"; but on other hand, she approves of the royalist struggle to overthrow the Republic in Western France: "The Vendean leaders," she wrote in *Considerations*, "inspire a thousand times more respect than those Frenchmen who have excited the different coalitions of Europe against their country" (Staël 2008: 286) – in other words, the Jacobins and Napoleon.

It may well be, however, that these contradictions were not perceived as such at a time when the national habitus was still in the making. Staël, for her part, did not believe that the duties of the citizen should ever conflict with the rights of men, as her critique of the concept of *salut public* in *Current Circumstances* makes clear: "In any country that will adopt public safety as its supreme law, justice and human rights will not be respected" (Staël 1979: 261). She further elaborated on this point in a chapter of the same work entitled "Of political virtues and crimes," a chapter that according to Lucia Omacini, was originally entitled "Of Love of the *patrie* or of political virtues:"

> In republics, love of the *patrie* is seen as the first virtue; virtue, however, never means anything else than the sacrifice of oneself. But when the legislators declared that love of the *patrie* was the first duty, they meant one had to sacrifice oneself to that object in preference to any other and that the duties to the family coming second in a republic, a man's time, his fortune, his life belonged to the State, instead of his father, wife, or children. One could make a number of objections to this hierarchy of duties, and one could easily think of circumstances that would make the implementation of such as system unbearable. But even if one adopts it, it pertains only to virtue that is to self-sacrifice. Nowhere is committing an injustice counted among the services one owes to the *patrie*. (Staël 1979: 243)

Her hatred of the radical Jacobins hinged on that point: private virtue should never be sacrificed to the common good. It also explains why the Revolution is reduced to its initial phase in *Delphine*. Her comments on those years in *Considerations on the French Revolution* vividly convey her enthusiasm for "the boasted charms and splendor of Parisian society [...] from 1788 to the end of 1791" (Staël 2008: 252). After two years of what she viewed as an era of positive reforms, however, the Revolution had veered off course. In the novel, therefore, all else is either omitted – the proclamation of the Republic in August 1792, for instance – or the focus is placed on negative events – the September massacres that occurred in part as the result of the defeat at Verdun.[22] And yet, as praiseworthy as Staël's position of non-compromise on ethical issues and zero tolerance for violence may seem, it is difficult to blame exclusively the Jacobins for the Terror, as she did. After all, she had supported the two measures Higonnet (1998: 33) views as their biggest mistakes: the "Civil constitution of the clergy" and "[d]eclaring war on April 20, 1792." Her explanation for the fundamental difference before and after 1792 cannot be sufficiently emphasized: if everything went so splendidly during the initial phase of the Revolution it was because "[a]s political affairs were still in the hands of the higher classes, all the vigors of liberty and all the grace of former politeness were united in the same persons." (Staël 2008: 252)

---

22 The last letters dated 8 September 1792 refer explicitly to "the massacres that have blooded Paris: all is pain, all is crime" (Staël 1995: 441).

3.1.4 *Delphine*'s reception

The novel's reception in the press close to the government is interesting to the extent that it underscores the fundamental disagreement between Napoleon and Staël in matters of morals and social mores. Gautier accounts for this discrepancy through the relative importance each of them grants to the individual and his rights in Staël's case; and to society as a whole, in Napoleon's case. According to Gautier (1921: 108), Napoleon described *Delphine* in the *Memorial of Saint Helena* as the product of "a vagrancy of the imagination, a disorderliness of the mind, a metaphysic of feelings." Although one may perhaps interpret Delphine's quest for happiness as a call for individual freedom, the message is rather blurry in the novel. But as Gautier points out, the preface contains a much more striking appeal to liberty. Anticipating negative reviews of her novel, Staël dismissed them in advance with the following thoughts:

> [F]or a long time to come, most literary judgments published in France will go on being mere partisan praise or calculated insult. Therefore I think that writers who brave these judgments known in advance to express what they think good and true, have chosen their public; they speak to the France of silence and enlightenment, for the future rather than to the present. In their ambition, they also aspire perhaps to the independent opinion, to the considered approval of foreigners [...]. (Staël 1995: 8)

On the one hand, she deplored the absence, worse the impossibility, of freedom of expression, of objectivity in Napoleonic France; on the other she appealed for redress to the *France silencieuse*, a concept she coined in *Current Circumstances*, and to foreigners.

The central role played by Parisian high society in *Delphine* accounts for its success in that milieu and for Bonaparte's displeasure with it. Although *Delphine* is set during the revolutionary period, the Revolution, seen here through the salon lens, appears strangely distorted, reduced to the point of insignificance. Staël claimed (1995: 9) to have purposefully omitted all references to political events in her novel, but not in order to conceal her opinions. However, by reducing French society to Parisian high society, she was sending the message that this high society was still playing a crucial role in French politics. According to Angelica Goodden (2008: 25) Staël's salon had served as "an instrument of political work, the rival of the [Revolutionary] club" during the Revolution. Its political power was still feared during the Directory and was the reason for her first exile: one of the Directors, Paul Barras (1755–1829), the man who introduced Bonaparte to Joséphine, thought in 1797 that Staël would be harmless away from Paris, that "the only real necessity was to keep her beyond the reach of the salons in which she could exert such influence" (Goodden 2008: 77). Gautier (1921:

105) similarly maintains that "salon life still played a considerable role" in 1802 Paris. The novel was thus a reminder that the salon was still a force to be reckoned with and that Staël's own power should not be ignored.[23] Napoleon was aware of high society's potential role as a political counter-power. He knew that he "had France behind him – that was his strength; but [that] he could not count on Paris" (105).

Contrary to her claim of having left politics out of her novel, Staël attacked Napoleon's reforms of divorce and religion directly. It remained legal to divorce during the Empire but the *Code Civil* legislation was much stricter than the laws passed in 1792, in particular for women. Lebensei, who married a divorcee in the novel, praised a more flexible legislation. Napoleon had reintroduced Catholicism in France; Staël was mocking the official religion of France through the character of Matilde and had M. de Lebensei proclaim the superiority of his own faith. Chateaubriand, who had written a review of *On Literature* in the *Mercure de France* declined to do the same for *Delphine* probably for that reason: "You took away the means to serve you efficiently by refusing to review my book [*The Genius of Christianity*] last year... You understand that for that reason, I cannot talk about your novel in *The Mercure*," he wrote her in a letter (quoted by Gautier 1921: 116). Joseph Fiévée (1767–1839), who wrote the review instead, violently attacked Staël for her lack of patriotism:

> The French [...] will certainly feel no gratitude for the way she treats them; all of her love these days is for the British [...]. Minds that soar above this world have no *patrie*, but Madame de Staël has other reasons to have none. Born in a country that no longer exists,[24] married to a Swede, French by accident, she never knew a *patrie* except through illusion and may thus be incapable of conceiving of it in any other way. (Quoted in Gautier 1921: 114)

Delphine not only stirred passions at a time when Bonaparte was doing his best to quell them, it stood as a reminder of the political task ahead: "France is not yet a nation: this country will have to go through a long period of calamities to form a public spirit" (Staël 1995: 375), Lebensei wrote in *Delphine*. But actually,

---

23 "The coterie spirit was all-powerful; aristocrats from the *Faubourg Saint-Germain,* who did not associate with bankers and financiers, stayed away from Mme Récamier's salon. Mme Moreau had her own court, opposed to the official courts at the *Tuileries* and *Saint-Cloud*. Mme de Staël, by contrast, was unique in that she had numerous friends in all cliques, even among the entourage and family of the First Consul; she was the link between old world and new; she was, all by herself, Public Opinion; in the universal disarray, she set the tone for salon life, she alone encouraged the manifestation of some kind of public spirit." (Gautier 1921: 105–106)

24 Fiévée seems to assume that Staël was born in Switzerland, "a country that no longer exist [ed]" as a result of its annexation to France. She was born in Paris, however.

as Napoleon saw it and Elias underscores, it was the presence of a "good society," of the Parisian *monde*, that most clearly indicated that "the integration of [the] country was incomplete" (Elias 1996: 49).

Napoleon had the excuse he needed to forbid Staël from returning to France: if she did not love the country, why should she want to live there? He let her know that if she tried to return, he would have the police escort her back to the border.[25] In spite of her friends' entreaties in spring and summer of 1803, he remained inflexible in his decision, while at the same time leaving them the faint hope that he might change his mind later. By 1803, the law was on his side. Although Staël was born in Paris, although Coppet was part of a *République helvétique* under French control between 1798 and 1813, she was no longer French according to the *Civil Code*. For a woman whose sense of identity was grounded in the life she had led in Paris from childhood onward, who viewed Paris as her "country," it was hard to accept. In one of her last works, she wrote extensively about the emotional distress she experienced as a result of her 'exile,' a term that clearly conveys her refusal to accept the foreign label that was imposed on her.

Thus forced to stay in Switzerland, Staël settled in Geneva. In *Ten Years of Exile*, she would recount that she was at the time "living by preference and circumstance in the company of English people, when news arrived that war had been declared" (Staël 2000: 67). Staël never made a secret of her Anglophilia. She had fond personal memories of the "four months of bliss salvaged from the shipwreck of life" during her exile at Juniper Hall, Surrey, in the spring of 1793.[26] She also liked Great Britain for other reasons that Paul Gautier enumerates: Enlightenment philosophers had praised its freedom and its institutions; Jacques Necker loved England and she adored her father; the country's religion and customs were her own; "its aristocracy offered the most perfect examples of human superiority[27] through its rich and sumptuous way of life, through its enlightened taste for the arts, through its liberalism" (Gautier 1921: 126). Finally, the tyrant Napoleon detested it, and now he also wanted to invade it. For the first time ever, British citizens were being arrested in France. Staël was upset and did not hide her opinions. But "[s]he was unaware that she was being watched closely in Geneva, that all her careless remarks were being reported to the First Consul." (128) Her indignation over the arrest of private British citizens in France

---

25 See Gautier (1921: 115–118). Napoleon also had *Delphine* banned from the Leipzig book fair for fear of bad publicity. No one needed to know that Staël did not support his regime.
26 See Appel (2006: 91).
27 In *Ten Years of Exile*, for instance, Staël contrasts Napoleon's temper-tantrums to the dignity of the English ambassador, Lord Whitworth. (Staël 2000: 67)

during the war testifies to her belief that "as private citizens not serving with the forces, nobles and gentlemen had nothing to do with their country's wars" (Elias 1996: 334). It documents, in other words, her pre-national understanding of the army, her view that the conduct of war was "a matter for nobles and career officers, together with units from the ranks of the poor who were recruited into military service for pay" (334).

Although she had not yet received authorization to return, Staël left for France in September 1803. She stayed away from Paris, settling in the neighboring village of Mafliers instead, where she resumed her social life in the company of a few friends. A month later, however, she was on the road to exile. According to Staël's own testimony in *Ten Years of Exile* (Staël 2000: 69), it was the rivalry, jealousy, and calumny of another woman writer, Félicité de Genlis (1746–1830), that precipitated this first real exile. In *The Influence of Literature upon Society* (Staël 1835: 85), Staël had dismissed much of the contemporary literary production authored by French women. She had praised Isabelle de Charrière's *Caliste*; Sophie Cottin's *Claire d'Albe*; and Adélaïde de Souza's *Adèle de Senanges*, and, almost as an afterthought, extended a few congratulatory remarks to Madame de Genlis for her works without mentioning any one in particular.[28] In the preface of *Delphine*, she had resumed her critique of contemporary French novels which she deemed "mediocre" compared to her own *ouvrages*. So much self-assurance could easily have been perceived as arrogance on Staël's part. Genlis had led the charge against *Delphine* by attacking its "immorality" (Gautier 1921: 131). She had now found a better way of getting rid of this annoying rival.

Although heartbroken, Staël left for Germany determined to make the best of her travels. She would avenge the humiliation of exile by reaping Europe's homage, she would return glorious and more famous than ever, she would also ignite the forces of opposition to the Corsican despot. In Metz, she met with her friend Charles de Villers (1765–1815) to prepare for her trip and left two weeks later for Frankfurt accompanied by Constant and two of her children, Auguste and Albertine.[29] After Frankfurt, her trip took her to Weimar, where she met Goethe, Wieland and Schiller, Leipzig, and Berlin, where she was welcomed and invited to all high society events and to court. Staël's trip to Germany thus had the positive effect of extending her fame beyond France: "She left Germany [...] in better shape than she had France: she was no longer famous just in France but already worldwide. From then on, if Bonaparte attacked her all of Europe would know

---

28 She praised Genlis's "skill in descriptive scenery and observation in sentiment" (Staël 1835: 85). On these women writers, see Cohen (1999); Reid (2010).
29 On Staël's trip to Germany, see Appel (2006: 155–200).

about it and pity her misfortunes." (Gautier 1921: 159) In Berlin, she also met August Wilhelm Schlegel (1767–1845), who liked neither France nor its literature, but whom she convinced to accept the position of tutor of her children. He would be part of her household for most of the rest of her life and play a central role in the Franco-German intellectual exchange that developed in Coppet between 1804 and 1810.

On the way back to France, news that her father was gravely ill precipitated her departure from Weimar but she arrived too late in Coppet. Jacques Necker had passed away on 9 April 1804. Staël had planned to reflect on her travel experiences in the German states in a book she would write upon returning to Coppet. But the grief she felt in the spring 1804 after losing her father made it impossible for her to work on that project and she spent the summer editing and publishing her father's manuscripts instead. By winter, as the hoped-for authorization to return to Paris failed to arrive, she decided to travel. Having received assurances from the French government that she would be free to travel as she pleased, she left for Italy in December, visiting Milan, Rome, Naples, Florence, and Venice, before returning to Coppet in June 1806. Her second novel, *Corinne, or Italy*, is based on her Italian voyage.

3.2 Divided allegiance: cosmopolitanism and nationalism in *Corinne, or Italy*

Published in April 1807, *Corinne, or Italy* has been deemed "one of the three most important novels of early French Romanticism," not only because of its timing but also because of its innovations in the area of narrative techniques.[30] Also path-breaking is the topic of the novel: the story of a female genius, Corinne, in whom many critics have seen the author's idealized self-portrait.[31] *Corinne*

---

30 *Corinne* appeared in 1807 at a time when the genre was becoming "popular, both reflecting and influencing society" (Goldberger 1987: xxxv). "Staël introduces the third-person, omniscient narrator [...] who was to become typical of the Romantic novel. At first Corinne, serving as Oswald's guide to Italy, speaks at length. Gradually, all indications of direct discourse disappear, and the reader becomes aware that the voice of the author is increasingly dominant, until in the last sentence of the novel Staël speaks to us in the first person. Thus it may be said that *Corinne* is in a real sense the first nineteenth-century novel." (Goldberger 1987: xxxvi)

31 "Corinne is an idealized Mme de Staël, with 'her ravishingly beautiful arms,' 'her tall full figure, reminiscent of Greek statuary,' and 'her inspired expression.' She is sensitive, gay, intelligent, graceful, and even modest! [...] How can we fail to recognize her in [...] the love of glory that torments Corinne's soul: 'When I wished for glory, she tells Oswald, I always hoped it would bring me love' [...]." (Gautier 1921: 198–99)

centers on the passion of a young and gifted heroine for a man who ends up betraying, and destroying her. In a study of the national habitus, the novel deserves our attention for another reason: the main protagonist's attempt, and ultimately, her failure to bring two distinct nationalities into a harmonious form of individual identity.

Written between 1805 and 1807, the novel finds its place in Staël's literary production between two works in which she developed her ideas on modern nations, *On Literature* and *On Germany*. It has been viewed mostly as a novel on gender relations in post-revolutionary France,[32] but in light of the increased importance the concept of nationality acquired in those years, and of the way in which new laws and decrees in that area affected Staël personally, it also deserves to be read not only as the continuation of the writer's endeavors to understand and define "the national character," but also, because it is a work of fiction, as an effort on her part to put a human face on this new concept, to retrieve and analyze feelings and emotions associated with national belonging. Turning to *Corinne* to examine the issue of national identity is also to acknowledge that feelings and emotions associated with national belonging were already on Staël's mind a decade before she wrote *Ten Years of Exile*, the work most commonly associated with this topic. As we will see, the novel stages the encounter between several competing understandings of national identity, and, as it unfolds, points to the relegation of pre-revolutionary conceptions of the self, both aristocratic and cosmopolitan, to the benefit of the modern sense of national belonging.

3.2.1 Cosmopolitanism and the national character

Corinne tells the story of a young and gifted heroine who falls passionately in love with a man who proves less than worthy of her, but the binary structure of the introductory chapters, each devoted to main protagonists of different nationalities, already points to the centrality of the national theme in this novel. Book I focuses on Lord Oswald Nelvil, a "Scottish peer" who travels in order to escape his Romantic *mal du siècle*;[33] and book II on Corinne, a celebrated Italian poet-*improvisatrice* crowned on the steps of the Capitol on the day of Oswald's arrival in Rome. In book I, the theme of national identity is first intro-

---

32 See Gutwirth, Goldberger (1991).
33 His "wounded sensibility no longer had any taste for the illusions of the heart" (3); "[...] he let the days go by without reserving a moment for himself, giving his time over to others out of melancholy and goodness." (Staël 1987b: 6)

duced indirectly through comments on travel that describe its negative effects and underscore the centrality of the national language in one's sense of identity:

> Travel, whatever else may be said of it, is one of the saddest pleasures in life. When you feel comfortable in a foreign city, it is because you have begun to make it your home; but passing through unknown countries, hearing a language you scarcely understand, and seeing human faces unconnected with your past or future, is to know a solitude and isolation without respite and without dignity. (Staël 1987b: 6)

The narrator, however, also takes a stand on that issue by offering objective comments that contrast British and Italian mores and highlight their incompatibility. It is the case for instance when, in a sentence than aptly summarizes the plot of *Corinne,* she offers the following insight on gender relations: "Nothing could have been more opposed to an Englishman's customs and opinions than focusing the public eye on a woman's fortunes." (Staël 1987b: 19) More crucially, Oswald is presented as embodying the national character Staël ascribed to "Northerners" in *On Literature,* and then later again in *On Germany:* introverted, inclined to melancholy and solitude, he is also, of his own avowal, "quite biased against Italians,"[34] and quite so against the French as well.[35] Corinne is his Southern opposite: extroverted; community-oriented, thriving in the limelight. Each of them also represents what Staël viewed as the two distinct literary traditions produced by these opposed national characters, the Romanticism of the North, of Ossian for instance, on the one hand; and the Classicism of Rome and Athens, of Corinne, on the other.

In *Corinne,* however, Staël ascribes newness and originality to the South instead of the North. She also has her heroine make a case for distinct national literatures, so for instance when Delphine argues that "[a] nation's theater must be shaped by its own imagination, character, and customs" (Staël 1987b: 122). In general, northern imitation is condemned and southern eloquence praised. The tension between an innovative Romanticism and a sterile Classicism takes the form of a spirited exchange between Corinne and Count d'Erfeuil. Whereas the latter views the French classical tradition as a standard of perfection and therefore also as a model worthy of imitation by other nations, Corinne makes the case for "natural color," "originality of feeling," and innovation:

---

34 Oswald "thought them [the Italians] flighty, unable to feel deep and enduring attachments" (Staël 1987b: 33). He declares, for instance, that "infidelity itself is more moral in England than marriage in Italy." (Staël 1987b: 97)

35 Lord Nelvil paints Count d'Erfeuil, a French nobleman, as frivolous and selfish (Staël 1987b: 47). He is also later depicted as superficial, with a short attention span and an inability to judge independently (358); as obsessed by the fear of being overlooked in society (382).

'I find it hard to believe [...] that the whole world would do well to lose every bit of natural color, all originality of feeling and mind. And I dare say, Count, that even in your country this literary orthodoxy, if I may put it that way, stands in the way of all felicitous innovation, and ultimately can only make your literature very sterile. Genius is essentially creative, stamped with the character of the person endowed with it. Nature, which has refused to make two leaves identical, has provided souls with more variety still; and imitation is a sort of death, since it strips us of spontaneous existence.' (Staël 1987b: 113–114)

As these lines indicate, and as Suzanne Guerlac (2005: 46) points out, in *Corinne or Italy* "individual character and national character are superimposed as the title of the novel suggests." As heir to the great Italian poetic tradition, Corinne is a link to Italy's classical past but she is first and foremost a creator and "[i]t is precisely as poet, writer, and *improvisatrice* that our heroine becomes identified with Italy and that Italy becomes a nation in the novel" (48).

When Prince Castel-Forte introduces Corinne to an adoring crowd at the Capitol, he insists on the modern side of her national identity. She is the perfect Italian, the embodiment of an accomplished contemporary national type that all should emulate: "To foreigners we say,'" declares the Prince, "'Gaze on her, for she is the image of our beautiful Italy; she is what we would be except for the ignorance, envy, discord and indolence to which our fate has condemned us.'" (Staël 1987b: 25) The topic of Corinne's life performance at the Capitol, "The Glory and Bliss of Italy," underscores the centrality of the national theme in the novel and the content of her improvisation echoes the Prince's comments, both as an homage to past artists and poets, and as a discreet evocation of Italy's current political subjection.[36] But the singularity of Corinne's talent lies in her ability to electrify the crowd: she "reaches the height of eloquence as an artist of improvisation and her eloquence engenders enthusiasm" (Guerlac 2005: 48). Guerlac rightly states that for Staël "eloquence, or literature, represents a means of bringing forth the general will, which lies at the heart of any possibility of a nation or a community" (49). At the Capitol Corinne is assigned the task of generating national unity, of mobilizing "everything that strikes the senses" (Staël 1987b: 122) to elicit feelings of national belonging. But if, unlike Chateaubriand, Staël praises patriotic enthusiasm, like him she defines the "national character" in relation to the customs and mores of the superior class, of the elite of the nation only. In *Current circumstances* this class bias is well illustrated

---

36 "Is Rome not now the land of tombs!" she asks, for instance. (Staël 1987b: 30). Goodden attributes the "constant see-sawing for and against Italy" in *Corinne* to editorial reasons. Staël had originally planned a critique of Italy, but her editor Nicolle, who had already published a book in the same vein that year, did not want to publish another one. See Goodden (2008: 167); Castillo (2006: ch.2).

by her comments on the revolutionary Republicans' inability to govern, but her restricted, class-based understanding of the nation is also found in *Corinne* where the national character is presented as the product of the noble exception through Oswald, the British aristocrat, and Corinne, the Italian aristocrat of the mind.

With regard to the issue of national language, Staël's message is a little more confusing. On the one hand, the notion that citizens of the same nation speak the same language is affirmed and almost taken for granted. On the other hand, the main protagonists in the novel are multilingual and have lived in different countries: Oswald speaks not only English, but also French and Italian and so does Corinne. Staël's class-based understanding of national identity, and her choice of multilingual and multicultural characters therefore seem to imply a conception of identity more akin to eighteenth-century enlightened cosmopolitanism than to modern nationalism. Is national identity viewed as a given, as a necessity, as a necessary evil, or as something to be resisted in *Corinne?* A close examination of the relation between Oswald and Corinne may provide a few answers to these questions.

Staël's choice of a heroine that is, initially at least, clearly cosmopolitan, signals a pre-revolutionary way of relating to the national. For as hard as Corinne tries to assert her Italian identity in the scene at the Capitol, she ultimately fails in her attempt to be and be seen as Italian only: the moment she sets eyes on Oswald and turns to glance at him, she loses her crown; and when the young man picks it up, the other national part of her identity manifests itself: she thanks him "in English with the pure native accent that can almost never be reproduced on the Continent" (Staël 1987b: 32). As we will see shortly, other factors underscore Corinne's multilingual, multinational, and multicultural sense of identity. But more important perhaps is the fact that this pre-revolutionary understanding of the national character is also questioned and challenged from this scene onward through Oswald. Whereas Corinne's national identity is shown to be shaky from the start, Oswald is presented as much more grounded and stable than her, to wit his initial reaction to Corinne at the end of the ceremony when he characterizes her as "the most charming of foreigners" (33), that is, as someone interesting and different, interesting because of her difference, but "foreign."

From the moment they meet, Oswald does his best to make Corinne fit into a single national mold, his own. During their first encounter, for instance, he is less impressed by the fact that she is perfectly bilingual than intrigued by his suspicion that she may be British – only a native can speak English as well as she does, he reckons – and when they meet the next day, he "gently reproache[s] her for not speaking in English" (Staël 1987b: 36). At that point, however,

Corinne clearly does not want to fit into a single national mold. She seems, in fact, to choose Italian as her language of conversation and to characterize herself as Italian precisely because she rejects, or represses, the British part of herself. Ironically, however, her explanation as to why she would rather speak Italian than English undermines a second time her professed allegiance to Italy: "[...] when a person has spoken two or three different languages over a number of years as I have," she says, "one or the other is called forth by the feelings one wants to express" (36). In asserting that language is a matter of private choice, Corinne explicitly rejects Oswald's nationalist conception of language, conveying instead her adherence to a supra-national conception of identity.

Through Corinne, then, Oswald's modern understanding of national identity is initially resisted, presented as a construct that can and should be transcended not only through multilingual and multicultural life experiences but also through the embrace of universal moral values. At the beginning of the novel, Corinne is a cosmopolitan, someone who believes in moral universals, such as "self-sacrifice, dedication, and heroism," and in whom the very best features of different nations blend to form a harmonious whole: "She saw through non-sense with the finesse of a Frenchwoman, and depicted it with the imagination of an Italian, but kindness [an English trait for Staël] pervaded everything she said" (Staël 1987b: 38). As far as the national tale is concerned, however, the point of the novel is to underscore the un-sustainability of this eighteenth-century ideal in the modern age and the concurrent necessity to be a national, or more precisely to derive one's sense of identity from one national set only. As the plot unfolds, as love operates his destructive charm, Corinne's cosmopolitan asset turns increasingly into a liability, the gift of dual nationality into a curse.

The primary cause of Corinne's downfall is, not surprisingly, her embrace of generous universal values, or more precisely selflessness pushed to the limits. Under the influence of passion, she is willing to sacrifice everything to Oswald, to become, as she puts it, his "slave." But as shocking as this abnegation may seem, as tempting as it is to regard it as an endorsement of women victimhood, it is important to remember that selflessness was a central concept in Staël's political philosophy. If upper-class manners, tastes, and customs formed the core of the French national character in her eyes, a single value separated the old from the new French: their ability or inability to put the well-being of other people before their own. In the novel, the issue comes up in a short exchange between Corinne and Count d'Erfeuil, in which the count warns her about the predictable outcome of her love affair with Oswald. Instead of heeding his advice, Corinne stands her ground, and goes on the attack, rejecting his logic of self-interest as morally flawed. The kind of passion she feels for Oswald, she tells him, "delights in the total sacrifice of the self" (Staël 1987b: 188).

The way Staël saw it, the problem was not with selflessness itself, but with its constant clash with its opposite, the selfishness, tenacious defense of one's own interests and privileges, which, together with arrogance, inconsistency, guile, vanity, and an ignorant chauvinism in matters of language and culture, defined the old French aristocratic ethos. As she presents it, the French national character was based on aristocratic manners, tastes, and customs, but split in two depending on one criterion: the aptitude or inaptitude for self-sacrifice. Extreme egocentrism and lack of altruism, these were the salient characteristic of an old aristocratic habitus best exemplified in the novel by the characters of Count d'Erfeuil, M. de Maltigue, and Mme d'Arbigny. D'Erfeuil, for instance, who preaches self-interest to Corinne, is also arrogant (Staël 1987b: 9), superficial (11), vain (116); convinced of the superiority of the French mores, language (37) and culture (113), in a word, terribly chauvinistic.[37] Similarly, Madame d'Arbigny, the woman for whom Lord Nelvil wasted his time in France, is a conniving, manipulating woman of great intelligence, but of disreputable morality and primarily moved by self-interest (Staël 1987b: 212, 220). As for M. de Maltigues, he states his Old Regime beliefs and principles more clearly perhaps than any other character in the novel (224–225). Staël had fought this narrow conception of French identity since the early days of the Revolution and staked her political dreams on the union of the upper bourgeoisie and the progressive aristocracy. In *Corinne*, Lord Nelvil's French friend represents this new exemplary Frenchman: Count Raimond, offers a sharp contrast with Old Regime aristocrats because of his ability to straddle past and present; to reconcile "pride in his ancestors" and "a rational mind;" and to adhere to "the new philosophical ideas" (Staël 1987b: 210). But the quality that makes him most different from them is his admiration for selflessness, his belief in self-sacrifice :

> Count Raimond came from the most renowned family in France. In his soul was all the knightly pride of his ancestors, and his rational mind adopted the new philosophical ideas when they enjoined personal sacrifice. He had not been actively involved in the Revolution, but he loved what was virtuous in each party; courage and gratitude here, love of liberty there: everything unselfish pleased him. The cause of oppressed people was just in his eyes, and his generosity of character was further heightened by the greatest carelessness of his own life. (Staël 1987b: 210)

---

37 "'Lovely foreign lady,' the Count went on, 'would you have us admit to our country the coarse barbarity of Young's *Nights* from England, the Concetti from Italy and Spain? After such crossbreeding, what would become of the French taste, and the elegance of French style.'" (Staël 1987b: 113–114)

Not surprisingly, given the weight Corinne ascribes to this quality, the propensity for altruistic behavior is in fact the trait on which Staël grounds her distinction between old and new aristocratic habitus.

Direct and honest (211), Count Raimond is loyal to his friends and his country, but when France becomes a republic, his patriotism fades away together with the monarchy: "[...] there is no France any longer. The ideas and feelings that made one love her do not exist anymore" (214). With this novel, then, Staël seems to have wanted to show that a woman of genius could fill this patriotic void. In that regard, Corinne plays in Italy the role of national unifer her creator had dreamed of playing, and might have played in France, had Bonaparte not stood in her way. By 1807, however, Staël knew from personal experience that the new French nation she had envisioned had been a dream, and that Corinne's cosmopolitanism was doomed as well, at least according to the novel. The parallel between Count Raimond and Corinne makes them therefore appear as figures of a recent past and of a wished-for future that was not to be.

3.2.2 The national habitus in *Corinne*

National identity plays a crucial role in Corinne's and Oswald's life stories, but it takes these two characters a long time to talk to each other about their past. Only halfway through the novel does Corinne finally explain why she speaks English so well: she is the daughter of an Englishman, Lord Edgermond, and his Italian wife, but she lived in England for many years following her mother's death and her father's remarriage. Only halfway through the novel does the reader learn why Oswald feels so melancholy: Lord Nelvil left for France as a twenty-one-year old with his father's blessing for a visit that was supposed to last a few months only. Contrary to his expectations, however,[38] life in revolutionary Paris was so exciting in 1791 that he decided to stay much longer. He made a good friend in the person of Count Raimond, and even seriously considered marrying his sister. His *mal du siècle*, his guilt and grief, have a precise origin: the knowledge that he betrayed his father and country by remaining in Paris instead of going back to England as promised; and that his disobedience and failure to act as a responsible British citizen contributed to his father's premature demise. Oswald, in other words, learned early on a lesson Corinne understands only at

---

38 "I thought I would never come to like the country; I share the prejudices inspired in us by sober English pride. I feared ridicule of all the cults of heart and thought; I detested the art of deflating all impulse, of disillusioning all love. That highly vaunted gaiety seemed essentially quite sad to me, since it gave the deathblow to my most cherished feelings." (Staël 1987b: 209)

the end of the novel: individuals owe their allegiance to one nation only; failure to comply with that golden rule brings shame and unhappiness. So vividly has this precept been impressed on him, the narrator tells us, that he becomes a model citizen with a particularly acute sense of national belonging:

> His cruel remorse when he deviated from the line of conduct he had mapped out for himself further strengthened his innately austere principles. In many respects, he was rather tightly bound by English morality, by the customs and opinions of a country where one feels all the better for the most scrupulous respect of duty as well as law. In short, the despondency born of deep sorrow leads us to love what is in the natural order of things, what goes without saying, and so requires no new resolution or any decision contrary to what fate has marked out for us. (Staël 1987b: 237)

The story of Lord Nelvil's life is thus of particular interest because of the new way of being and of defining oneself as a national it contains.

As a moral tale on the dangers of playing loose with one's national identity, Oswald's life story cannot easily accommodate a mixed national like Corinne as a wife. Testimonies pile up throughout the novel against this bi-national marriage. First, a relative visiting Rome recommends against it: "Believe me, my dear Oswald, only Englishwomen are right for England. [...] As lovable as Corinne is, I think like Thomas Walpole: *what do you do with that at home?*" (Staël 1987b: 133). The realization that his diseased parents would have disapproved of his union to Corinne causes such grief to Oswald that he becomes seriously ill. Once cured, a new obstacle arises, of a religious nature this time: Corinne is a devout Catholic and Oswald a Protestant. "If only you had the same religion, the same country as I!" Oswald exclaims (167).[39] They both display a great deal of religious tolerance, however. Oswald does not object when Corinne spends a week in a Catholic convent to prepare for Easter. Later in the novel, they both attend an Anglican religious service aboard a British ship in the Bay of Naples, thereby putting their relation to a first test.[40] But then Corinne admits that she hated the British way of life in the seven years she lived in England, that what other women praised as "domestic bliss," she regarded as a form of self-denial, as the obliteration of "every form of superiority" (259).

That Corinne's Italian habitus is fundamentally incompatible with the British national habitus is made abundantly clear in the letter Oswald's father

---

39 Anglicanism and Catholicism are both praised. Corinne's defense of Catholicism may be seen as a conciliatory gesture towards Napoleon and France. See Staël (1987b: 181).

40 "Oswald was concerned with Corinne and her reactions; but from time to time he was distracted by the pleasure of being in his native land once more. For are not ships and the sea indeed a second homeland for the English?" (Staël 1987b: 200)

wrote to Lord Edgermond to explain his change of heart regarding the marriage of the latter's daughter, Corinne, to his son, Oswald. According to Lord Nelvil, Corinne has such a "need to please, to captivate, to attract attention" that "our country life, our domestic practices, would inevitably thwart all her tastes;" that "Italy alone is right for her" (Staël 1987b: 329). Oswald's father expresses the fear that "she would inevitably lead my son away from England," which would be a real crime since a "man born in our fortunate country must be English first and foremost: he must fulfill his duties as a citizen since he has the good fortune to be a citizen" (329). In the worst case scenario, Corinne could even contaminate England with her foreignness. In order to make her happy, Oswald "would try to introduce foreign ways into his household" and "[s]oon he would lose that sense of nationality, those prejudices [...] that bind us together and make of our nation one body, a free but indissoluble association that cannot perish until the last one of us is dead" (329–330). Lord Nelvil senior therefore trusted that the national habitus would perform its magic with a little help from his friend, Lord Edgermond: "[...] I venture to beg you, dear friend, that should I die before my son marries, do not let him meet your elder daughter before the younger one is old enough to attract him" (330).

As if these ominous pronouncements from beyond the grave were not enough, Lady Edgermond, Corinne's father's second wife, also warns Oswald that a marriage to Corinne would be anything but "restful," that both of them would be unhappy precisely because their union would upset the "natural order of things" (1987b: 334). But Oswald lets once again his indecisive nature be his guide.[41] As his father predicted, he is attracted to Corinne's half-sister, Lucile, as soon as he sets eyes on her: "Oswald was deeply moved by her reserve, her constraint; and his imagination set in motion just a short time ago by eloquence and passion enjoyed the picture of innocence, and seemed to see around Lucile some sort of modest aura that was deliciously restful to the eye." (319) In the end, the most convincing argument against marrying Corinne is that it is easier not to marry her, to choose Lucile instead, as that young British lady encapsulates the promise of an unproblematic relationship, a union where "things go without saying," where "the natural order of things" takes its course.

---

41 "In the end, he did once more what he had done so many times: he put off the moment of decision, telling himself that he would go to Italy to have Corinne herself gauge his anguish and consider what he should decide. He believed that duty forbade his marrying Corinne. He was free from ever taking Lucile as his wife. But how could he find a way to spend his life with his friend? Did he have to give up his country or whisk her off to England with no thought to her reputation or her fate?" (Staël 1987b: 334)

Staël's deep understanding of the national habitus, of that instinctive inner mechanism that is the foundation of the modern sense of identity, is one of the most fascinating aspects of this novel. In the pages describing Oswald's return to his country, for instance, the narrator pauses to reflect on England's hold on him in the following terms:

> As he approached England, all the memories of his native land invaded Oswald's soul. The year spent in Italy had no connection to any other period of his life. It was like a dazzling apparition that had struck his imagination without completely changing either the opinions or the tastes that had shaped his existence until that time. He was himself again, and although he missed Corinne enough to preclude any sense of happiness, he was recovering a rigidity of thought that had vanished under the intoxicating wave of Italy and the arts. (Staël 1987b: 315)

The national habitus may be dampened through, and during one's experience in foreign countries, Staël tells us, but it endures, regaining its hold and power almost magically once the foreign experience is over, making it then appear as a separate parenthesis in one's life, as something as unreal, as fading as a dream. Paradoxically, the foreign experience also brings to consciousness the reality of the national habitus, the unconscious love for one's country: "Ultimately, he felt at home in his native land: those who have never left are unaware of the many ties that make our country dear to us." (Staël 1987b: 316)

By choosing this British character to exemplify the modern national, Staël demonstrates her understanding of the Grand Tour's purpose. Since the early eighteenth century, the gentry's ritual visit to continental Europe was meant to immunize young aristocrats against the lure of foreign countries and to reinforce their sense of loyalty to Great Britain.[42] This is an astute choice on her part since England was historically the first European country to witness the emergence of the national habitus:

> One of the few countries in which, so far, a parliamentary state structure and an individual personal structure have become attuned to each other in a comparatively friction-free way is Britain. The long process through which this attunement was reached can clearly be traced in British history. In fact, it has been happening very slowly since the time when the son of the puritan dictator had to give up the reins of government to the newly installed king who, however, inherited considerably reduced power-chances. (Elias 1996: 291)

Corinne, on the other hand, is an incomplete national. As she languishes in Italy, as Lord Nelvil's letters grow fewer and colder, she decides to leave for England

---

42 On the Grand Tour, see Burgess and Haskell (1967).

without announcing her visit. In London, she is welcomed in her banker's home and does not get in touch with Oswald, who, she has learned, is also in the city. She also stops writing to him so as not to betray her presence in England, a situation that makes him, of course, more receptive to the notion that she may already have forgotten him (Staël 1987b: 339). Indeed, Corinne has such a hard time dealing with her awkward situation and finding a justification for her presence in Great Britain that she promptly falls ill. As mentioned earlier, there is no real opportunity in the novel to settle the question of whether Corinne could actually have become a true English lady. But the pages describing the weeks she spends in London suggest an affirmative answer since ironically, her illness marks the birth of her patriotic feelings towards England: "[...] in the home of simple honest merchants, she had developed a genuine taste for English ways and customs." (339) The loving care and tender affection bestowed on her by this adoptive family make her realize that her stepmother's strict and boring ways are the exception, not the rule. But it is too late. When she recovers and goes to the theater she sees "suddenly, in the box facing hers," Lord Nelvil, his "gaze [...] fixed on Lucile," her little sister now transformed into "the most beautiful person in England" (341–342). Heartbroken, Corinne sees Oswald and Lucile exit the theater together at the end of the play, and then watches night after night, as his carriage is parked in front of her London home during the following weeks.

Oswald's true identity is finally revealed to her when she sees him stand review with his regiment at Hyde Park. Hidden in the back of a carriage, she observes her lover in his own element for the first time, in his true, patriotic environment, in uniform at the head of his admiring troops, as a marching band plays "God save the King." Moved by "the famous air that touches all English hearts so deeply," Corinne cannot help but feel pangs of patriotism herself: "Oh! estimable country who should have been my country, why did I leave you? Amid so many virtues, what did more or less personal glory matter? And what glory, Nelvil, was as good as being your worthy wife!" (Staël 1987b: 346). But as she watches Oswald help Lucile mount a beautiful horse and ride off with him, she understand that her own fate is sealed. The warrior component of the national habitus is further emphasized in the novel when Oswald's regiment is sent to war shortly after his marriage to Lucile. Away during the next four years, it is thus not in marriage that Oswald finds happiness, but in fighting for his country instead: "he flushed with joy when the clash of arms began, and it was only then that the weight on his heart lifted, allowing him to breathe easily." (384)

Meanwhile Corinne, now a shadow of her former self, has returned to Italy and settled in Florence. In a final scene that parallels her improvisation at the

Capitol, she hosts a recital of her last poetry at the Academy but the contrast between these two public events could not be greater. Too weak to recite her last song to her "fellow countrymen" (Staël 1987b: 415) and "[l]ovely Italy" (416) herself, she has a young Italian girl do so in her place. She dies in peace a few days later after forgiving Oswald "for breaking her heart" (418). Commenting on the novel's ending, Glenda Sluga (2003: 249) rightly argues that "Corinne's death is the ultimate sacrifice for the sake of the man who must devote himself to his 'self,' to his duty and his *patrie*." From Oswald, she adds, Corinne has learned that "[d]uty to the social good, expressed in the notion of patriotism, is an active virtue" reserved from men; from her sister, that "self-abnegation" is the passive virtue of women (249).

The modern reader may find fault with Staël's generalizations on national identity, the North-South dichotomy and the sets of oppositions derived from it: introverted vs. extraverted; domesticity vs. public sphere; rigidity vs. flexibility, etc... But her analysis of the psychological hold exercised by the national habitus denotes a great talent of observation and still rings true today. Independently of the accuracy of the national traits themselves, characters of British, French, and Italian nationality are shown to be under the spell of the national habitus, men in particular. The Nelvils, father and son, for instance, make it a point of subjecting themselves to the "natural order of things," of never questioning "those prejudices [...] that bind us together and make of our nation one body" (Staël 1987b: 329 – 330). The early Corinne, the Corinne of the Capitol, by contrast, stood for something more generous, for universal values that transcended the Nelvils' national biases: enthusiasm for beauty and life, the willingness to self-sacrifice in the name of liberty or love, etc... But as the novel tells us, hope to see these supra-national aspirations realized, the weight of the national habitus lifted, is faint. Not only is the balance tilted in its favor by definition, through inertia, love can also be a tool in its service, as Corinne's willing attempt to fit into a national mold that can only destroy her indicates.

Corinne's dual national allegiance, emotional and cultural to Italy, rational and political to England, reflects Staël's own dilemma: her love of France and its brilliant society and her admiration for Great Britain's political institutions. But as Sluga (2003: 248) notes, in the end, "Oswald's happiness [...] represents the victory of the bourgeois view of the world (his surname ends with the suffix 'ville'), over the cosmopolitan Corinne (whose surname ends with 'mond')." Staël's *Corinne*, we may therefore conclude, registers the diminished impact of the forward-looking mental orientation that had informed the Enlightenment's concept of civilization as a universal ideal and its replacement by a narrower, more exclusive, way of understanding oneself and one's relation to others, as nationals. The novel neither praises nor indicts the modern way of relating to the nation; it registers the difficulties associated with the process of becoming a modern national.

3.2.3 *Corinne*'s reception

Corinne's reception in France in spring 1807 was overwhelmingly positive, an immense success.[43] The relations between Napoleon and Staël had gone through a period of calm in 1805 (Gautier 1921: 170). The Emperor had authorized her trip to Italy, which was under French control at the time, and given signs that France might want to settle the huge debt (two million) owed her father. But tensions returned in the spring of 1806 after Staël left Coppet for France, circling Paris for the next six months but unable to enter the capital, except once briefly at night (Gautier 1921: 188). That her single infringement on Napoleon's orders was duly reported to the Emperor by Fouché, the Minister of Police, shows that Staël was under constant police surveillance while in France. According to Gautier, her mail was read and there were even spies in her salon (184– 192). Informed about her every move, sometimes by her own private correspondence, Napoleon grew more and more convinced of his political enemy's bad intentions. For the spring of 1806 alone, Gautier found ten letters the Emperor sent from the battlefield to Fouché in which comments on Staël appear, most of the time to call her names: "this element of discord" (175), "a real raven" (184), a bad French woman, an enemy of the government and of France, or "this crazy Mme de Staël." These letters reveal how much he feared her power, her talent for organizing opposition and fomenting agitation: "Everday I acquire new evidence that it is impossible to be more evil than this woman, more inimical to the government and even to France, this country she can't live away from." (Quoted in Gautier 1921: 187)

   Was the Emperor paranoid or did Germaine de Staël represent a danger for the most powerful man in Europe? Gautier clearly thinks that she did. Not only did her friends make regular wishes for Napoleon's death in battle, they also thought a great deal about how to get rid of him through other means. Fouché duly informed Napoleon of their activities but did not intervene (Gautier 1921: 190). On the contrary, efforts were still made to enlist Staël's support for the regime at that time. She was formally told that all her requests – the authorization

---

43 "Any book that displeases [the authorities] can be the target of violent attacks: such is the case of all of Mme de Staël's books since 1800 but their success has nonetheless endured. She is, with Chateaubriand, the most famous, [...] the most discussed writer." (Balayé 1968: 28)

to live in Paris, the reimbursement of Necker's funds – would be granted, should she feel so inclined and insert a little praise of Napoleon in the novel she was writing, *Corinne* (Gautier 1921: 194). She did not. She was willing to do her part, to refrain from antagonizing Napoleon publicly, but she considered that she had shown enough good will by staying clear of French politics in her novel and by writing a love story that did not take place in France and whose main characters were not French. She would go no further, she would not be bought; she would not flatter the tyrant. *Corinne* therefore only increased Napoleon's conviction that Staël was an enemy of France. Not only had she refused to even mention his military accomplishments in Italy – unlike Stendhal later in the *Charterhouse of Parma* – she had also once again put England, the enemy nation, on a pedestal. Just after the French navy had been annihilated by Admiral Nelson at Trafalgar, she had "tactlessly apotheosize[d] the British navy" in *Corinne* (Goodden 2008: 159) and made the French look ridiculous. Napoleon was still enraged years later in Saint Helena: "I cannot forgive Mme de Staël for having demeaned the French in her novel," he wrote in the *Memorial*. (Quoted in Gautier 1921: 195) There is a lot of exaggeration in this assessment, however: *Corinne* is not by any means as anti-French or pro-British as these comments imply.[44] But it is not as a-political as Staël claimed either. The scene of Corinne's coronation at the Capitol, for instance, certainly brings to mind and mimics a more famous coronation, Napoleon's self-crowing as Emperor of the French in May 1804. Through *Corinne*, then, Staël was sending Napoleon a reminder of a conviction she had stated so many times in her political writings: that the power of ideas is stronger than military might. Unsurprisingly, the coveted authorization to reside in Paris was denied and Staël had to return to Coppet. In the following years, she continued to proclaim her opposition to the Napoleonic regime all over Europe until its definite fall in 1815.

---

44 Gautier describes two Frenchmen who are presented as ridiculous, Count d'Erfeuil and M. De Maltigues, but he does not mention Nelvil's friend Count Raimond, another Frenchman, who is painted in positive light by Staël. Gautier's comments also seem a bit too focused on the Staël-Napoleon rivalry: "She was saying to Napoleon: 'The nation you are fighting is the bravest, the most generous, the most virtuous on earth. It is civilized, you are barbaric; it defends its homeland and humanity; you are only defending your horrible pride and your ambition.' Anti-French, Anglophile, such is indeed *Corinne*." (Gautier 1921: 198)

Conclusion

Cosmopolitanism, patriotism and nationalism are key themes in Staël's life and works but her writings themselves contain scarce evidence of the kind of patriotism found in Gouges's works: a quasi-religious devotion to the nation. Delphine writes at length and eloquently about the nation, but argumentatively, as a philosopher more than a citizen. In spite of her republican rhetoric, the sense of emotional attachment to the France born of the French Revolution is not there. The ambiguous critique of the aristocratic ethos in *Delphine* indicates that Staël's feelings of belonging were not vested in an abstract nation, but in a local kind of setting, the Parisian salon, and in the aristocratic and intellectual elite that inhabited it. Her sense of self and identity thus appears more akin to young Chateaubriand's than to Gouges's – even if 'the place of her youth' is an urban setting and his, a rural one. In that regard, it is interesting to note that the rural setting in which Delphine and Léonce spend their happiest hours together, Bellerive, is an estate lacking any kind of link to native soil or ancestry and that in this chosen place of residence Delphine feels a stronger emotional bond to the interior – she redecorates the place – than to the exterior, to nature. But what the novel most clearly indicates is that Staël's ideal conception of French identity was one that would mix Old Regime culture with Enlightenment principles.

This idea was first developed in *The Influence of Literature upon Society* [1800] where Staël argued that "French gayety and French taste" were the defining characteristics of the pre-revolutionary "national character" (Staël 1835: 61–62), and these features the product of an institution, the absolute monarchy. As this form of government's principle was "to please or to displease" (62), she explained, the relations between the aristocracy and the royal authority were shaped by "ties of the most delicate nature and prejudices artfully conducted" (63). For instance "[t]he point of honor compelled the nobility to decorate the most abject submission with the forms of liberty," and "[o]nly grace could give the appearance of choice to obedience" (62–63). Consequently, the dominant class in France was attuned to "the more subtle nuances" and ruled by the fear of "ridicule" (62). At the same time, these flaws had a positive effect because of the "kind of perspicacity" they generated, and in particular the talent for observation so well documented in seventeenth-century literature (62). The court culture that embodied national culture in Old Regime France, Staël pointed out, had many flaws: "The French nation was, in some respects, too much civilized; its institutions, its social habits had usurped the place of natural affections." (70) Court culture bred conformism; was detrimental to independent thought (70);

and encouraged people to take nothing seriously.[45] But in spite of these flaws, it still defined the French character, *l'esprit français*.

Staël viewed the Revolution as a major disappointment because it had failed to bring about the cultural revolution she had hoped for: as *Delphine* illustrates, it had not bridged the gap between the aristocracy and the bourgeoisie. The novel ends in 1792 because the rest of the Revolution was best forgotten, as she explained in *Current Circumstances*. France, born centuries ago of the encounter of Northern barbarity and Southern civilization, had fallen prey once again to barbarians as the "lower orders of the people [...] made an invasion upon the superior classes of society" (Staël 1835: 37). The Revolution had thrown the baby away with the bathwater, eradicated grace, good taste, and gaiety, and replaced the old French character with "a disgusting vulgarity" in manners (71). Like the invaders of the past, the new barbarians had destroyed and conquered: "[A]ll we have suffered, all we condemn in the revolution," she added, anchoring with this "we" her sense of identity in a solidarity with the "civilized" class, "arises from that fatal necessity of confiding the direction of affairs to these conquerors of civil order" (37). In the same work, she also explained that the French, who had suffered humiliations during the Old Regime and had been kept at bay by the civilized upper class, were a people full of resentment, whose mindset was still ruled by structures of authority and command: "A man who, in any kind of situation he may have been, has viewed himself as inferior, this man can never achieve equality; he will be the tyrant, the despot, the persecutor, never the equal of the one, who, at the bottom of his soul, he once thought ought to be his master." (Staël 1979: 37) Although the Revolution's efforts to destroy prejudices and biases were justified, violence was unavoidable: "The horrors and the confusion of the Revolution had brought to power the most ferocious souls, the basest characters, the most limited minds; but far from creating political equality, Robespierre's reign only brought about a kind of inverted aristocracy." (10)

As compelling as this account of the French Revolution may seem, it has the disadvantage of creating classes more than describing those that actually existed at the time. Staël's rhetoric of *classes dangereuses* would have us believe that the *sans-culottes* were in power during the Revolution but they were not. As Higonnet has shown, the various political groups that led the Revolution at some point – Monarchiens, Feuillants, Girondins, Montagnards, Thermidoriens – were all Ja-

---

45 "A spirit of ridicule attaches itself to one who may hold an object in the world in high estimation; it laughs at all those who, advanced to a serious period of life, still confide in unfeigned sentiments and weighty interests." (Staël 1835: 70)

cobins, all shared the same sensibility, turned ideology under political pressure.[46] For that reason, Higonnet also rejects the notion that the Jacobins were "men of the blood, driven by an anarchic or sadistic impulse that aimed to liberate some socially imprisoned human spirit" (Higonnet 1998: 129). Not only were they not *sans culotte*, they also feared and despised popular violence the same way Staël did: "Indeed a tolerance for direct violence separated the Jacobins from the *sans-culottes*. Robespierre chose never to witness an execution." (131) [47] Moreover, "once in power," each of these Jacobin factions realized "how politically dangerous it was to let the Revolution unfold toward an unfettered universalism" (118). Even if by "lower classes" Staël meant Montagnards like Robespierre, her description does not fit since the latter were not by any means uneducated, unprincipled, or uncivilized. On the contrary, "Jacobins, especially in Paris, in both club and Convention, were highly educated men who could with ease rattle off this Voltairian idea of toleration or that idea of Rousseauean general will [...] to justify what really mattered to them." (Higonnet 1998: 41–42) In that regard, the fact that Staël met Robespierre at her father's house in the early days of the Revolution is more significant than the negative portrait she later painted of him in *Considerations on the French Revolution*.[48] Had the manners and politics of the future advocate of the Terror been those of an uncivilized barbarian, he undoubtedly would not have been invited to Jacques Necker's home, one of the most distinguished salons in Paris. And yet, the remedies Staël proposed to avoid revolutions in the future were derived from the notion that "human follies occur when men who do not know how to write adopt Enlightenment philosophy as their religion." (Staël 1979: 270)

Staël obviously errs when she places the blame for the Terror on the lower classes – who were not in power – and in one and the same move demotes Ja-

---

46 Higonnet defines Jacobinism as "the quintessence of a single (if always changing), complex, divided, but ultimately liberal sensibility – or *esprit révolutionnaire* – that was superimposed on threatening, inherited, and unspoken apprehensions which perniciously denied consciously held principles, and eventually overwhelmed them." (Higonnet 1998: 8)

47 "They [the Jacobins] carefully distinguished between left-wing *hypocrites du patriotisme* (the supposedly egalitarian leaders of the *sans* culotte movement who claimed to be more revolutionary than even the Jacobins) and right-wing hypocrites (the supposedly Christian but in reality, sanguinary, nonjuring Catholic clergy). Also to be despised were 'arch-hypocrites,' former Jacobins who had gone over to the side of immobilism." (Higonnet 1998: 81)

48 "I once conversed with him [Robespierre] at my father's house, in 1789, when he was known merely as an advocate of this province of Artois who carried to extremes his democratic principles. His features were mean, his complexion pale, his veins of a greenish hue; he maintained the most absurd propositions with a coolness which had the air of conviction [...]." (Staël 2008: 372)

cobins like Robespierre to the rank of uncivilized barbarians. But the question she grabbled with – how could such a generous, universalist movement descend into terrorism? – is an important one and one that still puzzles historians today. Commenting on the grisly September massacres, Darnton, for instance, writes that "[I]t is there" and "must be incorporated in any attempt to make sense of the Revolution" (Darnton 1996: 27). For Higonnet, the "inherited social atavisms that structured their [the Jacobins'] sensibility and that ran directly against the grain of their Enlightenment ideas" (182) account for this violence. His explanation, in other words, echoes the one Staël gave, with the important difference that it applies to a *Monarchienne* like her as much as to a Montagnard like Robespierre. Indeed, all revolutionaries ended up resorting to the same logic of exclusion – you're either with or against us – to the same finger pointing and demonization of their former friends once they became their political enemies.

Seen from the vantage point of Elias's theory of nationalism, the Jacobins' inability to deal with political enemies "through verbal duels" instead of the guillotine highlights, as Gouges's case already did, the problems personalities used to the hierarchy of command and obedience experience when institutional change demands that they adjust. Having been ruled all their lives, they prove incapable of envisioning political life as all-inclusive, and, as the history of the Revolution shows, are condemned to simply replacing those who ruled before them. Gérard Minart (2003: 29) writes that Bonaparte came to power with "[...] one objective, one political goal: to create – or recreate – unity among the French," and that it was one of his "greatest and noblest ideas." Although he succeeded in breaking the circle of violence for a while, the same observation applies to him as well. As Elias notes, "[t]he disintegration of self-control in political battles means *ipso facto* the end of the multi-party system and its probable transformation into a dictatorial or monarchical autocracy" (Elias 1996: 293).

It is undeniable that, as Guerlac (2005: 53) contends, "*Corinne ou l'Italie* de Staël opposes a concept of the nation elaborated in relation to language and literature to a Napoleonic spirit recently on display in the conquest of Italy when *Corinne* is published." But to fully appreciate the opposition between literary and military genius Staël constructs, it must be seen for the simplification it is – an erasure of Napoleon's role as statesman – and replaced in the political discourse from which it emerged. In 1798, when Staël wrote *Current Circumstances*, she and her friends at the *Institut* wanted a new constitution so as to strengthen their hold on power. "The constitution," she stated, "must be modified so that all its powers, cleverly combined, give the Republicans all the strength they need to maintain the republic, and then captivate public opinion through all means that can ensure its control" (Staël 1979: 333). It was the legitimate fear that Bonaparte might want to play a political role that gave rise to her critique of the "military spirit" and to her admonition that the military should step aside: "Nothing is more worthy of admiration than military success, than the invincible valor of generals and soldiers, but nothing is more opposed to liberty than the military spirit" (289).

But did Staël truly speak for liberty? Did literature, as she conceived of it, really "leave out the manipulative nature of artful speech, and the possibility of political deception," as Guerlac (2005: 50) contends? In *Current Circumstances* [1798] Staël argued that in a divided nation, one had to "find a way of reconciling interests and principles, the opinions of the victors and the tranquility of the vanquished" (Staël 1979: 275). As she saw it, the first priority in France was to "instill a public spirit" in the nation, not to establish republican institutions and to develop public instruction, as the *Idéologues*, claimed.[49] For one thing, that would take too long, and for another it was putting the cart before the horse. If republican institutions were to take roots in the country, she argued, the people had to be enlightened first: "When an idea is well implanted in all heads, people ask for the institution that consecrates it" (274). The task of enlightening the nation, of shaping "public opinion," she claimed, was perfect for writers. They would "make public opinion move much faster than national education" (276), and as long as they were sincere and credible, as well as independent from the government, their "free thoughts" would elicit "free adherence" as well as "enthusiasm, joy, exaltation" among the public (276).

What these comments reveal is that Staël did not believe in the common people's ability to develop patriotic feelings on their own any more than Chateaubriand did, and furthermore, that her prescriptions for the well-being of the republic were no less authoritarian than Napoleon's. What she proposed instead of the military dictatorship he put in place was nothing less than an intellectual dictatorship. Public opinion the way Staël envisioned it was a substitute for political partisanship (Staël 1979: 106–112). What she meant by "shaping public opinion," was to make opinion, "to implant ideas in all heads." In that scheme, writers were supposed to manufacture consent, not to promote the free exchange of ideas. In fact, the great advocate of liberty had no qualms arguing in favor of a censorship of the press (113–123). In her national model, the people were not actors but the passive and enthusiastic recipients of republican propaganda conceived and delivered by the enlightened elite. In her polit-

---

49 William H. Sewell (1994: 192) points out that the *Idéologues* were not necessarily more democratic than Staël. Sieyès, for instance, whom she was close to during the Directory and the Consulate, "in spite of violently democratic rhetoric of *What is the Third Estate* [...] profoundly distrusted the people and was an advocate of government by expert representatives who would deliberate rationally and choose the wisest course on the people's behalf."

ical model, only one party ruled: "the republican party must use all means [...] to ensure that no other party enters the government [...]" (132). Clearly, Staël's conception of the republic was far from democratic.

Minart (2003: 54) argues that Bonaparte owed his success to his responsiveness to the people's desire for civil peace, something "Benjamin Constant and Germaine de Staël" did not understand because they were "locked up in their salon, surrounded by intellectuals, removed from the heartland, separated from social reality." As mentioned earlier, Staël did recognize the need to overcome political divisions and to create unity in France, but she also viewed France from above. Whereas she imagined the people as adoring crowds that could be moved by an intellectual genius, Napoleon, who dealt with soldiers, with common people on a daily basis, had a better knowledge of them and, in the end perhaps, a more democratic conception of the nation than she did. In part because he succeeded where she had failed, Germaine de Staël came to hate him. The effects of a national habitus she so well described in *Corinne* in the case of Oswald surface in the logic of exclusion and the language of nationalist hatred she increasingly resorted to when she talked about Bonaparte.[50] During a second visit to Austria a year after the marriage of Napoleon to Marie-Louise, for instance, she wrote that she "saw those Germans, whom [she] had known to be so upright, depraved by the disastrous misalliance that seemed to have tainted the very blood of their subjects by mingling the blood of their ruler with the African race of a Corsican" (Staël 2000: 132).

Ironically, in the eyes of the French who exiled her although she was French by birth, Staël was the foreigner. She did not love France the way a French person should; she lacked the blind love for the *patrie* that makes you wish it to be victorious always and she even turned against France, siding with its enemies, and expressing her preference for the literary and political institutions of other nations. This nationalist reception of Staël's works during her life time is matched by the unease with which historians and literary critics have dealt with it over time, as Godechot's assessment of *Considerations on the French Revolution* in the lines below illustrates:

> Germaine de Staël did not understand it [the Terror] because she was not really integrated to the French Nation. Undoubtedly, she was born in Paris, but her parents were Swiss, her

---

50 Chateaubriand used similar rhetoric in his pamphlet *Buonaparte and the Bourbon* [1814] to characterize Napoleon: "The foreigner, not yet a king, wished to have the bloody corpse of a Frenchman as a stepping stone to the throne of France." (Chateaubriand 2004: 6) "Absurd in administration, criminal in politics, what then did he have to seduce the French, this foreigner?" (18).

grand-parents Prussians, she was married to a Swede, sometimes she claimed to be French, sometimes to be Swedish, sometimes Swiss. She did not see that, without the gigantic effort in Year II, France would have been crushed, as it did later in 1814, 1815, 1870, 1940 [...]. What happened in Italy during the "thirteen months" in 1799 – 1800 is sufficient evidence. In fact, *Mme de Staël did not understand the events of Year II because she was not quite French.* Savary was not entirely wrong when he wrote to her: 'Your book is not French'. Germaine de Staël was more European than French. (Godechot 1983: 30) [My emphasis].

We may therefore perhaps attribute the "routine indifference" (Isbell 1994: 3) with which Staël's literary production has been met in France as an effect of nationalism itself, of the deeply held feeling that it is difficult to love Madame de Staël and France at the same time. It is surprising, however, that her opposition to the Revolution's "great men" – Robespierre and Napoleon – would turn Staël into a foreigner but not Chateaubriand, who hated the Jacobins and Napoleon just as much. Apart from religion, which is an insufficient indicator of national belonging in the post revolutionary age, what distinguishes her from other writers is ancestry. Staël, it would appear, was the victim of the Napoleonic redefinition of citizenship, or more precisely of the inclusion of *jus sanguini* in the law defining citizenship. Meant to grant citizenship to children of French parents born abroad, the law seems to have functioned against her, as if her birth to Swiss citizens had made her ineligible for French citizenship.

Part II: **The Post-Revolutionary Field**

Chapter IV
Through Stendhal's Eyes:
The National Habitus in the Making

–*Nous nous anglisons; –et nous
volons; –et nous bêtisons.*
(Stendhal 1929a: 87)

Investigating national identity in Stendhal's *oeuvre* may seem a paradoxical project. In many regards Stendhal's life and work testify if not to an outright lack of interest in this issue, at least to a position on it that is better characterized as the bird's-eye view of a cosmopolitan thinker than as the narrow lens of an ethnocentric writer. It is after all no secret that Henri Beyle (1783–1842) spent more time outside of France during his life than any French writer of his generation. As a young man, he fell in love with Italy, saw himself as a Milanese, and sometimes wished he had been born in Italy instead of France. Nowhere is the outright dislike he felt at times for his country of birth more strikingly conveyed than in this March 1820 entry of his diary: "I will never live in France. The French give me *la pelle di cappone* [goose bumps] by dint of disapproval, remoteness, displeasing, and contempt." (Stendhal 1982c: 43) Stendhal's reputation as a cosmopolitan thinker and his recurrent outbursts of anti-patriotic sentiment might partly explain why so little critical attention has been paid to the issue of national identity in his work. And yet, he devoted a remarkable amount of time thinking about France and the French, so much so in fact, that the two works that frame his prestigious career as a novelist can be described as writings about the nation.[1] The first, *Chronicles for England,* is a collection of book reviews and essays written between 1822 and 1829 to inform a largely upper class British audience of the social, cultural, and political state of France. They were translated into English and published in the British press, in the *Paris Monthly Review,* the *New Monthly Magazine,* and the *London Magazine.*[2] The second, *Memoirs of a Tourist,* is a travel narrative written for a French audience that appeared in 1838. It recounts the impressions, reflections, and the experiences of a French "tourist"

---

1 *The Red and the Black* appeared in 1830 and *The Charterhouse of Parma* in 1839.

2 *Chroniques pour l'Angleterre*, the scholarly edition in seven volumes (plus index) of Stendhal's essays for the Bristish press, was published between 1980 and 1995. Quotes in English are from this edition. An abridged edition of these essays in one volume (of nearly thousand pages) also appeared in 1997 under the title *Paris-Londres*. This book is the subject of a collection of critical essays published in 2001, *Stendhal, journaliste anglais.*

as he travels through France. Stendhal was convinced that France had considerably changed since 1789. He sought to understand in which ways this process was occurring, to assess how far the French still had to go to fulfill the ideals of the French Revolution. The exhaustive descriptions and astute analysis of French society found in both works provide prime material for analyzing the formation of national identity through Stendhal's eyes. This chapter centers on an examination of his views on *le caractère français* and follows him as he explores its transformation since 1789. Stendhal viewed the nation at once objectively, as a political and cultural entity subject to rational enquiry, and as the lines quoted above suggest, subjectively, as an object of love – or, in that particular case, of profound dislike. Read in the historical context in which they were written, his negative reaction to France is best understood as expression of the nation's failure to live up to the ideal image the writer had of it. As he explained in *Memoirs of an Egotist* [*Souvenirs d'égotisme*], the Bourbon Monarchy had tarnished, "dirtied," France (Stendhal 1982d: 517). A brief recall of Stendhal's life sheds light on these feelings.

Unlike Gouges, Chateaubriand, and Staël, Stendhal did not experience the French Revolution as an adult, but as a child. Henri Beyle was educated at home by private tutors until 1796 when he entered the *école centrale*, a modern school his grand-father had been instrumental in establishing in Grenoble. As a teenager, he developed a passion for literature and music and a more pragmatic affection for mathematics: he planned to study at *Polytechnique*, a Parisian institution of higher learning created in 1794 devoted to "la patrie, les sciences, et la gloire." Earning the first prize in mathematics in 1799 allowed him to leave Grenoble for Paris, where he arrived on 9 November 1799, or 18 Brumaire, the day of Bonaparte's military coup. Once in the capital, however, *Polytechnique* was no longer as appealing as it had been from afar. After several months of *far niente*, an illness forced him to accept the hospitality of the Daru family, wealthy relatives of his grandfather.[3] Ill at ease in their salon, which he found "stinky with decency," he developed an early allergy to high society but made the acquaintance of two cousins who were to influence his destiny for many years to come, Martial and Pierre. Pierre Daru (1767–1829) was a published poet – he was elected to the *Academie française* in 1806 – and a military man. A commissary to the army since 1793, he had risen through the ranks and was chief commissary to the Army Reserve for the second campaign of Italy, when, at the family's request, he secured a clerkship at Ministry of War for Henri. When Martial and Pierre left for

---

3 The Daru had made their fortune during the Directory. They owned and lived in a private mansion in Paris that had belonged to Condorcet, the hotel de Bissy.

Italy with Bonaparte in the spring of 1800, Henri followed – as a private citizen since he had not yet enlisted – entering Milan in June in the footsteps of a victorious army whose perilous crossing of the Alps would soon be the stuff of legends. Thanks to Martial's and Pierre's protection, Henri was soon promoted to the rank of second lieutenant and able to parade in uniform for the nearly two years he spent in and around Milan. Thus began Stendhal's love affair with Italy.

Back in France in 1802, the nineteen-year-old ungratefully resigned his army commission, opting instead for a life of leisure, entertainment, love... and debts for the next three years. In 1805, he followed an actress to Marseille and worked in a bank for a while. When his liaison with Mélanie Guilbert cooled off, he returned to Paris in the hope of repairing the damaged relationship with his powerful cousin, now Intendant-General of Emperor Napoleon's military household, and obtaining a well-compensated position with the *Conseil d'état*. To improve his chances of success, Henri joined the same masonic lodge as Pierre in August 1806 but the latter remained insensitive to his cousin's requests. When Martial (1774–1824) left for the campaign of Prussia that fall, Henri followed him – once again without assignment. After Napoleon's entry in Berlin in late October 1806, Pierre did this time come to the rescue, appointing him temporary assistant to the Commissary of War. Henri spent the next two years in the German states of Brunswick and Westphalia, filling positions of increased responsibility in the administration of the occupied states. On sick leave in Paris during the winter of 1808–1809, he left for the Campaign of Austria where he witnessed the "horrifying butchery of war." Following Napoleon's victory at Austerlitz, he assisted Martial in his functions of intendant of Vienna, but aimed higher than this temporary position. Coveting a position in Spain, he requested his transfer and waited in Paris in the spring of 1810, only to learn that he was being sent to Lyon.

Before he even had time to pack, however, the twenty-seven year-old Henri received good news: he was appointed auditor to the *Conseil d'état*, as Inspector of the Crown's accounts, furniture, and buildings. This was the beginning of a new exciting life full of evenings at the opera, visits in the salons of the prettiest women in Paris (Mesdames Gay, Tallien, and Récamier) and love affairs with divas. In the summer of 1811, Henri was about to accompany Martial, who had been appointed intendant of Rome, to Italy, but the trip was cancelled. Henri took off by himself and stayed four months in Italy where he started thinking about a book on Italian painting. Upon his return, he incurred the wrath of Pierre Daru, now a Baron in the newly created imperial nobility, who was scandalized by his cousin's unauthorized leave of absence and his lack of professionalism.

Henri behaved himself in the following months, and then, perhaps to be forgiven, asked to participate in the Campaign of Russia.

He left Paris for Vilnius, Lithuania, in July 1812, carrying letters from Empress Marie-Louise to her husband, and was assigned to supplies and logistics. In September, he witnessed the battle of Borodino and, a few days later, the fire of Moscow. Then, the most horrific experience in Henri's life began: from mid October 1812 to 31 January 1813, the day he got back to Paris, he shared the horrors of war and the pains of hunger in freezing cold weather with the rest of the *Grande Armée* as it retreated from Russia.[4] He did not have much time to recover from this trauma. In April, he was ordered to take part in the campaign of Prussia and was at the battle of Bautzen. In June, he was named intendant of a Polish province, where he fell seriously ill, and by August he was back in Paris. He obtained an authorization to go and rest in Southern France and pushed a bit further to Italy. By the end of the year, he was back on the job, taking part in the defense of Grenoble, but for Napoleon the end was near. By February the Cossacks were in France and, on 1 April 1814, the Emperor abdicated.

4.1 The French character in *Chronicles for England*

For Stendhal as for many of his contemporaries, the French Revolution marked a point of no return in the history of France. Its impact on the French character was extreme: it destroyed the old French identity and shaped the new one. One of his most pressing concerns in his *Chronicles for England* was to correct common misconceptions about his country, and in particular the distorted views of the French Revolution that Edmund Burke and Germaine de Staël had popularized in England: "The perusal of the works of MM Dulaure et Bailleul, who were both actors, and in no inferior capacity, in this eventful drama, will give much juster ideas on the subject." (Stendhal 1982a: 82) He also recommended "that [François-Auguste Mignet's *History of the Revolution*] be read in England, a country that has been poisoned by all the nonsense found in Mme de Staël's *Considerations on the Revolution*" (Stendhal 1988: 45). In one of the earliest texts he wrote for the British press, Stendhal deplored the political bias found in most French historical writings: "It may be laid down as a general rule that true historical knowledge freed from party spirit and bad faith [...] is [...] rare in France [...]" (Stendhal 1982a: 252). He wished if not for more objectivity, at least for more balance. So far, only the voice of the Revolution's opponents

---

4 On the effect of the retreat of Russia on Stendhal, see Berthier (2010: 207–209).

has been heard, he reasoned, it was time to let its advocates have their turn. He was not alone in thinking that way. By the end of the 1820s, numerous accounts of the Revolution had been written and history, Stendhal noted with satisfaction, had become "the most brilliant part of French literature" (Stendhal 1991a: 36).

Reading and reviewing these new books on the French Revolution, Stendhal became sort of a historian himself. Those he recommended to readers for an accurate assessment of the Revolution include now forgotten works such as Rabaut Saint-Etienne's *Précis de l'histoire de la Révolution française*; Madame Roland's *Mémoires*; Dulaure's *Esquisses historiques*; Bailleul's *Examen critique*; and Mathieu Dumas's *Histoire de la guerre de la Révolution*. But he also reviewed the better-known products of the then emerging Romantic historiography: *Histoire de la Révolution* by François Auguste Mignet (1796–1844), which he praised as "one of the best and satisfactory publications that have appeared upon the subject" (Stendhal 1982a: 202); and *Histoire de la Révolution française* by Adolphe Thiers (1797–1877), which he found well-informed, but written in a pretentious, off-putting style (Stendhal 1983: 69; 1991a: 55). Stendhal's book-reviews highlight the merits and demerits of these works while at the same time providing insights into his own understanding of the Revolution. Novels are also presented as a source of information on the Revolution because of the subjective light they shed on these events. In his review of Louis-Benoit Picard's *Le Gil Blas de la Révolution*, for instance, he congratulates the "accurate and diligent observer of men and characters," adding that "[w]ith M. Mignet's admirable history of the principal events of the French Revolution and M. Picard's novel, which traces their influence upon the various classes of society, one may form a most just and satisfactory idea of one of the most singular periods in the world's annals" (Stendhal 1983: 38).

4.1.1 Of Frenchmen, old and new

Stendhal was particularly drawn to Jacques-Charles Bailleul's *Examen critique de l'ouvrage posthume de Mme de Stel* [sic] *ayant pour titre Considérations sur les principaux événevements de la Révolution française*, published in 1818, because its author had been directly involved in the power struggles of the period and had acted as a "courageous enemy of Robespierre." Bailleul's personal experience and his reliance on first-hand factual information, he thought, strengthened his credibility as a historian, as did his willingness to acknowledge unpleasant truths. But Bailleul's political stand also corresponded to his own: both refused to let the revolutionary excesses of the Terror void the Revolution's accomplishments, as Staël had done in their opinion in *Considerations on the*

French Revolutions.[5] Bailleul also wrote about the Revolution with a passion that echoed Stendhal's own, an enthusiasm he often found lacking in the young historians' works.[6]

In sharp contrast to Chateaubriand's global rejection of the Revolution and to Staël's partial acceptance of it, Stendhal's writings on the French Revolution signal a new attitude characterized by a willingness to accept it in its entirety, to acknowledge and embrace its mistakes and more importantly to highlight its accomplishments. According to Berthier (1987: 30), "mass mobilization [*la levée en masse*] during the Convention was for Stendhal one of the most beautiful moments in modern history, a spectacle of rare grandeur in the annals of humanity." This openness leads to a radically different understanding of the "horrible period emphatically named the reign of Terror." Its origin is no longer located in a depraved human nature, as Chateaubriand argued,[7] or in the government's take-over by uncivilized barbarians, as Staël contended, but in circumstances: the political instability caused by war and conspiracies, and the political inexperience of the revolutionary leaders, men of the lower classes sincerely devoted to the republican ideal:

> The government of that day was beset on every side with plots and conspiracies – some in the very seat of power, others at the most distant points of the territory [...]. From the desertion of the noble and of the wealthy, who hated the republic, [...] magistrates were of necessity drawn from the humbler classes of society, and it was no infrequent occurrence to see much more than the municipal powers arbitrarily entrusted to the discretion of masons, shoemakers, carpenters, and other artisans [...]. These persons, as it was natural to suppose, not only committed the most signal follies, but, urged on by excessive distrust, from ignorance and the novelty of their situations, they rushed into a sea of blood to escape their own fears. (Stendhal 1980: 272, 274)

Stendhal is thus so far the first of the writers examined in this book to defend Jacobin leaders; for him they formed "the only class that was sincerely devoted to the republican system" (Stendhal 1980: 274). In spite of their shortcomings,

---

5 Jacques Félix-Faure's analysis of Stendhal's marginalia on his copy of Staël's *Considérations* (1974) yields interesting insights in that regard.

6 "After perusing these two volumes [by Thiers] [...] I questioned some old Jacobins on the subject. All rendered justice to the young historian though they blamed him for being too cold and philosophic. These Jacobins seem not to have grown a day older since 1792. The danger faced by their country, which at that period roused their youthful hearts, still continues to be the sole object of their thoughts." (Stendhal 1991a: 54)

7 Even later in life, as he commented on Mirabeau in 1821 in his *Memoirs*, Chateaubriand continued to view the revolutionaries as "the monstrous abortions of Nature depraved" (Chateaubriand 1848: http://wikilivres.ca/wiki/Chateaubriand%27 s_memoirs,_V,_12).

these men were heroes and their failings paled next to their great accomplishments. In a 19 March 1837 entry of his diary, for instance, he defended George Danton (1759–1794) when La Fayette accused him of being corrupt. Even so, even if Danton did benefit financially from the Revolution, the two millions he stole were little compared to what he had achieved: "Without him, [...] civilization was delayed by fifty years. Danton being corrupt, one cannot have any illusions about the character of this great man. But are illusions needed when it comes to the man who saved the *patrie?*" (Stendhal 1982b: 291). The elite, by contrast, had done its best to destroy the Republic and the country. Aristocrats, who, like Chateaubriand "had sided with those who had invaded the *patrie*," had simply betrayed it (Berthier 1987: 31). A "dukomaniac" bourgeois like Staël had "such 'blind respect for the nobility' [...] that she 'glorified the most ridiculous facts and silly characters of the Old Regime as perfect models of grace and wit'" (Félix-Faure 1974: 37). For Henri Beyle, she was "a renegade who acted hand in glove with *émigrés* and foreign powers in league against Napoleon" and who pursued "all the great men of our revolution with a vile and preposterous relentlessness" (37).

Stendhal's political definition of the Frenchman in *Italy in 1818* testifies to a forward-looking attitude typical of the Enlightenment and the early revolutionary era: "The foreigner is not someone separated from us by a river or a mountain. It is someone whose principles, wishes, and feelings are at war with our principles, wishes and feelings. M. de Chateaubriand, for instance, is a foreigner for me." (Quoted in Berthier 1987: 21) When faced with the central question of "whether France still grounded its identity in Catholicism or was committed to building a political order turned towards [...] the universalism of Reason" (Birnbaum 1993: 10), Stendhal unambiguously chose the latter. In fact, as early as the 1820s, he provided the blue-print for the interpretation of the Revolution that was to become its official account during the Third Republic.

At the time, however, this narrative was novel and had a militant character: it stood as a rejection of the Restoration government's official policies of forgetting described by Sheryl Kroen (2000: 39–76). It also testified to Stendhal's determination to keep the Revolution alive by reminding his readers of its most important dates and by underscoring its significance for France and for the world: "The existence of this great assembly [the Convention] presents the most curious thing in modern history. It is interesting to every nation; for had this Convention been subdued in 1794, Mexico would not now be free." (Stendhal 1991a: 54) Stendhal was convinced that the French Revolution had brought more change to

France within a few years than the monarchy in centuries (1983: 74).[8] One of its greatest merits was to have brought to the fore people used to facing real needs and therefore capable of action:

> The best eulogium that can be made of the French revolution is to state that it rescued from frivolous, useless, and worse than useless pursuits, hundreds of men of superior talents, and afforded them, in the wide field of public affairs, numberless opportunities for the exertion of their energies, which otherwise would have remained dormant, or have been employed upon laborious trifles. (Stendhal 1982a: 274–276)

In *The Life of Henry Brulard*, Stendhal wrote that by 1811 he considered that "energy was only to be found [...] among the class which battles against real need" (Stendhal 2002: 24). The ascent of the lower class, its gradual incorporation into the national mold was, in his view, inevitable and just a matter of time. The common people had already proven themselves as citizens and as soldiers during the revolutionary wars, as Stendhal pointed out in his review of Tissot's *Mémoires historiques sur Carnot*. Carnot's "brightest title to glory," he wrote, was "his having raised in 1794, as if by enchantment, and out of the bowels of the earth, as it were, fourteen armies of eighty thousand men each, and without the aid of pecuniary resources" (Stendhal 1982a: 274). As opposed to Napoleon who "dreaded to awake the passions of the people and make an appeal to their patriotism [...] Carnot made a frank and generous appeal to their love of country and horror of foreign invasion and the starting of a countless multitude into armed existence was the immediate result" (1982a: 274). Except for Western France, a province that was still in "a state of comparative barbarism" due to the "unbounded sway exercised by the priests and nobles" (1983: 40) the largest segment of the French population, the peasantry, had greatly benefitted from the Revolution. Unlike the peasants of Vendée, who "fought with desperation, thinking that they were fighting in their own cause against the soldiers of the republic" (40), the vast majority of rural France was deeply attached to the Revolution's principles because it was "the class which has gained the most by the revolution" (1985: 244).

Like George Sand in *Nanon*, Stendhal attributed this attachment to the sale of clergy lands because it had allowed half of the French peasants to purchase small plots and to enjoy the right to own property. Not only had living conditions improved in the countryside as a result, land ownership had also helped the

---

8 "The fact is that in Paris a man of sixty entertains on all subjects, ideas totally the reverse of those which regulate the conduct of his son, a young man of thirty. The Revolution formed the character of the latter, but the father is still the man of 1785." (Stendhal 1991a: 306)

peasantry progress in the areas of education, citizenship and morality (1991b: 180). Owning land was an incentive for peasants to learn more – so as to improve their farms; to be interested in politics and suspicious of the church – out of fear of losing their land, should the clergy return to a position of political power; and to deal honestly with others. "One of the finest qualities of the French peasantry and small tradesmen is probity ," he declared, "There is scarcely any pilfering in villages." (Stendhal 1988: 277) The last point underscores Stendhal's materialist ethics: moral behavior is derived from practical common sense, not from religion. According to him, this new moral sense was itself the outcome of the greater equality among the people brought along by the Revolution. Of all the revolutionary principles, he regarded equality as the best anchored among the French: "In France, all adore equality […]; what they [the French] want above all, is political equality." (1988: 118) The acquisition of land was a first step towards greater equality, the introduction, in 1810, of a solid currency a second.[9] The next step would be education and political equality – the right to vote.

In spite of the satisfaction Stendhal took in noting the significant progress towards greater social equality, the lower classes provided unsuitable material for assessing the Revolution's impact on French national identity. Like all writers examined so far, Stendhal viewed the upper class as the embodiment of the *caractère français,* as the restricted meaning of "society" in the quote below illustrates; like Germaine de Staël he believed that the national character was shaped by political institutions, as his brief history of the Revolution indicates:

> For the last thirty years French society has changed according to the phases of the government. It may be said to have been almost annihilated under the reign of terror. On awaking from the state of apathy in which it remained during the sway of the parties represented by Robespierre and Danton, it assumed a reckless and inordinate gaiety. Then followed the aristocracy of wealth, which arose under the Directory when all sorts of adventurers, gamblers, and swindlers, whose manners had been formed during the last years of the reign of Louis XVI assembled around the director Barras. Dishonesty and unbridled immorality were the characteristic traits of society from 1797 to 1800; after which the ambition of General Bonaparte introduced into France a moral and almost prudish severity. Never have the public morals in that country been so pure as from 1800 to 1809. At this latter period the foolish desire of having a court, and the mania for imitating the kings of Europe, took possession of Napoleon. (Stendhal 1985: 245)

---

9 "Since the *assignats* have been replaced by coined money, this immense majority of the French nation have gradually increased their comforts, and are now perfectly at ease, and without any inquietude." (Stendhal 1985: 298)

The Revolution, he argued, had irremediably changed the *caractère français*, but his British audience was unaware of it: "The notions generally entertained in England of French society" were still "derived from those descriptions of it which appertain to a period anterior to the revolution [...]" (Stendhal 1985: 244). In order to enlighten the readers of his *Chroniques pour l'Angleterre* on the nature of the differences between the pre- and post- revolutionary national character, Stendhal used the same comparative approach as Staël: "Nothing can be more different than the light, gay, careless Frenchman of 1788 and the reasoning and political Frenchman of 1828." (Stendhal 1991b: 238) Like her, he viewed its development in pre-revolutionary France as intimately linked to the absolute monarchy and, like her also, he saw pluses and minuses in the old aristocratic way of life. Those flaws and qualities were not exactly the same for both of them, however. For Stendhal, the absence of political liberty had led the aristocracy to devote itself entirely to pleasure and entertainment, hence its "spirit of light, graceful, and witty badinage" (1982a: 252). What he found most attractive in this sociability was less the refined character of aristocratic manners that charmed Staël than the joy and happiness implied by the nobles' propensity for wit, fun and laughter, "the spirit of derision and gaiety which belongs to the French nation" (1991a: 120). This was the aspect of the aristocratic way of life that Stendhal would have liked to see preserved in post-revolutionary France. These fun-loving aristocrats were "people one would have been so happy to live with" (1980: 296).

Unlike Staël also, the flaws he zeroed in were not of a moral, but of a practical nature: the inability to take anything seriously because "a long habit of submission to absolute power has rendered [the Frenchman] indifferent to all serious ideas [and he] only wishes for amusement [...]" (1988: 272); and a lack of practical common sense originating in the long engrained habit of observing court rituals. During the absolute monarchy, "[a] Frenchman [...] could not allow himself the simplest movement, the most insignificant step, without thinking about the rule good company prescribed for this movement or step" (1980: 296). Long used to relying on etiquette and protocol for the smallest details of life, aristocrats were no longer capable of relating naturally to the physical world; over time they had become "pitiful in action." Latching on to one of the central tenets of the *Idéologues'* philosophy, the relation between body and mind, Stendhal established a correspondence between these pitiful bodies, entirely deprived of the most basic freedom, the liberty to move and to act, and their "narrow, feeble minds" (1980: 296). "Attention to hundred little things," he wrote elsewhere (1982b: 61), "is truly what makes these people shrink."

In order to illustrate this important point, Stendhal selected King Louis XVI's botched attempt to flee France in 1792 as an example. Nothing, he pointed out, should have been easier for courtiers who had all possible means at their disposal to get the King safely to Austria, and yet, because of their excessive attention to detail, they managed to have the King arrested instead (1980: 296).[10] In one of those great ironies of history, the enslaved aristocratic habitus that allowed absolutism to thrive for so long was thus responsible for its demise. It was not the Revolution that had destroyed the monarchy; it had run out of "energy" and self-destructed. Stendhal found it crucial to contrast the courtiers' inability to act, to carry out their mission successfully, to the people's common sense and efficiency. Drouet, a simple, uneducated post-master had recognized the King from his likeliness on a banknote and taken appropriate measures to have him arrested (1980: 297), an event that clearly showed that "energy had now found refuge in the lower classes of society" (1982b: 61).

Napoleon Bonaparte had found the secret of galvanizing this nation awash with energy. Stendhal had the greatest admiration for the clean break with the fossilized aristocratic model Napoleon had achieved: "What merit Napoleon had to get us out of this pettiness! Immediately, one sees a different school!" (1982b: 61). The Emperor, who had an enormous work capacity and expected the same of his collaborators,[11] emphasized work ethics, efficiency, and results not only in warfare, but also in public administration and business. Stendhal admired Napoleon's achievements in the area of modernization. Reviewing a book on canals, *Des Canaux navigables en France* by M. De Pomeuse, he underscored the Emperor's entrepreneurial spirit: "Napoleon did much for France in this way [...]. The moment the construction of a canal was finished, he sold it to a company, and with the produce commenced another." (1982a: 97) He also commented on the construction of roads in Western France, nodding approvingly at the result:

> Napoleon, to humanize them [peasants in Vendée] a little, had the country traversed by two great roads, intersecting each other at right angle. The result of which has been, although La Vendée is not yet as civilized as Alsace or Franche Comté, yet it is nearly on a par with the Nivernois, the Bourbonnais, and other provinces in the interior of France. (Stendhal 1983: 40)

---

10 Stendhal detected the same lack of common sense in Staël. In the margins of the passage of *Considerations* in which she narrates her arrest in 1791, he wrote: "And so, as soon as Mme de Staël wants to act, she does something foolish, and in this case, out of vanity: she takes a six horse-drawn carriage." (Quoted in Félix-Faure 1974: 43)

11 In *Memoirs of an Egotist*, Stendhal recalls Pierre Daru's grueling work schedule as well as the Emperor's exacting demands and rough manners with his collaborators.

Young men were busy and active then, Stendhal observed nostalgically; they learned from experience, valued work, and had the opportunity to become real men (1988: 132). He embraced work as a positive value and the work ethics he had (reluctantly) acquired in the imperial administration would stay with him all his life. (His correspondence shows how seriously he took his responsibilities as a Consul of France during the July Monarchy – to the point of being a bit over-zealous). Men who, like Stendhal, had grown up in Napoleonic France had made all kinds of contributions to their country, in stark contrast to the depressed dreamers of Restoration France: "They don't know what to do with themselves; they read novels, or *sentimental philosophy*, and soon fall into an utter weariness of all things; in short, into the spleen." (1988: 133)

Less known in England, and just as significant in Stendhal's eyes, was the "moral rigor" Napoleon had introduced into the French upper class. It was he who "forced [them] to adopt not only a regularity of conduct in public, but even a strict propriety in the private relations of life" (1983: 56). This moral reform, "as strange as it may appear to the compatriots of Burke and the readers of *The Times* as it was edited during the war" (1983: 56), was viewed by Napoleon as a necessity, both as a way to deflect criticism of his regime[12] and as a means towards greater efficiency: "He was anxious to avoid being incessantly annoyed in the midst of his important occupations by the frivolities and scandal of a licentious court." (1983: 56) What his English readers did not realize, he insisted, was how pure mores had been in France during the First Empire at least until 1809.

For the Napoleonic regime also had serious flaws for Stendhal. 1809 marked a turning point in his attitude towards Napoleon, the beginning of a disillusion originating in his disappointment with the Emperor's "foolish desire of having a court" and his new "mania for imitating the kings of Europe" (1985: 244). That same year, he noted in his review of *Voyage en Autriche en 1809, avec la Grande Armée*, "several French generals, indignant at the state of slavery in which they were held, plotted the downfall of Napoleon" (1980: 254). Stendhal, who viewed liberty as "the most important asset, the most irreducible need" (Ansel 2003: 400), faulted Napoleon with an unforgivable sin: his hatred of liberty. The Emperor acted as a despot in 1802, Stendhal wrote in June 1825, when he crushed the Jacobins, who were "for the most part good people," and sided with the Catholics, who were mostly "cowards" (1988: 225). He took away freedom of expres-

---

12 "This despot, in founding a new court, dreaded above all things the effect of ridicule, which in France is mortal to all it touches, and which would eventually have been called into question had his new-made nobility aped the follies and vices of the old noblesse." (Stendhal 1983: 56)

sion and restored censorship so that during his reign the press was "enslaved by the despotism of glory" (1982a: 307). Literature also suffered as the Emperor sought to control the flow of ideas by appointing old fashioned critics like Julien-Louis Geoffroy (1743–1814) who "wrote the theatrical articles for *Journal des débats*, a paper charged [...] to resuscitate all the old ideas swept away by the Revolution" (1983: 214). Napoleon, who "dreaded nothing in this world so much as education" (1980: 85), smothered educational reforms so much that "the education of the French youth, which was excellent from 1794 to 1802," became "debasing under M. de Fontanes and Napoleon, from 1802 to 1814" (1985: 301). In that regard, women had fared even worse than men, as Stendhal noted in his review of Mme de Rémusat's *Essai sur l'éducation des femmes*. Napoleon was "not successful in introducing any material reform in the system of female education – a system which has been less affected than any other by the modifying process of the Revolution. In fact, female education in France at present is nearly as absurd as it was fifty years ago." (1982a: 231)

In religious matters, Stendhal maintained, "[t]he question of the re-establishment of the Catholic faith in France d[id] not exhibit one of the best points of Napoleon's character" (Stendhal 1991b: 56). Bonaparte had acted with utmost cynicism and simply used religion as a means of political control. In one of his reviews, he reproduced a conversation that took place between the First Consul and M. Thibaudeau, author of *Memoirs on the Consulate, 1799–1804*, at the time this issue was being discussed. According to the latter, Napoleon would have expressed, or rather feigned, emotion upon hearing the ringing of church bells – "such is the force of early habits and early education!" – before outlining his real reasons for restoring Catholicism: "I said to myself: What an impression must this make upon the minds of simple and credulous men! What can your philosophers and metaphysicians say to this? A nation must have a religion; and that religion should be in the hands of the Government." (1991b: 56) In the same passage, Stendhal criticized the Concordat as a "measure [that] occasioned the restoration of the Jesuits" (56), and elsewhere he complained that it had also served the interests of their political allies, the Royalists. That was not the smartest thing Bonaparte had done since he had thereby "himself created the party which overthrew him" (85). Finally, Stendhal was sensitive to the fact that the moral rigor Napoleon had demanded of his entourage and that he had himself praised, had come at a cost. It had widened the gender gap in France, leading to even less equality and less liberty for women. Now that husbands "assumed a haughty tone, their pride being raised by the whim of the despot, who 'resolved to have morals,'" it had become the "rule [...] that no wife should appear anywhere without her husband." (1991a: 130)

As far as liberty was concerned, the fall of the Empire had thus been a good thing. At least in theory, the constitution of the restored Bourbon monarchy guaranteed political liberty and freedom of expression. In practice, however, the Restoration had not turned out to be the just and constitutional regime the *Charte* had supposedly promised. The constitutional government existed on paper only and it had taken less than ten years for corruption to undermine political freedom.[13] This situation was all the more deplorable, Stendhal thought, that corruption also destroyed the French's confidence in democratic institutions: "Great numbers of Frenchmen of mature age, who entertained sober and reasonable patriotic sentiments as long as they saw any chance of a real constitutional government with two independent chambers being established in their country, have now resigned these sentiments as chimerical, and only seek for an opportunity for themselves." (Stendhal 1985: 295) The government had also gone back on its promise to grant freedom of expression. Plays were subject to censorship during the entire Restoration and the theaters controlled by the police as they were under Napoleon. Liberal song writers like Pierre-Jean de Béranger (1780 – 1857) and journalists were often arrested and sent to a prison that came to symbolize the regime's inability to cope with freedom of expression, Sainte-Pélagie. Censorship of the press brought down the Restoration regime in 1830, but Charles X had wanted to censor it four years earlier. In 1826 already, Stendhal worried "about a plan for a law against the freedom of the press, which [wa]s to be brought forward in February" and he wondered whether the government would accept the deal offered by the Jesuists: "non-restoration of the censorship, in return for the prohibition of publishing new editions of Voltaire and Rousseau." (Stendhal 1991a: 339) He was willing to concede that Restoration France was a peaceful and prosperous country, but in his eyes the Bourbon kings had had little to do with these fortunate circumstances. They were simply harvesting fruit from seeds planted by the previous regimes (1982a: 276). The French people knew that, and as long as Restoration government accepted the status quo, "they look[ed] upon the Bourbons *comme un inconvénient, mais comme un inconvénient peu embarrassant*" (Stendhal 1985: 298).

The central problem in Restoration France, Stendhal argued, was precisely this disconnection between the government and the people. The two kings and their entourage, who had lived in exile during the Revolution and the Em-

---

13 "The two chambers have been established in France only ten years, and yet already is the Chamber of Deputies bought and sold. Such an assembly, thus devoted, is one of the surest support of absolute power. It is cheating the people with a show of freedom; for the voting of taxes by those very persons who are to share in their produce [...] furnishes the wily and the rapacious with a *prétexte honnête* for selling themselves." (Stendhal 1985: 267)

pire, were like foreign bodies grafted on a nation that had moved on. The monarchs did not understand how much the French had changed since the Revolution; they did not share the French people's values in matters of religion and morals, education and politics. Louis XVIII had brought back his Old Regime mores from abroad; with him "returned the manners of the old court," the "reign" of royal mistresses, first Madame Princetot and then Madame du Cayla (1983: 58). Moral rigor had fled the court and only "[t]he wealthy Bourgeois still preserve[d] the bias towards good, given them by Napoleon." (1983: 58) Charles X was even more out of touch, more old-fashioned and undemocratic than his brother. As early as 1824, Stendhal accurately predicted that it was "more than probable that he [would] resume the ideas he entertained before 1789" (1985: 250). Not only was these two kings' worldview outmoded, they were also condemned to hang on to it due to a court protocol that prevented them from ever hearing sincere and true opinions.[14] Reviewing a book on the state of the French monarchy in 1824, Stendhal praised the author, François de Montlosier (1755–1838), for putting his finger on the problem that plagued France: "'People of the Third-Estate who have more wit and money than the nobility'" (1982a: 211). "Never, perhaps," Stendhal concluded in October 1826, "were so acute and intelligent a people as the French, ruled by so silly a government" (1991a: 336). That was the France that gave him the creeps.

4.1.2 Assessing change in Restoration France

For Stendhal, France had entered modernity, the age of reason and science, but its kings still lived in Old Regime France. Louis XVIII wrote in outdated French and his book, *Relation d'un voyage à Bruxelles et à Coblentz, en 1791*, was in the style "of a lady's waiting-maid" (1983a: 127). Besides, this poor King "was perfectly sincere in his belief of *divine right*; for this monarch, though learned, was incapable of reasoning" (1985: 258). Charles X had "no capacity for public affairs" (1985: 250). Judged by the modern standards of governance put in place by their predecessors, these monarchs were inept. They did not recognize, promote, and reward merit, as Napoleon had done. From the start, Louis XVIII had acted unfairly and divisively by firing capable men – like Stendhal – who had served the previous regime. As a result the administration of public affairs

---

14 "[T]o swerve from this protocol would be considered in France a breach of what are called *les convenances*, and be looked upon as ridiculous, even by the liberals. From this it results that a Bourbon prince is condemned never to hear the accents of truth and sincerity, – never to know the charms or utility of real conversation." (Stendhal 1985: 262)

was entrusted to people who lacked experience and abilities; the government, to incompetent royalist ministers. Jean-Baptiste de Villèle (1773–1854) definitely lacked "the qualities necessary to captivate the hearts of Frenchmen" (1985: 268) but Charles X maintained him in power because he was convinced that he was "the only man in France who possesse[d] sufficient financial talent to accomplish so arduous and important a measure as the indemnity to the émigrés" (1985: 288) – a measure Stendhal strongly objected to. As far as he was concerned, the 1825 law on the "*milliard des émigrés*" was fundamentally unjust. It compensated, at tax-payers' expense, aristocrats who had weathered the revolutionary storm in exile and returned to France during the Consulate. A month before the vote, he reported on a new book that contained speeches by three members of the assembly, Constant, Foy and Girardin, who opposed the bill as well. He praised Constant in particular for having written a witty passage proving "in the clearest manner that, after having returned under Buonaparte in 1801 – after having vied with each other in crowding his anti-chamber – *after having sworn allegiance to him*, they [the émigrés] c[ould] not boast of their fidelity, and still less of their heroism, but simply of their prudence" (Stendhal 1988: 114).[15] The bill, he contended, had been a strategic mistake that had fueled a lot of resentment and was largely responsible for the strength of a liberal opposition that shaped public opinion between 1815 and 1830 through its control of the press – as Liberals owned newspapers with the largest circulation, including *Le Constitutionnel*. Piling up mistake upon mistake, the Royalists in power gave Liberals increasingly more reasons to oppose the government, as it revived old wounds, instead of healing them, so for instance when it honored as "heroes" former counter-revolutionaries who had fought against the First Republic's armies (Stendhal 1983: 41). He also mocked the Ultra party not only for the "want of capacity" already noted, but also for its "want of unanimity" (1985: 288). Had not Chateaubriand fought hard against Villèle in 1826–1827 in the hope of replacing him? Had he not "thought to play the same *golden* game as M. de Villèle?" (Stendhal 1985: 270) – i.e. make millions while in office.[16]

The Bourbons' belated efforts to rally the French to their regime by capitalizing on their partiality for military uniforms had failed miserably as well. The French expedition to Spain had been a pastiche of warfare given the weakness of the adversary, the luck of the French army, and thus the ease with which

---

15 Stendhal was not all praise, however: "Happy would it be for the public, and for M. B. Constant himself, if his works on religion were written with the same fervour and the same talent!" (1988: 114)
16 But Chateaubriand "had too much poetry in his head to make a good financier […] and succeeded only in ruining himself and the husbands of his mistresses." (Stendhal 1985: 270)

the monarchy had been re-established in that country. Far from rallying the French to the regime, the Spanish war had made them fall out of love with warfare (Stendhal 1991a: 238). Between 1815 and 1825, Bonapartism and the French predilection for military glory were already in decline (1988: 234). Disregard for the new professional army had done the rest (1991a: 239). In Stendhal's eyes, one main factor accounted for the French people's growing disaffection with the military: the new social make-up of the troops. Soldiers were now uneducated draftees from the poor peasantry who fought for money, no longer the volunteers of the Republic's army, who had come from the land-owning peasantry, had been somewhat educated, and had fought for the *patrie* (1985: 247). Patriotism could only be on the wane when officers were "looked upon as mere soldiers of fortune; such men as Walter Scott has described, fighting for those who pay them best" (1991a: 238).

The most egregious flaw of the Restoration government was its support of the Roman Catholic Church and its religious policies. Stendhal monitored the Jesuits' return on the social and political scene with a mixture of disbelief and concern. In 1823, he commented on the Jesuits's efforts to regain their former power, noting that "the Jesuits [we]re making such silent, yet gigantic strides towards power" (1982a: 230). In 1824, he remarked that the Society of Jesus "was becoming every day more powerful and adroit" (1983: 166). A year later, in January 1825, he voiced his indignation at the prospect of a take-over: "Now come the clergy and noblesse, who, in the intoxication of triumph, aim at reducing us to the state of the *roturiers* before the revolution." (1988: 62) In December of that year, he wrote a mock constitution ridiculing the Bourbon Monarchy and denouncing the Jesuits' growing power:

> France is, in fact, governed by a constitution, consisting of four articles:
> Art. 1: The laws shall be made by two chambers, appointed by the ministry.
> Art. 2: Five journals shall enjoy free permission to speak on all subjects, except the follies of the royal family.
> Art. 3: Promotion in the Royal Guard shall be made, and all places shall be filled up, solely on the recommendation of the Jesuits, who overawe the ministers.
> Art. 4: The Jesuits and the 25,000 young priests who are devoted to them, may commit every crime, murder excepted, without being prosecuted by law. (Stendhal 1991a: 44)

By 1826, he conceded defeat: "France is governed by Jesuits [...]." (1991a: 68) With a quarter of representatives in the house supporting the Jesuits – "108 of the 420 members composing our Chamber of Deputies under the control of M. Ferdinand de Berthier" (46), he figured that the devout party had become a political force to reckon with.

This development was a dangerous threat to equality and liberty. The law gave the Jesuits preferential treatment when it allowed them "to go armed in the street, whilst we are strictly prohibited from bearing arms." (328). In the provinces, the Jesuits had taken over municipal affairs and were now in a position to "appoint the *garde-champêtre*, the justice of the peace, the officers of the *gendarmerie*, the mayor, the priest, and the sub-prefect [...]" (325). They are "our masters everywhere," Stendhal complained: "except in Paris [...] one must pay them homage or be exposed to their vexations" (328). The Jesuits' rise to prominence was also as a factor of social division, particularly in local politics and in education. In the provinces, the clergy was doing its best to regain control of vital records, a function that the townships had taken over during the Revolution. Stendhal relished that power struggle, however, because it pitted the clergy against of the aristocracy – most mayors, like M. de Rênal in *The Red and the Black*, being aristocrats during the Restoration – and thus weakened the royalist party. He also found the clergy's attempts to regain control over the hearts and souls of the peasantry funny and ludicrous at times, so for instance when Abbé Hulot, denounced and sought to prohibit dancing "that national and innocent amusement, the looking forward which cheers the peasant through his labours" (1983: 70).

Education, by contrast, was a serious matter. Stendhal worried that the new generation being taught in Jesuit institutions would have little in common with the previous one, neither intellectually nor morally (1982a: 210). People like him, who had benefitted from an enlightened education in the schools of the Republic, had a strong moral sense. But the young men now being trained for the priesthood, peasants for the majority of them, would become hypocrites like Julien Sorel, the hero of *The Red and the Black*. Those young peasants who made up "five sixths of the clergy in France" (242) did not become priests out of religious zeal, because it was their vocation. For them, the priesthood was a way of earning a living. The Church might be kidding itself that it was winning the hearts and souls of the French, Stendhal reasoned, but it wasn't. It was breeding hypocrisy instead. In Restoration France, the Church had simply replaced the army as the avenue of social mobility for the semi-educated landowning peasantry. He found some comfort in the thought that this new development was not necessarily a bad thing: religious despotism, he reckoned, would not last as long as military despotism had (Stendhal 1983: 55).

In Paris, the *parti dévot* had tried to take control of higher education since 1822 and appointed professors of its liking, but higher education remained in good shape. *Polytechnique*, an institution of higher learning created during the Revolution, was a European center of modern education. The thousands of young graduates this school had produced were men of science and reason, a mode of thinking incompatible for Stendhal with faith and religion.[17] This school and the colleges of law and medicine ensured the on-going production of a young elite that was close intellectually to the *Idéologues* and familiar with the works of contemporary philosophers.[18] In his review of Cabanis's *Oeuvres complètes*, Stendhal listed the three works he viewed as the best and most influential philosophical works of his time, Cabanis's masterpiece, *Rapports du physique et du moral de l'homme*; and two books by Destutt de Tracy, *L'Idéologie* and *Commentaire sur Montesquieu*. These works, he claimed, "form[ed] a principal part of the education of the rising generation in France" (1982a: 118). Stendhal was confident that, like him, college students [*la jeunesse des écoles*] shared their anthropocentric worldview, their materialist philosophy, their conviction that religion was incompatible with science, that it had been, and still was, an impediment to human happiness, the only worthy purpose in life. These students, "whose minds [we]re imbued with the writings of Voltaire and Roussseau, and the political pamphlets of Benjamin Constant," not only kept the Enlightenment legacy alive, they were also Republicans at heart: "they dreamed of the King of France being reduced to the dimensions of a President of the United States of America" (1985: 300). The middle class origin of these students was another positive sign, an indication that education was spreading in France, since the Parisian schools attracted young men from "the middling class of persons, who follow no profession or trade, but live in the provinces upon a competence of from 6 to 10000 francs a year [...]." (300)

As for the rest of France, Stendhal believed that religion had largely lost its appeal there as well, as he continuously remarked: "In France, nothing is as rare as faith. Everyone is afraid of being taken for a dupe" (1991a: 210); "The majority of the French look with a mocking eye upon both Jansenists and Jesuits. Indifference to religious matters is more than ever the distinctive trait of the French character." (1983: 66) France, he declared elsewhere, was "of all the countries in Europe, most free with respect to religious opinion" (1991a: 342). As far as he was concerned, the clergy's efforts to re-convert the French population were doomed, "[t]he efforts of Messieurs Grégoire, Lanjuinais and other respectable characters [...] to root out [...] this indifference to former sentiments [...]

---

17 Stendhal expressed this view when commenting on Collin de Plancy's *Dictionnaire infernal*, a book on magic, Satanism, etc...: "To the philosopher who adopts Hume's system, this volume will not be unacceptable, as it will furnish him with a well-chosen collection of the absurdities flowing from a belief in things which we do not see." (Stendhal 1983: 164)

18 The *Idéologues* granted primacy to reason and sensory experience, from which will [*volonté*] and memory [*mémoire*] were derived. They were not concerned with phenomena outside the purview of sensory experience and did not deal therefore with religion.

w[ould] be unavailing." (1983: 66) In 1828, he guessed that "the Catholic religion, as it is arranged by the Pope, [wa]s not believed by three men, or twenty women, in a hundred" (1991a: 184). In each and every social class, he recorded the same indifferent attitude towards religion. Among the educated elite, those who claimed to be Catholics were so only in name: "they may admire the morality of the gospel but, as to the peculiar dogmas of the Church of Rome, if they do not openly despise them, they at least consider them of little if any importance." (1983: 66) The upper classes were "averse to devote their children to this profession" (1982a: 242); they did not let their children become priests, a sure sign of their disaffection with the Church. For them, religion was for show, for children and servants (1985: 292). But even shopkeepers were of opinion that religion was something for those beneath their station! (1982a: 236).

In *Chronicles for England,* as elsewhere in his work, Stendhal's assessment of the progress of freedom is based on political factors – the form of the government, the political class's ability to resist cooptation by power – and on social ones. With no time or money for education, for instance, the working class has little experience of freedom.[19] As mentioned earlier, his understanding of freedom is grounded in a materialist ethics derived in part from the Enlightenment philosophy, in part from their heirs, the *Idéologues,* the proponents of a kind of "reasoning, palpable enough, which, in France is in everybody's mouth" (Stendhal 1985: 208). Like Condillac (1715 – 1780) Stendhal viewed moral sense as a product of experience, not as an innate feeling.[20] Like Helvétius (1715 – 1771), one his favorite Enlightenment philosophers,[21] he took 'interest' to be the principle of human action, a term that does not mean selfishness but the 'pleasure' associated with generous, altruistic behavior, with a concern for others and for the common good (1980: 86). For Stendhal, the "generous souls" – *âmes généreuses* – have a duty to act morally, in accordance with what they believe to be true or good, and to do so because it is in their own

---

19 In *The Charterhouse of Parma,* Stendhal provides an example of what he means by the difficulty to think experienced by the lower class. On the battlefield at Waterloo, Fabrizio notices that his new friends, the canteen-woman and Corporal Aubry, "as they debated, [...] repeated the particulars of his story three or four times" (Stendhal 2006: 64) and he can't help wondering why: "Why go on repeating what we all three of us know so perfectly well? Fabrizio said to himself. He did not yet know that in France this is how the common people go in search of ideas." (2006: 65)

20 "The philosophy of Condillac is based upon, and recommends a continual recourse to experience. The German philosophy of Kant rejects experience and appeals upon all occasions on the *sens intime.* But when one objects that he does not find this *sens intime* in his mind, the arrogant answer is then God has left you an imperfect being." (Stendhal 1983: 104)

21 See Stendhal's review of *Pensées sur la philosophie d'Helvétius* (Stendhal 1980: 84 – 87).

best interest. If they don't, the self-contempt they will feel for not living up to their own expectations will be a source of unhappiness. To explain what he means, Stendhal gives the example of two men standing on a river bank who see a child drowning. The first regrets it but does nothing; the second, the *âme généreuse*, the moment he "conceives of the possibility of this generous action, his pleasure obliges him to throw himself into the water and to attempt it. If he does not, he will be pursued by the remorse of having contributed to the death of the unfortunate child: he will be pursued by his self-contempt." (1985: 208) A moral individual, a generous soul, thus understands that his or her happiness is irremediably bound to the happiness of others:

> In almost all the circumstances of life, a generous mind perceives the possibility of certain actions, the idea of which a common mind is incapable of comprehending. The moment the possibility of accomplishing these actions becomes visible to a man of generous sentiments, that moment it also becomes his *interest* to do them, and if not done he feels the stinging of self-degradation, and consequently becomes unhappy. This principle of Helvetius is true even in the wildest aberrations of passion, and even in suicide. In a word, it is contrary to the nature of man, it is even impossible for him, not to do that which he thinks may conduce to his happiness, the moment the possibility of doing it is offered to him. (Stendhal 1980: 86)

The heroes of Stendhal's novels are these generous souls who take the liberty to act in accordance with their beliefs and the expectations they set for themselves. For some, it comes easy: in the *Charterhouse of Parma*, as naïve as the sixteen-year old Fabrizio Del Dongo may be when he decides to fight with Napoleon at Waterloo, this young man with "too much fire for prosaic souls" recognizes that his happiness depends on his ability to live up to the self-imposed challenge of fighting for liberty:

> I saw that great image of Italy rising up from the slough in which the Germans have kept it covered. She was stretching forth her bruised arms, still half weighted down by chains, towards her king and liberator. And I, I told myself, the as yet unknown son of that unhappy mother, I shall leave, I shall go either to die or to conquer with that man marked by destiny, who sought to cleanse us from the contempt cast at us [...]. (Stendhal 2006: 32)

Other characters must learn that liberty and happiness come from one's heart, not from some external idea of duty, as Julien Sorel first believes in *The Red and the Black*.[22] In that case freedom is an education, an exercise that requires

---

22 For Goldstein, Stendhal's Julien Sorel demonstrates that "a psychic apparatus conceived on sensationalist lines had conspicuous weaknesses and vulnerabilities, that it lacked protective armor and full control over its processes – that it was, in a word, disaggregated." (Goldstein

honest soul searching, commitment, and self-discipline on the part of the individual, for as Stendhal, quoting Jeremy Bentham, writes in *Memoirs of a Tourist*: "One deserves liberty only when one knows how to conquer it." (1929: III, 318) Some succeed – Julien learns that playing a role will never make him happy; others, like Mathilde de la Mole, don't.[23] The Stendhalian hero is a free individual who does not need society's encouragement or approval to find his or her own happiness. Gina Pietranera in *The Charterhouse of Parma* is another generous soul who acts as her heart, not social convention, dictates. Count Mosca, by contrast, is not a bad man, but a "vulgar soul" who "believe[s] himself obligated to seek before all else the happiness of Count Mosca della Rovere" (2006: 288). He therefore lacks virtue, or more precisely "what the Liberals understand by *morality* (to seek the happiness of the greatest number)" (288).

The altruistic side of Stendhal's conception of individualism is so important that he uses it to divide the political field of Restoration France in two: a Liberal is the generous soul that "wishes for the happiness of the greatest number;" and a Royalist, or Ultra, one who "wishes evil for the greatest number of people for the pleasure of a minority" (quoted in Ansel 2003: 400). Or so it goes in theory, for ironically "the liberal party led by Marchesa Raversi and General Conti" (266) lacks this very virtue in the novel, and so did the Restoration Liberals according to Stendhal. Seeking to explain the Liberals' puzzling rejection of his conceptions of individualism and freedom, he mused that Hélvetius had done himself a disservice by calling his central concept 'interest,' a word bound to be misinterpreted as narrow self-interest or egoism and for that reason, "not to mention around polite ears" (1980: 86). In Stendhal's opinion, it was precisely the mistake Benjamin Constant made when he claimed that individualism was detrimental to society, that "if every individual was its own center, all individuals were all isolated" (1985: 209), a misunderstanding all the more regrettable that it had led him to conclude to the moral and social necessity of religion. So sadly, the Liberals, these members of the French upper class who could have been the "happy few," who could have reaped the benefits of freedom, had chosen not to do so. They had become "charlatans," the opposite of "generous souls."

2005: 106) What Stendhal shows in the novel, however, is that this "uneducated" self can overcome weaknesses through new experiences.

23 "Julien [...] was tired of heroism [...] but Mathilde's proud soul always required a public, the presence of *all those other people*. In the middle of all her suffering, and all her fears for her lover's life (she did not want to survive him), she had a hidden need to astonish the public with the utter extravagance of her love, and the sublimity of everything she was trying to do." (Stendhal 2003: 450)

Stendhal's frequent recourse to the charlatan/dupe dichotomy to track the actualization of the rights of man in France is perhaps most striking proof of his sensationalist and republican convictions. As Jan Goldstein points out in *The Post-Revolutionary Self*, this rhetorical feature coined during the Enlightenment and commonly used by revolutionaries originated in the belief that the adoption of the *Declaration of the Rights of Man and the Citizen* had put an end to the Old Regime hierarchy of command and obedience, or, in Condorcet's words in his 1793 *Sketch for a Historical Picture of the Progress of the Human Mind,* to the division of "humanity into two races, the one fated to rule, the other to obey, *the one to deceive, the other to be deceived,*'" in other words charlatans and dupes. Summarizing Condorcet's argument and quoting him, Goldstein writes:

> A republican government can reasonably hope to attain among its citizenry not a complete equality of education or mental acuity but that adequate degree of equality that will enable every citizen 'To be no longer the dupe of those popular errors which torment man with superstitious fears and chimerical hopes; to defend himself against prejudice by the strength of his reason alone; and finally, to escape the deceits of charlatans who would lay snares for his fortune, his health, his freedom of thought and his conscience.' (Goldstein 2005: 98)

According to her, the "sensationalist experiment in political culture" conducted during the Revolution was meant to eradicate this divide. In an article she quotes, a journalist named Pinglin explained the reasoning that led to this project and the high stakes that were attached to it: the people's "docile, trusting, credulous" nature made them highly vulnerable to charlatans; but once duped they became "misanthropic," convinced that they were "surrounded by rascals," an attitude clearly inimical not only to individual happiness but also to the common good (quoted in Goldstein 2005: 98). Just as the republican festivals were meant to dispel religious superstition, the course in 'general grammar' taught in the central schools, open to sons of the working class as much as those of the bourgeoisie, aimed at counter-balancing the power of human imagination (Goldstein 2005: 97–98): "'Imagination without analysis,'" Condillac had declared, would be "'a source of opinions, prejudices, errors.' In the absence of the regulation provided by analysis, imagination would lead us to produce nothing but 'extravagant dreams' – as do in fact, those 'writers who rely solely on imagination'" (quoted in Goldstein 2005: 69).

Educated at the central school of Grenoble, Stendhal shared his teachers' sense of "responsibility towards possessors of a wayward imagination" (Goldstein 2005: 97). His vocation, if indeed he had one as Kete contends (2012: 73–106), was probably less to be a writer for the sake of it, than for the sake of educating others by relentlessly identifying and denouncing his contemporaries' failure to live up to the expectations of their revolutionary fathers. But as he noted, the healthy sensationalist philosophy that aimed at eliminating dupes and charlatans was under attack in the early 1820s. In his review of Victor Cousin's edition and translation of *Oeuvres de Platon* (1822), Stendhal lambasted the new guru for embracing a wayward imagination that real philosophers had the duty to combat. Cousin, he wrote, owed his success to his improvisations and oratory skills in public lectures and if, in terms of "poetic coloring, vicacity of invention, and fertility of imagination," he came right after "Chateaubriand, Casimir Delavigne, Lemercier and Pigault Le Brun," as a philosopher, he lacked "one of the most essential qualities of philosophy: common sense." (Stendhal 1982a: 38)

The French, he thought (wrongly),[24] were too rational, too used to clarity of thought and expression to be duped by a doctrine inspired by "the mysteries of German philosophy" (38). And yet, the Liberals, the very people Stendhal felt closest to politically, were suddenly regressing in that area. A prominent liberal politician like Benjamin Constant was publishing on religion. Stendhal admired Constant's intellect and political courage. In his first review of his book, *De la Religion*, he had praised him as "one of the most intellectual men in France" and "the most distinguished and efficient member of the Chamber of Deputies" (1982a: 236). But, he regretfully noted, "[i]t is singular enough that M. Constant, who, in his place in the Chamber of Deputies displays such an acuteness of perception and force of reasoning in detecting and holding up to ridicule the errors and sophisms of Ministers, should, when he comes to write as a philosopher, stray into the same tortuous and obscure path." (238)

Stendhal made fun of Constant's definition of "religious sentiment" as "a modification of the religious sentiment which inspires an ignorant person with fear mingled with respect when he hears a thunder-clap" (236). Such sentiment, Stendhal joked, had no reason to be after Benjamin Franklin's invention of the lightning rod! Constant's main contention that religious feeling was a universal response to a deep human need, may have applied in the past, but it no longer did in the modern age when scientific explanations alleviated fears formerly caused by unknown natural phenomena. In his second review of the book,[25] Stendhal made clear that Constant's goal was to undermine sensationalist philosophy, "the philosophy which has reigned in Paris for the last thirty years"

---

24 On "Cousinian Hegemony," and in particular the institutionalization of Cousin's philosophy through its adoption in the *lycée* curriculum, see Goldstein (2005: 182–232). Also Spitzer (1987: 71–96), "Victor Cousin: the Professor as Guru."

25 *"De la Religion* de Constant," followed by a related article: *"L'Aristocratie Parisienne."* Stendhal (1985: 196–229)

(1985: 208) and he mocked his efforts "to refute it by mystical arguments" (208). But he was worried nonetheless. Until Constant published *De la Religion* only conservatives like Chateaubriand had defended the view that religion was a necessary foundation of society. Now, Liberals were giving in to the same kind of inconsistent, unscientific reasoning on the topic of religion. Even more disappointing, the young people he had befriended in Delécluze's circle and admired for launching the independent newspaper *Le Globe* were becoming *Cousinistes*.[26] Unlike Constant, the *Cousinistes* had the merit of denying the universality of religious sentiment and of acknowledging that the French, in general, were not a religious people (Stendhal 1991a: 345). But they too were losing their reason, giving in to mysticism and *obscurantisme*, the very opposite of the sane philosophy Stendhal subscribed to: "Distrust everybody – me to begin with – believe nothing but experience;" realize that "[t]he moment I become obscure, I must have become absurd without knowing it" (Stendhal 1988: 100).

Stendhal noted that Protestants figured prominently among the Liberals who were speaking out in favor of religion. At some point (Stendhal 1983: 66), he had painted them as the only true believers in France, but he was wary of a "liberal aristocracy" that had, in his view, decided to take advantage of circumstances for political gain. Now that the Jesuits had made religion fashionable again, they were competing with them on their turf. The *Société de la morale chrétienne*, founded in 1821 by liberal members of the house of lords [*chambre des pairs*], including the Duke and Duchess de Broglie, Staël's son-in-law and her daughter, had gained so much influence that "a debutant who will *brusquer la gloire*, and wants consideration in the drawing-rooms of the Duchesses *à-la-mode*, must get admitted into the society *de la Morale Chrétienne*, and choose the mottos of his works in the Bible" (1988: 38). Stendhal probably did not know that Staël had wished to make Protestantism France's official religion – her *Current Circumstances* were not published during his lifetime – but he clearly saw that the liberal aristocracy was moving in that direction, that "[t]he Aristocracy [...] [wa]s attempting to get up a kind of Protestantism" (38). As Sacquin (1998: 38) argues, however, the Protestants' assertiveness in a period of "Catholic re-conquest" had more to do with survival than with fashion. Stendhal himself admitted that much when he commented on the violent reaction to the *Société de la morale chrétienne*'s creation in the press controlled by the Jesuits (1985: 292) and when he suggested that the Protestants might make a few converts given the

---

26 Alan B. Spitzer, commenting on "the polemic between Stendhal and Armand Carrel over the former's pamphlet, *D'un Nouveau Complot contre les industriels*," underscores the "chasm dividing the literary-moral sensibility of the forty-two year old charter member of the Happy Few from that of the young prophet of the new industrial order" (Spitzer 1987: 168).

Catholics' unreasonableness (1988: 274). This religious revival was ridiculous nonetheless, he thought, and the attempt to convert the French to Protestantism just as doomed as the Jesuits' efforts to bring them back to the bosom of Catholic Church. He chose, therefore, to watch these salon wars of religion with amusement from afar, describing them as a form of entertainment for a bored Parisian high society (1983: 66), as "a way to kill time" (1988: 276).

Stendhal had a great deal to say about all current impediments to progress. For a start, he denied the existence of the problem Staël, Constant, and Chateaubriand, all these "possessors of a wayward imagination," had sought to cure with religion: there was nothing wrong with individualism. On the contrary, there was not enough of it. Too many obstacles distracted individuals from acting freely, in accordance with their acquired sense of morality when circumstances demanded it. Unafraid to name the traitors by name, Stendhal painted a "sketch of the liberal party, sold or to be sold" (1985: 296). Most liberal politicians had sold out to the government or were about to do so: in addition to endorsing religion, they were being seduced by government honors and positions. Even the liberal press he had counted on for the political edification of the French (301), seemed to him much more accommodating than it has been previously (296). Commenting on the launch of another liberal periodical in 1823, *Le Mercure du dix-neuvième siècle*, Stendhal remarked that the owners of this new publication, "MM Jouy, Jay, Tissot, Etienne, Aignan, Andrieux, &c.," in other words the cream of the liberal crop, would have gladly rallied to the government, had they been offered a chance. (Stendhal 1982a: 136) Charlatans were everywhere, among political figures of all parties, Bonapartists (1983: 55–57) and Liberals (1988: 134); among scientists (1985: 252), high society ladies, and regretfully so, particularly among the opinion-makers, the journalists (Le Hir 2007).

True to his philosophical convictions, Stendhal sought to understand the elite's inability to free itself from the constraints of deception and self-deception. As mentioned earlier, the flaws of *le caractère français* during the Restoration were for him remnants of Old Regime mores. High society had not yet learned to wean itself from fashion; the very tool Louis XIV had used to enslave the aristocracy still reigned "paramount in France" (1991a : 248). In his review of the Duke of Choiseul's *Mémoires*, he underscored the crucial role fashion had played in shaping expectations of proper behavior during the absolute monarchy, and hence also what passed as ridiculous traits, *ridicules*, in seventeenth-century France:

> The omnipotence of fashion is merely one of the effects of absolute monarchy. Louis XIV was not only absolute in power, but his real greatness, which escaped the observation both of Voltaire and Montesquieu, consisted in the control he exercised over public opin-

ion, and that among all classes of society. [...] Molière was the minister of opinion under Louis XIV, and his business was to excite laughter at the expense of every Frenchman who did not scrupulously imitate the pattern assigned to his particular class. This is the point on which Molière's comic humor turned [...]. (Stendhal 1991b: 50, 52).

Stendhal even mused about the possibility of comedy in a society that no longer assigned specific social roles, as absolutism had done, now that "peculiarity of conduct [wa]s no longer regarded as an offence" (1991b: 52). He wondered whether liberty meant less gaiety, less laughter. In Molière's days, he explained, it was easy to recognize *ridicules* and to laugh at them, but what would happen in a society where the lines were blurred? Nonconformity to standard norms of behavior would no longer elicit spontaneous laughter; it would raise questions, be met with doubt and reflection instead of automatic condemnation.[27]

This scenario was a far-away prospect, however, for in reality, liberty had made little inroad in France. Granted, the French had had little opportunity so far to experiment with freedom: "Napoleon [...] tried to convert us into the feudatories of the middle ages. Danton and Robespierre wanted to make us citizens of Sparta and Rome" (1988: 62). But as it was, the French had "no love for liberty;" they did not "understand it" (246). The constraints imposed on Restoration France by fashion, the greatest impediment to the progress of freedom, could be felt everywhere: in philosophy, with the displacement of rationalism with mysticism (1991a: 344); in moral life, given that "[m]orality, in France, has hitherto been merely an affair of fashion" (1991b: 50); in religious life, now that religion was "the mode" (1988: 38) and had returned to a country where it had been practically extinct; and of course, in social life. It was ironic that at a time when individuals had more freedom than ever to behave as they wished, they chose to follow fashion and imitate others rather than be themselves.[28]

Stendhal observed the discrepancy between being and appearance everywhere in high society. In that milieu, inauthenticity and hypocrisy reigned supreme: "Everything is become stage effect and affectation among this unfortunate people. Is it impossible for a nation to reach a high point of civilization

---

27 "Before the audience laugh at any character in a comedy, they say: 'but, perhaps, the man is happy in his own way?'" (Stendhal 1991b: 52)

28 Stendhal hardly ever mentions clothing when he speaks of fashion, except to criticize women who follow it as 'Parisian dolls,' but the numerous studies devoted to fashion in nineteenth-century France – to the proliferation of women fashion magazines; French male artists' preference of the distinguishing extravagance of the British dandy over the increasingly standard black suit of bourgeois men, etc... – demonstrate the accuracy of his observation. In his days, London was the center of male fashion (Mérimée purchased his clothes exclusively there) and Paris of women fashion (his Spanish friend Madame de Montijo dressed there).

without getting into the state in which no step, no motion, can be left to the guidance of nature, and to the impulse of the moment, and in which, consequently, every act is a lie?" (Stendhal 1988: 188) Mores that had been natural and charming in the age of the absolute monarchy had now lost their moorings in the social order that had created them. Deprived of their benign innocence, they were out of place in the post-revolutionary world. A parody of the past, high society no longer embodied unity, but disharmony between self and the world. The contemporary upper class lacked the refinement of mind and feeling of its former incarnation: "In proportion as the necessity of *acting a part*, at all times and in all places, becomes more obvious and imperative in Parisian society, delicacy of mind disappears with fearful rapidity." (258) Imitation condemned it to coarseness and inauthenticity: "We are never permitted in France [...] to do what one likes, or what the feelings of the moment dictate. There is always a certain model of *bon ton*, a certain ideal pattern, which must be kept in view, and upon which all must fashion themselves. This is the most striking absurdity of the French character." (1988: 106)

L'inconséquence, fickleness and inconsistency, was an attendant flaw of this love of fashion, and the most distinctive feature of the *caractère français* at the time (1991a: 146). Stendhal defined it as "the French privilege of being mean but with good grace" (120) and he saw it as particularly problematic because it went to the heart of his understanding of identity. In the modern age, the self ought to be whole, thought ought to match action, but the contemporary self was split: a good and kind external behavior did not necessarily imply a virtuous self. In high society in fact, the either/or prescribed by logic was replaced by the coordinating conjunction: social niceties *and* immorality; social niceties as the coat of immorality. The display of "excessive sentimentality" in conversation, for instance, could very well point to an actual inability to feel, a thought Stendhal conveyed through the striking image of a slave trafficker crying over a dog's broken leg (1985: 266). Inconsistency touched everyone, and perhaps most those who were dependent on the good graces of others (1991a: 120). This flaw was compounded by a tendency to doubt everything, even the truth (310). As long as there were charlatans, there would be dupes, so the fear of being taken advantage of, of being thought naïve and gullible, would endure. Interestingly, this characteristic also explained the French people's lack of religiosity.[29]

Apart from the Old Regime aristocracy, the contemporary British upper class provided another point of reference in Stendhal's depiction of *le caractère fran-*

---

29 "The Frenchman is not naturally either mystical or chimerical; and he has always such a dread of being duped, that he takes care to believe very little." (Stendhal 1991a: 342)

çais. Focused exclusively on high society, his comparison of national differences and biases was meant to challenge preconceived ideas the two nations had about each other by "reflecting habit" (1982a: 283), viewing what one habitually took for granted in a new light, as like Adolphe-Jérôme Blanqui (1798–1854), the future economist and brother of revolutionary Louis-Auguste, had done in his travel narrative on Scotland. Arguing that it was unnecessary to deal with the vulgar nationalist hatred born of a false sense of patriotism (283) because this kind of chauvisnim was only found in the lower class,[30] Stendhal compared attitudes toward rank, money, leisure, work, and government, among others, in the French and the British upper class. Rank, he thought, mattered more in England than in France (1968b: 254–255). Across the Channel, it was highly valued not only by the upper class but also by society at large, as "the British people's exuberance at the sight of Queen Victoria" amply demonstrated (254). Such a manifestation of unanimous admiration for a king or queen was "a phenomenon utterly incomprehensible to the vast majority of the French" (254), Stendhal maintained, for in France, rank in itself was found rather unattractive: "For never w[ould] French vanity allow a privileged class of nobles to take root in public opinion, and exact, as a matter of hereditary right, the deference and submission of their fellow citizens." (Stendhal 1985: 300) Consequently, the obsessive curiosity for the private life of aristocratic celebrities in England was seen as rather ridiculous in France, including by Stendhal himself. In his view, divergent attitudes towards money corresponded to these divergent attitudes toward rank. The British viewed money as a means to a higher rank; the French rank as a means to fortune: the prospect or expectation of personal benefit explained their tolerance of rank, a fact that Stendhal deeply regretted as it was in his view far too costly for the nation during the Restoration. Unequal access to rank in both countries accounted for these opposite priorities: rank was open in England, its aristocracy admitted "all men of great talents into its ranks" (1991b: 96), but not in France. The British, viewing rank as an end, tended to open it to talent. The French, viewing it as a means, tended to restrict access to it.

As a result, the British valued work and took it seriously; the French mocked those who did. Stendhal makes this point through a fable that could be entitled 'British ant and French grasshopper meet inventor:' "The Frenchman [...] who only wishes for amusement, assails the inventor of the machine with jokes

---

30 This comment is somewhat surprising because anti-British sentiment was far from being restricted to the common people during the Restoration, originating as it did in France's military defeat at the fall of the Empire. As Stendhal himself pointed out (1980: 262; 1982a: 136), the liberal press had made "vulgar patriotism" and England-bashing its trade-mark.

and ridicule, well or ill timed. The Englishman, [...] encourages the projector of the machine" (1988: 272) in the hope of saving or making money. As a result also, the British were self-reliant, did not expect their government to provide for them, and took care of their own business, as Stendhal explained in one of his sketches of French society in 1826:

> It is curious to observe the striking differences between the two most civilized nations in the world. I have often thought that in France we know a great deal more about England, than the English know of us. The reason is plain. You English are all very much occupied, because you attend to your own business yourself, while the peculiarity of our Government is that it affords its subjects an immense deal of leisure-time. In France the Government does everything for the people; even settles their disputes in the theatres. (1991a: 338)

Another related flaw in the French national character was an extreme cautiousness in social relations[31] and practical matters – a great disadvantage in business.[32] The French relied on authority in all aspects of daily life, as the following anecdote, first told by Paul-Louis Courier (1772–1825), and retold by Stendhal in *Chroniques* illustrates: a horse-drawn carriage is being driven too fast, thereby endangering the safety of its passengers. How do they react? They complain that the police should do something about it. When the narrator suggests that they should ask the driver to slow down, they refuse for fear of getting in trouble. For Courier, the anecdote painted a "'faithful picture of the French people. They trust to their police for everything; and whenever they are required to show the least resolution and moral courage, rather than make an effort so unnatural to them, they have recourse to personal courage, which never fails them'" (Stendhal 1991a: 340). The French expected not only the police, but also the government to take care of things rather than taking things in their own hands: a meager salary in a government position that flattered their vanity because of the power it gave them over others seemed preferable to them than earning five times more money in private business (1988: 344–348). Once again, Stendhal reached the same conclusion: the French did not love freedom, did not know how to be free.

Like any description that attributes specific characteristics to an entire nation, or even in this case to its upper class only, the neat contrasted picture Sten-

---

31 In his review of Montigny's *Le Provincial à Paris ou esquisse des moeurs parisiennes*, Stendhal attributes this caution, a new trait in his view, to the fear of losing one's government position (Stendhal 1983: 120).

32 "Nothing can be more absurd than the constant prudence which the French observe in trivial matters. It is this which precludes all chance of our ever being formidable rivals to you in the manufacturing and shipping interests." (1991a: 340).

dhal draws of the French and the British involves stereotypes that are not only questionable but also questioned by contradictory statements. The French, for instance, are said to be too reliant on authority on the one hand, but also to always try to break the law on the other: "French vanity always piques itself on doing that which is prohibited." (1991a: 340) They are said to be uninterested in work and business in one place, but mostly preoccupied by industrial and commercial ventures in another (1983: 166); to be joyful and gay by nature here, and overcautious and prudent there. They are characterized as happy-going grasshoppers in one review, and as "half-British" ants in another – as people who require "something of sterner stuff [than reckless frivolity] to move them" (74). The value judgment passed on these characteristics also varies from text to text. Fickleness and inconsistency are flaws in the passages quoted above, but qualities in the lines that follow: "This inconsistency of the French character, this want of accordance with itself, which is indispensable to be witty, and to avoid being dull and ridiculous, is precisely that which has ever made the French people the most lively and agreeable in the world." (1991a: 120). Last but not least, Stendhal criticizes his fellow citizens for relying too much on the government to earn a living and claims that it was not the case for him: "I never believed that society owed me anything. Helvetius spared me this giant nonsense. Society pays for the services it sees." (1982d: 878) Nonetheless, a few days after the July revolution, he was asking for a *préfet* position in the new administration and, already envisioning an appointment in Quimper, Finistère, even wrote an address to the population! (Berthier 2010: 349)

In the end, these contradictions reflect the complexities of Restoration France with its bizarre mix of revolved past in government and high society on the one hand, and of unknown future – industrialization and the emergence of the lower classes on the national scene – on the other. Stendhal's *Chroniques* reveal the difficulty of assigning stable characteristics to this evolving nation and of defining French identity in any precise way, particularly for a writer fraught with anxiety about the transformation he is witnessing. Stendhal understood the self as the product of a private history that it was difficult to uproot, but he also he chose to face these contractions. He felt most at ease in situations where he could be honest with himself and others, in social circles where real exchange occurred, like the *grenier* of Etienne-Jean Delécluze (1781–1863), or in the company of artists like Giuditta Pasta and her friends. Unlike famous contemporaries he despised, people who like Staël and Chateaubriand had distinguished themselves by raising social hypocrisy to an art in his eyes (1982a: 141), he refused to play the social games he knew were necessary for success and advancement: "'Ah! If only you were more industrious...' Destutt de Tracy told him, but he found it too boring to have to call on important people night after night, to wear silk stockings and waste nearly an hour each time in their waiting rooms" (Berthier 2010: 210). He would have liked to see his merits acknowledged and his services rewarded, Berthier adds, without having to tout them in society. He knew that "merit is nothing without the art of showcasing it" (210), but he could not bring himself to follow the rules of polite society. In fact, his natural ways, and in particular his inability to hold his tongue, shocked even his friends in Destutt de Tracy's salon, where he went every Sunday for ten years because he liked hosts and guests (La Fayette, Ari Scheffer, Augustin Thierry, Victor Jacquemont). Berthier (365) provides a good example of the kind of faux pas he was capable of: when he was appointed Consul in Italy, Mérimée had to remind him not to talk about religion with his new boss the ambassador, since he was a devout Catholic, and above all, not to use his miniature guillotine to cut his sugar cubes in front of him!

Stendhal felt reasonably confident that the Bourbon monarchy would not succeed in erasing the legacy of the revolutionary era, in returning France to the Old Regime, given the French people's distrust of church and the nobility: "Aristocracy is much more likely to gain ground at New York and at Boston than in Paris" (1988: 246), he declared. On the positive side, the Parisian schools continued to offer an outstanding scientific education. The increased freedom the French enjoyed during the Restoration had worked against the monarchy's best interest and served the liberal opposition more than the Royalists. The Restoration, or more precisely "the fall of Napoleon" had been favorable "to the progress of liberty, or rather to the birth of liberal sentiments, which now enjoy the immense advantage of being in fashion with our young men" (1988: 130). On the negative side, the Restoration monarchy certainly delayed the completion of the transformative project started in 1789. The gap between the government and the people was a corrosive force. It bred immorality and hypocrisy in the generation of young people who were coming of age in Restoration France and not only in Catholics seminars. The students were free-thinkers in Paris, but once they returned to their province as lawyers, physicians, or engineers, it was a different story. They had to hide their thoughts and feelings, to act hypocritically, particularly in towns where "the party who wish to establish theocratic government in France" was powerful, which was the case in southern, more than in northern France (1985: 285). Sooner or later, these young professionals would give up the beliefs of their youth, especially if they were ambitious (285). Time was also of the essence: how long would the regime last? Would nobles and priests continue to strengthen their power, or would the government be overthrown?: "No one can say whether ten years hence we shall be ruled by a despot, or led by the priests [...], or whether our king will merely possess the power of a President of the United States." (1991b: 96) The educated provincial elite could certainly not be counted on to start a revolution, but they would applaud to a change of regime given their preference for a constitutional monarchy *à l'anglaise* – minus church and aristocracy (1988: 300). Should Charles X, his heirs, and an increasingly corrupt ruling class stay in power, would the French people's attitude toward religion change? Who could predict "the result of the moral experiments" that had been made "on the religion of the French since 1815?" (1983: 66).

For all the reasons mentioned above, Stendhal thought that the French Revolution started in 1789 was far from over in the 1820s. He sometimes wondered whether the Restoration regime would last and for how long, but the prospect that a revolution might put an end to it, which, as we saw he considered, did not seem bright. The July Revolution of 1830 was therefore as happy a surprise as could be (Berthier 2010: 348). Like his friend Delacroix, Stendhal was overjoyed to see the tricolor float over France again. He praised La Fayette's courage and admired the heroism of the plebs – *la canaille:* "After fifteen years of glaciation, something great had finally occurred: the splendors of history were revived" (Berthier 2010: 349). More pragmatically, Stendhal thought that the new government might want to appoint him to an administrative position and since his old acquaintance François Guizot (1787–1874) was now Minister of the Interior – he would resign a few months later – he wasted no time paying him a visit. Although, as we saw, he would have preferred to become a *préfet* somewhere in France, he was appointed Consul of France in Triest, Italy, in September 1830, then, in March 1831, demoted, with the same title but a considerable pay cut, and sent to a small town in the neighborhood of Rome, Civitavecchia. Berthier (364) writes that "Stendhal was convinced that Guizot and his friends at the *Globe* (the 'globules') were more or less hostile to him and had acted against him, taking a shabby revenge for having made light of them" in his pamphlet *Of a new Plot against Industrialists* [*D'un nouveau complot contre les industriels*]. Perhaps, he had indeed mocked his former liberal friends too much.

4.2 Identity nationalization as inescapable universal process

As early as 1810, Berthier (2010: 423) tells us, Stendhal would have liked to explore the French provinces "to study the national character in all its facets." *The Red and the Black*, published in 1830, played on the opposition between the province, in this case Franche-Comté, depicted mostly in book I, and Paris, in book II. Stendhal's ambition, however, was not limited to his native province, and nearly three decades after he first had this idea, he finally realized his project. The three volumes of *Memoirs of a Tourist* (1838)[33] recount a voyage through France that lasted from 10 April 1837 to February 1838; or even 22 July 1838, since *Travels in the South of France* [*Voyage dans le Midi de la France*], from 8 March to 22 July 1838, actually recalls the continuation of these peregrinations.[34] The first volume of the *Memoirs* covers Stendhal's trip from Paris to Bourbonnais, Burgundy, Lyonnais, Provence, and Touraine;[35] the second Brittany, Normandy, and, following a stop-over in Paris, Provence in August;[36] the third, Dauphiné, Savoie, Lyonnais, Provence, Languedoc, Roussillon, and Gascony.[37] *Travels in the South of France* (1839) starts in Poitou-Charentes and continues South to Aquitaine, Languedoc, Roussillon, and Provence.[38]

In literary criticism, *Memoirs of a Tourist* was initially seen through the prism of the Paris-Province dichotomy and presented as evidence, by Victor Del Litto (1978) for instance, of the poor opinion Stendhal allegedly had of the French provinces. But this view has been increasingly challenged if only to point out, as Yves Ansel does (2000: 132), that the French capital is far from being cast as an ideal place in Stendhal's works, and in this one in particular. Anthony Zielonka similarly argues that even in *Lucien Leuwen*, where the province of Lorraine is described in unflattering terms, "the preference for Paris is never unequivocal" (1983: 50). Contrary to Del Litto, Cécile Meynard (2005: 12–13) believes that the province, not Paris, is seen as representative of France by Stendhal in *Memoirs of a Tourist*. In *Chronicles for England* already, Stendhal had noted the Parisians' contempt for the rest of France. Weighing the pros and cons of this bias, he had concluded that it was justified to the extent that talent was concentrated in Paris, and unjustified, to the extent that the Parisians' sense of superiority was really inflated (Stendhal 1991b: 73). Hundred and fifty years

---

33 Henri Martineau's 1929 edition of *Mémoires d'un touriste* in three volumes is used here. The only translation available in English is a "cut version" of the work (Stendhal 1962). It is used whenever possible, otherwise references are to the French edition and translations mine.
34 Quotes are from Abbott's 1970 translation.
35 It covers the period of 10 April to 23 June 1837 and the following cities: Verrières, Sceaux, Fontainebleau, Montargis, Nevers, Moulins, Autun, Chaumont, Langres, Beaune, Dijon, Chalon-sur Saône, Lyon, Vienne, Valence, Montélimar, Avignon, Nivernais, Bourges,Tours.
36 From 25 June 1 to September 1837, he explored the cities of Nantes, Vannes, Lorient, Hennebon, Ploërmel, Rennes, Saint-Malo, Granville, Paris, Tarascon, Nîmes, Grenoble, Vizille, Briancon, Grenoble.
37 In September 1837, the tourist visited: Chambéry, Aix-les-Bains, Genève, Lyon, Avignon, Marseille, Gênes, Toulon, Marseille, Nîmes, Montpellier, Béziers, Perpignan, Bordeaux.
38 From 8 March to 22 July 1838, Stendhal visited the cities of Angoulême, Bordeaux, Toulouse, Agen, Bordeaux, Bayonne, Pau, Tarbes, Auch, Toulouse, Carcasonne, Narbonne, Montpellier, Marseille, Toulon, Grasse, Cannes, Marseille, Valence.

later, another *provincial*, Bourdieu, noted in the preface of *Distinction*, the resilience of the phenomenon identified by Stendhal, namely "the persistence [...] of the aristocratic model of 'court behavior,' personified by [the] Parisian *haute bourgeoisie* [...]" (1984: xi). In *Memoirs of a Tourist* Stendhal twisted the stick in the other direction by almost completely neglecting the capital city and centering his "monologue on French identity" (Crouzet 1978: 36) exclusively on the rest of France.

4.2.1 On becoming 'British'

The narrator of *Memoirs of a Tourist* tells his readers that he writes to document the rapid change he sees occurring in France in the late 1830s: "It is because France is changing fast that I dared write it." (1929: I, 305) The process of change described and criticized by Stendhal in this work, is the instauration of the regime of oneness characteristic of modern national identities. The target of his critique of modern France is this process of identity standardization, of modern national identity, described by Calhoun in *Nationalism* when he argues that to live under the national regime means living under the regime of oneness, one nation, one language, one race, one gender. A brief dialog on the title page of the first volume of *Memoirs of a Tourist* attests to the significance of the issue of identity leveling in this work: " – We're turning British; – and we steal; – and we're getting dumber." This statement is echoed hundreds of pages later in the following remark: "In France, we're turning British and ours sons will have even less fun than us" (1929: III, 87). Although 's'angliser' refers to a process of identity change that affects the French, this process applies to all individuals who live in democratic or semi-democratic states. Through the verb 's'angliser,' the narrator simply recalls that the British were the first to experience liberty and identity leveling as well as to invent tourism, the Grand Tour, as a cure to the boredom this sameness produces. Although a negative light is shed on this process – 's'angliser' sounds like 's'enliser,' to get bogged down – although England is "an unpleasant country" – the tourist is not a nationalist. Instead of proclaiming France's superiority, he predicts nationalism's disappearance by mid-century: "People will say things like this in 1850: The French and the British nations [are] united by deep esteem for each other (national hatred having found refuge among the idiots of both nations)." (1929: I, 271) This is quite an insight considering that from the July Monarchy onward England and France finally ceased to be hereditary enemies on the battlefield and have fought all their wars on the same side ever since.

The tourist is not a scientist. The issue of methodology – on the basis of which criteria should change be assessed? – comes as an afterthought in the *Memoirs*. It is addressed a few hundred pages into the work, in a passage that deals with the various branches of the science of man. The tourist reports on the classification of human races established by Amédée Thierry (1797–1873) and William Edwards (1777–1843),[39] the brother of Stendhal's friend Edouard. Both thought that three human races could be found in France, Gaël, Kimri, and Ibère, an hypothesis the tourist is willing to test. This race theory is presented as an amusing topic of conversation at the end of a dinner party in Lyon while the guests enjoy "eight or ten different kinds of Burgundy wine" (1929: I, 210). The tourist also tells us that it is a useful therapy against *"haine impuissante:"* instead of being angry at someone and focusing on your anger, you center your attention on that person's physique in an effort to determine whether he is a Kimri, Gaël, or Ibère (1929: II, 137–138). As if the contexts in which this new science is discussed did not provide sufficient indication of the tourist's doubts in it, the narrator makes his position clear. He finds this new science a bit obscure: "As soon as you throw yourself into the study of races light disappears; you feel you're in a dark place. Nothing is worse, in my mind, than lack of *clarté* [brightness and clarity]." (138) Besides, his common sense – based on dog cross-breeding! – tells him that his chances of finding pure representatives of these races are limited, an intuition confirmed through field work: the pure samples of the Gaël race the tourist thought he had identified in Brittany turned out to be from the Alps! Concluding to the ineluctable racial and ethnic metissage of his country, Stendhal dismisses racial anthropology long before its official birth in the 1850s, the heyday of Arthur de Gobineau (1816) and Paul Broca (1824–1880).

The tourist divides France in two along an East-West line that goes from Dijon to Nantes, a division that may seem arbitrary with regard to geography, but not to his own sense of history. It marks the current border of civilization, understood as the area where political and economic change has already occurred; it separates an already Anglicized Northern France, deemed uninteresting and therefore excluded from the travel narrative, from the Southern provincial France described in the *Memoirs*. According to Le Bras and Todd (1981: 269) a very similar East-West line was already used in the 1820s to separate literate France in the North, from illiterate France in the South. Located in the North, "Paris is a republic," a statement that implies that the South is not (1929: I, 123). But apart from this accepted division of France in two, the tourist adopts

---

39 On Thierry's and Edwards's race theories see Venayre (2013: 55–62; 251–262).

Stendhal's methodology, as laid out by Berthier (2010: 249): he "claims the enduring right to say accurate, even profound things, while dressing them up in irony, humor, even bad temper, and in a sprightly tempo, without wearing the heavy clogs of the 'specialists' who want to be taken seriously."

In the introduction of *Memoirs of a Tourist*, the narrator describes himself as a Northerner, a Parisian, writing for other Northerners, and a business man, a *marchand de fer*, an iron salesman, traveling through France for his job. Through the nature of the tourist's business, Stendhal indirectly refers to the legislatives debates on the development of the railroad system [*chemin de fer*] in France at a time when the question of their public or private financing was being decided. Jaume (1997: 7–8) mentions and discusses a speech Alphonse de Lamartine (1790–1868) gave at the Chamber of Deputies on 10 May 1838 in which the republican poet denounced the "sixty or eighty iron manufacturers who bully the country with impunity" and expressed his opposition to the railroad's privatization.[40] If, seen in that light, the tourist objectively appears to be one of those "bullies," he is actually a 'slave' to his father-in-law, the laziest of men, who owns the business, lets him do the work and pockets "two thirds of the profit" (1929: I, 11). Mr. L, the name given to the tourist in the foreword (1), or Philippe, as his father-in-law calls him (13), is a "victim of work" (4), an indecisive man pushed around by relatives he admits to not loving, although this lack of affection causes him remorse; a man to whom things happen more than he makes them happen. At age thirty-three, including twelve years in the iron business, he is wealthy but he made a fortune "without realizing it" (1929: I, 114).

Stendhal, or H.B., who intervenes as editor in the foreword, tells his protagonist's life story several times, at length in the introduction, including in a note that reads like a balance sheet,[41] and in shorter form later on in the work. Mr. L received a good education but his intense studies of classical languages and mathematics robbed him of his childhood (1962: 5). At age sixteen, he got a job as a Customs officer thanks to his father's connections and he worked very hard, "ten to twelve hours a day" (6), until he was overheard singing a song by the liberal songwriter Béranger one day (1929: I, 114) and banished to Martinique as the result of this seditious activity. As a "victim of the Jesuits," he was welcomed by everyone on the tropical island and enjoyed living there

---

40 "Private companies will create aristocratic railroads that will exclude the people; the State will make you democratic railroads where everyone will travel at everyone's expense." (Lamartine quoted in Jaume 1997: 9) Stendhal thought the same way (1929a: 291).

41 "Left for the colonies at age 19; 6 years in the colonies; 6 years of married life; 2 years as a widower. Total 33 years." (1929a: 14).

a great deal (114). Unfortunately, the climate did not agree with him, he got sick, went back to France, where he arrived already healed. He was ready to go back to Martinique when his father decided to marry him to the daughter of a business associate. He got married, behaved as a good husband, but found little joy in marriage. When his wife passed away, he mourned her death but realized a few months later that he "was much happier alone" (12): "I was so ashamed after this discovery that I became a louse for the first time. I turned into a hypocrite" (1962: 12). He thought of going to back to Martinique at that point but decided to postpone his project after being told by a friend that he "would be a monster if [he] abandoned this unhappy father in grief" (12). Although aware that his father-in-law "had not felt any sorrow whatever at the loss of his daughter" (12) and that he only "began to love [him] with passion" (11) when faced with the prospect of losing the man he depended on for his income, Philippe continued to work to avoid public infamy. He hoped, however, to be able to go back to Martinique in the long run, and this time not to make a living, but to enjoy life (1929: I, 114). Condemned by society to play the part of a hypocrite, like everyone else around him, conscious that his good reputation hinges on his ability to continue to hide his real thoughts (16), Mr. L views and uses writing as a way of telling the truth (15). The editor of his travel narrative, in fact, apologizes to the reader: the author's "shortcoming," he writes, "is to call a few too many things by their right names" (1962: 3). The author himself worries about the reception of his work for the same reason: "I realize that, unfortunately, I shall be sharply criticized and all because of the same vice: my absurd love of truth, a trait that makes me so many enemies" (1970: 177).

These biographical indications – in particular the loveless relationship to a father who left him "some small parcels of land worth one hundred fifty thousand francs, encumbered with eighty thousand francs debt" (1962: 15), or the forced exile due to liberal sentiment – support Béatrice Didier's claim (1988: 86–87) that the fictive "I" of the *Memoirs* is for a large part Stendhal himself.[42] Besides, references to Stendhal's life sometimes slip into the tourist's narration. In Toulouse, a young Spanish girl looks like "Pepita, Gina Pietragrua's sister," his former lover (1970: 68); in Pau, the eyes of a young Béarnaise remind him of those of "Archchancelor Cambacérès who, for Monsieur Daru's sake, was so kind to me." (1970: 138) But the merit of the traveling salesman's fiction is to combine two positions that would seem incompatible, that of the advocate of po-

---

42 Thierry Gouin (1999: 30) writes that the fiction of the traveling statesman is absent in *Travels in the South of France* but a note indicates that "the author is 35 years old, travels for business, and is an iron salesman." (1930: 1)

litical and economical change, and that of the critic of that change. This seemingly contradictory stand signals the narrator's and the author's overall support of change, seen as irreversible, but at the same time the need for a position from which to monitor its effects. Mr. L describes himself as a full and successfully participant in the modern economy, as someone who loves money (1929: I, 14), but at the same time, narrator and author are literally "in irons" [*dans les fers*] as participants in, and as advocates of, the new economic and political system, and metaphorically, as prisoners and as critics of that system. The salesman is aware of the paradox of his condition since he attributes his success in his job to the fact that he hates it: "Since I do not care for commerce in general, and iron trade in particular, I always behave with perfect self-control." (14)

The tourist seems to be a Liberal – since he was demoted for singing a song by Béranger – and even of a Jacobin, since the current constitutional monarchy, he claims, is the political outcome of the French Revolution: "What is there to change to our constitution? Since 1830, we are finally enjoying the reforms put in place by Mirabeau, Carnot and the other great men of 1792" (1929: I, 321). He expresses admiration for "the growing prosperity France is enjoying under Louis-Philippe" (320) on the basis of personal observations in the area of economic development and praises "the king's wisdom and the current administration" (1929: III, 287) for its handling of the popular riots in Paris in 1830 and in Lyon in 1831 and 1834. But these comments, of course, are to be taken with a grain of salt. The tourist's mention of the workers' plight, the fact "that they have been starving for six months (from November 1836 to July 1837)" (287), belies the rosy picture of the economic situation he initially paints. Similarly, his comments on the workers's politization and radicalization, due to the government's inaction and failure to address the problem, contradict his congratulatory remarks. Stendhal, in fact, had offered a much less flattering and more honest appraisal of political life during the July Monarchy in *Lucien Leuwen* a few years earlier and it is clear that, in his eyes, the current regime left much to be desired. The moral and religious character of the 1833 Guizot law on public instruction, for instance, could not have pleased him since it went against his own educational principles. The goal of this law was not to teach students how to learn, or to develop their own judgment, but to be the passive recipients of values the State wanted them to have.

The tourist takes the opposite road as these passive students. He develops his views on France on the basis of his observations. What does this self-described modern Frenchman tell us about the national habitus in *Memoirs of a Tourist?* First that material well-being plays a considerable role in it. An advocate of material progress, the narrator is so deeply attached to his comfort that it even shapes his aesthetics, his conception of architecture in particular. A real town has to have a sheltered walkway, a portico, for instance (1929: III, 16). Physical comfort is a must. The capital rule in architecture is not beauty, but functionality. Importing architectural styles from other regions is therefore viewed as an error for that very reason: "Since the death of the Gothic, French architects have never had the genius to invent a church adapted to France." (1962: 232) Second, that the modern national is an urban creature. Going against the grain – each French province is usually viewed as a distinct and separate rural entity at the time – the tourist emphasizes the urban character of provincial France, comparing theaters, town halls, and other public buildings in cities like Nantes, Tours, Bordeaux, Lyon, Marseille, Toulouse, and many others. Furthermore, what interests him in these cities is not what tourists are supposed to be interested in, namely the relics of the past. In fact, he only visits museums and churches "under protest" (1929: III, 197) and when he does, in Marseille for instance, he apologizes to his readers for having "against his firm resolve [...] written at some length about this museum" (1970: 211). Instead, the purpose of the *Memoirs* is to assess change, or more specifically how provincial towns compare to Paris in terms of civilization, whereby civilization is understood in strikingly materialist terms as the ability to make people feel good physically: "You may say what you please; but when you want to be materially comfortable, you must must not leave the boulevards [town center]!" (1970: 181)

Each city is put to the test through the tourist's ritual visit to cafés, town squares, and theaters. The assessor is a consumer who rates the quality of service – is it prompt and courteous? – the quality of the product – do they serve good tea, good coffee? – and sometimes even the quality of the ingredients. Thus several passages are devoted to water quality, found better in Toulouse than Bordeaux (1970: 67); hot enough to make tea in Marseille (1970: 197) but definitely not in Tours (1929: I, 426). A few towns are deemed unworthy of the test. In those cases, the narrator brings and makes his own tea – for like a real Englishman, our tourist drinks more often tea than coffee. To show that he really means to rate civilization in terms of consumer satisfaction, and to preempt the reader's temptation to take these observations as tongue and cheek, the narrator confirms that it is indeed his intent: "The reader will perhaps have noticed my habit of measuring the degree of civilization by the degree of hot I am served. My answer is that I believe only what I see and these little details are very important." (1970: 197–198) Although mentioned on two occasions only, another kind of information which is deemed important and "will be valuable in 1880" (1970: 77) is the price paid for transportation, meals, lodging, coffee, museum catalogues, and even tips to guides.

The *Memoirs* are sprinkled with comments on weather conditions that often bear on the tourist's reactions to the cities he visits. The "first whiffs of soft spring air" in mid-March (1970: 19) put him in a good mood and may encourage him to declare that "Bordeaux is unquestionably the most beautiful city in France" (8); but after feeling sick from "the cold and damp in Pau" (139) he decides "to go to Marseille in search of warmth." (140) Hygiene, size and comfort of accomodations, lighting, hospitality, quality and efficiency of service are the criteria used to rate hotels and inns. Speed, comfort, and company are deemed what matters most when traveling by horse carriage, steamboat, or train. As far as physical comfort goes, the Tilbury is the tourist's preferred means of transportation (1930: note 298). Traveling by stagecoach is a messy business because it takes time to unload and to collect one's luggage, but it is more suited to the tourist's project of getting to know provincials because it offers "the sight of humanity along the road" (1970: 171). All these details underscore the narrator's expectation of material comfort. Utilitarianism, materialism, consumerism thus already function in *Memoirs of a Tourist* as principles of vision – what art and civilization should be – and division – between the civilized and uncivilized world. An integral part of the economist vision of the world, these new modes of thought are those one would expect of a traveling salesman whose avowed goal is the pursuit of money, the accumulation of the financial capital necessary to live as a *rentier* in Martinique, but as mentioned earlier, they are also Stendhal's.

Before these new principles are ascribed directly to the new 'Anglicized' national habitus, the issue of social class must be addressed. To what extent are the narrator's tastes also shaped by his position in the social field? One notes, for instance, that these tastes are frequently and forcefully expressed as distastes, as *dégoûts*, that is, as tastes radically different from those of the provincials, but more specifically, those of the lower classes. The stench of the Marseille harbor (1929: III, 149); the funny "smell" in Saint-Servin church in Toulouse; the malodor of burnt fat in a Bordeaux hotel (1970: 59), or of garlic on the breath of his fellow travelers in Southern France (1970: 52) clearly bother the tourist more than they do the locals. Filth disgusts him: the border station between France and Savoy is a "disgusting hovel [*taudis infâme*] on the French side, and very comfortable, even heated in the winter, in Savoy (1929: III, 23). Our tourist is sensitive to bad lighting, to the "sadness of the small lanters on the wall" at the carriage stop in Orthez, near Montpellier; or in Bordeaux to the unpleasantness of dining in a "low-ceilinged room" that is "so dark, without any light whatsoever, that there can be no gloomier room even in Geneva!" (5). Similarly, sharp sounds, like the voices of "those hideous women who hawk fish on the streets of Paris" (44) are experienced as highly unpleasant. More generally, he is stunned by the "incredible vulgarity and filth of the common people"

(1970: 59), not only in Toulouse but also in "all these towns of the interior of France: the same rudeness, the same barbarous service" (172).

The narrator is thus filled with disgust and contempt for the coarseness of the *classes montantes*, a *grossièreté* also defined as a form of ego-centrism combined with as an obsession for material possessions. Those he remembers particularly well were his traveling companions between Dol and Saint-Malo, "rich, or rather newly rich bourgeois [who] talked endlessly about themselves and their possessions; their wives, their children, their handkerchiefs" and, who, because "the provincial's distinctive sign is that everything he has the honor of owning takes on the mark of excellence," bragged about their belongings the entire trip on end. (1929: II, 183) At one point, their insipid conversation and their bad manners irritated him so much that he exclaimed: "I had never seen the human species in such an ugly light before: these people overcame their baseness just about as much as pig wallowing in muck. Will it become necessary to court people of that sort to get elected to the House of Representatives? Are they kings in America?" (183) Not only does he compare them to "pigs wallowing in muck," but he also expresses his feelings towards them in strikingly violent terms: "I would have spent two weeks in prison to be able to give each of them a good thrashing" (184). This is a vivid illustration of the social resentment the narrator calls *haine impuissante*, the contained anger towards people perceived as socially distant. As if the image of the feudal lord administering corporal punishment to his subjects insufficiently impressed upon the reader the aristocratic nature of his own habitus, the tourist imagines how pleasant his trip would have been had he been traveling with a group of *légitimistes*, his political opponents, instead: "Their principles could not have been more absurd and more hostile to the *common good* but far from being hurt all the time, my mind would have enjoyed the charms of polite conversation" (184). One notes that these fellow travelers are not the poorest of the poor: we learn that they pay enough taxes to be eligible to vote under the restrictive election system of the July Monarchy when the tourist hears them "stupidly praising liberty" (184). Why is their understanding of liberty deemed "stupid"? Because it is based on a narrow sense of self-interest: they only vote for representatives who defend their own, personal interests. This conversation gives nonetheless the tourist an opportunity to define liberty in a more generous way when he proclaims his political allegiance to these "animals" in spite of his social affinity with the aristocratic elite: "Here, then are the people for whose happiness I believe we must do all we can" (184).[43]

---

43 Berthier mentions an earlier instance of Stendhal's ambiguous attitude towards the people:

As these comments illustrate, the aristocratic habitus is shaped by repression, by thought and body control. Polite, civilized, social intercourse requires a great deal of self-discipline on the part of the participants, and in particular the ability to keep at bay language and manners that would threaten the charmed illusion of commonality. But the narrator also justifies behavior control for pragmatic reasons: if you are afraid, for instance, it is best not to express your fear, as the Marseillais do, thereby increasing it (1929: III, 211). The narrator's approval and justification of these various forms of self-control seems to contradict his critique of Anglicization, understood as a standardization of identity that goes against *le naturel*, the spontaneous, unaffected and uninhibited forms of social behavior observed and admired among Southerners. The contradiction is nonetheless only apparent since it disappears once social class is taken into account: "Let's not forget however [...] that in places where *le naturel* is the rule if a gentleman (*homme d'esprit*) is more pleasant, an idiot (*sot*) is a hundred times more unbearable than anywhere else" (1929: II, 211). The case made on behalf of *le naturel* and against Anglicization in other words does not apply to all indiscriminately. Implicit in the Stendhalian critique of Anglicization is the notion that conformity to the dominant rules of social behavior is a good thing for most people, and a bad thing for the happy few only. Exception to the rule is claimed for the *homme d'esprit*.

Stendhal was keenly aware of his own ambivalence towards the world he was describing. He despised the old aristocratic ways but had aristocratic tastes himself. Thus in *The Life of Henry Brulard*, he wrote that he "loathe[d] the mob (to have any dealings with it), while at the same time [...] passionately desir[ing] their happiness as a *people* [...] (Stendhal 2002: 116). A little further in his autobiography, he confessed that he "would do anything to make the people happy, but [...] rather [...] spend fifteen days of each month in prison than live with the inhabitants of shops." (277) He was both a *républicain forcené* in theory and a dilettante in practice. At the same time, he understood that his "aristocratic taste" was not entirely a matter of personal preference but something ingrained in him since childhood that escaped his control, as he explained: "For it has to be admitted, although my opinions were then thoroughly and fundamentally republican, my relatives had passed on to me in their entirety their aloof and aristocratic tastes. This defect has remained with me [...]." (161)

---

on the one hand, eleven-year old Henri Beyle was so interested in revolutionary politics that he went to a meeting of the Jacobin society in Grenoble; but on the other hand, he found "these people he would have liked to love terribly vulgar" (quoted in Berthier 2010: 62–63).

One notes that Stendhal's critique of Anglicization is first expressed indirectly through the tourist's desire to leave Paris and France, a desire linked to his awareness of the complexities of modern social interaction: "Paris is a bit too complicated for me; I like to wear a straw hat and a nankeen jacket when I call on people" (1929: I, 114–15). If the project of flight to the colonies and the journey through France are thus cast as attempts to escape the demands of Parisian social life, the travel experience, and in particular the direct encounter with ways of life perceived as different, brings to light the Parisian social doxa, the unspoken social rules that govern the Parisian habitus. Anglicization, the narrowing of the range of allowed social behaviors the narrator observes and criticizes, is directly linked to political change in the *Memoirs*. But it is a term wide enough to also mean "Americanization."

4.2.2 Obstacles to real democracy

Memoirs of a Tourist appeared in 1838, three years after Tocqueville published the first volume of *Democracy in America* – the second volume on American society came out in 1840 only. In comments related to education in Paris, which is deemed excellent because it is "philosophical and devoid of any falseness," the tourist nonetheless criticizes students for their bad readings habits: they read "modern nonsense to be able to make conversation about every book when it comes out" but they "don't read the best books seriously: Bayle, Montesquieu, Tocqueville" (1962: 46). Stendhal had apparently read Tocqueville seriously and meditated on his sentence: "I know of no country where, in general, less independence of mind and genuine freedom of discussion reign than in America." (2000: 244) Not only did Stendhal agree with this evaluation of American democracy, he also used Tocqueville's approach to measure democratization in France. He watched for signs of the tyranny of the majority, commented on its negative impact on French public opinion, just as Tocqueville had done for America.

Assimilating constitutional monarchy and democracy, the narrator argues that the rights granted to citizens in a democracy have as their counterpart limitations imposed on individual freedom, which he bemoans in spite of his support of democracy:

> But the republican government, at it grants citizens many rights, is also forced to impose a number of obligations on them that would greatly bother me. So as to avoid disappointment, it must be clearly understood that the rights of the republic cannot exist without a great number of restrictions on individual liberties. In the United-States, I can name the king, the police commissioner, the street sweeper: but walking *too fast on Sunday* will

bring shame on me; it will be assumed that I am enjoying a walk instead of going to church. (1929: III, 162–63)

Stendhal's main target of criticism is the majority rule, the need to gain approval from the greater number. Pleasing as many people as possible has become the norm, not only in the political sphere, but also in all areas of daily life. For the narrator, social life is not ruled by reason in a democracy, but by the fear of displeasing, of doing "anything that might rub the shopkeepers on my street the wrong way" (1929: III, 162–63). Courting public opinion is not an option but an obligation in modern politics: "We are already like America here, obliged to pay court to the most unreasonable part of the population." (1962: 41) This state of affairs is bad for business and it is bad for the truth (1929: I, 290–91). The moral decline recorded on the cover of the *Memoirs* – "And we steal" – finds a concrete expression in electoral politics where the desire to win leads to fraud and corruption, to the purchase of votes through honors and privileges (1929: III, 316). Electoral fraud is a bad thing in itself but it also leads to the people's disaffection with democracy (120–21). Stendhal best described the terribly corrupt world of electoral politics in *Lucien Leuwen*, a devastating critique of the July Monarchy's politics of *juste milieu* and of its corrupt government – the King himself practices insider trading! The novel testifies to the writer's profound disillusion with the outcome of the Revolution of 1830 and offers an honest critique that mitigates the praise of the regime expressed, if only mockingly, in *Memoirs of a Tourist*. Commenting on the political meaning of the novel, Michel Crouzet describes (1983: 107) Lucien's initiation to politics as an initiation to "evil." Set under the reign of Louis-Philippe, who is characterized as "the greatest royal scoundrel" [*le plus fripon des kings*], the novel is for Crouzet a reflection of Stendhal's negative opinion on politics and on money's influence on political life (Crouzet 1983: 103): "As the tourist claims, 'political ideas are almost as despicable as money interests.'" (57)

A side-effect of the necessity to appeal to the largest number is the self-imposed censorship of personal opinion. The willing suppression of free personal thought can be observed in the case of elected representatives whose best interest is "to conform to a certain rule" (1929: III, 205) instead of developing and defending reasonable personal opinions. But it is evidenced elsewhere, and indeed throughout society, in the tendency to adopt available models of thought and conduct as one's own and in the irresistible appeal of ready-made opinions. Far from being restricted to politicians, the tyranny of public opinion has become the rule in Paris as much as in New York. "Journalism is excellent. It is necessary to political interests" (1962: 26), but the press also plays a significant role in the standardization of opinion and identities. Newspapers, the narrator insists, are useful and necessary for the conduct of political affairs and as a means of political education, but these important functions are undermined not only by the fact that the press tends to serve the interests of those who own it, but also, and more fundamentally so perhaps, by its role as the main manufacturer of public opinion (1929: III, 266–267). By providing ready-made opinions, the press feeds the inability to think for oneself:

> One of great misfortunes of Paris, one the great misfortunes of civilization, one of the most serious obstacles to the increase of happiness among men is the *uniformity of opinion*. This uniformity has advantages only on the political side. It harms the arts and letters [....]. In towns not subject to journalism, Milan, for instance, everyone goes to see the picture before reading the article about it, and the journalist had better take care not to be ridiculous when he writes about a picture on which everyone has an opinion. (1962: 26–27)

In Paris and other big cities by contrast, the press is subject to "a gloomy compulsion toward *phoniness* [*charlatanisme*], [...] *the one and only religion of the nineteenth century*" (1962: 27). Paradoxically, the narrator observes, information, now widely available through print matter of all kinds, contributes to intellectual laziness. This Frenchman who speaks to him badly about Calvin is just repeating what he has read in Michaud's biography, whose forty volumes he carries along with him everywhere (1929: III, 80).[44] This new habit of adopting other people's opinions instead of developing your own has deplorable consequences in politics and is absolutely disastrous in the arts. The law of unintended consequences is at work here again: instead of contributing to the development of a healthy political life, institutional progress leads social conformism. Sameness is everywhere. Conformity to rules and models, rather than individual judgment or taste, defines the modern national habitus. The desire to be accepted by others, the compulsive need to fit, to gain approval, can be observed in all social classes in Paris: "It's a desire that is always on the heels of the bourgeois, the semi-bourgeois, and the worker in and around Paris [...]" (205). Conformism turns Parisians into victims of fashion and clones of each other, common people like the two old ladies who switch "from brandy to absinthe because it's in good taste" (211), as much as the social elite. The Parisian, the narrator comments, "if he belongs to good society, is always the same" (1929: I, 115).

In Marseille, or Bordeaux, the tourist notes, no one, not even the social elite understands these new codes of behavior: "The rich man in Marseille [...] is not even aware of the rule he is breaking; speaking out of turn in a salon doesn't

---

44 A first edition of Louis-Gabriel Michaud's *Biographie universelle ancienne et moderne* appeared from 1811 onward; a second edition was published in 1843.

make him blush at all" (1929: III, 207). It is therefore the Southerners' unselfconscious behavior – their *naturel* – that reveals the Parisians' "insidious hypocrisy" (1930: 11), "this obligatory artificial veneer that imparts a certain baseness and even nastiness to the Parisians' social customs" (1929: I, 41). Yet, for the Southerners seeking fortune in Paris, this unselfconscious behavior is also a recipe for failure: "The Marseillais is absolutely incapable of exercising the Parisian's first qualification to success in life: knowing how to be bored [...]." (1970: 196) In the capital, mastery of the new codes of social interaction is a necessary condition for success, even if it means doing nothing and suffering from boredom.

The narrator knows that to speak one's mind freely, to express one's opinions is frowned upon in Paris, which is why he usually chooses to remain silent: "I know well enough what I lack to be esteemed in Paris. Hence, I never talked when I had to do business, which is why I am seen as a man of remarkably few words." (1929: III, 281) He also views hypocrisy as a social necessity: "I learned [...] that one must [...] conceal, as though it were the most baneful advantage, any passion one might feel" (1970: 170). At the same time conformism has its price, the repression of enthusiasm, passion, spontaneity, and imagination: "This fine art has perhaps made me less awkward at times," the tourist confesses, "but it has robbed me of my charming travel reveries" (170). The same tension can be detected in other choices he makes. His love of material comfort, for instance, leads him to select "an admirable clean, English country inn kept by Monsieur Delhomme" (1970: 33) in Lesparre near Bordeaux, but the host and hostess are "gloomy" and offer "a sample of the 'gentlemanly' manner instead of the straightforward frankness" characteristic of Southern hospitality. The product of the social leveling the tourist observes everywhere is *ennui*, boredom: "It's inevitable: a general blandness is attached to all things modern; everything, it seems, pushes us further into boredom" (1929: III, 176). With social capital now key to success in Paris, knowing how to be bored has been elevated to an art: "Monsieur de Villèle once told one of his clerks that the quality a man in his position needed most was the ability to learn to be bored." (1970: 196)

The desire to conform also turns the modern national into a self-conscious and fearful creature. The Parisians, who live first and foremost in the eyes of others, are subject to all kinds of fears: fear of the unexpected (1929: I, 115); of being taken for a fool (117); of having personal opinions (1929: I, 40, 41; 1929: III, 281). What gets lost in the process is the "divine unexpected" [*le divin imprévu*] the narrator views as the primary source of beauty and love and as one of the greatest charms of life (1929: I, 107). In this dull and boring social environment where people look and act the same, it becomes more difficult to stand out. According to the narrator, the only thing a person asks of his neighbor "is to show that you regard him as the most important person in the world" (115). The desire to be acknowledged and "to be pictured as a highly-regarded man of wit in the mind of the public," leads to new mannerisms, body postures and tones of voice.[45] The tourist immediately recognizes this characteristic of the new habitus: a few people bother everyone else in a reading room in Marseille by conversing in an affected manner as if they were alone? They are British aristocrats who flaunt their superiority of rank by offending others (1930: 261). A young man in Toulon puts on airs and graces to let his merit transpire? That means that he is a Parisian for sure (289).[46] As indicated in chapter III, Staël maintained that the fear of being overlooked was a characteristic of the aristocratic habitus, but here Stendhal views it as a modern national trait. One way to reconcile these two positions is to consider that this trait belongs to the category of the "typically upper-class patterns [absorbed by] the middle and lower classes," (Elias 1996: 74) like dueling or the cult of ancestors.

The narrator is therefore fascinated by the absence of self-consciousness he observes among Southerners, a characteristic associated more specifically with the Spaniards, "the only people who dare do what they want without thinking of the audience" (1929: III, 304). This authenticity is a source of uniqueness and thus of beauty: if he loves the Spaniards, it is mostly because "they are no one else's copy" (304). This originality is rare in France, where "all nuances are disappearing in next to no time" (257), but the tourist encounters two specimen of it, one in Brittany in the presence of a young lady with a green hat whose perfect beauty mirrors her strength of character (1929: II, 37); and another in Normandy as he travels with a delightful woman, a fourty-year old farmer whose natural poise offers a stark contrast with the "Parisian dolls" he is used to (199). Assuming that beauty can only be found in these unexpected, magical encounters that take the breath away and produce surprised admiration on the part of the viewer, the process of identity leveling thus bodes ill for the arts.

According to Crouzet unity is the principle that presides over the formation of the nation in the account of its emergence laid out in *Memoirs of a Tourist:* "The Nation is constructed in a new coherence according to a principle of

---

45 There's an echo of Stendhal in George Sand's description of Tonine, a character in *The Black City:* "She is pretty enough, but her white hands and graceful airs don't make up for her narrow views and populist [*démocratique*] vanity, which is the worst sort." (Sand 2004b: 34)

46 George Sand builds Horace, the main character of the eponymous novel (1841), on that very character trait, the fear of being oneself, the necessity to copy: "Horace was *naturally affected.* Don't you know some people like that, who come into the world with borrowed personalities and manners, and who seem to be acting a part, even as they seriously play out the drama of their life? These people imitate themselves. [*Ce sont des gens qui se copient eux-mêmes*]." (Sand 1995b: 10)

unity, if not uniformity, grounded in an expectation of public interest." (1978: 54) Contrary to other writers who toured France in the 1830s and, as we will see in the next chapter, emphasized the singularity of each and every French province and the particularities of its inhabitants, Stendhal maintains that regional differences are disappearing fast, that "in fifty years, there may no longer be any Provencals or a Provencal language" (1929: III, 257). So are other identity markers. In the past, for instance, a person's clothing provided a sure clue of his trade and station. Today, people focus their efforts on erasing these clues, not only in clothing, but also in manners, and even in style, on merging into anonymity. A person is dressed appropriately if no one can remember what he wore (249). In short, far from being a Parisian prerogative, change affects all of France, not only in its political and economic dimension, but also at the social and individual level, in the way it shapes identities in the same mold. The tourist thereby underscores the paradox of democracy: political liberty reduces individual liberty because of the moral and social conformism it breeds.

The importance Stendhal grants to the military theme in *Memoirs of a Tourist* is of particular importance with regard to the issue of nation-building because it is "through the mediation of the army that a French man becomes a citizen" (Crouzet 1978: 55). To measure 'the degree of civilization,' as Stendhal does in that work, Crouzet argues (55), is thus to measure provincial men's "aptitude to serve as soldiers." It is worth noting, however, that in *Memoirs of a Tourist*, the French of the 1830s are often found lacking as soldiers. In Stendhal's eyes, class considerations, that were inexistent during the Revolution and the Empire, weakened the French army of July Monarchy. Once again, the military found itself plagued by an aristocratic lack of common sense deleterious to the accomplishment of great tasks. At a dinner in Toulon, for instance, officers departing for Algeria treat an old navy officer returning from the colony with "utter contempt" for misnaming a commanding officer. Feeling sorry for the latter, the narrator imagines what he should have said in self-defense, namely: why bother retaining the name of generals who have won no battles? (1930: 287–288). At the same time, the officers' aristocratic arrogance poses a real problem. By zeroing in on an irrelevant detail – the name of a general who has done nothing memorable – they miss out on important lessons they could have learned from a navy officer with a great deal of field experience, had their judgment not been clouded by bias: how to position a camp away from marshes and thus avoid deadly diseases that plague the colony's troops, for instance (1930: 288). Crouzet's observation on the role Stendhal attributes to the military in the formation of the nation is well-taken: the writer's critique of the July Monarchy's army only serves to underscore his ideal of the citizen-soldier in *Memoirs of a Tourist*. As the critic points out, Stendhal's topology of France is based on each province's patriotism in

1814–15: did they rejoice or not over the monarchy's return? (Crouzet 1978: 56) Furthermore, his "martial mania" also testifies to his concern for national defense. The undisciplined, unmilitary behavior of "several hundred soldiers wearing red trousers, marching in twos, threes, and fours, or resting stretched out under the trees" he saw on the road from Paris to Essones made him "angry" (Stendhal 1962: 21). Watching a parade in Marseille, he worried that "[t]he colonels are getting too fat to wage war" and wondered if "a man who has passed forty-five [can] wage war" (1970: 149). In Montpellier, he "spent two hours" observing "full-scale maneuvers in honor of May Day" and found that "the officers were well trained; but the poor soldiers were slack, timid and averse to moving" (1970: 173). He understands, Crouzet argues, that the nation's existence is premised "on the defeat of centrifugal energies and local disorganization" (Crouzet 1978: 56). If the soldiers the narrator observes in Toulouse (1929: I, 64) have a self-assurance that is presented as essentially French, it is also true that the tourist's admiration for the military originates more generally in the power and pride the status of citizen confers on those who are willing to die for their nation.

Far from being restricted to the French, this kind of nationalism applies to modern soldiers everywhere. In Nantes, for instance, the narrator meets with an American from Louisiana, M. Jam, who, as a seventeen-year old, took part in the battle of New Orleans against Great Britain in 1815 and whose account of the American victory over a British army twice as strong shows that faith in the nation gives the modern citizen-soldier "herculean" forces (1929: II, 46). Interestingly, the United States is presented as a model for France not only in terms of warfare, but also of colonization (1929: III, 251–252). The conquest of Algeria, which began in 1830 as a "whim" on the part of Charles X according to Stendhal, is mentioned on several occasions in *Memoirs of a Tourist*. Fernand Rude (quoted in Crouzet 1978: 44) found it strange that someone with a well-established anti-militarist reputation like Stendhal would "applaud" to French colonial expansion, but as Philippe Darriulat shows (2001: 60), colonialism was part of the republican credo not only during the Third Republic but as early as the July Monarchy. Without figuring as a major theme in the works of the novelists examined in the second part of this book, Algeria is mentioned in all of them. It is the setting of Mérimée's short story *Djoûmane* and the far-away country where young men who are unhappy in love go to find death in George Sand's novels.[47] In these three cases, colonization is acknowledged matter-of-factly; France's pres-

---

47 In the *Miller of Angibault*, Rose tells the story of her sister who went mad after her parents refused to let her marry the man she loved: "The young man enlisted and went off to get himself killed in Algiers." (Sand 1995c: 93) Similarly, when Henri Lémor thinks it is impossible for him to marry Marcelle, he considers going to Algiers. (Sand 1995c: 120, 136).

ence in Algeria is presented as a given that need not be justified. Crouzet, who considers that the war in Algeria is a "test for the civic spirit," a "proof of national worth" (1978: 56) for Stendhal, argues that the latter was rather skeptical with regard to the potential success of the colonial enterprise. The narrator's comments in the third volume of *Memoirs of a Tourist,* however, express more his impatience with the slow pace of colonization, due to an old and inefficient army, than disbelief. In fact, optimism and hopes for its future are clearly stated when Stendhal writes that "one day, the French will wake up and win ten battles in three months" (1929: III, 252). His comments on Algeria also reveal his own nationalism. Noting that the man most talked about in Marseille is Adbelkader, the leader of the Algerian insurrection, he feels "ashamed for France" (252).

Conclusion

In *Les Etats-Unis devant l'opinion française, 1815–1852*, René Rémond contrasts the French Liberals' enthusiasm for the young American democracy during the Restoration with their progressive disenchantment with it during the July Monarchy. In 1826, Stendhal still saw the United States as a beacon of hope for the world: "Since America is securing to herself the most reasonable of all governments, she will, 300 years hence, plunge into one depth of contempt all the nations of Europe, more or less degraded and brutified by despotism and aristocracy [...]." (Stendhal 1991a: 210) According to Rémond (1962: 682), Stendhal, whom he uses to illustrate his point, stopped equating liberty and happiness as early as 1828, probably under the influence of his friend Victor Jacquemont (1801–1832) who spent several months in the United States in 1826 but returned rather disillusioned with the new world. For Rémond, this disillusion originates in the French Liberals' conflicted attitude towards democracy: they were "Republicans out of principle" but "aristocrats in their mores" (679); they were deeply attached to democratic institutions but thought they could never be happy in a democratic society, as we saw in the case of Stendhal in this chapter. Rémond's conclusion, that "liberty and happiness are incompatible" for Stendhal (1962: 682), needs to be nuanced, however. For more than a statement of principle, it is an acknowledgement of the writer's own limitations, of his inability to make do without what constitutes happiness for him. But it does not preclude that liberty and happiness may be compatible for the generations to come. Moreover, as a nation concerned with common-sense and pragmatic action, the United States was still held as a model for France by Stendhal in the 1830s, as his comments on warfare and colonization imply.

Stendhal's forward-looking mental attitude, in fact, is best captured by his remark that the Revolution, "this great and imposing drama, which commenced in 1789, [...] may probably not be concluded until 1900" (1982a: 82). Although he occasionally uses the term *patrie* in the sense of "attachment to one's native land,"[48] his sense of identity is grounded in universal principles, those of the French Revolution; aspirations, the desire to see them implemented; and feelings, of love when principles and aspirations coincide, of hatred when they don't. Chateaubriand and Staël are deemed foreigners on that basis but Italians like Fabrice or Gina in *The Charterhouse of Parma* are not. Similarly, the relative merits of "French" sensationalism and "German" philosophy are weighed on the basis of their usefulness for implementing these universal principles, not of their national origin. There is thus, theoretically at least, no place for chauvinism or nationalism in this conception of patriotism. In practice, however, shows of patriotism are frequently found in Stendhal's writings, as expressions of national pride – in comments on the 1800 war of liberation in Italy – or of suffering – at the fall of the First Empire, after Waterloo – and more generally when political reality frustrates revolutionary aspirations.

Stendhal clearly sees that the modern political regimes, the constitutional monarchy and the republic, favor greater social and political equality, a trend reflected in his novels by the fact that characters are no longer from the upper class only, as was the case with Staël, but from all social classes. Similarly individuals are no longer defined by characteristics attributed to an estate as a whole, as was also the case with Staël, but on the basis of their own abilities irrespective of their class, political affiliation, gender, and region of origin. Stendhal's writings thus testify to a wider understanding of the concept of nation, one no longer limited to high society, but extended to society at large. He appears to agree with Staël on one point: the French do not understand liberty. But the way he sees it, her conception of liberty precludes equality: it means happiness for a few people at the expense of most. For him by contrast, equality is the essence of democracy, and thus a prerequisite for liberty and for the happiness of all. It is therefore a good thing that it has made great strides in France since the Revolution.

Equality, however, threatens liberty in insidious ways. One of Stendhal's major preoccupations in both *Chronicles for England* and *Memoirs of a Tourist* is to assess its progress and to warn of the dangers that threaten it. The impedi-

---

48 "For Julien, making his fortune meant, first of all, leaving Verrières: he hated his hometown [il abhorrait sa *patrie* (1964b: 43)]. Everything he saw there chilled his imagination." (Stendhal 2003: 23).

ments to liberty discussed in *Chronicles* tend to be associated with social customs inherited from the absolutist tradition, and to a lesser extent from the Napoleonic dictatorship, in a socio-political context that encouraged regression to a pre-revolutionary past. The obstacles discussed in *Memoirs of a Tourist* center on problems inherent to a democratic society and particularly difficult to root out when combined with the first. For Stendhal, freedom means being able to live in such a way that belief and action coincide, and to do so without the crutches of religion or the gaze of others.

The generous impulse to contribute to humanity's happiness that informs Stendhal's thought mitigates the critical tendency to view him solely as the *égotiste* he claimed to be. While it is true that "[i]n the quest for the self, no one has ever been more methodical, more systematic, or more perseverant" (Berthier 2010: 14) than him, his reflections on the individual are geared towards society at large. Perhaps more than any of Stendhal's writings, the *Mémoires* offer lessons in liberty for all. In this text, he identifies and analyzes the social forces that restrict freedom and he encourages his readers to acknowledge, and to resist, the appeal of ready-made thoughts and behaviors, in other words to stand up to the tyranny of public opinion and fashion. Stendhal's purpose in describing the genesis of the national habitus, in criticizing the regime of sameness brought along by greater equality, stems from his conviction that this process is preventable and reversible, that liberty is possible. He writes to let his readers know that it is up to them to shake their shackles and be free.

Chapter V
Looking Back: National Past and Culture in Mérimée

To say that one does not like
Mérimée is the same thing as saying one
does not like France. Mérimée is a
striking picture of what is most French
in France.
(Dutourd)[1]

The lines above are striking not only because of their overt nationalism but also because of their apparent inaccuracy. Like Stendhal, Prosper Mérimée (1803–1870) enjoys the reputation of being a cosmopolitan thinker (Augry-Merlino 1990), someone who spoke many languages,[2] had friends all over Europe, in England, Spain, Russia, Italy, loved to travel, and did so frequently. His most famous characters, Carmen and Colomba, are also better known for their exotic otherness than for their Frenchness. Similarly, Mérimée's preoccupation with difference, not sameness, with the description of particular local customs, the recording of disappearing languages, monuments, traditions, is thought to be the most distinctive trait of his literary and scholarly writings by most critics. Crouzet, for instance, opposes Mérimée's well-known tales of alterity to "this little-studied and embarrassing body of works, let's call them 'French novellas' as most of them refuse the exotic, or folkloric displacement, as they stage 'modern' people, or civilized and contemporary characters" (Crouzet, 1987: 43).

But as this quote also makes clear, Crouzet's division of Mérimée's work in two parts, one exotic and valuable, the other French and embarrassing, does not really invalidate Dutour's characterization of Mérimée' work as essentially French. Positing that the tension between alterity and Frenchness is the structuring principle of his literary corpus implies that the traditional focus on alterity is gained by de-emphasizing its Frenchness. Crouzet himself underscores elsewhere the significance national identity and patriotism had for Mérimée. To sup-

---

1 These lines attributed to Jean Dutourd are used as advertisement on the back of Roger Salomon's 1964 edition of *Colomba* published by Garnier-Flammarion. Unless otherwise indicated quotes from French texts and articles are my translation.
2 In addition to English, he learned Latin and Greek in school, and also spoke Spanish, Italian, and Russian.

port his claim that he *"absolutely* believe[d] in the idea of nationality" (1987: 57), he quotes this fiery declaration of patriotic love:

> It [the *patrie*] is the image of what is most tangible in the world, the flesh of our spirit, the heart of our heart ... the living amalgam of our ancestors, of our fathers, of us ... the vibration of all our voices... Language, traditions, science, art, letters, she kneads them all to make them French... People say I don't believe in anything, I believe in "Her," in our France.... If France was ever invaded, I would die. (Quoted in Crouzet 1987: 57)

Young Prosper went to a prestigious high school in Paris, the *lycée Napoléon*, where he was trained in the Humanities and established solid friendships with young men of the same intellectual and artistic milieu: Armand Bertin, future editor in chief of the prestigious *Journal des Débats*; Camille de Montalivet, future minister during the July Monarchy; and the sons of famous scientists: Isidore Geoffroy Saint-Hilaire, Alexis de Jussieu; and Jean-Jacques Ampère, his best friend. According to Jean Autin (1983: 18), all were part of a patriotic Parisian youth that skipped school to defend the capital at the fall of the First Empire – although they did not have much of a chance to fight for the *patrie* since the Russians were already in Paris by the time they were ready to march. The tension between seriousness and play found in Mérimée's literary works is already present in his teenage years. On the one hand, Prosper was a solid student, gifted for languages and drawing; and on the other, an adventurous spirit with a passion for out-of-the ordinary characters, bandits like Cartouche and Mandrin, or freebooters and corsairs like Duguay-Trouin et Surcouf (19). After his parents moved to the *Ecole des Beaux Arts* he lived in a building that had housed the Museum of French monuments between 1791 and 1816 and learned about the history of architecture from its founder, Alexandre Lenoir (22).

Prosper Mérimée was nineteen and going to law school when, in 1822, he met the thirty-nine year-old Stendhal (Maillon and Salomon 1978: lviii). The friendship that developed between two men so far apart in age was to last until the late 1830s and was based on their common anticlericalism, epicurean lifestyle, and interest in literature. According to Virginie Ancelot (1858: 65), whose salon they both frequented, they had opposite characters but their verbal exchanges were witty and delightful. Mérimée, in his portrait of Stendhal wrote that "[a]part from a few common tastes and distastes," they "did not share a single idea and agreed on very few things," and that, as a result, they spent their "time arguing with each other" (Mérimée quoted in Augry-Merlino 1990: 6). In the late 1830s, Stendhal would grow tired of what he viewed as Prosper's pedantic ways and nickname him "Academus," but in the 1820s, the two of them evolved in the same social circles and had many friends in common, the young historians Stendhal praised in his reviews, Thiers and Mignet for instance

(Autin 1983: 39). It was also Stendhal who introduced Mérimée to the salon of zoologist George Cuvier (1769–1832) at the *Jardins des Plantes* and to his daughter-in-law, Sophie Duvaucel, in 1828.

Mérimée's first short stories were published in 1824 in the liberal journal *Le Globe*.[3] His first plays were read in front of friends in Delécluze's attic and published as *Théâtre de Clara Gazul* in 1825. *La Guzla*, a volume of poetry supposedly collected in Dalmatia, Croatia, and Herzegovina and translated into French, but actually written by Mérimée, appeared two years later, again anonymously. In *La Création des identités nationales* Anne-Marie Thiesse (1999: 85–86) mentions *La Guzla* as an example of the "international patronage of a European culture" – the title of her chapter – and views the success of this hoax as evidence of the general enthusiasm for national cultures in the late 1820s. In his famous 1882 lecture "What is a Nation?" Ernest Renan (1823–1892) defined the nation in the following way:

> A nation is a soul, a spiritual principle. Two things, which in truth are but one, constitute this soul or spiritual principle. One lies in the past, one in the present. One is the possession in common of a rich legacy of memories; the other is present-day consent, to desire to live together, the will to perpetuate the value of the heritage that one has received in an undivided form (Renan 1882: 26).

In the previous chapters, our focus was on the present, in this one, it is on the past, on the "rich legacy of memories," or rather on its invention, in Thiesse's words, on "the process of identity formation [that] consists in determining each nation's patrimony and in diffusing its cult" (12). The crucial role Prosper Mérimée played in that regard is explored from different angles: an examination of his civil servant career, and of writings related to it, underscores the backward-looking attitude that grounds his understanding of culture as a dead and static entity; an analysis of his historical novel foregrounds the theme of national belonging, defined as an attachment to a secular state, while at the same time shedding light on the novelist's attitude towards 'civilization.' Two Corsican novellas help us define his conception of national identity. Finally, Mérimée's essay on Mormonism documents his reconsideration, at a later stage in life, of religious faith as a means of national cohesion and social order.

---

3 For an analysis of Mérimée's liberalism, see Schmitt (2010).

5.1 Mérimée and the invention of the national patrimony

In pre-revolutionary literature, exoticism was associated with far-away lands, Tahiti in Diderot's *Supplement to the Voyage of Bougainville*, the Mariana Islands in Rousseau's *New Heloise*, Mauritius in Bernardin de Saint-Pierre in *Paul and Virginia*. But increasingly after the 1789 Revolution, the French provinces were seen as exotic as well. In *"The Invention of Brittany"* [*"L'invention de la Bretagne"*], Catherine Bertho (1980: 45) points out that there was "no specific image of [...] any other province in French literature in the eighteenth century;" that "the emergence of the representation of the province dates back to the Revolution." After the Revolution, once the provinces lost their political autonomy to the benefit of the central state, they became the object of a discourse seeking to define and characterize them. The same political will to unify the nation, that, as Bourdieu shows in *Language and Symbolic Power* (1999: 42–52) made the imposition of French as the official national language possible, also contributed to the emergence of a discourse on the province. It first appeared "under the pen of administrators and scholars during the Republic, the Consulate, and the Empire" (Bertho 1980: 47), an expression of the State's need to ascertain its control over provincial France, and in particular to be reassured about the peasants' willingness and aptitude to contribute their share to the national economy. The post-revolutionary province and its administrative, scholarly, and literary representations are thus the product of the process of political integration by which France constituted itself into a single political community. Under favorable conditions, Bourdieu (1999: 223) tells us, regionalist discourse, one of the cultural expressions of the new configuration of political power in post-revolutionary France, has the peculiarity of bringing to existence the categories it produces – "Corsican," "Breton," "Occitan"- and, as we will see in this chapter, in this discourse the province appears as the remnant of a distant past, as a fossilized culture.

At the same time, a discourse on the necessity to preserve historical monuments emerged in reaction to the revolutionary destructions of monuments. André Chastel (1986: II, 410), who believes that the concept of "historical monument" was used for the first time in 1790 in France, mentions that Abbé Grégoire had denounced "vandalism" as "counter-revolutionary" as early as 1793 (414), but that "it took half a century longer to translate into official language the intuition that there exists a monumental patrimony that is essential to national consciousness" (424). The State's interest in the province stimulated a similar impulse on the ground, leading to the rapid development of provincial learned academies and societies. According Françoise Bercé (1986: II, 534–535), these *sociétés savantes provinciales* were often created by "an aristocracy uprooted by the

Revolution and the Empire" that found in archeology and local history a way of coping with loss of land and power. The province was thus subject to a double scrutiny, the external gaze of national writers, and the internal gaze of the local scholars [notables locaux], people who knew their province from experience and often saw it as their "'duty of honor to ... rehabilitate oneself and a pays that Parisian travelers such as Etienne de Jouy and Mérimée had 'mistreated' – that is, ridiculed or condemned to obscurity" (Gerson 2003: 93). In the case of historical monuments, this configuration led to conflicts of authority between central and local power. Olivier Poisson (1999) shows, for instance, that the foundation of the Société française pour la conservation et la description des Monuments historiques by Arcisse de Caumont on 23 July 1834 was a reaction to Mérimée's appointment to the position of Inspecteur général des Monuments historiques on 27 May the same year.[4] As Bercé notes (1986: II, 547), however, the power balance was clearly tilted in favor of State in the 1830s. State-sponsored institutions such as the Société d'histoire de France or the Commission des monuments historiques were created and the State moved to "récupérer" [take over] conservation and restoration projects that had been initially conceived and supported by local and private organizations. Mérimée, who understood the importance of this tug-of-war between local and central power over the rightful ownership of monuments, the legitimate interpretation of their meaning, and the determination of their value, recommended that his competitors be starved financially as soon as he became Inspector general (Bercé 1986: II, 548–549). Poisson sees evidence of this rivalry between public and private control of the national patrimony in his short story "The Venus of Ille." According to him, the characters in the tale, Alphonse Puygarrig, the unfortunate bridegroom, and M. de Peyrhorade represent real local scholars, Puigarri and Jaubert de Passa. Mérimée features their scholarly disputes over the inscriptions found on the Venus of Ille, refuses to take side, but wishes these "envious and ridiculous local archeologists" (1999: 34–35) the same fate as Alphonse in the story: that they be given a good thrashing by their statues! Over time, however, Mérimée's biases against regional scholars disappeared and he even made friends with several of them (Darcos 1998: 204).[5] The lessening of the tensions between center and periphery exempli-

---

4 Poisson bases his claim on the following lines in the first issue of the Bulletin monumental, the journal of the new society: "The protection of our ancient monuments should not be solely entrusted to a few influential men; the entire enlightened population of France should oppose their destruction." (Quoted in Poisson 1999: 28)
5 Stendhal's take on these turf wars was as follows: "One might say that the study of antiquities necessarily destroys a man's faculty of reasoning, so much so that scholars become simpletons,

fied by these friendships can thus be taken as an indication of the State's increased ability over time to exercise control over the national patrimony.

There were no struggles between local and central power about the nature of the discourse on the province. Like historical monuments, the province was seen, both locally and centrally, as a cultural patrimony, as a "treasure to be rescued," as "a precious inheritance handed down by ancestors in danger of being wasted by heirs unconscious of its value" (Bertho 1980: 47), a vision that justified and lended legitimacy to scholarly interest and research. Bertho, who examined the emergence and the evolution of a coherent, organized, discourse on the province in anthropological, economic, historical, and literary writings, notes that the criteria used to define the province are always the same: each is viewed as a rural entity, with people of the same race, speaking the same language, and living in a particular "landscape." In sharp contrast to Stendhal's *Memoirs of a Tourist* this scholarship in fact "completely fails to imagine rural customs as realities as subject to change and transformation as city ways or bourgeois habits" (47). Because both provincial *notables* and national writers adopted these criteria to define and characterize provincial identity, few writings of the period challenged these representations. As a result, the nineteenth-century discourse on the provinces tends to be highly stereotypical: it invariably opposes the living civilization it embodies to the dying provincial patrimony it tries to rescue.

Stéphane Gerson (2003: 278–279), arguing from the position of a "growing historiographical turn, which apprehends French politics and culture at ground level and shuns an exclusively top-down (and Paris-centered) perspective," shows that regionalist discourse cannot be regarded as imposed from the outside by the central power, even if the "French state [...] played a central role in this story." Another way of looking at this conflicted relationship is to put forth the idea that local writers contributed their fair share to the genesis of provincial stereotypes. Bourdieu, who argues (1980: 77) that "[i]f the region did not exist as a stigmatized space, as a 'province' defined by an economic and social (not a geographical) distance from a 'center,' it would not have to claim its existence," also shows that the attempt "to convert the stigma into an emblem" (1989: 152) does not subvert the logic of stereotyping. Symbolic violence, the contribution to one's own domination, does not come about as the result of passive submission or of unconditional embrace of exterior values. For him, it can only be explained by taking into account the position provincial notables occupied in the social space. Owing their dominant social position in the province to their mastery

---

then, pedants, and Academicians (that is, they don't dare speak the truth for fear of offending a colleague)." (Stendhal 1962: 257)

of means of expression (the French language and culture), local bourgeois had nothing to lose from the politics of national unification. It could only increase their social standing since they were the obligatory intermediaries between the central power and the province. On the other hand, as landowners or producers, they often had a vested interest in the local economy, which in turn explains why their writings encompassed social and economic aspects not addressed by their Parisian counterparts. The national literature produced by Parisians, even though it fed off provincial writings, was fixated on what it could use best, "the signs of otherness of a rural world collected at the level of customs" (Bertho 1980: 48), what is commonly referred to as folklore.

As a writer and a civil servant, Mérimée was a major producer of this discourse on the province. His short stories on Corsica and Southern France, his official writings, his published travel logs, all belong to the regionalist discourse described by Bertho. During the eighteen years he toured the provinces as *Inspecteur général des Monuments historiques* (1834–1853), his main activity consisted in identifying monuments of national interest all over France and in taking appropriate measures to ensure their safeguard and preservation for future generations. During his trips he regularly consigned his observations on provincial France in notebooks he published afterwards: *Notes d'un voyage dans le Midi de la France* in 1835; *Notes d'un voyage dans l'Ouest de la France* in 1837; *Notes d'un voyage en Auvergne* in 1838; and *Notes d'un voyage en Corse* in 1840. Born and raised in Paris, Mérimée had an opposite vision of the province as Stendhal. The latter saw modernity everywhere in France, the former viewed the province mostly as exotic and as "more foreign than Greece or Egypt" (Darcos 1998: 155), as a survival of the past. His administrative and creative writings have the performative function Bourdieu mentions: they turn living cultures into dead ones, provincial ways of life into cultural artifacts and relics of the past. They quantify, qualify, reify and ready the province for incorporation into the national cultural treasure, the *patrimoine national*. More subtly, state officials who crisscrossed the country were also exporting the official state language to the most remote corners of the provinces and imposing its use wherever they went at a time when the vast majority of the rural population did not speak French in everyday life. Mérimée's reports on the state of historical monuments in Brittany, for instance, contain numerous comments on language use. In Western France, he observes (1989: 68, note 2), not only is the diversity of Breton dialects an obstacle to communication and national unity, but French is also virtually unknown. In a village like Lanleff nobody, with the possible exception of the parish priest, speaks French (1989: 69, note 1).[6]

Mérimée's activities as a state official are thus directly related to the national project of cultural unification and political integration. As a civil servant, he had a sense of mission: his task was to contribute to the central state's political control over the entire national territory. In his dealings with local authorities, the Inspector general's allegiance was to the State. As Autin notes (1983: 194), he would rather have sacrificed a cathedral than negotiated from a position of weakness. His faith in the central state is also reflected in statements that convey his dislike of federalism, his praise of centralization, as well as in his tendency to send all moveable works of arts to Paris. The same way Dominique Vivant-Denon, the curator of the *Musée Napoléon*, collected works of arts and artifacts from conquered territories during the Empire for what is now the Louvre museum, the same way Mérimée's reflex was "to gather everything in Paris" (Autin 1983: 295). By affixing the 'national interest' stamp on monuments, churches, castles, artifacts that, for all practical purposes, belonged to diverse and local histories, the central State found a way to assert its power over the entire territory, to own and thus control the nature of the national patrimony and the content of the national memory.

Mérimée did not work alone. He was at the helm of a new administration exclusively devoted to the national patrimony and composed of scholars, many of them members of the very active *Commission des monuments historiques,* to whom he reported on a regular basis. The commission usually met weekly in Paris to discuss monuments from all historical periods and projects related to them, to organize excavations of Gallo-Roman ruins, determine the fate of medieval fortifications, Roman churches, Gothic cathedrals, etc... The symbolic domination exercised by the State over the entire nation is inscribed in the very form of these administrative writings, "rapports" addressed to a higher administrative authority, the *Commission des monuments historiques* or the *Ministre*. Mérimée understood and described his role as that of "safeguarding monuments of real interest for France, for history and the arts, shielding them from the whims of private interests so as to allow easy access for scholars and artists" (quoted in Autin 1983: 156). Once identified, monuments deemed of national interest were usually purchased by the State. Preserving their authenticity, their original state, was seen as a priority.

---

6 "Thus, only when the making of the 'nation,' an entirely abstract group based on law, creates new usages and functions does it become indispensable to forge a standard language, impersonal and anonymous like the official uses it has to serve, and by the same token to undertake the work of normalizing the products of the linguistic habitus." (Bourdieu 1999: 48)

But as André Fermigier notes (1986: II, 606–607), the concept of patrimony that informed the politics of conservation during the July Monarchy was also restrictive to the extent that emphasis was placed on monuments and artefacts dating back to France's earliest history: "[...] together with the legacy of the Celts and Romans, only medieval structures were seen as historical monuments deserving of preservation," as if "the memory of France ended with the last Valois" in the fifteenth century.[7] Fermigier questions these priorities but they make sense, not only for practical reasons, older monuments being in greater danger of becoming ruins than newer ones, but also for ideological reasons, and in particular in light of Seyiès's distinction between Celtic roots, seen as the nation's real origin, and a Frankish legacy viewed as aristocratic. Right and left also agreed on the necessity to preserve monuments from the Middle Ages, albeit for different reasons. The Royalists' affection for the period originated in feelings of "historical guilt" (Fermigier 1986: II, 607) for not having been able to prevent revolutionary vandalism, and Liberals considered that "medieval art was the only native art" (608).

Restoration was considered only when absolutely necessary and conducted by teams of specialists well-versed in architecture, archeology, and history. Budget figures testify to the progress and success of this nation-building enterprise. The Inspector general's budget increased from 80,000 francs in 1833 to 900,000 francs in 1853 (Autin 1983: 294). Mérimée was apparently a skilled manager who repeatedly convinced the government of the importance of preserving the national past and succeeded in obtaining funding for his restoration projects. As the concluding lines of his March 1836 report to his hierarchical superior indicate, he was not only conscious of working for "the glory of France," but also willing to use patriotic sentiments as a means of getting his way:

> Some will see them [these noble monuments] disappear with an indifferent eye; they will say that one may pray to God in a large barn as much as in a Gothic cathedral and that it is of no importance if all the works of art perish. But I have too high an opinion of our country to believe that she will resign herself to part cold-bloodedly with such a great share of her glory. (Mérimée 1989: 204)

As Inspector general, Mérimée created the first inventory of French national monuments. The most important ones appear on the 1840 list of *monuments classés*. They include "large abbeys and basilicas like Vezelay, Saint-Benoit-

---

7 Stendhal shared Mérimée's restricted understanding of the national patrimony: "I believe that there is nothing else for tourists to admire in France than thousands of gothic churches and beautiful remnants of Romanesque architecture in the South." (Stendhal 1929: I, 116)

sur-Loire or la Charité; castles like Chenonceaux, Langeais, Chambord; citadels and fortified cities like Aigues-Mortes and Carcassonne" (Autin 1983: 294). All royal residencies were added in 1848, Notre-Dame de Paris in 1862 only. Once placed on the registry, a *monument classé* is most of the time owned and in all cases protected by the State. If it is privately owned, the status of *monument classé* ensures the State's financial participation, usually for half, in maintenance and restoration expenses (Autin: 1983: 294). Mérimée's achievements in the preservation and the restoration of the national past are considerable. Paris owes him the Cluny Museum that opened in 1844 after he negotiated the purchase of Alexandre de Sommerard's medieval collections; of the Hôtel de Cluny and its Gallo-Roman public baths. In the castle of Boussac, not far from George Sand's Nohant, he found the six magnificent *Lady and the Unicorn* tapestries that now adorn a large room of the Museum of the Middle-Ages – others had already been cut in pieces and used for profane purposes.[8] His plan to highlight the beauty of the Sainte-Chapelle, a remnant of the Capetian royal palace, by disentangling it from the web of buildings that surround it, was not retained, but he successfully fought for its classification as a historical monument and its restoration. In the provinces, countless monuments and buildings were saved from ruin. In addition to those mentioned above (Carcassonne, Chenonceaux, etc...), the castle of Blois, the arenas of Nîmes and Arles, the Romanesque Church of Notre-Dame-la Grande in Poitiers, but also more modest sites, like the tenth century Morienval Abbey, the eleventh century church of Saint-Etienne de Vignory, Fontgombault Abbey, the Abbey church of Saint Savin in Poitou, the Priory of Serrabonne in the Pyrénées, Saint-Gilles near Nîmes, and many more.

All these projects required the assistance of an army of new professionals specialized in the preservation and the restoration of monuments, inspectors, architects, artists, but also simple workers. Fermigier (1986: II, 608) notes the positive influence these projects had on the revival of traditional trades, such as "stone cutters, masons, sculptors, stain-glass window makers, carpenters, joiners, roofers, painters, locksmiths." As Mérimée pointed out in a 20 December 1846 letter, monument restoration also had the great advantage of creating jobs, of "keeping the popular class busy" (quoted in Autin 1983: 179). During the Second Republic, he worried that the new regime might reconsider the centralizing policies of the previous administration. Bercé (2010: 167) sees in his support of Louis-Napoléon Bonaparte an expression of his professional integrity more than of his fear of revolutionary violence, of his deep conviction "that a strong regime was necessary to pursue the July Monarchy's policies, to continue

---

8 Mérimée did not succeed in purchasing the tapestries. They became state property in 1882.

to ensure the centralization of decisions, the only guarantee, in his eyes, of their good execution." Twice Mérimée made the case that an interruption of the restoration projects would not only create unemployment but also be a disservice to the State in light of its previous financial and educational investments (Autin 1983: 206). Twice he obtained satisfaction. Although he stopped touring France after being appointed Senator at the beginning of the Second Empire,[9] he continued to work for the *Commission des monuments historiques*. He could hardly have envisioned the importance artistic tourism, largely based on the visit of historical monuments, plays in today's French economy, but a detail shows that he already understood its potential economic impact. As long as provincial hotels and inns lacked comfort, he contended, tourists would stay away, and in their absence, monuments would continue to fall apart (Autin 1983: 289–290).

Fermigier (1986: II, 594) and Darcos (1998: 153) see a paradox in the fact that Mérimée, a known atheist, devoted most of his life to the restoration of churches. The assumption on which this paradox rests is that churches and religion are inseparable but Mérimée's task was, on the contrary, to separate them. In the various volumes of *Notes* on the provinces, religion is subject to the same scientific, scholarly gaze as other customs and practices. It exists as a trace of a distant past, objectified in churches, convents, abbeys, most of them ruins, or in bad need of repair. The relics of France's religious past are suspended between two functions: no longer houses of God, and not yet works of art, they are being restored. They are in the transitional stage needed for the separation from religion and the transformation into art to occur. The cut-and-dry, technical style of Mérimée's administrative writings captures well this moment of articulation between old and new in his notes, but personal commentaries tell the same story. Reflecting on his career as *Inspecteur général* in 1852, for instance, he confessed his inability to appreciate the monuments he had spent his career studying as works of art: "I regret I studied them too officially. I paid attention to architectural characteristics, additions and repairs, but their poetry escaped me" (quoted in Darcos 1998: 152). But by establishing a contrast between then and now, did he not imply that he had learned to view them as art by 1852? Did he not thereby acknowledge the predominant association of church and art as a substitute for the relation of church and religion? The opposition between these two functions comes through in another form in a brief note from 1850 ad-

---

9 Autin (1983: 229) writes that Mérimée belonged to "the ultra-conservative wing" of the Senate and that he was despised by republicans for his support of the Second Empire. He also detects traces of racism in comments about a trip to London in 1857: "London worries him: the city is becoming more and more noisy and it also attracts too many people of color – people from India in particular." (250).

dressed to his young friend and close collaborator architect Eugène Viollet-le-Duc (1814–1878). When he reminds him "what a nuisance it is to work in churches on Sundays" (Mérimée 1947: 144), he clearly opposes the seriousness of their own work to the futility of church services. This anecdote recalling how church services hindered Mérimée in his work stands as an apt metaphor for the obstacle religion represented in the construction of the secular nation-state. There is nothing paradoxical therefore about an atheist restoring churches. On the contrary, it is too important a task to entrust it to anyone but secular agents. Mérimée was perfect for the job.

Chateaubriand understood the museum's function very early. In the *Genius of Christianity*, he criticized Alexandre Lenoir's *Musée des monuments français* at the *École des beaux-arts*,[10] where Mérimée's family lived for a while:

> The French, we acknowledge, are under great obligations to the artist who collected the fragments of our ancient sepulchers; but, as to the effects produced by the sight of these monuments, it is impossible not to feel that they have been destroyed. Crowded into a narrow space, divided according to centuries, torn from their connection with the antiquity of the temples and of the Christian worship, subservient only to the history of the arts, and not to that of morals and religion, not retaining as much as their dust, they have ceased to speak either to the imagination or the heart. (Chateaubriand 1856: 521)

Out of context, Chateaubriand realized, these remnants of the past were deprived of their real meaning and ceased to live. His reaction illustrates Bourdieu's insight (2012: 352) that the creation of a national culture is the condition of cultural domination. The same way the creation of a national linguistic field reduces local dialects to deviant forms of expression, the same way Mérimée's efforts to create a national cultural field were turning Chateaubriand's living culture into a dead one.

Finally, the process of national memory construction must not only neutralize, but also reconcile different histories if it is to elicit national unity. The nation's memory must take the form of a "treasure" in which heroes and monuments from different periods of the nation's history, Gouges's great men, Staël's philosophes, Chateaubriand's knights, and Stendhal's Robespierre and Napoleon, are placed on equal footing so as to give the nation's "living members the choice between contrasting and antagonistic heroes [...]." (Elias 1996: 328) Louis-Philippe's decision in 1840 to transfer Napoleon's ashes to an establishment created by Louis XIV, the *Invalides*, offers a particularly striking illustration of this will to merge incompatible histories into a single national past. Whereas

---

10 On the *Musée des monuments français*, see Poulot (1986); Bonnet (2009).

the burning of castles, the beheading of statues of saints and kings, that occurred during the French Revolution (Gamboni: 2007) attests to fears associated with a recent past still perceived as threatening, the invention of a national patrimony and of a collective memory testifies to the State's mastery over it, and to its ability to tame it in a much more inventive way.

5.2 A history of violence and superstition

5.2.1 Violence and religion in *A Chronicle of the Reign of Charles IX*

Mérimée's first novel, *A Chronicle of the Reign of Charles IX* is a testimony to his early distaste of religion and to his love of the past. Published in 1829, this historical novel centers on the most tragic event of the wars of religion that tore sixteenth-century France apart, the Saint-Bartholomew's Day massacre. On 23 August 1572, between five and thirty thousands of Huguenots, depending on the source of the estimates, were murdered at the hands of Catholics. In the preface, the twenty-six year old novelist indicates that he drew from historical sources, memoirs by "Montluc, Brantôme, d'Aubigné, Tavannes, La Noue, etc" (Mérimée 1890: 2) to try and create characters as they were, lived, and acted at the time. True to the principles of Romantic historiography, Mérimée envisioned the retrieval of this (imagined) past as a means of informing the present: "To my fancy, it is curious to compare these manners with ours, and to note in the latter, the decadence of vigorous passions; hence no doubt a gain in quiet living and perhaps happiness" (1890: 2).[11] As these lines indicate, the temporal distance that separates France as it was in the sixteenth century and France as it is in the nineteenth century doubles as a measure of civilization's progress expressed here through the contrast between a violence associated with the past ("vigorous passions") and its taming in the present ("quiet living and perhaps happiness"). Claude Millet comments on the benefits of this operation in the following terms:

> Civilization, for all its sophistication, can only account for psychological barbarity if it integrates the terrifying power of myths, takes back popular poetry, constructs the memorial of the legendary barbarian world, keeps the temples of the idols it wisely destroyed. These temples are not monuments to faith, but places of panic, brutality, violence, destruction, built on the ruins of any kind of belief. Legends allow civilization [...] to retain the numi-

---

11 Corry Cropper's analysis of the novel, by contrast, emphasizes continuity between past and present – "the similarities between political tensions in the novel and those of Restoration France" – instead of discontinuity. Cropper (2004: 60)

nous terror of dark psychic forces, to maintain a sense of the numinous at the very moment when faith is evicted. (Millet 1999: 97)

Observed from the safe confines of a peaceful present, the ancestors' lack of physical self-restraint, the ambient violence of the historical period in which they lived, is the object of endless fascination and meditation for French Romantics, Mérimée included: "What attracted him to the Charles IX's reign was the toughness and brutality of this harsh and heated period, [...], a flamboyant era of conflicts and blood, likely to produce exceptional beings and dramatic actions."

In an effort to explain his interest in this gruesome topic, Mérimée proposes a theory of moral relativity in the preface to the novel, arguing that "[...] about 1500, a murder by dagger or poisoning inspired nothing like the horror it does today" (1890: 2). "What is criminal in a state of advanced civilization," he adds, "is only a bold deed in a state more backward, and in a state of barbarism it may perhaps be a laudable action" (3). The St. Bartholomew's Day massacre is difficult to justify, he acknowledges, "for it was a great crime, even for its own days" (4). What makes it worse with hindsight, in his opinion, is that "the larger part of the nation took a share" in this terribly bloody event or sympathized with the murderers (4). The explanation he then suggests to account for this great crime and for the wide-ranging support it enjoyed among the French population goes to the heart of our topic since it involves defining the nation: the Huguenots, he argues, were viewed "as foreigners and enemies" (4). Mérimée himself, of course, does not subscribe to the vision of France as a Catholic nation, and his point in the novel is instead that associating state and religion is a recipe for disaster. Recalling the St. Bartholomew's Day massacre is for him a way to make a case for the separation of church and state.

In the preface still, it is interesting to see Mérimée paint the French monarchy's dilemma in 1572 in political, not in religious terms, and in particular reject the commonly held notion that Catherine of Medici's religious fanaticism led to the massacre. Pointing to the French monarchy's weakness at the time, he argues that the young King's authority rested in his ability to keep in check the two parties that opposed him. It was not, therefore, in Charles IX's or in the Queen Mother's best interest to eliminate one party, the Huguenot faction led by the Admiral Gaspard de Coligny, unless they were also able to eliminate the other, the Catholic faction led by the Duke of Guise. Perhaps, the novelist suggest, their plan had been to have the Duke of Guise murder Coligny only to turn against him afterwards. But if it was, their plan had faltered: the King lost control of events, and Guise, who was loved in Paris, used his prestige to foment the popular insurrection that led to the St. Bartholomew's Day massacre two days after Coligny's murder. Such, in any case, is the plotline adopted by Mérimée.

The novel takes place immediately before and during the St. Bartholomew's Day massacre. Bernard de Mergy, a young Protestant, is on his way to Paris where he hopes to meet with Admiral Gaspard de Coligny and to enroll in his army. His brother, George, has renounced his faith, converted to Catholicism, and now serves the King. When the two brothers meet in Paris, they argue about religion. Bernard criticizes his older brother for abjuring his faith, a conversion that has cut him off from his family, but George tells him to attach no weight to his conversion for he is, in fact, an agnostic: "Papists! Hugenots! What is there on either side but superstition? I cannot believe what reason shows me to be absurd" (Mérimée 1890: 66). George goes to church to see pretty women and reads Rabelais during mass. But he is loyal to the King and views both Protestant and Catholic leaders as his enemies and potential usurpers. The King seems to share George's position on the importance of leaving religion out of state business. When Bernard is introduced at court, Charles IX inquires about his religion but only "for curiosity's sake:" "The devil take me if I care of what religion are those who serve me well!" he declares (108). That those words are deemed "memorable" by the narrator provides a sufficient indication of his position. Similarly, when the King later decides to have Coligny murdered, it is for political, not religious reasons. He fears the power of a man some already nickname Gaspard I.

Reason may be invoked in religious matters but not when it comes to honor in *A Chronicle of the Reign of Charles IX*. Duels take place for all kinds of unreasonable reasons. When Béville questions the virtue of his friend de Rheincy's mistress, a duel takes place on the spot in the dining room. For good measure and for no reason, witnesses also duel, injuring or killing each other in the process. A noble woman's beauty and value are determined by the number of duels fought for her. Diane de Turgis, the Catholic countess Bernard falls in love with, has caused "scores" of them (54). At first, Bernard does not understand the subtleties of honor. At court, when Diane drops her glove for him to pick up, he is so taken by her beauty that he just stands and stares. He has to be told by another courtier, Vaudreuil, that Diane's current suitor, Comminges, has gravely offended him when he brushed him in his haste to return a glove that was meant for him. Reason is on Bernard's side: the room was crowded and Comminges probably did not mean to insult him. Not so, according to Vaudreuil, who insists that Bernard's honor is at stake because Comminges offended him twice, first by picking up the glove only Bernard was entitled to pick up; and second by pushing him. Bernard's suggestion that he'll just ask Comminges to apologize is ridiculed – his rival never admits to any wrong – so he ends up challenging him to a duel. For his first duel in Paris, Bernard must thus fight a formidable man, someone skilled at dueling and known to have killed countless rivals or pseudo-rivals. But Bernard is lucky: he is the one who kills Comminges and 'inherits' the beautiful lady. Even ladies are prone to violence either indirectly when they encourage men's violent behavior, or in Diane's case directly since she is said to have challenged a woman rival in duel. Human life, in short, has little value for these aristocratic characters who are friends one second, and mortal enemies the next. Dueling, a pre-modern practice that contests the State's monopoly of legitimate violence and goes against the revolutionary belief in the value of human life obviously exerts a fascination in post-revolutionary France, as attested by the development and the predilection for the historical novel of the period.[12]

The aristocratic world depicted in *A Chronicle of the Reign of Charles IX* is one of cough manners, moral cruelty and physical violence. In the first chapter, for instance, officers are depicted as constantly drinking and eating too much, and associating with *courtisanes*, such as Mila and Trudchen, in public. Ladies at court fare no better as far as virtue is concerned. They hide their affairs, but they are all known to have lovers. Theft is common practice. Captain Dietrich Hornstein steals Bernard's beautiful black stallion after partying with him; Mila steals his money after spending the night with him. When Comminges is killed, his witness, Béville, steals his watch. Weapons are used not only in duels but to resolve the slightest disagreements, a pistol and an arquebus for a questionable hotel bill, for instance. People must always be on the lookout. Coligny's supporters don't want him to open a letter because they fear it may contain poison. Diane believes in talismans and practices white magic with Camille, an old woman, so her lover will heal. Many scenes depict animal cruelty. When Coligny insults George de Mergy by telling him that a man "who has denied his faith has lost the right to talk of his honor," the latter is so furious to be unable to challenge the old man to a duel that he takes it out on his horse, which ends up "drenched in sweat and blood" (1890: 163). At the royal hunt, the court enjoys "the pleasant spectacle of dogs devouring the entrails of the deer" and "the king looks like a butcher" (133).

Of all the characters, George, the agnostic, is the only man with a strong moral sense. Charles IX is cunning and false with Coligny, professing his love for him while at the time plotting his murder (1890: 191). Aware that Coligny offended George, Charles IX suggests that he avenge himself by murdering him,

---

12 During his love affair with Emilie Lacoste, Mérimée was challenged to a duel by an angry husband and shot in the arm. Prosper refused to defend himself which may indicate that he regarded dueling as an antiquated practice.

but George declines: "A gentleman's honor is not mended, but ended by assassination" (200). He warns Coligny anonymously instead. On 24 August 1572, when he gets the order to lead the slaughter of Huguenots in Paris, he first tries to convince his men to disobey orders. When he fails, he takes leave of his troops with these words: "Farewell, cowards! I thought my men were soldiers but they were just assassins." (227) He resigns as captain and is thrown in jail. From the wars of religion, then, a modern hero emerges, George de Mergy, a secular man who refuses to side with Huguenots or Catholics, a loyal servant of the State, but one who does not shy from disobeying the King when he uses religious hatred as a means to govern. This plot allows Mérimée to date the secular tradition in France all the way back to the sixteenth century and to make an early reasonable, historically-grounded case for the separation of church and state. Christian Chelebourg (2010: 44–45) identifies a similar intentional anachronism on Mérimée's part in *Inès Mendo*. Don Luis de Mendoza renounces his aristocratic lineage for the sake of happiness as early as 1640 when in fact "in the classical age, no tragic hero would have so contemptuously ignored his lingeage or preferred his *happiness* to the rules of dynastic honor." In both cases, the novelist's strategy is to describe a past dominated by church and aristocracy that was so uncivilized that it necessarily contained within itself the seeds of a more civilized present.

In *A Chronicle of the Reign of Charles IX* religion is the source of this barbaric past full of superstition and fanaticism. Diane uses her influence over Bernard to try and convert him to Catholicism until it is almost too late for him to flee the massacre, thus endangering her lover's life. Bernard escapes to La Rochelle where the Huguenots are depicted as just as unreasonable and just as savage as the Catholics in Paris. Mérimée's position on the disastrous consequences of religious fanaticism is well illustrated in the last scene of the novel when the war it has caused destroys the Mergy brothers. Bernard, who fights on the Protestant side does not recognize his brother when he gives the order to fire on him. True to his principles, George rejects the assistance of both priest and pastor as he dies of his wounds, while his friend Béville, also mortally wounded, asks for a priest. The scene provides an opportunity to mock the clergy: "In a minute or two Béville died in the arms of the monk who assured his hearers that he had distinctly heard in the air the joyful cries of the angels who received the soul of this repentant sinner, while the devils returned a howl of triumph from underground as they carried off the spirit of captain George" (1890: 308). Here, the monk's dubious testimony is clearly questioned by the narrator's skeptic and ironic report, a deconstruction that successfully keeps the irrational at bay.

5.2.2 Taming the superstitious mind: the fantastic tales

The fantastic short story, a genre in which Mérimée excelled, is a particularly appropriate medium for this kind of deconstruction. In *Frederigo*, a sinner by that name, a young man addicted to gambling, wine, and women, succeeds in tricking Jesus Christ himself into admitting him to paradise. In the *Souls of Purgatory* Don Garcia Navarro and Don Juan de Maraña are even worse rascals than Frederigo. The two Salamanca students lead a life of complete debauchery, getting drunk on a regular basis, seducing, exchanging, and betraying young innocent women, killing their relatives violently, while tricking a priest into vouching for their good manners and their innocence. They escape murder in Spain by enrolling as soldiers in Flanders, where their bravery at war miraculously erases their debt to society and earns them their parents' forgiveness. But nothing changes: their life of violence and lust simply just goes on elsewhere. Nothing is sacred to them. Don Juan promptly gambles away the gold coins his dying captain, Gomare, had destined to masses for his soul's repose. Back on the battlefield he shudders when catching sight of Gomare's rotting corpse whose "lifeless eyes filled with congealed blood seemed to look at him menacingly" (Mérimée 1978a: 705). Don Garcia, by contrast, shocks even tough soldiers with his blasphemies. But just as he is defying God and death and even denying the existence of the soul (1978a: 707), a vengeful brother cut his atheist discourse short. Mortally wounded Don Garcia refuses to see his death as a punishment for tempting fate or as divine retribution: "nothing is more natural than a soldier killed by an arquebus" (708). Like George de Mergy he remains faithful to his principles to the last, suggesting that his friends celebrate his passing with an orgy instead of a mass. Don Juan, deeply saddened by his friend's death, amends his ways but for a few months only. When the death of his parents makes him wealthy again, he returns to Spain to pursue his life of debauchery in grand style. In the inventory of conquests and cuckold husbands he establishes as methodically as Mérimée catalogued monuments, only God is missing. He thus decides to kidnap a nun and the one he chooses to steal from God turns out to be his first lover – who soon gives in to his entreaties. But as he waits for the day of her kidnapping to arrive in the castle of his youth, the painting of the tormented "souls of purgatory" in his bedroom haunts and terrifies him. On his way to the convent, he is stopped by the vision of his own funeral procession and other hallucinations that give him such a fright that he faints in the street. When he regains consciousness, he confesses his misdeeds to a monk and to Sister Teresa, who dies of a broken heart. He gives his fortune to the poor and becomes a monk, Brother Ambroise. But a few years later, the vengeful brother who killed Don Garcia, challenges him to a duel. He refuses at first but ends up killing him. To repent this last horrific crime, Don Juan spends the rest of his life in devotions and dies as "venerated as a saint" (728).

It is this kind of pious ending that has led a few literary critics, Pierre-Georges Castex in *Le Conte fantastique en France*, for instance, to doubt Mérimée's professions of secular faith and to argue that his attraction to the supernatural and the fantastic genre revealed a superstitious mind (1951: 248). But who is the hero in this tale? Don Garcia, who lives his life to the fullest, takes responsibility for his misdeeds and dies unrepentant and at peace with himself, or Don Juan who succumbs to his fears and visions? Obviously Don Garcia, who, like Mérimée, according to Pierre Glaudes (2008a: 103) "considers that pre-logic or archaic forms of thought, influenced by magic, myths, or fables, testify to a state of civilization that belongs to the past" and "for whom religious zeal [...] is of the same order as superstition and fanaticism." The dream of unbridled individualism, the desire to yield to primitive instincts, encapsulates civilized man's predicament, the regret for a life imagined as so much more exciting and fulfilling than life in the nineteenth century, but dismissed as no longer possible except through the medium of fiction: "How can one resist the powerful attraction of a primitive energy that sweeps away all taboos, of the weightlessness imparted by the absence of any moral sense when one must live in accordance with the refined manners of extreme civilization?" (Glaudes 2008a: 132)

In "La Passion pour l'Archè," Antonia Fonyi (1999: 198) points out that *Carmen* "begins with the narration of the quest for an *antique world* that has become so foreign to the *modern world* that even the memory of its location has been forgotten." Indeed, in short stories like *The Venus of Ille*, *Lokis*, or *Djoûmane* the reader is invited to embark on a quest for a supernatural past, but she is also given the opportunity to do so safely. In these tales, the irrational is kept at bay through a layered narrative frame in which rational characters – usually incredulous scholars and men of science – encounter phenomena that they cannot explain yet, but are in the process of deciphering, or that they know cannot actually exist. In *The Venus of Ille*, an antique statue with the gaze of tigress kills a bridegroom who has imprudently put his wedding ring on her finger. In *Lokis*, Count Michel Szémioth, the son of a bear and a woman, embodies man's dual nature, the tension between savagery and civilization. In this case primitivism wins as well: the count kills his bride on their wedding night and escapes to the forest to live with the wild beasts. In *Djoûmane*, the incredibly bizarre and cruel events observed by a rational officer turn out to be a dream. Customs and practices that appear so strange, so foreign, so exotic to contemporaries of Mérimée because of their settings in faraway lands like Lithuania or Algeria[13] owe their fascinating character to their symbolic death. The delicious moment of doubt and fear is only possible because it is neutralized as soon as the story ends and the reader returns to a safe environment. Catherine Huet-Brichard offers a similar appreciation of Mérimée's exotic short story:

> In the end, the truth in *La Guzla* is probably to be found in the confrontation between editor and poet, barbarian and civilized, man of the present and man of the past: the desire for a relation to the world that may be characterized as holistic is expressed in the poems; the irreversible break with that relation to the world in the commentaries. (2008: 73)

As Darcos (1998: 66) also points out, even in tales that feed on the supernatural, the ending "always ends up denouncing the superstition the narration brought into play. Lucidity and irony return, dispelling the fantastic's chiaroscuro." Mérimée was clearly fascinated by the irrational but he did not succumb to it, as he explained in a 3 November 1856 letter to Mme de la Rochejacquelein: "I like to imagine ghosts and fairies and I could make my hair stand on end by telling myself ghost stories. But in spite of the very physical sensation I feel, this does not prevent me from not to believing in ghosts, and in that regard, so strong is my disbelief that I would not believe in them if I saw one." (Quoted in Darcos 1998: 67) As he pointed out, he saw a huge difference between fact, "the things he viewed as real," and fiction, "the things he liked." Darcos (1998: 499) sums up Mérimée's position on religion and science accurately when he writes that religion and all forms of superstitions offended his reason; that he always demanded and relied on "historical evidence." In fact, the very act of writing fantastic tales demonstrates the writer's mastery over the uncanny forces he conjures up and a similar willingness on the part of readers to engage in a pretend game.

5.3 *Colomba:* **savage past and modernity**

In literary criticism, Romantic literature tends to be seen as a reaction to modernity, as an attempt to escape social fragmentation. The exotic appeals to a modern imagination, it is said, because it represents a way of regaining a sense of unity through the encounter or fusion with imaginary others. For sociologists and historians, by contrast, the constitution of modern national identi-

---

13 Is the choice of these two exotic settings, Lithuania, where Stendhal was stationed during the Napoleonic wars, and Algeria, a quasi-French province during the Second Empire, a clue that Mérimée may have subscribed to the idea of the *"grande nation"*?

ties is premised on the individual's ability to imagine him or herself no longer in relation to a set of horizontal, real or imagined, social relations, but to vertical axis, an abstract entity called the national State. In *Colomba* these two understandings of identity, the modern national and the traditional communitarian sense of self, confront each other in the person of Orso, who successfully negotiates the turn to modernity, and of Colomba, who does not.

Colomba, Mérimée's famous short story, is often seen as a perfect illustration of the Romantic predilection for local color and exoticism, but, as we will see, the tension between alterity and Frenchness also structures this exotic novella. Crouzet (1987: 26) defines Mérimée's exoticism "as a constant movement through the space of closed cultures, of peoples rooted in the double strangeness of their archaism and impermeability, a quest for an elsewhere that is also a quest for the primitive and for the origin." In the Romantic age, he argues, this fascination for otherness fulfills a cathartic function: it is a kind of mourning ritual for all the facets of life that had to be given up in exchange for civilization. In that scheme, then, modern man is the prey of conflicting desires – on the one hand, the need for civilization, on the other, the yearning for unbridled primitive passions that exotic fiction is meant to fulfill. Peter Robinson, who underlines the popularity of exotic fiction in the second quarter of the nineteenth century, recalls that the *Revue des Deux Mondes*, where *Colomba* first appeared in July 1840, "had originally been founded [in 1831] as a bi-weekly travel journal depicting, for the civilized world of France, exotic landscapes and adventures in what today we call the Third World" (quoted in Clark 2000: 189). That curiosity for faraway cultures and the desire to live out primitive fantasies played an influential role in the success of these stories is undeniable. But the notion that Romantic alterity is constructed in opposition to the "civilized world of France" needs to be qualified. Crouzet's statement, for instance, is ambiguous in that regard: alterity, difference, and otherness imply a relation to something, but the way he sees it, "*l'individuel*" is both self and other, self to the extent that it represents modernity's supreme value, and other, insofar as it stands for an ideal that can only be imagined, attained through fiction. For a sociologist like Calhoun, by contrast, the individual is attuned to the present, rather than turned toward the past, to the universal discourse of nationalism instead of the escapism of the past. Two contradictory scenarios on modern identity thus emerge. For the literary critic, the Romantic individual seeks to escape modern fragmentation and to regain his former sense of unity through the encounter with imaginary others. For the sociologist, by contrast, the individual is modern only to the extent that he is able to break with the past, that he is capable of learning how to derive his sense of identity without the web of concrete relationships that previously defined who he was, that is in the first place through the abstract category of the nation. It is the scenario that my reading of Mérimée's *Colomba* is meant to foreground.

Mérimée's novella is named for Colomba Della Rebbia, a young Corsican woman who has vowed to avenge her father's death. The plot can be summarized in a few lines. Convinced that her neighbors, the Barricinis, are responsible for her father's murder, Colomba tries to talk her brother Orso, a lieutenant freshly returned from the battlefield of Waterloo, into following the Corsican tradition of personal justice, the *vendetta,* and avenge blood with blood. But Orso, who has returned to Corsica to marry his sister and sell off the family's property, is more interested in his new love for the very civilized Miss Lydia Nevil, a young lady from England he met, with her father, on the boat to Corsica. When he rides ahead to greet his guests as they near his village of Pietranera he is ambushed by the Barricinis. Acting in self-defense, he promptly shoots and kills them. He must spend a few days in the *maquis* in the company of bandits, but is soon cleared of any wrong-doing. All ends well. Colomba can proudly proclaim that her brother acted like a true Corsican and avenged their father. Orso marries Miss Nevil and leaves Corsica forever.

In *L'Image de la Corse dans la littérature romantique francaise,* Pierrette Jeoffroy-Faggianelli notes that Mérimée's novella combines three themes, "vengeance, feuding families, and bandits" that were found separately in previous works of Corsican inspiration and that all three are related to the *vendetta* (1979: 352). Comparing *Mateo Falcone* and *Colomba,* she further points out that the central theme of both novellas is male honor: "In *Mateo Falcone* a father kills his son for transgressing the code of honor. In *Colomba,* a son avenges his father's honor and death. In both case, despite this chiasm, the plot centers on the father and the father's honor." (355) But as she also acknowledges, it is the young woman, not the man, who takes it upon herself to preserve the father's honor and the Corsican tradition in *Colomba.* Noting that "the son is fallible in both of Mérimée's Corsican works," she wonders whether the son ought to be seen as an embodiment of the new forces of change. But she leaves the question unanswered, turning instead to Colomba, "the primitive heroine who symbolizes continuity and permanence" (355). It is an interesting question nonetheless: why is it that in both stories sons reject the Corsican code of male honor, even if they do so to different degrees, and in different ways?

Mateo's son, Fortunato, fails his father because he is seduced by modernity's materialism: he betrays his family's honor for a watch. He is ten years old and may not seem guilty of a crime punishable by death, but from his father's vantage point of view, he is. He has upset Corsican customs, he has, as David Charles points out, "stolen a watch that he should have inherited,"[14] and thereby shaken the tradition of filiation and his father's sense of identity. For Chelebourg (2010: 51), this lack of commitment to filiation applies to young Romantics in general and to Orso in particular. It is worth noting that in *Colomba* as well as in *Mateo Falcone* the breech of tradition is mediated through money. When Colonel Nevil tries to slip a gold coin into Orso's hand, the young man warns him "never to offer money to a Corsican, for there are some of my compatriots impolite enough to throw it in your face" (Mérimée 1998: 169). Money, in short, is a modern value, an abstract category that stands in opposition to, and threatens to destroy, the 'web of concrete relationships' that defines Corsican identity. In that regard, Mérimée's observation that there is an incompatibility between traditional male honor and money is confirmed by Bourdieu (1979), who, in his work on Algeria, discusses the difficulties people raised on the Mediterranean sense of honor experience once they are transplanted in a world where the acquisition of a capitalist habitus is a precondition for adaptation and survival.

Nationalism is an equally serious threat to identities defined by kinship. Nationalist discourse, Calhoun writes, "differs sharply from the discourse of kinship and the ideology of honor of the lineage" (1997: 46), and as if he were thinking of *Mateo Falcone*, he adds: "it offers the chilling potential for children to inform on their parents' infraction against the nation" (45). French law demands that the criminal hiding in Mateo Falcone's haystack be turned over to the police; Corsican honor that hospitality be granted to him. By complying with the former, Fortunato thus unwittingly informs on his father, reveals him to be a man who puts honor before law. At the same time, it is not Fortunato's breech of customs but Mateo Falcone's savagery that shocks the reader in *Mateo Falcone*: how can a father kill his only male son for acting like a child?[15] Male honor the way Mateo Falcone understands it can only be rejected as cruel and immoral. What *Colomba* tells us, however, is that the successful re-negotiation of identity from the ideology of kinship to the ideology of nationalism is premised on the preservation of a male sense of honor. In the novella, the theme of male honor is primarily developed through Orso, a character critics tend to view as a man of divided allegiance, half Corsican, half French, when he is better seen as a model of successful adaptation to the national mold.

---

14 In "*Mosaïques. Les Orientales* de Mérimée," David Charles rightly sees Fortunato's theft, "as a way to save time" (1999: 116) and links it to the lazy Corsican peasants' practice of burning fields so as to save effort and pain. In my opinion, this "theft" of time is an expression of the modernist refusal of social hierarchy, a rejection of the logic of filiation.

15 As opposed to Fortunato, Chilina, the little girl who serves as a reliable liaison between her outlaw uncle in the *maquis* and Colomba exemplifies adherence to Corsican tradition.

Orso is not the only Corsican male in the story who frees himself from a Corsican identity based on lineage, the elder Barricini does as well. But he is from the start opposed to the Corsicans who have tried and failed, namely the two outlaws who live in the *maquis*, Castriconi and Brandolaccio. Like Orso, the two bandits left Corsica and lived on the continent for some time. Given Mérimée's views on religion, it is hardly surprising that Castriconi, a former theology student known as *le curé*, proves incapable of adjusting to the national regime: religion does not necessarily promote nationalism. But the army does, which is why the case of the second bandit is more interesting. Brandolaccio, formerly known as Brando Savelli served under Orso Della Rebbia at Waterloo and yet he deserted and returned to Corsica. Very subtly, the text offers an explanation for his desertion, that is, for his failure to act as a true national: rather than serving France, Brandolaccio was serving Napoleon, "our poor compatriot" (Mérimée 1998: 221). As we will see shortly, Orso della Rebbia's attitude toward military service is quite different from Brando's. Before, however, let us highlight the important role social rank plays in Mérimée's assessment of Corsican men's ability to acquire a sense of national identity.

On route to Corsica, Colonel Nevil and Miss Lydia initially dismiss the possibility of entertaining any social relations with Orso Della Rebbia. They do not hear, or do not believe, the ship's captain when he describes his relative as an officer whom Napoleon would have promoted to Colonel, had he remained in power. The Nevils allow the captain to take Orso on board under the assumption that social relations between them are impossible.[16] But when they find out that Orso is indeed a lieutenant, civility requires that they treat him as such. Military rank alone does not explain the ensuing friendship. What changes the Nevils' attitude toward Orso is the revelation that, as a '*caporal*,' he belongs to old Corsican aristocracy. From then on, they treat him as an equal. Once Lord Nevil realizes that he has doubly wounded the young man's honor, he has to find ways to "make a man with a pedigree stretching back to the year 1100 forget his impertinence." As for his daughter, she immediately starts "to find something aristocratic about him" (170).

The text's emphasis on these pre-modern roots would seem to preempt a reading of *Colomba* as a nationalist tale. But what it reveals instead is a keen understanding of nationalism on Mérimée's part: his awareness that "nationalism works, in part, because national identities and the whole rhetoric of nationalism

---

16 "[...] they concluded that it must be some poor wretch whom the skipper wanted to take on board out of charity. If he had been an officer, they would have been obliged to speak to him, to mix with him; but, with a corporal, one need not stand on ceremony, and he is a person of no consequence [...]." (Mérimée 1998: 166)

appear commonly to people as though they were already there, ancient, or even natural" (Calhoun 1997: 12). Nationalism in that sense is not nation-specific, but related to the ability to conceive of oneself and the world along national lines. As Mérimée describes it, the friendship between Orso and Sir Thomas transcends the age-old rivalry between England and France. Consider, for instance, that Orso does not feel any hatred or any need to avenge his father upon learning that Nevil fought and nearly killed him during the Spanish campaign. Similarly, the fact that Della Rebbia and Nevil faced each other in combat at Waterloo does not impede their friendship in the least. On the contrary, this common experience on the same battlefield feeds their mutual respect. Like old aristocracy, it is a source of what Bourdieu calls "equality in honor." The cordial relationship that develops between them is possible in spite of their different nationalities, and despite the fact that they were on opposite sides in one of the greatest butcheries of the century only four years earlier.[17]

In a sense, then, we could interpret the text as intimating that modern male honor, the product of courage and bravery at war, somehow escapes the parameters of national identity. But it is, on the contrary, profoundly rooted in nationalism, measured by a supreme test of allegiance: the *pro patria mori*, that is the willingness to selflessly sacrifice one's life for the sake of an abstract national entity.[18] Granted, Mérimée's *Colomba* detracts the reader from gaining such insight. By turning enemies into friends, it downplays the foundational violence inscribed in the modern sense of male honor to a grotesque extent; by directing attention instead to a "bizarre," "savage" Corsican cultural practice, the *vendetta*, it discourages the reader from making a logical comparison between these two expressions of wounded male honor. But if we do compare the modern and the traditional codes of honor in which male identities are grounded, two essential distinctions impose themselves: first, modern male honor emanates from an allegiance to national institutions (the army, administration, justice) and the old Mediterranean honor from an allegiance to a web of concrete, personal, relations in which such institutions are superfluous. Second, and this is perhaps where the clash between the two senses of honor is most visible, traditional male honor is founded in memory, in the ability to never forget insults to one's name. Thus, Mérimée's Corsicans may forget the nature of the offense that deserved punishment, but not the offense itself. As Ernest Renan famously

---

17 Waterloo took place in 1815; Orso's father died in 1817; the plot is set two years later.
18 Still today, it is this test that most distinctively separates a nation in two gendered halves: men must subject to it when their country goes to war; and women don't have to. Thus, women who rightly, if perversely, demand to be granted the same right to die for their country as men, are actually protesting their exclusion from the realm of honor as a male privilege.

claimed, the modern sense of national identity, by contrast, is premised on the ability to forget, in the first place in this case the recent and arbitrary character of nation-based identies since Nevil, who fought in the British army, is actually Irish, and Orso, who fought in the French army, from Corsica, an island acquired by France in 1768 only. But it is also imperative not to remember the brutalities that may occur in the name of the nation. It is this "off and on" modern sense of male honor Della Rebbia and Nevil exemplify. They possess the ability not so much to forget, as to ignore the blood that has flown between them in battle recently. Even death is de-personalized under the national regime.

Apart from the transformation of male honor, other elements support a nationalist reading of *Colomba*. Corsica's integration to the French nation-state is attested by its institutional and administrative structure (*départment, Préfet, commune, maire, gendarme*) and its adherence to French law. In Ajaccio, the State's authority is represented by *M. le préfet*, a man who, true to stereotypes, finds Corsicans uncivilized and is eager to make friends with distinguished British tourists. What his visit to the Nevils reveals, however, is that the dominant political division of the mainland is reproduced on the Corsican island: when Orso Della Rebbia refuses to talk to the Prefect he does not snub a French official but a political enemy: "As a liberal, Orso had no wish to talk to a henchman of the regime" (Mérimée 1998: 180). Just as significant in this brief encounter is the Prefect's refusal or inability to envision Orso's hostility toward him on those terms. For the Prefect, a native of Corsica returning to his island can only have ulterior motives, and he sees it, therefore, as his duty to preempt any temptation on Orso's part to 'go native' again: "Having spent so long in the French army, you cannot have failed to become thoroughly French, I don't doubt, Monsieur" (Mérimée 1998: 181). The Prefect has his doubts, of course, or else he would not need any reassurance. His words are meant as a not-so-subtle warning to Orso to behave, to forget about avenging his father. Orso, who has no intention of doing so, does not understanding this part of the Prefect's message: "I find him most odd, with his pompous, mysterious airs" (181), he tells Lydia later on. But when Miss Nevil explains what the Prefect meant Orso has good reasons to feel insulted by his words and to react angrily.

In addressing Orso as he does, the Prefect reveals his bias toward the Corsican province, the view that it is hopelessly retrograde and that nature tends to have the upper hand over culture in the shaping of identity: a former savage remains a potential savage. In addition, the fact that he expresses this fear openly shows that he is unaware of the insult he is inflicting upon Orso when he refuses to treat him as a fellow citizen. Seeing his French identity questioned by the Prefect, Orso has in fact no choice but to accept the Corsican identity that is imposed upon him. Hence his response: "Do you think, Prefect, that a Corsican needs to have served in the French army in order to be a man of honour?" (181). The Prefect, in short, is as responsible for shaking Orso's sense of identity as his sister Colomba, for forcing him to be someone he is not, or, as he puts it himself, to play the role of a "some stage brigand straight out of the *Ambigu-Comique*" (216).

The problem with this interpretation of the pointed exchange between the Prefect and Orso is that it conflicts with the one forcefully recommended by the narrator between the Prefect's question and Orso's response: "It is scarcely flattering for Corsicans to be reminded that they belong to the Great Nation. They wish to be a nation apart, and they justify the claim sufficiently well for it to be conceded to them" (181). Where I claim that Orso is insulted by the Prefect's questioning of his Frenchness, the narrator tells us the opposite, namely that Corsicans don't want to be French, or to be reminded that they are. Other factors, however, support my interpretation. *Colomba,* for instance, shows Corsican politics during the Restoration to lack any local specificity, to be based on the same opposition between Royalists, supporters of Louis XVIII, and Liberals, their political opponents, in Corsica as well as in Paris: the Della Rebbia are Liberals and the Barricinis, Royalists. Corsica's integration and participation in French politics is not a new phenomenon. The hatred that had long existed between the two families, we are told, disappeared for several generations until it was re-ignited not by age-old rivalries, but by modern politics. There is nothing specifically "Corsican," in short, in this new conflict. In Pietranera as in Paris a single political event shapes politics, the fall of the Napoleonic regime.

In a few pages, the narrator provides a surprising amount of information on the political nature of this conflict. The reader learns that Orso's father, Ghilfuccio Della Rebbia was a decorated army captain, then colonel, who benefitted from the support of one of Napoleon's generals during the Empire. In 1812, this general's protection led to the selection of a Della Rebbia as mayor of Pietranera, instead of Giudice Barricini, a lawyer who was well positioned for the job and had every reason to believe he would become mayor. Thwarted by the Imperial regime, Giudice became a natural ally of the Restoration government: "At the fall of the Emperor in 1814, the General's protégé was denounced as a Bonarpartist and replaced by Barricini. In turn, the latter was stripped of office during the Hundred Days; but after that tempestuous period, amid much ceremony he again took possession of the mayor's seal of office and the register of births, marriages, and deaths" (191).

In Pietranera and Paris, political power shifted from the military to the legal elite during the Restoration, leading to the dismissal of military personnel, the army of *demi-soldes* to which father and son Della Rebbia belong. On the other hand, "an unrelenting campaign of petty harassment" (192) came to shape local politics, leading the vanquished camp into further opposition to

the regime. Pietranera is shown to mimic Paris to the extreme in its political behavior: here too, for instance, a funeral can lead to an insurrection. When Colonel Della Rebbia defies the mayor's orders and buries his wife according to her
own wishes – that is in the wood instead of the cemetery – the two camps fighting for her remains are not moved by traditional Corsican values. As the mayor's
report on the riot documents, the two warring parties consist of Frenchmen engaged in a national political struggle:

> Needless to say, the particulars of the incident were recorded, and the mayor submitted a
> report to the Prefect, in his loftiest style, in which he depicted divine and humane law as
> trampled underfoot – his dignity as mayor and that of the parish priest slighted and insult-
> ed – with Colonel della Rebbia at the head of a Bonapartist plot to change the order of suc-
> cession to the throne and inciting the public to take up arms against one another, crimes
> under Articles 86 and 91 of the Penal Code. (193)

It is difficult to overlook the irony of this passage: a Royalist uses the Penal Code
put in place by Napoleon to accuse his enemy of being a dangerous Bonapartist!
More subtly, reminding the reader of the Penal Code is also a way to recall that
Corsica was home to this great legislator and thereby to contradict the stereotype
of an uncivilized Corsica the novella foregrounds. Moreover, the mayor's preten-
sion to turn a local incident into a national affair may be mocked by the narrator
– "The exaggerated tone of the indictment detracted from its effect" (193) – but
the recourse to the competent authority of the Prefect is not. By turning to him,
Barricini acts as a member of the national community, as a French citizen.

Colomba, in sum, is as much about French identity as it is about Corsican
identity. The description of Corsican people and customs is produced against a
French sub-text that reveals the novella's belonging to a nationalist discursive
web.[19] It tells a story that concerns all modern nationals; it underscores the necessity of abandoning the traditional sense of identity based on kinship and of
replacing it with the modern national sense of identity. This transition is eased
by the fact that nationalism is also a male ideology of honor that "defines national strength in terms of potency and military power" (Calhoun 1997: 112).
Orso's political thinking offers an irrefutable proof of his modern sense of identity and this new mode of thought is even shown to apply to Pietranera as a
whole in the subtle mimicry of Parisian politics that informs Mrs. Della Rebbia's
funeral scene. Corsica's otherness in *Colomba* is as staged as the main charac-

---

19 In *Nationalism* Calhoun (1997: 3) suggests that nationalist discourse depends, for its production and for the shape it ends up taking on individual cases, "on a more global, indeed
*inter*national rhetoric." Thiesse makes the same point.

ter's identity when he endorses the costume of a Corsican brigand. In that regard, *Colomba* can best be characterized as a performative text that stages otherness so as to better elicit proper national behavior on the part of readers. Finally, a brief examination of the characters' ability to conform to the imperative of defining oneself in terms of one nation, one language, one race, one gender, reveals that non-conformity to the regime of oneness is punished by extinction in Mérimée's text. Too closely invested in the traditional order, half man, half woman, Colomba flunks the test. She is therefore condemned to remain single and childless.

5.4 State and religion in *The Mormons*

Mérimée's thoughts on the nation occupy a great deal of space in his novellas, scholarly writings, and his correspondence, but not, however, as a focus of sustained attention. The exception is a little-known essay on the Mormons that features nation-building as its main theme.[20] Published in four installments in the *Moniteur Universel* at the end of March and the beginning of April 1853, *The Mormons* is a sixty-page long history of the Church of the Latter Day Saints.[21] The documentary nature of the piece is obvious. For its composition, Mérimée relied on very recent English and American sources, including *Le livre de Mormon, histoire sacrée des peuples aborigènes de l'Amérique*, John Taylor's translation of *The Book of Mormon* published in 1851 in Paris. But Mérimée's interest in that particular topic is puzzling, given that "[f]or him, no doubt about it, God does not exist" (Fonyi 2008: 78). Raised in an anti-clerical household, his reputation as a Voltairian free-thinker was already well established during the Restoration, at a time when it was not particularly popular or wise to be known as an atheist. In 1844, shortly after his election to the *Académie Française*, the publication of *Arsène Guillot*, a short story mocking a high society lady's effort to convert a dying prostitute, created a scandal among the Catholics, leading many of

---

20 The note Mérimée sent to Turgan on 28 December 1852 to request information on the Mormons reads as follows: "I am a very poor theologian. If you have any books that might enlighten me, I will read them with pleasure and will let you know what I think. I heard that a Mormon Gospel has been translated into French. Could you try to find out where it is possible to get it?" (Mérimée 1945: 478).

21 Following the original publication in *Le Moniteur Universel*, *Les Mormons* was included in *Mélanges historiques et littéraires* in 1855, and in 1930 in *Etudes Anglo-Américaines* edited by Georges Connes – the edition used here. Translations are mine.

those who had supported him to regret it.[22] Mérimée was upset about the expansion of neo-Catholicism from the 1840s onward but he refused to compromise, did not convert to Catholicism, and remained faithful to his secular principles all his life. Why his interest in the Mormons, then? Why would a well-known anti-clerical intellectual like him treat the topic of religion in a serious, scholarly manner? What becomes clear upon closer examination is that *The Mormons* is not about religion per se but about the use of religion in state-building. Set against the backdrop of Mérimée's *Correspondence* between 1848 and 1853, my reading of this text shows that it is primarily a reflection on the Revolution of 1848. Focused on the relation between politics and religion, it highlights Mérimée's grasp of the significance of belief as a prime factor of social and national cohesion.

The Mormons opens as a religious satire, a ten-page long critique of "superstition" that confirms Mérimée's secularism. The aspects of the new religion provoking his most sarcastic comments are those that fall within the purview of his professional authority. They are, in a snapshot, the language of its sacred texts – bad syntax, bad style; a doctrine that is full of contradictions and based on a bad plot – *une farce mal ourdie* – and a ridiculous theory of translation, all unbearable weaknesses for a scholar of culture and language (Mérimée 1930: 37–38). By contrast, he finds great interest in the history of the Mormon people.[23] His goal in this essay is to tell the truth about the Mormon Church, a truth that cannot be found in its religion but rather in its history. Factual observation and objectivity preside over his historical investigation. The sources consulted bring "accurate and unbiased information" (25) thanks to a book by Mayhew; "the distinct benefit of personal and thoughtful observations" gathered by Gunnison (25); and a

---

22 "As a result [of the short story's publication] I am being seen as an atheist, a scoundrel, etc...," he wrote to an unknown correspondent on 22 March 1844 (Mérimée 1945: 61). The next day he told the same thing to Mme de Montijo: "M. Molé, who voted for me, says he regrets it and the most furious is M. De Salvandy, who knows how to reconcile debauchery and religion in practice, but is the most moral and pious man in theory. This outburst of false devotion angered me at first, but now I find it amusing" (68). In the same letter he also described the renewal of religious fervor in France: "You can't imagine what this neo-Catholicism movement looks like. We are moving so fast towards the greatest extravagance that we'll be back in the Middle Ages before we know it." (68) In a 12 April letter to the same lady, he described the "L'abbé de Ravignan," as "the flavor-of-the-day preacher," who "has already brought to communion nearly two thousand bearded young men" (77).

23 "On the other hand, the history of this sect seemed interesting to me." (Mérimée 1930: 25)

description of Mormon customs based on another work by Sansbury.[24] Thus recast, the history of the Mormons is about state-building. The point of the essay is to trace the development of a nation-state, from its creation to its blossoming into a prosperous and peaceful society.

The contrast between Mérimée's negative opinion of Mormon religion and his high-opinion of Joseph Smith, as architect of the Mormon state, could not be more striking:

> As for me, I have no doubt that as soon as he realized how powerful he was, his main goal was to create a state of which he would be the legislator and the leader [...]. I don't think one can refuse one's admiration to an illiterate young man, a man without education, who, with audacity and perseverance as his sole resources succeeded in transforming deserts into blossoming colonies (40).

The initial imposture, the lies and flattery used to rally disciples – ["*les jongleries*"] – are not ignored, but the focus of attention is elsewhere: on political leadership and on results. The intelligence and courage of the man, his organizational talent, his grasp of the power of association are duly noted and praised; the strategies that account for his rise to power examined in detail. Two of them stand out: first, his ability to reconcile "the authority of a theocratic regime with the business activities typical of mercantile republics;"[25] and second, his reliance on principles that are "at once religious and political; for he excelled in the art of always prescribing what would contribute to the sect's enlargement as a duty to Heaven" (40). These principles include requiring absolute obedience to him as a prophet; the use of active propaganda; and the intelligent redirection of private interests towards those of the community. All these principles are geared toward a single goal: the creation and development of an independent state built on the union of all church members (39).

As Mérimée recalls the tribulations of the new church as it moves from Ohio to Missouri, and on to Illinois, and its struggles in the face of calumny, envy, fanaticism, persecution, betrayal, and murder, his sympathy for the Mormons grows: "The Mormons forced their most cruel enemies to admire their courage and their invincible perseverance" (Mérimée 1930: 50). Smith's murder while in the custody of the State of Illinois is deemed "shameful for his enemies"

---

24 The sources quoted in the essay are: Mayhew's *The Mormons, or the Latter day Saints*, published in London; Gunnison's *The Mormons in the Valley of the Great Salt Lake*; and Sansbury's *Expedition to the Great Salt Lake*.
25 "He combines the authority of a theocratic government with the activity characteristic of merchant republics; he knows how to flatter the pride of his sect by convincing its members that they are the object of God-Allmighty's exclusive preferences." (Mérimée 1930: 39)

and plain stupid. Their "detestable rage turned a charlatan into a martyr and a god" (66). But the foundation laid by Joseph Smith was solid and Brigham Young took over easily: "He is seen as a talented man, better educated than his predecessor, and just as skilled in handling the singular nation he has been called upon to lead." (68) Mérimée's description of the community's exodus to Utah reads like an epic. Admiration for the leader is transferred to the disciples, the hard-working, well-organized, disciplined, kind, generous, honest, happy men and women who braved the Wild West's dangers for the sake of their faith and the future of their community: "Misfortune and religious faith had united the members of this sect who now seemed a family. On the road, everyone left his wagon to help when someone else's turned over or broke. The rich shared his bread with the poor. If such deeds brought the Mormons the reproach of communism, let us hope this is the only kind of communism Europe will ever know" (76).

As the preceding sentence suggests, Europe was very much on Mérimée's mind as he wrote *The Mormons*, France in particular. In the very last sentence of the essay, he compares the young Mormon State to "our old society," concluding that Old Europe is after all just as good as the new world. But following as it does such an enthusiastic account of the Mormons' socio-political accomplishments in Utah, the line seems a bit disingenuous. The small Mormon settlement in Deseret truly looks like the ideal state: free of war and political oppression; economically prosperous thanks to trade and hard work; with no unemployment, no poverty; and no social divisions, all concrete achievements that strong leadership and, paradoxically in Mérimée's eyes, religious faith, made possible. All France had in common with the young Mormon State in 1853 was the tight political control exercised by the new Emperor.

As Corry Cropper points out, the parallel between the history of the Mormons, as Mérimée tells it, and the history of the Second Empire is too obvious to be overlooked. The timing of his interest in Joseph Smith's story cannot be pure coincidence, especially since he viewed both Louis-Napoleon Bonaparte and the Mormon leader as impostors, the former as a caricature of his uncle, the latter, as a "religious charlatan." And yet, against all odds, both men succeeded in their quest for political power.[26] *The Mormons*, however, is not a cri-

---

26 Cropper interprets *The Mormons* the same way Scott Carpenter (2009) does *The false Demetrius:* as a critique of the Second Empire. Granted, the temptation to read these texts as oppositional writing is great. It originates in the legitimate assumption that revealing usurpation is the same thing as denouncing it. Scott Carpenter concludes his examination of the "oppositional potential" of *The false Demetrius* by saying that this potential was not realized. In my view, for a good reason: Mérimée believed in the Empire.

tique of the Second Empire, a regime that was only a few weeks old when the text was published. Besides, Mérimée was not only an early apologist of the regime, he also saw and ridiculed *l'imposture* in *Les Mormons* and in real life while at the same time praising *les imposteurs*.[27] Mérimée was too modern, too attached to science and secularism to envision anything like the Mormon State as his own ideal form of government. But in 1848, he did not view the Republic as an option either. The reference point in Mérimée's text is not, therefore, the Second Empire, but the Second Republic.

His correspondence with Madame de Montijo documents what a traumatic experience the 1848 Revolution was for him. His job was suddenly at stake, most of what he had taken for granted in his life in question. The extreme fragility of France's political institutions, of the State he had served, came to him as a shock and a total surprise. On 8 March 1848, he wrote to her that "[t]he Revolution was the work of fewer than six hundred men who for the most part did not know what they were doing or what they wanted" (Mérimée 1946: 258). Those who initially applauded the Revolution, the National guard, the small shopkeepers, the opposition, etc..., were already having second thoughts a few weeks later as bankruptcies were starting to occur and "anxiety [wa]s at its peak" (258). By mid-March, he wished for a strong government and for a strong leader.[28] By the end of March, he was deploring the proliferation of political clubs, and in particular, the rebirth of "the famous name of *club des Jacobins*" where "the wildest proposals" were being discussed (269). His greatest concerns at that point were the rarity of money and the unpredictability of workers he found "always so threatening" (269). By the beginning of April, he thought that "[w]hatever may happen, liberty [wa]s lost in this country," that it would "not survive anarchy or the rage for order that may follow it one day" (273). Chaos was everywhere: people had stopped paying their taxes, thefts went unpunished, private property was no longer being protected. Even a police state, he thought, would be better than the current anarchy.[29] By June 1848, he was taking active part in politics for

---

27 Mérimée did not shy from criticizing Napoleon III openly in letters to friends and acquaintances whenever he disagreed with him, on the Mexican war (Darcos 1998: 389) for instance, but in a more general manner every time the Emperor relaxed his authority. At times, he found "the imperial couple reckless" (379); or "Napoleon III's liberal ideas [...] irresponsible and risky," (389) – the risk being, of course, that the beloved regime might collapse.

28 This predilection for powerful leaders is also reflected in his admiration for Bismarck several years later: "I like the great man in him. I also find him necessary: necessary to prevent his King from acting stupidly." (Quoted in Darcos 1998: 388)

29 In a December 9 1851, letter to Francisque-Michel, he stated: "Souvarof said: the bullet is dumb; the bayonet is strong. But the bullet is not that dumb, it keeps the gawkers quiet." (Mérimée 1947: 265)

the first and only time in his life: as a National Guard, he was fighting arms in hand against the revolutionary faction of the young Republic. On 28 June, he reported that he "spent the last five days living and lying on the Parisian sidewalk with all the honest people in town" and gloated that they had triumphed over the "revolutionary army put together by Lamartine et Ledru-Rollin, and preached to by Louis Blanc" who had tried to establish a communist "government of the guillotine" (339). He proudly noted that no one, among the "honest people," had sought to take advantage of the situation to impose "any kind of pretender;" that they had just fought "to take or preserve" and to "save their skin" (339 – 340). In the face of social turmoil and economic bankruptcy, security and the preservation of property had become Mérimée's major concerns.

His horror of chaos and revolution explains why democracy and the republic, the two political options debated at the time, were equally unappealing to him: "The former want to get to a government that is wise and well-ordered. The latter do not believe that a repeat of 93 is possible and want to start a republic again. I see no real enthusiasm or even deep convictions on either side." (1946: 264) As mentioned earlier, Mérimée was too enamored with the idea of a strong central state to admire American democracy; and, as his comments on the 1848 Revolution make clear, he thought the French incapable of establishing any kind of republican government that would differ significantly from the First Republic. He approved, as we saw, of a "communism" defined by benevolence and charity, as in the Mormon case, but loathed the idea of a socialist Republic. In Paris socialism always meant theft and destruction of property. That prospect frightened him out his wits (Darcos 1998: 311). As for democracy, which he equated with federalism, it was too weak a form of government. Defending a centralization "that had placed France's fate in the hands of the Parisian people" at a time it was under attack, he argued that federalism "would even worsen our situation" (269). Mérimée's dislike of these two political options remained constant during in life. In 1848, he expressed his rejection of both in a striking formula: "All one can predict with certainty is that we face the choice between anarchy and tyranny, these are the options" (269). And he added: "The example set by America frightens me terribly" (273). In 1867, he still thought that democracy the American way meant chaos; the republic the French way chaos and dictatorship: "Constitutions and liberty fit us, if you'll excuse my language, like cuffs on a pig." (quoted in Darcos 1998: 379) *Les Mormons* provides indirect insights into the origin of Mérimée's fear of American democracy. The story of the Mormons documented its weakness since the central state had proved incapable of protecting religious minorities and of exercising control over its entire territory, of preserving its national integrity. The way he saw it, it had allowed a different kind of state to rise within the state itself. "Democracy," he concluded rather cynically in 1867, "is nothing but the art of sawing the branch on which one is sitting" (quoted in Darcos 378).

It is tempting to dismiss Mérimée's political views as those of an old conservative foggy plagued by undue pessimism, but his political thought is more complex than would appear at first. Democracy and the Republic are not seen as inherently bad, the problem is that they don't work and the question is why. In 1848, the response he came up with was lack of education: "We ought to do two things, educate the people and create institutions related to the expectations set by its victory" (1946: 264). Unfortunately, at that particular point in history neither France nor the United States had the educated citizenry democracy demands. In France, the task was daunting: "I don't really understand how it would be possible to do two things at once that cannot be left to improvisation" (264). In the United States, where institutions of higher education existed, the problems, in his view, were the poor quality of education and the gullibility of an American public ready to believe "all the mystifications and extraordinary stories published by their newspapers" (1930: 29). The paragraph in *The Mormons* Mérimée devotes to Solomon Spalding, author of *Manuscript Found*, the alleged source of the *Book of Mormon*, is telling in that regard: "M. Spalding, graduate of an American university with a strong taste for history books had the fantasy of writing one. [...] He chose the history of America as his subject, I mean, ancient, very ancient history. It is plain to see, that lacking documents, he used his imagination instead." (26) In addition to the central lesson conveyed in *The Mormons*, namely that in the absence of education, superstition reigns supreme, his correspondence reveals another interesting insight on his part; namely that unequal access to education is a factor of social division. In a society where education remains unequally distributed among the population, it simply functions as a rare good, just like property or money, and causes "envy and hatred of superiorities" among the lower class (1946: 293). And since deprivation feeds resentment, unequal access to education is a factor that increases the risk of revolutions.

Mérimée considered therefore that, in the absence of mass education, the most pressing task in France was to secure order, to establish a strong government. In 1848, he initially doubted that a real leader would emerge from the revolutionary turmoil. There were plenty of men with generous ideas, he said, but none who had enough experience and talent to run the country. Then he watched, incredulously at first, Louis-Napoleon Bonaparte slowly rise to power. He saw his election as President of France in December 1848 as a first step in the right direction. He deemed the military coup of December 2 1851, a good thing,[30] and he welcomed the Empire a year later. The Emperor's marriage to Eugénie, daughter of Mme de Montijo, Mérimée's old friend and confidante, propelled him to the center of imperial power. His long acquaintance with the Empress made him a favorite at court and a real insider. His appointment to the Senate in 1853 ensured a civil servant career and financial security as long as the regime would last.[31] Pierre Trahard recalls that "starting in 1853 he was a regular visitor at court where he was treated as a friend" and "a willing participant in official receptions and ceremonies" (Trahard 1930: 17).[32]

Mérimée admired and respected Napoleon III the same way he admired Joseph Smith. But he also drew an important political lesson from these two adventurous trajectories. Both showed that "extravagance" was an effective political tool – whether in the form of Joseph Smith's new religion, or of Louis-Napoleon's political farce. The secular, anti-clerical intellectual thinker Mérimée was and remained all his life,[33] realized with a shock that belief, faith in a religion or in a political myth – was an all-powerful instrument of social cohesion, a tool of sorts for manufacturing consent, for uniting divided people and for attaching them to a particular political regime, to a particular nation-state. Mérimée himself was not among the dupes, of course. He also knew that his friend Isidore, the nickname he gave the Emperor, was not among them either.[34] But the 1848 Revolution had taught him that the construction of the secular state was a longer-term project than he had originally thought. The Mormon experiment offered a short-term alternative to the costly and lengthy process of mass education. It demonstrated that there was another side to religion than intellectual oppression; that it too, could unite people, attach them to the state, and make them prosperous. Mérimée resented but feared the social and political power of the

---

30 Victor Hugo, horrified by Mérimée's position, refused to have any further contact with him.

31 An urban legend attributed Eugénie's paternity to Mérimée. Some have argued that he played a role in her marriage to Louis-Napoleon.

32 He felt admiration for the Emperor and even more for the Empress: "he sometimes mocked the former, whom he nicknamed Isidore, but never the latter." "How vulgar," Trahard comments, "did the selfish egoism of the French bourgeoisie seem to him compared to these princely virtues!" (Trahard 1930: 17)

33 Friends who tried to convert Mérimée, including Empress Eugénie, were rebuked. His conversion to the Augsburg faith on his deathbed is usually seen as a kind gesture toward the Lagden sisters, two lady friends he had known since his childhood and who took care of him during his illness. (Darcos 1998: 498–99)

34 Darcos recalls an anecdote that shows that Mérimée remained true to his anticlerical principles during the Second Empire. When Napoleon III asked him to support Champagny's election to the Académie française, he reportedly said: "No, Your Majesty, I cannot vote for a clerical." (Quoted in Darcos 1998: 422)

Catholic church. He was unhappy, he explained in April 1844, about his "fall out with the bigots" for that very reason (1945: 75). But he loathed "bad company too much to associate with these devout and philanthropist rascals who rule[d] the salons" (75), and, in the late 1850s when pilgrimages were in fashion, "ridiculed his era for flaunting its devotion" (Darcos 1998: 377). He understood, therefore, that the Emperor could not afford to display his anti-clerical views openly, that in a Catholic country, he had to play the Catholic card, which he did, and which Mérimée accepted. But while a short-term goal may have involved using the influence of the Church to prop up the nation-state, the long-term goal was to separate education and religion. A detail suggests that the Emperor probably knew of Mérimée's ideas on education and that the long-term project of educating the nation was discussed: in 1864, he offered Mérimée the *ministère de l'instruction publique* (Darcos 1998: 380). Mérimée refused, conscious perhaps that his anti-clerical views would be a liability. But Victor Duruy, who then accepted the position, began acting on the project of separating education and religion and creating educational institutions better attuned to the nation's needs.

Conclusion

It is difficult to tell if Mérimée foresaw the Franco-Prussian war. Bismarck, whom he met at the imperial summer residence in Biarritz in 1867, seemed to him "a great man" (Autin 1983: 304). But at the same time he also expressed concerns about Prussia's ambitions. In 1860 already, he confided to an English friend that he viewed a Franco-British alliance against the "Kraut-eaters" as more necessary than ever (Autin 1983: 281). As war with Prussia broke out in July 1870 and things went badly for France right away, Mérimée wrote his old friend Adolphe Thiers on 15 August: "Like all Frenchmen of my generation I have a French disposition and the account of our disasters has made me endure hours of anger and furor against the designs of providence, which are singular, to say the least." (Quoted in Autin, 327)[35] On 2 September, Napoleon III surrendered to Bismarck at Sedan; on 4 September, the Republic was proclaimed; on 8 September, Mérimée left Paris for Cannes, never to return.

Did he die out of love for the *patrie*? The timing of his death, on 23 September 1870, and the testimony of his physician, Dr. Maure, would seem to indicate

---

35 According to Autin, Mérimée and Thiers disagreed on politics during the Second Empire, but were both patriots: "[...] until the end, they would meet in Cannes or Paris to evoke the topic that, in the end, was dearest to their hearts: the fate of the *patrie*." (Autin 1983: 264)

that he did in fact die of a broken heart: "'France is dying; I want to die with her. Make sure that Thiers saves what he can of France,'" he is reported to have said many times on his deathbed (quoted in Autin 1983: 327). France's defeat caused him such insufferable grief that it had brought this deeply-felt outcry of patriotism a few days earlier:

> All my life, I have sought to stay clear of prejudice, to be a citizen of the world more than a Frenchman, but all these philosophical garbs are useless. I bleed today through the wounds of those stupid Frenchmen, I lament their humiliation, and however ungrateful and absurd they may be, I still love them. (Quoted in Trahard 1930: 233)

Pierre Trahard, who quotes these lines in *Vieillesse de Mérimée*, expresses concern that "this ultimate confession" of patriotic faith might damage Mérimée's cosmopolitan reputation. In a note, he therefore urges his readers to weigh it against an impeccable, fifty-year long record of struggle against religious and national biases (Trahard 1930: 234). But he need not worry, for what these lines so splendidly lay bare is the peculiarity of the national habitus. Under normal circumstances, its perfect compatibility with the "cosmopolitanism," the openness to the world, so many critics have viewed as characteristic of Mérimée's life and work; and simultaneously, under abnormal circumstances, in times of national crisis and war, the replacement of this love of others by an exclusive love of the nation – and even of fellow citizens who may not be loved at all under normal circumstances ("those stupid Frenchmen").

As we saw in this chapter, the patriotism Mérimée expressed in 1870 was present earlier on in other guise in his writings. As Inspector general of historical Monuments, he played a major role in the production and the circulation of the scholarly discourse aimed at constituting the nation by transforming the provincial past into a cultural artifact. More than "a prophet of the modern museum" (Darcos 1998: 222), he was the inventor of the concept of *patrimoine culturel*, a concept particularly revealing of the backward-looking, static understanding of culture that replaced the forward-looking, dynamic understanding of civilization that had prevailed in the revolutionary era. In his administrative writings and in his travel logs, the fossilization of the province, its representation as rural entity fixed in distant past, and the transformation of remnants of France's feudal or religious past into works of art, are expressions of the central state's assertiveness, of its increased ability to exercise control over the entire nation. A similar process occurs in the historical novel where the wild freedom of aristocratic ancestors, their lives full of unbridled passions and violent acts, are depicted so as to better underscore the distance from, and the difference with nineteenth-century customs. The fantastic and the supernatural also have the status of relics of a long gone past in short stories like *The Venus of Ille, Lokis*, or *Djoûmane*. For Mérimée, the "primitive energy that sweeps away all taboos," "the weightlessness imparted by the absence of any moral sense" are attractive in fiction, but clearly not as palatable in real life when communists want to steal your property or anarchists burn your house![36] In short, the violent past appeals to him only when and because it is tamed, when it has "the beauty of death" – as Michel de Certeau puts it.

Why was Mérimée so attached to the state? Jürgen Habermas has argued that the welfare of the state matters primarily to those who have a stake in its existence, those who derive profits from it in the form of jobs, education, or other benefits.[37] As a civil servant all his life, Mérimée clearly had a vested interest in the preservation of a strong, centralized state. The fact that he held on to his job under various governments has led some commentators to view him as a political opportunist who always supported the regime that best supported his personal interests.[38] But the fact that he pleaded with the government to continue or start major restoration projects on several occasions – in May 1848 when he proposed the creation of an *atelier national* to restore the Cathedral of Chartres, for instance – would seem to indicate the contrary; that he thought that what was good for him, was also good for others; or at least that people with good jobs do not make revolutions. As he recognized in *Les Mormons*, however, the wide majority of the people in France still needed crutches to become true nationals. In the absence of education, religion would have to do.

Following the fall of the Second Empire, a consensus emerged in France as to why the Germans had won the war: their education system was better.[39] Public opinion, however, was sharply divided as to what made it better. Those who

---

36 Mérimée reiterated his fear of communism on 12 January 1851 in a letter to Mme de Montijo: "Not a single one of them knows what he wants, except for the Reds who want to take other people's money. Being the only ones who act in accordance with their doctrine, I fear that they may well succeed one day." (Mérimée 1947:156)

37 Habermas emphasizes the use-value of citizenship: " [...] to remain a source of solidarity," he writes, "the status of citizenship has to maintain a use-value: it has to *pay* to be a citizen, in the currency of social, ecological, and cultural rights as well." (Habermas 2001: 77)

38 Trahard is one of them: "Mérimée rallied behind the Empire as he had rallied behind all other regimes, out of indifference or interest [...]. In short, he accepted, but he protested and he did so less out of fecklessness than lack of convictions. He had too little faith in the power of words, programs, and ideas; he made do too easily with all regimes provided they guaranteed his material future and his liberty, to indenture himself to any party or government. [...]. Those who believed in theories, those who defended a political or social ideal, utopists and apostles alike, never failed to debase this opportunism." (1930: 12)

39 See Ozouf (1963); Ringer (1992).

thought France too secular argued that it was because the German school system was faith-based. Those who viewed France as too religious contended that it was because it was science-based. The Third Republic found a way of acknowledging the importance of both faith and science and of reconciling the two: it adopted a science-based curriculum but turned republicanism into a new religion. Mérimée would have liked this elegant solution. The history of the Mormons and of the Empire helped him gain an insight articulated more recently by Marcel Gauchet: that "religion is a form of pure politics," that "to exist as a meaningful whole, the members of a society must identify 'a point of absolute power' in relation to which the nature of their association is defined" (quoted in Behrent 2004: 33).

Chapter VI
National Belonging in George Sand's Novels

> *But what about* France! *That word had
> been so important at the time of my birth
> [...]. From childhood on, provided you
> had all your faculties, you had felt a
> sense of your country's honor.*
> (Sand 1991b: 563)

In the book she devotes to the creation of national identities Anne-Marie Thiesse briefly mentions George Sand's contribution to this process of identity formation. As epigraph to a chapter entitled "Identifying ancestors," she quotes the following lines from Sand's preface to her *Rustic Legends:* "'The peasant is thus, if one may say so, the only historian from pre-historical time we have left.'" (quoted by Thiesse 1999: 19) Going back to Renan's dual conception of the nation as "present-day consent" on the one hand, and "rich legacy of memories" on the other, Sand's contributions to the process of national identity formation would thus be of the same nature as Mérimée's, i.e. related to the invention of a common symbolic patrimony more than to the "daily plebiscite." But if the historico-anthropological approach identified by Thiesse is set in the wider context of Sand's political thought and of her analysis of nineteenth-century French society, the other aspect of her contribution to the process of national identity formation emerges: her sustained reflection on the means of attaching everyone to the nation, making it thereby possible to see that these two facets are actually two sides of the same coin in Sand's work.

Already in *Jeanne* (1844), where the passion for antiquities led Sand to discover Celtic monuments in the center of France, it was not only through the desire to contribute to a census of the national patrimony – by establishing a list of monuments, local legends, superstitions, and customs – that the issue of national identity was raised. For Jeanne, the heroine, is not only heir to a past that links her to a pagan and Christian history, from the *fades* of popular mythology to Joan of Arc (Naginski 2000), she is also a modern French citizen, the daughter of a Bonapartist whose legacy she claims with much more passion than those who, in the novel, directly benefited from the Emperor's largesse. When Marie asks her why she hates the British, Jeanne, in her naïve ways, offers an explanation meant to demonstrate that a strong emotional attachment to the nation may exist in spite of a limited worldview and education:

Your late daddy who was a great military man (so they say), waged war against them, and your mommy, who was always scared he would be killed, hated them to death. And then, my mother cried, and cried when the Emperor was dismissed and *put in an iron cage* by the British, and I, seeing her crying, cried too. She also used to get mad when people said that the British had brought an English king from their country to Paris to order the French around. That's why, Mam'selle, I was so surprised when I came here to hear your mom say that she liked Louis XVIII, the British king; and I did not know what to think [...] when I saw the portrait of the Emperor moved to the attic. But I put it in my room without telling anyone and I don't think there's anything wrong with that. (Sand 1986: 199)

Jeanne's patriotism is such, in fact, that she categorically refuses to marry a rich Englishman, as good and generous as he may be, because in her eyes he represents not only perfidious Albion, the traditional national enemy, but also the modern enemy, the Royalists' ally in the fall of the Napoleonic Empire. As we will see in this chapter, the Sandian conception of the nation as "daily plebiscite" is particularly evident in the novels Sand wrote after 1848, in the aftermath of the Republicans' defeat and of the lessons she drew from the fall of the Second Republic. To examine national identity in the works written by the mature novelist is to give oneself the means of understanding that these works belong to a single project and at the same time to question the critical vision that traditionally divides George Sand's life in two, her revolutionary years up to 1848, and her grandmother's years, encapsulated in her "Good Lady of Nohant" image, afterwards.[1]

6.1 George Sand and the Republic

In her essay on "Families and communities in post-revolutionary France," Claudie Bernard (2005) argues that the two main institutions on which society rested in nineteenth-century France, the family and the nation, did not live up to the expectations people had placed in them: "[T]he Nation can be constraining and oppressive, does not treat all its members on the same footing, and is taint-

---

1 This opposition is found, for instance, in Naomi Schor's *George Sand and Idealism* (1993). Michael Garval, in 'A Dream of Stone,' questions this dichotomy, showing, in the chapter he devotes to the evolution of George Sand's image (2004: 112–157), that this dual image became a standard under the influence of the press and in an environment rather hostile to women but not until the end of the century. Philippe Régnier (2004: 146) makes a similar point: "[...], far from blooming in the literary field's margins, as legend has it, Sand occupies a dominant position in it, and this domination [...] only increased as realism and naturalism emerged at the bottom of the field during the Second Empire."

ed by internal strife. Similarly, the disappointment with bourgeois family, never free, never fair, never loving enough, almost seems inseparable from the family itself." (Bernard 2005: 261) Nineteenth-century writers, who, like the Saint-Simoniens and the Fouriéristes, felt a strong need to remedy "this double deficiency of nation and family," turned to "associations" as a new form of mediation between the individual and the state (261). From the mid-1830s to mid-1840s, Sand was friend with numerous republican philosophers and political thinkers who envisioned a better society: Michel de Bourges (1797–1853), her republican lawyer and lover; Giuseppe Mazzini (1805–1872), founder in 1834 of *Giovine Europa*, a movement that sought to create a federation of European republics; Félicité de Lamennais (1782–1854), a former priest and early advocate of the separation of church and state who became a republican philosopher; and particularly Pierre Leroux (1797–1871), a Christian socialist philosopher, whose idea was "to organize family, property and nation 'in such a way as to serve the indefinite communion of man with his neighbors and with the universe.'" (Bernard 2005: 268) Leroux, Bernard argues, played a crucial role in helping George Sand "gradually emerge from the mal du siècle" (270) characteristic of her novels of the 1830s, *Lélia* in particular. Her focus on political and social issues and her trust in the possibility of social improvement are reflected in the central role working-class characters play in her late novels of the July Monarchy, *Le Compagnon du tour de France* and *Horace* in 1842, *Jeanne* in 1844, or *The Miller of Angibault* in 1845. Her involvement with causes related to the betterment of humanity also took the form of a collaboration on numerous projects meant to familiarize the public with humanitarian, republican, and socialist ideas: her support of Leroux's *Revue indépendante* in 1841; of the printing association he established at Boussac, not far from Nohant in 1843; of working class poets in the 1840s; of a republican newspaper *L'Eclaireur de l'Indre et du Cher* in 1844. After the June repression of 1848 she also petitioned the government on behalf of Republicans who had been arrested or forced to leave the country, asking for leniency and, in several cases, providing them with financial support. She spent considerable sums of money in support of causes that were dear to her heart, as much as "the equivalent of £ 1,000,000 earned from her writings" according to Donna Dickenson (1995: xxv).

6.1.1 Republican patriotism

In *Les Patriotes, La Gauche républicaine et la nation,* Darriulat (2001: 8) shows how French Republican identity developed between 1830 and 1870, crystallizing around five values that have formed the core of the national credo in France ever since the Third Republic: "universal suffrage, reference to the Enlightenment, secularism, involvement with social issues, and patriotism." The Revolution of 1830 led to a split of the liberal camp: those on the right of the political spectrum who seized power viewed it, like Mérimée, as a restoration of the constitutionality of the monarchy following its violation by Charles X, whereas for Republicans like Stendhal and Sand it was the continuation of the 1789 Revolution. For them, patriotism and republicanism went hand in hand.[2] Too young to have experienced the glorious moments of the 1789 Revolution, the Republicans of the July Monarchy, who grew up with memories of Waterloo and a wounded sense of national pride, initially believed that history was resuming its course after a thirty years hiatus, that the Revolution of 1830 would lead to "a general uprising of nationalities – a spring of the people [...] against old monarchies" (Darriulat 2001: 18–19). "Wars among kings [we]re not national wars" (100), but wars of liberation from the monarchical yoke were.

In the early 1830s these young Republicans did not have a clear political doctrine or program but they shared a common "romantic sensibility" that led them to believe in the virtues of the people and to face the future with confidence (Darriulat 2001: 9). The terms 'nation' and '*patrie*' thus belonged to the "domain of feelings and passion, to a subjectivity hardly permeable to the logic of reason. There was no need to define the nation; its existence was sufficiently demonstrated by the feelings of a people ready to die for her" (111). But as Darriulat further shows, republican attitudes toward the nation were contradictory as well. On the one hand, the nation was not seen as an end in itself but rather as an intermediary stage between the state of barbarity and the bright future of universal happiness. Helping other nations who shared the aspiration of freedom from tribalism or from autocratic regimes was thus seen as a sacred duty. In France, this conviction took the form of support of wars of liberation and, as we saw in the chapter on Stendhal, colonization; in the United States, of the doctrines of Manifest destiny – and more recently of the political will to "export democracy" to the world. On the other hand, however, the nation was bound to remain an empty, powerless entity as long as the State served the interest of a few, instead of reflecting the will of the people. The necessity for a nation to have a political identity, to be a republic, was the logical consequence of this premise.[3]

---

2 "To be a patriot is to be on the left, and in the end, a republican. That's how contemporaries saw it." (Darriulat 2001: 15)
3 "Patriotism, a natural virtue among peoples, may become a vice if it is placed in the service of a degenerated State." (Darriulat 2001: 115)

By tracing the Republicans' reactions to foreign and domestic events from 1830 to 1870, Darrriulat shows that a narrow form of nationalism soon replaced this initially open, forward-looking attitude. Disappointment with the outcome of the Belgians insurrection of August 1830, which led to the creation of a new monarchy instead of a republic, resurrected the rhetoric of the "*grande nation*" and the desire to annex Belgium (30). Anger over the French government's inaction during Poland's uprising of November 1830, produced a new kind of nationalist, even xenophobic discourse pitting Russian barbarity against French civilization (43). As the dream of a republican Europe vanished, Republicans focused their attention away from the international to the domestic sphere, and here too there was cause for disillusion. Not only did the July Monarchy last much longer than predicted, its policies also contradicted republican expectations in every respect. By 1835, it had violently repressed workers' insurrections, reintroduced censorship, and arrested republican leaders. More profoundly, it embodied a new type of aristocracy based on wealth, *l'aristocratie des écus*, that adhered to 'British' ideas incompatible with the Republicans' values of generosity and solidarity France supposedly embodied. Just as Louis-Philippe's foreign policy of "peace of all costs" (Darriulat 2001: 20) had annihilated the dream of a democratic Europe, so too the *entente cordiale* signaled a humiliating subjection of France to England. Nationalism took on a new meaning as the Guizot government was increasingly seen as the "foreigners' party" and Republicans started viewing themselves as the "national" party (112). Darriulat also argues that by 1840, after France's exclusion from the London treaty, patriotism ceased to be the prerogative of the Republicans, as it had been in the early 1830s; that "it belonged to everyone" from then on (15, 91).

The Republicans' critique of Great Britain hinged on the contrast between their own idealist vision of the nation, "supposedly generous and philanthropic," and the economist, "merchant and egoistic" model England symbolized in their eyes (Darriulat 2001: 104). As opposed to the market, which was of concern only to the few people who had a vested interest in it, the nation was supposed "to concern everyone, owners and workers, the educated and the peasantry, civil servants and soldiers united as citizens" (112). In a context where "Anglophobia was one of the dominant themes of the republican discourse in the years 1835 – 1848" (104), attitudes towards England provide a useful indictor a writer's politics: thus Mérimée's Anglophilia in *Colomba*, where the Nevils embody civilization, places him out of the republican camp; while Stendhal's fears of Anglicization in the late 1830s and Sand's critique of England in *Jeanne* point to their inclusion in it.

In 1824, the target of Stendhal's early critique of the economist vision of the world in *Of a new Plot against Industrialists* was not England but his liberal friends in France. The core of Stendhal's critique of capitalism was its reduction of all forms of capital to one, economic capital (Le Hir 2007). But the critique of liberalism in the republican press took on nationalist overtones in the context of increased commercial and colonial competition with England during the July Monarchy. In George Sand's works, this critique takes the form of an affirmation of "the primacy of feelings so as to better proclaim the superiority of moral, over material interests" (Dariullat 2001: 112), with the goal of contributing to a better world. Against a liberal individualism associated with the defense of narrow, selfish, material interests, Sand's novels of the 1840s extol the common good, the virtues of love, fraternity, and solidarity that simple people instinctively possess and adhere to, because they are involved with the real world through their work and unspoiled by money interests.

In the *Miller of Angibault*, for instance, Grand-Louis, the main protagonist, embodies the people in all its aspirations and virtues: disinterested love, honesty, devotion to the poor like Piaulette and the downtrodden like Cadoche, but also common sense and good judgment, and above noble and productive labor. Money, on the other hand, corrupts absolutely: Uncle Cadoche, who stole a pot of gold, has lived his life as a beggar for fear of being found out and losing it. M. Bricolin, the nouveau riche, is evil incarnate, a man with no feelings and no scruples, a father who sacrificed his elder daughter's sanity on the altar of wealth and is ready to immolate his younger daughter as well. Henri Lémor famously reduces the achievements of the 1789 Revolution to naught in the novel: it has led to the "universal *sauve-qui-peut* to which the corrupting effect of money has reduced all humanity" (Sand 1995c: 111). Instead of doing away with all forms of inequalities, the Revolution has created new ones.[4] The peasants' current obsession with money, however, is presented as a generational aberration. Mère Bricolin and Grand'Marie, who have been friends for sixty years and symbolize the people's good instincts, form an alliance with the young, and help re-establish traditional peasant virtues in the community when they help Rose and Grand-Louis realize a union deemed all but impossible until the end of the novel. Mother Bricolin has seen the deleterious effects of the obsession with money close up: her husband lost his mind together with his pot of gold; and her son, who stopped respecting her once he received his inheritance, was responsible for her granddaughter's raving madness.

Sand's intent in this novel is to show that inequalities can only disappear if aristocrats and bourgeois sincerely renounce their privileges for ever, it they

---

4 "They say the world is much changed these past fifty years; I say nothing has changed but the ideas of some of us have." (Sand 1995c: 52)

adopt the people's common sense and virtuous way of life. Marcelle de Blanchemont happily accepts the loss of her fortune as a precondition to her marriage with Henri Lémor, a bourgeois who has himself renounced "his businessman father's mercenary ideas" and sold his inheritance "for a pittance to a man whom father Lémor had ruined through the most rapacious and disloyal schemes of an unpitying competition" (Sand 1995c: 107). Both believe in a moral and social regeneration through work, "in a religion of fraternity and community in which all men will be happy through mutual love and rich through self-deprivation" (111). Once free of the burden of his aristocratic lineage and of his fortune, Marcelle's son Edouard "will get a good education" from his stepfather and "the miller will teach him his craft" (297). In order to achieve national unity, society has to find its balance. The rich must get closer to the people through work; the working class closer to the rich through education.

6.1.2 George Sand's project of national unity[5]

As the 1848 Revolution broke out, George Sand rushed from Nohant to Paris, where she soon played the role of an "unofficial information minister" (Dickenson 1995: xxiv). At the height of her political activism, in May 1848, she published, in *The true Republic* [*La Vraie République*], three articles that clearly demonstrate the importance of the national question in her political thought since they have as titles and subjects: "The religion of France;" "The Dogma of France;" and "The Cult of France."[6] If, as Michelle Perrot indicates in her presentation, these texts "illuminate Sand's religious ideas and highlight the burning desire of Republicans and many socialists to reconcile religion and democracy" (Perrot 1997: 451), they underscore above all the great significance Sand granted to the affective dimension of national belonging. In her eyes, no faith in the republic is possible without a transfer to the nation of "the sincere and profound faith" (454) of the Gospel, of a Gospel "freely understood and interpreted," whose new motto is "Liberty, Equality, Fraternity" (459).

This conviction was for Sand the outcome of a reflection on the history of France recently consigned in *Story of my life*. It was neglect of religious feeling,

---

5 This section was previously published in French: "Le Sentiment d'appartenance nationale dans l'œuvre de George Sand", in *Romantisme* n°142 @ Armand Colin, 2008.
6 These three articles were published in *La Vraie République* on 11, 12, and 13 May 1848 under the title "Questions de demain" [Questions for tomorrow]. They appear under the same title in *George Sand. Politique et Polémiques (1843–1850)*. Translated quotes from these articles are mine.

of man's instinctive aspiration toward an ideal beyond the confines of his own universe, that had led to the fall of the First Republic and of the First Empire. The revolutionaries, who initially believed they could count exclusively on Enlightenment philosophy, understood their mistake too late since they waited till 1794 to establish the cult of the Supreme Being.[7] Similarly, the First Empire fell for want of a common faith, or more precisely because of the new meaning the word *patrie* took on when losing "faith in herself" to "only believe in Bonaparte," France ceased to be "the safeguard of the common good" to "become the guarantee of each individual's interests" (Sand 1991b: 314). Sand then elaborates on this point, explaining why this change matters:

> The common good, in our societies where inequality reigns, is yet of a higher order than material possessions. It consists of honor and liberty, and although less than humanity has a right to desire and expect, remains the ultimate foundation of all ideals, the point of departure in the quest for the integrated world humanity longs for. Everyone can take this noble quest to heart; everyone can work for this dawning of fraternal equality. It is still a very abstract idea, but sublime abstractions rule the souls of men and exalt their character by elevating their thoughts.
> Individual interests produce quite a contrary effect. No government constituted on an individualistic principle can satisfy everyone, no one being exactly alike, and the infinite degrees of inequality in fortune and rank create as many adverse interests as there are men engaged in the struggle. (Sand 1991b: 314–315)

And summarizing her thoughts, Sand concludes: "It was for want of a social religion not for lack of genius or patriotism that Napoleon failed in his design." (315)

A follow-up on the project sketched out in April 1847 when she began writing *Story of my life*, the three texts on France's religion, dogma, and cult, aim at assimilating religion and politics, or more precisely at erasing what Sand calls "that chimera, prejudice, which makes the [...] words [...] religion and philosophy, into opposing and irreconcilable terms " (1991b: 344). In these lines, one may undoubtedly detect the influence of Lamennais and Leroux with whom she was in close contact in the 1830s and 1840s and who played an important role in her religious evolution. But her relations with Lamennais[8] cooled off

---

7 "And let us even suppose that [...] the French might have persisted in believing themselves to be totally philosophical – which is not probable, *because in 1794 they had outlined a religion and accepted the wording* – that philosophy, which would have matured by being challenged, and that solidarity in the face of danger, which would have been engraved on all hearts as synonymous with homeland, would have imbued us with a strength that would probably not have broken at Waterloo." (Sand 1991b: 344) [my emphasis]

8 On Sand and Lamennais, see Rubat du Mérac (1994); Hamon (2005: 67–112).

due to disagreements and stopped when she met Leroux in 1836, and by 1845, she had freed herself from Leroux's influence as well.[9] The most decisive factors guiding her line of thought and providing materials for her novels afterwards were her personal experience of political life during the 1848 Revolution and the deep disappointment of witnessing the Second Republic's fall, as evidenced by her correspondence with Armand Barbès, her republican friend (Perrot: 1997). This sustained letter exchange also shows that Sand had reached such a point of intellectual and political maturity by then, that she no longer any needed master or guru – as the relation of equality between the two letters writers makes crystal clear – and also, in light of the duration of this letter exchange – from May 1848 to Barbès's death in 1870 – that the political situation of France and its future never ceased to be on her mind during this entire period. Isabelle Naginski (2003–2004) examines Sand's handicap in a literary field structured by the opposition between a dominant "realism" and an "idealism" deemed old-fashioned and associated with Sand's name. This "idealism," however, takes on an entirely different dimension when the political project that informs it is taken into account. Barbès who understood better than anyone else Sand's insistence on approaching the social world from a subjective, intuitive angle, through the heart's voice, as much as from an objective vantage point, did not hesitate for his part to speak of Sand's "genius" (Sand 1999: 116).

To Sand's growing interest in society and politics during the post-1848 period corresponds a similar disenchantment with established religion. In "Le triomphe de la liberté de conscience et la formation du parti laïc," Philippe Boutry traces her religious trajectory, from her deep devotion as a teenage girl to her increased disaffection with the Church from the 1830s onward, an evolution he sees as illustrative of a general trend, as symptomatic of the declining influence of Catholicism in French politics in the 1830s. Sand's post-1848 literary project finds nonetheless its organizing principle in the political axiom theorized in the three texts on France's religion, dogma, and cult of France. As Bernard Hamon points out in *George Sand face aux églises*, the right way to envision the reconciliation of religion and politics was not, for her, "to invent a substitute religion in order to preserve the nation's unity and avoid civil discord" (2005: 138). Her rejection of any "substitute religion" is clearly expressed in *Nanon* through the heroine's feelings of alienation during the celebrations commemorating the 10 August 1792 sack of the *Tuileries* palace in the town of Chateauroux. This "republican fête" appears to her as "purely fanciful," as a "senseless performance" (Sand 1901: 167). To create a new republican religion that would replace Catholicism was not what Sand

---

9 On Leroux's influence on Sand's religious conceptions, see Hamon (2005: 31–85, 112).

had in mind. It was instead to make the nation itself the object of love and belief, to restore the affective dimension of the Republic, to give a firm and unconditional basis to the faith in the nation by instilling in everyone the desire to contribute to a France where "fraternal equality" would reign. It meant, in other words, finding the means of eliciting Renan's "daily plebiscite," or to use Sand's terminology in the last of these three texts, "the free and spontaneous consent of all" (Sand 1997a: 464). Hamon argues that Sand never realized her "dream of a religion redefined to conform to republican values and freed of the paralyzing supervision of the Church, or Churches," (2005: 138). But that dream, I argue, finds its expression in the national religion that was to become one of the main pillars of the Third Republic: the secular belief in the nation.

It is thus not a coincidence if, in the very first pages of *Story of my Life*, Sand places her autobiographical project under the aegis of "solidarity," defined as "the source of progress for the human mind which is most alive and serious" (Sand 1991b: 73),[10] and envisioned as the modern equivalent of Christian "charity," eighteenth-century "sensibility," and revolutionary "fraternity" (Sand 1970 : 9). "The recital of struggles in the life of each," she writes, "is, therefore, a lesson for all; it would mean health for all if each of us could analyze the cause of our suffering and realize what has saved us" (74). Applied to her own case and developed in *Story of my life*, this thought explains the extraordinary importance she grants to what some critics have mocked as "the story of her life before her birth," that is the account of the suffering her close relative – grandmother, father, mother – had to endure before the unique individual in which the contradictions that so bitterly opposed them were annulled could see the light of day.[11] In Sand's story, the main obstacle to a national unity symbolized by the marriage of the noble father and the plebeian mother, is not Mme Dupin de Francueil's aristocratic bias towards commoners, even if she is descended from Maurice de Saxe. Nor is it economic interest. She does not object to her son's choice of Sophie Delaborde as a wife because of the young woman's lack of title or wealth. It is not her reason, but her heart that rejects her. The older Mrs. Dupin, Sand gives the reader to understand, did not want her son to marry a woman who

---

10 The adjective Sand uses in French is "religious," not "serious": "La source la plus vivante et la plus *religieuse* du progrès de l'esprit humain, c'est […] la notion de solidarité." (1970: 9)

11 Examining reviews of Sand's *Histoire de ma vie* in his preface to her autobiography, Georges Lubin considers that "some of them were not inappropriate" (xxi). Armand de Pontmartin's 1855 criticism that "the amount of place devoted to the father was […] excessive" and pointed to "an obvious composition flaw" seemed particular pertinent to him: "Some have claimed that a better title would have been *Story of my life before my birth*," he commented. (Lubin 1970: xxi)

had already loved.[12] She feared that a fickle woman would not bring happiness to an only son she adored. Sand's family story therefore points to the novelist's conviction that the great republican dream of fraternal equality has to do with the heart. Moreover, through the change of heart that occurs when baby Aurore is placed in her grand-mother's lap,[13] this personal anecdocte enacts the miracle that occurs when hearts open up, thereby demonstrating that the dream of fraternity is within reach.

By approaching the issues of national reconciliation and national unity from a personal vantage point, through her autobiography, Sand is in a better position to highlight the crucial role of feelings when it comes to instilling a sense of national belonging: only love and solidarity can give life to a nation. Moreover, to the extent that the suffering described in *Story of my Life* is the direct product of a precise historical context, the revolutionary Terror and Napoleonic wars, it offers an exemplary lesson. The readers can generalize from Sand's individual case, understand that there are no social conflicts that can't be solved when love of others is involved; they too may hope and change. That Sand wrote *Story of my Life* with this goal in mind is clearly stated at the beginning of the book when she addresses and challenges the people to speak up, to "escape from oblivion" by following her example and writing their life stories: "Thus, you artisans who are beginning to understand things, you peasants who are learning to write, don't forget your departed ones any longer. Hand down the life of your forefathers to your sons [...]. Write your stories, all of you who have understood your lives and probed your hearts" (1991b: 86). This duty to remember is not a gratuitous exercise. To write down one's life story is not only a way of proclaiming one's dignity and one's presence in the national community, but also, by working through this raw material, an apportunity to be transformed, wherever one may be, and thereby to contribute to the collective betterment of the nation.

Sand actually completed herself the project she had assigned her fellow citizens. Contrary to what one might think, she did not do so in her rustic novels only – when, for instance, she tried "to save the furrow of Germain, the 'expert plowman' from oblivion" in *The Devil's Pool* (Sand 2004: 96). She did it in a more general, all-encompassing fashion, for all of France, and to such an extent that it is tempting to read retrospectively the passage of *Story of my Life* quoted above as a kind of preface for her future work, serving the same function as Balzac's

---

12 Sophie already had several children from different fathers.
13 Elizabeth Harlan cast doubt on the veracity of Sand's account, seeing it as a product of the writer's imagination or wishful thinking (Harlan 2004: 6–8). But whether this event ever took place or not Sand's belief in the power of love cannot be doubted.

"Foreword" in the *Human Comedy*. In the novels she wrote after settling down in Nohant in 1848, Sand's concern was less to prove something, than to experiment, to trace paths, to give hope, to present French men and women as they were and as they might become under the beneficial influence of solidarity, and of the religious feeling of love. Barbès understood Sand's project of national unification so well, that seeking to make amends for his role in the "improvised, unjustified, and hopeless attempted coup d'état that only led to her friends' arrest" (Perrot 1999: 9) on 15 May 1848,[14] he wrote the following lines to her from his exile in The Hague in August 1867: "48 could have been saved if we had listened to you. What we needed was more love. France is a country of love, and who knows? Those we called reactionaries might have loved us if we had known how never to threaten and to show that we were capable of love." (Sand 1999 144)

Love, this all-powerful social force in Sand's work, is found in two forms, as she tells us in *Horace:* "the noble passion" that "exalts and strengthens us in the beauty of our feelings and the grandeur of our ideas" and the "harmful passion [...] that returns us to egotism, fear, and all the pettiness of blind instinct" (Sand 1995b: 149). As she further explains, "[e]very passion is either legitimate or criminal, depending on whether it produces one or the other effect, although society, which bestows humanity's seal of approval, often sanctifies the harmful and proscribes the good" (149). Seen from that vantage point, it becomes easier to understand the crucial role Sand grants to the process of sentimental education in her work of maturity. In novels like *The Marquis de Villemer* (1861), *The Black City* (1861), *Mademoiselle de la Quintinie* (1863), *Mademoiselle Merquem* (1868), *Cadio* (1868), *Malgrétout* (1870), *Nanon* (1872), or her last, unfinished novel symptomatically entitled *Marianne* (1876), love relationships are painted as works in progress, as the product of a labor meant to challenge love, to make it overcome obstacles, and past suffering.[15] Commenting on *The Marquis de Villemer*, Lucienne Frappier-Mazur notes that the memory of the past in Sand is "both antidote and antithesis to mourning" – since "once the loss has been accepted, it is liquidated" – because "it leads to the blending of social classes, the equality of genders and the inclusion of the feminine [...]. Far

---

14 Perrot explains that "the perfect understanding that existed between Sand and Barbès had been undermined [...] by the 'stupid day' of 15 May [1848]" (Perrot 1999: 9).

15 Commenting on *Mademoiselle de la Quintinie*, Gilbert Chaitin explains why Sand's *roman à thèse* is not just about abstract ideas but "joins the ideal and the real, the spiritual and the material, the abstract and the concrete, the political and the aesthetic, in sum the story and the idea" by "making the struggle over the thesis *be* the story [...]" (Chaitin 2004: 81).

from erasing it, one must cultivate memory with an eye to a better future." (Frappier-Mazur 1992: 173)

These remarks apply as much to the rustic novels as to the novels mentioned above, to Landry and Fadette in *Little Fadette* (1849); Madeleine and François in *The Country Waif* [*François Le Champi*] (1850); or Tiennet and Thérence, Brulette and Huriel in *The Master Pipers* [*Les Maîtres Sonneurs*] (1853). The gaze does not stop on the past, it takes note of it, and turns toward the future: Sylvinet leaves to serve his *patrie*; François, the abandoned child, finds "dignity and love of work" (1980b: 4); two communities with opposite ways of life, the sedentary peasants of Berry and the lumberjacks of Bourbonnais, learn to understand each other and to fuse in *The Master Pipers*. The difference between *The Country Waif* and *Mademoiselle Merquem* is not that the first is a rustic novel but not the second: they both have the same rural, provincial, setting, and female protagonists, Madeleine Blanchet and Célie Merquem, with similar characters to the extent that they share the same altruism, the same ability to give. Where they differ is in their social milieu, and consequently also, in the nature of the obstacles the protagonists have to overcome to reach the harmony they dream of. The beautiful, learned, and wealthy Célie is the embodiment of the educated and independent woman; Madeleine, the peasant woman, lacks education and autonomy. But in spite of these differences, both have one important thing in common: they have never experienced love and must learn how to love, a lengthy education of the heart at the very core of each novel.

In these novels, the nature of the learning process depends on the characters' pre-existing qualities. Altruists, the Marquis de Villemer, Caroline de Saint-Geneix, Sarah Owen, learn to think of themselves; egoists and libertines, the Marquis de Villermer's brother, Montroger in *Mademoiselle Merquem*, Horace in the eponymous novel,[16] and Adda Owen in *Malgrétout*, to think of others. Illiterate characters, Abel dans *Malgrétout*, Cadio, François le Champi get an education; Lucie de la Quintinie learns to distinguish between dogma and true religion. In most cases, the educational process yields positive results; very few characters remain impervious to change and are left to their own device for

---

16 *Horace* is particularly interesting in that regard because, as the concluding lines of the novel show, even an individual as selfish as the main protagonist has the ability to change: "Horace himself became an excellent young man, steady, studious, inoffensive, still a bit declamatory in his conversation and bombastic in his style, but prudent and reserved in his conduct. [...] Finally, having less literary success than talent and needs, he courageously decided to finish his law degree; and now he is working to build a clientele in his native province, where he will soon be, I hope, the most brilliant of lawyers." (Sand 1995b: 329)

that reason.[17] In practically every scenario, characters that strive for self-improvement and come to terms with their past are rewarded with a wished-for marriage initially perceived as impossible. This plot line may be seen as a sacrifice to bourgeois conventions on Sand's part, but as Frappier-Mazur points out, there is a better way to interpret the frequent recurrence of misalliances: as a means "of putting an end to the ideology of lineage" (1992: 172). Let us add that in novels where noble characters are absent, the theme of misalliance is used to destroy popular biases against people who do not neatly fit into the local social organization (*fades, charbonniers,* foundlings), in other words to integrate to the community those who were at first excluded. It is also interesting to note that requited love does not mean selfishness but that it tends instead to lead to new forms of solidarity. In *Mademoiselle Merquem*, for instance, Clélie is part of a sea-side community from the start – she rescues shipwrecked sailors and passengers – but love also opens up Armand's eyes to those around him and makes him see Stephen's loneliness. Realizing how cruel he has been in misusing the painter's friendship, he becomes a sincere and devoted friend, which in turns allows Stephen to open up, to see the world with fresh eyes, and in the long run to become a true artist. As Bernard observes:

> What saves the domestic garden from […] degradation, in many of Sand's novels, is that it grows into a 'community,' halfway between private and public spheres. Contrary to Lélia and other early heroines, who were solitary, powerless, and suicidal Edmée de Mauprat, Yseult de Villepreux, Fadette, Brulette, Tonine or Nanon, whatever their station in life act in order to preserve their love commitment, and their action reaches far beyond their ménage: towards a collectivity, extended family, village, factory, working town, whose example, they hope will have repercussions on society at large. This is the utopian component of Sand's 'familialist' feminism. (Bernard 2005: 274)

In short, the sustained character and the cohesion of Sand's literary project during the Second Empire appears once her novels are examined from the vantage point of the "free and spontaneous consent of all," as a project devoted to the acquisition of feelings of national belonging.

6.2 Patriotism and nationalism at times of war

The religion of love that is the central theme of these novels, and in which Sand's conception of the happy nation is grounded, does not imply any pacifism on her part. She believes in national self-determination and thus also in the necessity of

---

17 It is the case, however, for Joset in the *Master Pipers* and Count de Remonville in *Malgrétout.*

wars of independence. One of her complaints about Napoleon, for instance, is not that he waged war too much, but, on the contrary, that he demeaned himself by concluding peace treaties with European monarchies and thereby shattered the peoples' nationalist aspirations.[18] This "passionate citizen" (Hamon 2001: 7) viewed war as legitimate, even as necessary, when it was fought in the name of liberty, of national independence, or whenever the *patrie* was in danger. In *Story of my Life*, she defended the wars of the First Republic when "[h]eroic martyrs of freedom [...] had an incontestable and glorious mission for all times and from all points of view – that of safeguarding the national territory" (Sand 1991b: 149). During the Second Empire, she proclaimed her support for the nationalist struggles waged in Italy and Poland (Hamon 2001: 327–399). But Sand's nationalism is best exemplified in the texts she wrote before and during the Franco-Prussian war. Her writings of the period have in common to take place in a precise temporal setting, at a historical moment when France's national sovereignty was threatened: the revolutionary wars in *Cadio* (1868) and *Nanon* (1872); France's invasion at the fall of the First Empire in *Francia* (1872); the Franco-Prussian war in the *Diary of a Traveler during the War* [*Journal d'un voyageur pendant la guerre*] and her correspondence with Gustave Flaubert.

The nationalist theme is fully developed in *Cadio*, a novel set during the Chouans wars of 1793–1795 that Royalists from the Vendée and Brittany fought, together with their British allies, against the armies of the First Republic – which is probably the reason why a few republican characters are Anglophobic in that novel. This revolutionary epic centers on the political education of the nation, on the progressive conversion of people of all classes to the cause of the Republic. In this *roman dialogué*, Sand identifies the philosophical, social, political, religious and human conflicts that stand in the way of the "true republic," while at the same time working toward their resolution. Over the course of the novel, Cadio, the Breton bagpiper, loses his naive religious faith and his dreamy poetic personality; rallies behind the revolutionaries out of admiration for Henri de Sauvières – thus once again showing that attachment to the nation is a matter of the heart; rises through the ranks in the republican army to become, like him,

---

18 "We had addressed these nations in our propaganda; momentarily affected by the wonders we were working, they went back to their selfish preoccupations when we ourselves provided the example of a hurried return to the past. The seeds of revolution that these nations possessed were less ready to flower than ours, but had we properly nurtured them, they would have overthrown their despotic governments. They watched France deny her beliefs and crouch beneath the wing of a man stronger and more powerful than all the despots of Europe. How could they believe in the brotherhood of republics? They again adopted the hostility of contending monarchies." (Sand 1991b: 316)

an officer; turns for a while into a revolutionary fanatic; but in the end, having matured and been saved by love, becomes a real citizen.

Written two years later, *Malgrétout* marks a departure from this earlier optimism in its treatment of the issue of national belonging. Apart from *Jeanne*, Sand's work is relatively free of the ambient Anglophobia of the period. Most of her British characters are presented in a positive light – Ralph in *Indiana* (1832), Jacques's friend Ralph in *Le Diable aux champs* (1857), Lord B*** in *La Daniella* (1858), and Sarah Owen in *Malgrétout* [1870]. In that novel, however, the notion that one should belong to one nation only is clearly expressed. Although an accomplished woman in all respects, Sarah, who is British through her father and French through her mother, worries about her dual citizenship: "I lack nationality [...] I don't have the genius of any of them" (1992b: 13). If belonging to two nations is perceived as an identity flaw in *Malgrétout*, cosmopolitanism, presented as a lack of attachment to any nation, is severely criticized and associated with selfishness, ambition, lack of morals, and the inability to love for the characters of Médora in *La Daniella* and of Camille d'Ortosa in *Malgrétout*. In that novel, Camille, a character in which some critics have seen a portrait of Empress Eugénie, goes through a process of self-criticism: "I was educated in Madrid, Paris, London, Naples, and Vienne, that is to say, not educated at all" (1992b: 112). Also noteworthy in *Malgrétout* are the doubts expressed by the main protagonist with regard to the possibility of lasting love: "I love him with all the energy of my heart," Sarah Owen says of Abel, "and I may be very happy; I may just be gathering strength for sorrows I'll never know; but I don't want to delude myself" (1992b: 176). Nonetheless, and in spite of this cautionary stand, the struggle goes on, the conviction remains that the beloved ideals are still worth fighting for, as the novel's preface makes clear:

> On veiled horizons, shrill and woeful voices are proclaiming that the world is dying, that powers are collapsing, seawaters rising, that the social vessel will soon be just a wreck; but those whose heart did not die in fear are conscious of the universal vitality whose powerful wind sustains and lifts them up. How far is the shore? Why ask? Nobody knows; but all can act and some will: those who still love the *patrie* and still believe in human perfectibility. (1992b: 12)

One could hardly state more clearly that love of the *patrie* is what this novel is about – just as it is the topic of her other works of the early 1870s.

6.2.1 National identity *in Nanon*

Published four years later than *Cadio*, *Nanon* revisits the topic of the 1789 Revolution to describe its effects on the ordinary life of peasants in the *Creuse*.
This second novel on the Revolution, set this time in central instead of Western
France, tells the story of the eponymous character, retracing the trajectory that
led her to become "less of a peasant, that is to say more of a Frenchwoman"
(Sand 1901: 318). In *The Civilizing Process*, Elias praises George Sand for her excellent depiction of the old feudal provincial ways in her novel *Mauprat*.[19] The
passage that attracts his attention and that he quotes at great length is one in
which Sand describes the difficulties people used to a particular social universe
have adjusting to a new one. As one of "the last debris [...] of that race of petty
feudal tyrants," old Mauprat leads a life of "exactions" and "organized brigand-
age," but he does "not ask for money [...] because money represents for him [...] a
commerce with things and people formed outside, an effort of foresight or cir-
cumspection, a market, a sort of intellectual struggle, which jolts him out of
his apathetic habits, in a world of mental effort, and to him this is the most painful and disturbing thing of all.' (Sand, *Mauprat*, quoted in Elias 2000: 242) How
to change mental habits is an issue also taken up in *Nanon*. Substituting country
folks in flesh and bone to the poetic allegories of the peasantry still found in
Cadio, Sand reflects in this novel on the means to attach the rural population
to the nation in a more concrete fashion. She offers an astute analysis of the national habitus when she points out that institutional change – the passage from
a feudal to a republican system – does not suffice to transform a nation of peasants into a nation of citizens. She shows, through the villagers' reactions to the
Fête of Fédération, that liberty, even if it brings joy to the village, is at first an
abstract and difficult concept to understand. The meaning of the celebration escapes them as well as Nanon, even if they are eager to understand:

> The little brother explained to me that the principle cause of the rejoicing was that all
> France was to be under one and the same law thenceforth, and he impressed it upon
> me that, from that moment, we were all children of the same fatherland. He seemed hap-
> pier than I had ever seen him, and his joy passed into my heart, although I had as yet very
> little knowledge on which to form a judgment of so momentous an event. (1901: 54)

---

19 "And if we can believe a poetess, George Sand – and she expressly confirms the historical
authenticity of what she says – there were still a few people leading these untamed feudal lives
in provincial corners of France right up to the French Revolution, by now doubly savage, fearful
and cruel as a result of their outsider situation. She describes life in one of these last castles that
had by now taken on the character of robbers' caves less because they had changed than
because society around them had done so [...]." (Elias 2000: 242)

Accustomed to their servitude, fearful of the unknown, and incapable of adjusting to change, the old folks die: "When the men of the law appeared and notified him of the new order of affairs, the prior had been stricken with apoplexy. He died in the night." (50) Similarly, Nanon's great-uncle had been "a serf so long, that he could not conceive another kind of life or different habits. He was so shocked and worried that he died a week after monsieur le prieur." (50–51) For Elias, this inability to adjust to radical change is nothing out of the ordinary but on the contrary the norm:

> Becoming accustomed to doing without an order of things in which a symbolic ruling figure bears the responsibility for a nation of subjects, and adjusting to a regime which lays however limited a responsibility on each person is a lengthy process that requires conditions that are as crisis-free as possible and takes at least three generations. (Elias 1996: 291)

The fact that the adaptation process takes a long time also explains why freedom and the new way of life the Revolution brings along are a source of uncertainty and anxiety not only for old people, but also for young ones, Nanon in particular. Their attachment to the nation must therefore be constructed in as "crisis-free" a way as possible, which means incorporating instead of destroying meaningful pre-existing bonds.

Since love of religion and land are what matters most for the villagers in *Nanon*,[20] religious markers must not be erased from daily life, but maintained: the church bells must continue to ring, until such time at least as the association with religion disappears and a secular meaning takes its place.[21] Similarly, freedom has to be experienced concretely to be understood: owning land, as a result of the clergy's expropriation, allows country folks to learn how to live freely, to define themselves as individuals. A necessary condition to the creation of a bond with the abstract entity of the nation, individualism is presented as something that has to be learned as well in Sand's novel. Nanon's ambivalence towards her new status of landowner indicates that it is a difficult apprenticeship.

---

20 Land and religion are the country folks' main concerns: "Among us, with whom everything was a matter of barter – work on one side, payment in produce on the other – money was not a seductive dream; [...] we thought about owning a meadow, a bit of woodland, or a garden, and we said : 'That is a right of those who work and bring children into the world.' Piety alone held the peasant back." (Sand 1901: 13)

21 "As the monastery was no longer a parish church, mass was not said there; but, at the request of the inhabitants, the prior caused the Angelus to be rung in the morning and evening and at noon. They had long ceased to say their prayers, but there is nothing that the peasant likes better than the sound of his church bell. [...] Later, when the monastery bells were requisitioned to be made into cannon, there was great consternation." (Sand 1901: 92)

When Émilien asks her if she regrets her serfdom and her misery, as her great-uncle did, she responds that she is happy to own a house, but also conscious of having a responsibility, the nature and extend of which she still ignores. She also fears that she might become someone else in the process and thereby lose the web of social relations that make her who she is.[22]

Émilien tries to alleviate her fears and to convince her that she has nothing to lose and everything to gain with the following reassuring words: "The peasant of today, you see, is between two very different things: the past, when many people preferred to suffer rather than to help one another, and the future, when by helping one another, they will cease to suffer." (1901: 65) Of aristocratic birth himself, Émilien views love as a new, republican religion, and based on his experience, as something incompatible with Old Regime mores. Throughout the novel, the peasants' ability to love, which is best illustrated by Nanon's altruism, is sharply contrasted with the affective void of aristocratic life, best exemplified in the novel by Madame de Franqueville, an aristocrat who "never petted her [daughter Louise]" or "even love[d] her older son [Émilien]" (95–96). The lack of maternal love is not presented as a personal flaw on the part of "this beautiful matron," however, but, like in Gouges's *Madame de Valmont* and *The Convent, or Forced Vows*, as a defect inherent to an aristocratic family model that treats children as things to be disposed of at the father's will, and where family relations cease as soon as the offspring leaves the house (95–96). Whereas Gouges emphasized the deprivation of individual freedom inherent in this conception of the family, Sand underscores its psychological effects on children, starved for the love and the affection they would need to become well-ajdusted adults. Her point is not, however, that the birth mother alone is capable of providing that love. It may also come from substitute parents, such as Nanon's great-uncle, as it does in many of her novels. Even a young girl like Nanon can provide some of the affection Émilien craves through the friendship that develops between them.

---

22 "I see what it will be necessary to do to repair this place and keep it in repair, and I know that my cousins won't help me much. They will not have any feeling of attachment for what is not theirs. They will be jealous of me perhaps. They have a way of laughing at me because I take more care of them than they do of themselves. You know very well that, if they are a little uncivilized, they don't pretend to be anything else, that they destroy more than they repair, and that they are always pleased when a day has passed, provided they don't to talk of the next day. Well, perhaps they are right, and I am going to take a great deal of trouble for which they will not be particularly grateful to me. I am so young! Is it possible that at my age I have in my charge an estate worth a hundred francs? They will tease me. What do you advise me? Perhaps you think as they do." (Sand 1901: 62–63)

Unloved by his parents and by the monks he lives with, Émilien suffers particularly from not being loved by his father, M. de Franqueville: "If my father had written to me himself, if he had asserted his claim to my obedience with some show of affection, I would have sacrificed everything, not my conscience, but my honor and my life." (117) This is why things are clear in his mind and in Sand's as well: on the one side, a feudal system that privileges the interest of the dominant group in every respect, demands blind obedience from all, from peasants because might makes right,[23] and from aristocrats in the name of honor; and on the other hand a republican nation that grants every individual, without consideration of social origin, the right to own, to love, to examine and judge freely. As far as Émilien is concerned, therefore, the nation is his true mother, the only one worthy of love, the one he is willing to die for if need be. Although his family pressures him to behave as prescribed by the aristocratic code of conduct, he enrolls in the revolutionary army, and proudly loses an arm which he views as his gift to the new Republic. Love of the nation, Émilien tells us clearly, ranks higher than all other forms of love when the *patrie* is in danger: "[I] am no man's son when it is a question of betraying France. [...] I am no longer a noble, I am a peasant, a Frenchman!" (117) If placing love of the nation above of other forms of attachment in moments of crisis is the peculiarity of the national habitus, it is precisely what French aristocratic émigrés like M. de Franqueville, Émilien's father, are incapable of doing. These pre-nationals do not love their country, they think of their interests and those of their caste first. As for the dupes that obey them, they are just slaves.

6.2.2 Nationalism in *Francia*

In Sand's mind, the distance between a free and an enslaved people is immeasurable, nothing else but the very distance that separates civilization from barbarity.[24] This is the main theme of *Francia*, a novella set in 1814–15, that begins at the fall of the First Empire, on 13 March 1814 to be precise.[25] In *Story of my life* Sand had devoted a few pages to Napoleon's "inexplicable" defeat in 1814 and 1815, arguing that "If a royalist party had not emerged to sell our country

---

23 The carter who drives Nanon to Chateauroux expresses this Old Regime mentality of passive obedience: "When the government orders me to do thus and so, I am ready to obey." (1901: 149)
24 In these novels, the foreigner is really the military and political enemy, not a figure of feminine alienation, as Syvlie Charron Witkin (1995) suggests for some of Sand's novellas.
25 Paris surrendered on that day. In the absence of an available English version of *Francia*, translations are mine.

and betray it, the whole universe united against us could not have defeated the French army" (Sand 1991b: 590). Considering that Francia is the name of the old kingdom of the Franks, it makes sense to see the protagonist's relation with the Russian prince Mouzarkine as a symbol of France's treason by the aristocracy in 1814. This betrayal is graphically depicted in the opening scene of *Francia* through the contrasted reactions to the victors' military parade of the patriotic working class on the one hand and of the unpatriotic elite on the other. The crowd of Parisians, who would have gladly fought against the enemy had they not been prevented from doing so, feel hurt in their national pride, as they suffer the shame and humiliation of defeat.[26] Offering a "gloomy, sorrowful and sometimes menacing welcome" (Sand 1980a: 3) to the foreigners, the Parisians use the compact mass of their bodies to express their hostility[27] and "exclamations of hatred and rage" (5) when Mouzarkine's horse hits Francia. The unpatriotic Royalists, by contrast, treat the Russians as allies and friends:

> When the military parade reached the boulevard, the scene changed almost magically. As the enemy was getting closer to the rich neighborhoods, middle ground was found, the foreigners could breathe; and then all of a sudden, they all merged, not entirely without shame and scruple. The royalist element threw its mask away and dashed into the victors' arms. (Sand 1980a: 7)

A comparison with Staël's reaction to the first occupation of Paris in 1814 underscores how different her sense of national belonging was from Sand's. "It would be altogether wrong to feel surprise at the grief experienced by the French on seeing their celebrated capital occupied in 1814 by foreign armies" (Staël 2008: 595), Staël wrote in *Considerations*, a laconic comment that establishes a distance between "the French" and herself, or rather, from Sand's vantage point, puts her in the position of a royalist traitor. Staël's "insupportable grief on seeing Paris occupied" sounds hollow in light not only of her professed "esteem" and "unqualified admiration" of "the foreigners for having shaken off the yoke" (566), but also of her personal encouragements to the Czar to send his Cossacks to Paris. More than "moral inconsistency" (Goodden 2008: 271), these conflicting feelings reveal Staël's inability or unwillingness to take responsibility for

---

26 "We lost this time as always by denying the people the right and means to defend themselves, by distrusting them, by refusing to provide them with weapons. Silence was therefore their only protest; sadness, their only glory." (Sand 1980a: 2)

27 "The crowd was becoming so dense that had it closed up on the victors [...], they would have been smothered without being able to use their weapons." (Sand 1980a: 4)

the consequences of her actions.[28] How could she, who had "been instrumental in turning the tide against the despot" (Goodden, 221) feel grief once the enemy was in Paris? When it came down to it, even barbarity *à la russe* was preferable to civilization *à la Napoléon* for Staël. The Russians may still have been "what we call barbarians," but as she used the term "to designate [...] a certain primitive vigor that alone can stand in place of the surprising power of liberty in nations," it was more a compliment than an insult. (Staël 2000: 155). Napoleonic France, by contrast, was just one of those "nations [...] which have learned no more of civilization than the art of explaining power and rationalizing servitude" and are therefore "made to be conquered." (Staël 2000: 148)

Sand obviously saw things differently. She meant 'barbarian' when she wrote it. A standard theme of the nationalist rhetoric, hatred of foreigners, finds its way in *Francia*, through the opposition between civilization and barbarity. In the opening scene of the novel Mouzarkine is already presented as a "barbarian prince" (Sand 1980a: 28), as "a reflection of the type and taste of the barbaric Orient" (8). The Russians, the narrator argues, may seem civilized because they speak French, because they master the Old Regime art of proper social behavior, but they don't know the first thing about real, post-revolutionary French values.[29] The French love freedom, the Russians live in servitude. Even a prince like Mourzakine is a slave, forced to live according to the whims of his uncle Count Ogokskoï. This selfish man is utterly incapable of loving anyone, he only knows how to exploit other human beings, so for instance when he steals his nephew's mistresses. These two Russians' entire "science of life" consists in "crushing the weakest to unite with the strongest" (Sand 1980a: 23) The French may also "yield to masters" once in a while, but they "get tired of them with marvelous ease" and know how to "sacrifice [their] personal interests to the need of being [them]selves again" (24).

When Mourzakine mentally compares the Muscovites' heroism, because they burnt down their capital city rather than seeing it occupied by the French, to the latter's cowardice, because they opposed so little resistance to the Cossacks when they entered Paris, the narrator intervenes and protests, observing, as

---

28 This is probably the kind of contradiction Stendhal had in mind when he noted that Staël did not think: "In France, if you write well [...] you may say anything, thought itself means nothing anymore. Look at the works of Mme de Staël and Chateaubriand. These famous writers do not think." (Stendhal, *L'Italie en 1818*, quoted in Félix-Faure 1974: 34)

29 "In those days, no one was less akin to a Frenchman than a Russian. Here, we called them 'Frenchmen of the North' because of the ease with which they spoke our language and complied with our customs; but never was identification more far-fetched and impossible. They could only take from us what did us the least justice then, our kindness." (Sand 1980a: 22).

Sand had already done in comments on the 1812 fire of Moscow in *Story of my Life*,[30] "that the Muscovites did not destroy the city themselves; that an enslaved people does not have to be consulted;" that it is "heroic willy-nilly and cannot brag about involuntary sacrifices." (Sand 1980a: 9)Whereas the French trust in merit, the Russians are forced to resort to cronyism and nepotism to get ahead: "Protection, from wherever it may come, was a vital condition for any future among the poor Russian nobles in those days. Ogokskoï had been carried by the fair sex, Mourzakine was protected by his uncle." (Sand 1980a: 38) Smilarly, the Russians are subject to "the blind cult of absolute power" (23), but the French believe in reason and democracy. The Russians are "deprived of the right to speak and thus los[e] the need to think" (Sand 1980a: 137) but the entire Parisian population enjoys freedom of thought and speech because Paris is "a temple of truth where people think out loud and where they teach each other what to think about everything (137).

Even if Mourzakine was ever able to overcome all these cultural differences, he would still be a foreigner, an enemy because "[h]e had been duly baptized a Russian through the French blood he had spilled" (Sand 1980a: 23). The battle of Moskowa, where Mourzakine "spilled French blood" two years earlier, plays a pivotal role in the love affair that develops between this foreign enemy and the young Parisian woman he has hurt during the parade. Following the incident with his horse, the prince sends a servant to inquire about Francia's health, and she, in turn, asks for permission to call on him because she thinks she might have seen him on the battlefield. When Francia and her younger brother, Théodore, meet with the Russian officer, it is the young boy, Dodore, a typical Parisian urchin who has much in common with Hugo's Gavroche, who tells how they ended up in the midst of war. Their mother, Mimi, was an actress who had taken them along when her company was on tour in Moscow. During the retreat from Russia in 1812, they all fled with the French army, but mother and daughter were separated at the battle of the Moskowa. The children made it back to Paris with the help of an old soldier, Moynet, but Mimi disappeared.

---

30 "Supposing that before burning Moscow, Rostopchin had taken the advice of several rich and powerful families, the population of that vast city would nonetheless have been obliged to submit to the sacrifice of house and home; and one may well doubt that they would unanimously have consented to that, had they been consulted, had they any claims to make and rights to uphold. The Russian war was the ship tossed by the storm, which threw its cargo overboard to lighten the ballast. The Czar was the captain; the sunken cargo, the people; the ship to be saved, the sovereign's policy. If ever authority has profoundly despised and discounted the lives and property of men, the ideal version of such a system is to be found in absolute monarchy." (Sand 1991b: 556)

Francia, who remembers seeing a Russian officer before being wounded, thinks that this officer may have been Mourzakine. The children therefore hope that he might have information on their mother's whereabouts. Mourzakine actually knows that Mimi died during the battle but he promises to do his best to help them because he is interested in Francia, whom he recognizes as the young French woman he saved at the time. For him, the encounter comes at the right time. He just had to give up his Parisian mistress, Marquise de Thièvre, because his all-powerful uncle and master, Count Ogokskoï, wanted her. The young Cossack has no difficulty seducing Francia: she has led the life of a *grisette* out of financial necessity for a few years and immediately falls in love with him. After only three days of happiness, however, her lover disappears. News that Napoleon is still fighting brings joy to Dodore, who lets his sister know that he is going to fight so that the enemy never reenters Paris. Francia declines his offer to join him on the barricades and goes searching for her lover instead. Because she heard him mention her name, she asks to meet with Madame de Thièvre, who being eager to know if it is true that Francia is Mourzakine's new mistress, agrees to see her. During the meeting, however, she also brings a devastating piece of news to Francia: her lover is actually her mother's killer; Mimi "was crushed under his horse's hooves" (Sand 1980a: 144).

The next day, as Paris learns of Napoleon's capture, Francia falls gravely ill. Her doctor reassures her that Mimi is still alive, that the jealous Marquise just wanted to hurt her, but he also recommends that she end her relationship with Mourzakine and he finds new accommodations for her. But when the Russians return to Paris, the young officer succeeds in convincing his lover that he did not kill her mother and they resume their life together. Although he does not wear his uniform in public to alleviate her fears of being seen "as a traitor of the *patrie*" (Sand 1980a: 159), Francia suffers nonetheless because of the way her countrymen treat her, her doctor, for instance. A nagging sense of self-loathing takes a hold of her, due in part to jealousy towards the Marquise, in part to the self-contempt she feels for loving "an enemy of [her] country" (161). Mourzakine tries to comfort her by taking her to see a play, but a chance encounter with Moynet's nephew, Antoine, only increases her sense of shame and her conviction that she "deserves the contempt of all honest people" (161). To make matters worse, Count Ogokskoï takes a sudden fancy to her and tries to kidnap her. Francia then realizes with horror that Mourzakine, who had just offered her a dagger, knew about the Count's intentions. She manages to escape, Antoine finds her and brings her back to his uncle's house.

Moynet, the brave soldier, serves as the civics teacher in the novel. Once Francia has confessed her love for her Russian prince, acknowledged that she is living with him although she knows he killed her mother, her surrogate father heaps reproaches on her:

> "You are a heartless coward," he told her; "you betrayed your country and your mother's memory. You gave yourself to the man who killed her! Here, stop crying, kept woman of the enemy, lest I put you out to join the other prostitutes in the street! The other harlots? No, I'm mistaken, how could I forget... whores are better than you! The day the enemy marched into Paris, not a single one of them went to work... Ah! I blush in shame for you! For me as well, who brought you all the way back from over there. I would have done better to shoot you in the head! What a fine piece of wreckage from the *grande armée* we have here, what a striking illustration of our crushing defeat! The enemy must have a high opinion of us indeed! (Sand 1980a: 194)

Insensitive to Francia's pain and to her pleas to stop insulting her, Moynet carries on for a long time, painting her life as over while at the same time forbidding her to commit suicide, an act that would only add to her cowardice in his eyes. In spite of his warning that no Frenchman will ever want to marry her, "to have a Russian's leftovers" (197–98), he nonetheless asks his nephew if he would. This is a desperate solution since Francia had already rejected Antoine, who loved her, but who did not conform to her standard of beauty at an earlier point in her life. To Francia's consternation, even Antoine hesitates, even he would be "ashamed of loving" her (200). In this miserable state of mind, Francia returns to Mourzakine's apartment with the plan of regaining some of her lost honor:

> I don't want people to say: "She was the mistress of the Russian who killed her mother and she loved him so much that she killed herself for him..." I want to be forgiven, to be remembered with respect when I'm be gone. I want people to tell my brother: "She acted despicably, but she redeemed herself; you can be proud of her and mourn her. You wanted to kill Russians, but it was not to be. She found a way. She avenged your mother." (Sand 1980a: 211)

As these lines clearly show, the murder Francia is about to commit is premeditated. She hides in Mourzakine's bedroom and waits till her lover returns and goes to bed. When he is deep asleep, she approaches him and, as she watches him, looks "into the deep abyss she has fallen into" (210). Then, shaking with fever and with a heart as cold as her body, she plunges the dagger he had given her in his chest, killing him instantly. The narrator, however, changes her story at that point. Francia, she tells us, was in a state of semi-consciousness when she acted; she did not know "where or who she was" (213) and by the time she made it back to Moynet's, she was gravely ill again. In her delirium, she confessed what she has done, but those who heard her confession made sure that it remained a secret for the justice system and also for Francia herself. When she recovered, not only didn't she have any memory of the murder she committed, her love for Mourzakine was also as strong as before. She was therefore told, and believed, that Mourzakine had left with the Russian army, that he forgot about her. She worked for a few months as a laundry woman in a hospital but died of consumption on 21 March 1815, the day Napoleon re-entered Paris.

Sand's tale shockingly reveals patriotism's perverse logic, the subordination of all forms of love to one, love of the *patrie*, in times of war. Neither Francia's love of her biological mother, the initial reason for her relationship with Mourzakine, nor her love of this dashing officer, are good enough reasons for betraying her true mother, France. Even a child, even Dodore who "awakens to life through patriotic pride" (Sand 1980a: 92), knows that it is a horrible thing to make friends with the fatherland's enemies, as he tells Francia:

> It's disgusting, you see, to throw yourself into the Cossacks' boots like that ... It's cowardly! I'm just poor, I have nothing, I am nothing, but I spit on the enemy's helmets. Our allies! What a joke! A bunch of brigands! Our friends, our saviors! Make me laugh! They'll set Paris on fire if we let them, you'll see. So, there's absolutely no reason to lick their boots! Don't go back to this Russian. (Sand 1980a: 87–88)

When Dodore has to go to "this foreigner" himself, just being in the Russian's house stirs his blood (128). Coveting with the enemy is treason and treason is like a contagious disease. It destroys those who loved you; it kills their affection, it replaces their love with shame and despair. To the hierarchy of love corresponds a hierarchy of crimes. There is no greater crime than treason, no worse offense than sleeping with the enemy: even prostitution (selling oneself to all men) pales in comparison to loving a foreigner. As innocently as Francia may have acted, she is guilty in the eyes of those who loved her and now despise her.

The plot also discloses patriotism's immorality. Social shunning teaches Francia that her crime cannot be easily forgiven and puts her on the road to murder. When it comes to the *patrie*, there are no half measures. The only way Francia can redeem herself is by being truly heroic in the national sense, by sacrificing the man she loves to the *patrie*. "Shame," "betrayal," "foreigner:" all this nationalist vocabulary leaves no doubt about Sand's patriotism. By giving Moynet's exalted nationalism free rein without intervening, by letting his demeaning insults stand without a commentary, by excusing Francia's murder of Mourzakine, and by letting Francia escape justice, the narrator indicates agreement with this patriotic logic. She also shows that once the national crisis is over and once Francia has become worthy of the *patrie* again, the violent nationalist rhetoric subsides and hostile attitudes toward her disappear. The doctor finds her a job, Antoine, Moynet, and Dodore love her again, and all mourn her when she dies.

Sand's comments in her *Diary of a Traveler during the War* and her letters to Gustave Flaubert during the Franco-Prussian war amplify the nationalist themes of her fiction and give it a more personal tone. In her war diary as in *Francia*, war against France is seen again as a clash between civilization and barbarity: "The military condition is a brutal constraint that repulses our civilization. [...] At this time, Germany asserts itself as [...] a brutal force, and let's not mince words, as barbarity." (1980c: 114–115) In a 17 March 1871 letter to Flaubert, the Franco-Prussian war is described once more as "a struggle of barbarity against civilization" (1980c: 191). In her *Diary*, the republican dichotomy opposing an idealist, generous France to a selfish, capitalist England, is adapted to underscore the contrast between a freedom and peace loving France and a materialist Germany that misuses its scientific advantage and its population for murderous purposes, an easy thing to do in a nation attuned to the hierarchy of command and obedience. Weighing France's chances of success against a nation that has made a "fatal material progress [...] in the industry of murder, of weapons of destruction, and of military science," Sand comes to a pessimistic conclusion: "discipline is a dead thing among us" because "[p]assive obedience seems incompatible with the progress each of us has made in the sentiment of self-possession." (1980c: 145) Sand also acknowledges that she adheres to the nationalist principle that personal opinion must be silenced "in the well-understood intention of defense" (Sand 1980c: 97) in times of war so as to offer a unified front to the enemy.

The pessimism found in *Malgrétout* is echoed in the *Diary* in comments from October 1870 regarding the fate of the newly proclaimed Republic. After Sedan, Sand questioned the wisdom of establishing a Republic at a time, when "the country [wa]s not republican" (Sand 1980c: 97), as she wrote on 9 October, in other words when so few French people were in favor of this form of government: "Is it true that only a republic can save France? Yes, I firmly believe it still, but a constituted and real republic, consented to and defended by a nation deeply imbued with the greatness of its institutions, jealous of maintaining its independence within and without. This is not what we have now." (151). A true republic, she believed, should not be imposed by a minority, as was the case with the Third Republic. If the nation did not will the republic into existence, if public opinion associated it with party politics, the people would never know that the republic was "an ideal, a philosophy, a religion" (160).

In December 1870, the same concern for national unity made her reject the Paris Commune as an ill-advised and doomed experiment: "It is a delusion to believe that knocking down the doors of the [Paris] *Hôtel de Ville* by surprise and insulting a few defenseless men turns you into the masters of a nation like ours." (203) A month later, Sand reiterated her belief that the republic had to be based on love and fraternity, not hate and violence (206). For her, the Commune was a missed opportunity: the "reds" had been too self-righteous, too impatient, the Second Republic's failure had not taught them anything about to the use of violence (251–52). They had even forgotten basic lessons of the French Revolution, namely that "a society based on the sacrosanct respect of the principle of equality, embodied in universal suffrage and freedom of the press" (253) does not have to act rashly. By doing so, by resorting to "violence, hatred, and insult," the *Communards* lost "the right to call themselves our brothers" (253). Their punishment was therefore well deserved.[31] In a very long 14 September 1871 letter to Flaubert, in which she reaffirmed her republican principles and her faith in France, Sand once again compared what the Commune could have been, had "[a] patriotic fanaticism [...] been the first sentiment of this struggle" (Sand 1921: 222) to what it actually was, an "[u]nfortunate *international*" rebellion (221).

In spite of the grief caused by the French defeat of 1870 and by the Commune, Sand was not ready to conclude to the people's incurable stupidity, as Flaubert did.[32] She tried instead to prove to her cynical young colleague that the revolutionary proletariat did "not even represent the people of Paris," (1921: 215), that the Parisians were not "ferocious," but just "ignorant and foolish" (215). More fundamentally, she objected to his vision of the people as separate from writers like them, or from the rest of society, insisting that all appearances of social distinctions were illusions: "The people, you say! The people is yourself and myself. It would be useless to deny it. There are not two races; the distinction of classes only establishes relative and for the most part illusory inequalities." (213) She was not willing, in short, to abandon her principles and her beliefs: "For me, the ignoble experiment that Paris is attempting or undergoing proves nothing against the laws of the eternal progression of men and things, and, if I have gained any principles in my mind, good or bad, they are neither

---

31 "The scorn of France is perhaps the necessary punishment for the remarkable cowardice with which the Parisians have submitted to the riot and its adventurers. It is a consequence of the acceptance of the adventurers of the Empire; other felons but the same cowardice." (Sand 192: 196)

32 Flaubert wrote, among other things, in his 8 September 1871 letter to Sand: "I believe that the crowd, the common herd, will always be hateful" (1921: 208). "The idea of equality (which is all the modern democracy) is an essentially Christian idea and opposed to that of justice." (1921: 208–209) "The first remedy will be to finish with universal suffrage, the shame of the human mind." (1921: 209)

shattered nor changed by it" (195), she wrote to Flaubert on 28 April 1871. When he mocked her idealism, she fired back on 14 September 1871:

> And what, you want me to stop loving? You want me to say that I have been mistaken all my life; that humanity is contemptible, hateful, that it has always been and always will be so? And you chide my anguish as a weakness and puerile regret for a lost illusion? You assert that the people has always been ferocious, the priest hypocritical, the bourgeois always cowardly, the soldier always a brigand, the peasant always stupid? ... Ah! We are entirely different for I have never ceased to be young, if being young is always loving. (Sand 1921: 212)

At the same time, there were new lessons to be learned from the Commune. Never an unconditional supporter of universal suffrage, Sand had sided with Louis Blanc in 1848 when he had argued that education should be made a pre-condition to universal suffrage.[33] The Commune reinforced her in her conviction that universal suffrage as practiced during the Second Empire had given peasants and workers a sense of entitlement, and hence a right they may not have deserved. But if the government were to try to roll back universal suffrage (1980c: 215), farmers would fight back by withholding taxes and "the charming proletariat created by the Empire" would not see any reason to go to school now that it already had the right to vote (1921: 202).

Would education help anyway, Sand wondered? Although she believed in the necessity of education for all, she also confessed her misgivings in that re-gard to Flaubert: "[C]ompulsory education, which we all desire out of respect for human rights" would not be, she knew, "a panacea, [...] an infallible remedy for our woes" (1921: 216). She even worried that education might result in less morality and honesty, as "evil natures" would "find in it only more ingenious and more hidden means to do evil" (1921: 216). As opposed to her, Flaubert fret-ted that being able to read would not develop, but diminish the people's intelli-gence, since, according to him, newspaper reading "dispense[d] with thinking" (1921: 209). By February 1871, Sand, who had initially resisted the Third Republic, was sincerely hoping that it would last. But even if it did not, it was no reason in her eyes to despair of France (1980c: 398). In the long letter initially written to

---

33 On 27 September 1870, Sand wrote in her *Diary:* "Louis Blanc had a true revelation of the future when, in 1848, he consented to universal suffrage provided it was proclaimed with this restriction: free and mandatory schooling is to be understood in such a way that any man who will not know how to read and write three or five years from now will lose his right to vote." (Sand 1980c: 51) Two weeks later, she stated her own position more clearly: "As for me, it is with regret that I saw it [universal suffrage] being established in 1848 without the prerequisite free and mandatory education." (Sand 1980c: 163)

Flaubert, but transformed into an article for the newspaper *Le Temps*,[34] she exhorted her fellow citizens, to love each other, to believe in liberty, equality, fraternity, and to form one nation:

> Frenchmen, let us love one another, my God! My God, let us love one another or we are lost. Let us destroy, let us deny, let us annihilate politics, since it divides us and arms us against one another; let us ask from no one what he was and what he wanted yesterday. Yesterday, all the world was mistaken, let us know what we want today. If it is not liberty for all and fraternity towards all, do not let us attempt to solve the problem of humanity, we are not worthy of defining it, we are not capable of comprehending it. Equality is a thing that does not impose itself; it is a free plant that grows only on fertile lands, in salubrious air. It does not take root on barricades, we know that now! [...] Let us desire to establish it in our customs, let us be eager to consecrate it in our ideas. Let us give it for a starting point, patriotic charity, love! It is the part of a madman to think that one issues from a battle with respect for human rights. (1921: 220–221)

But in spite of her deep and primary concern for her nation, Sand had not lost sight that the further step was Europe: "Let us also wait, not for a war of extermination, not for a heinous revenge [...]; on the contrary, let us wait, for a republican and fraternal alliance with the great nations of Europe" (Sand 1980c: 309).

Conclusion

Just as the diversity of social settings in Sand's writings invites a sociological reading of her work, so too the diversity of geographical settings encourages an approach focused on the description of landscapes and regional particularisms that makes the construction of the nation easier to grasp as "a rich legacy of memories" than as expression of the "free and spontaneous consent of all." But if one considers her post-1848 work as a whole as an expression of the political project that informs it, that is of the desire to transform France into a true republic, the issue of national belonging as "daily plebiscite" emerges clearly, as does Sand's patriotism.

As we saw, virtually all the themes and tropes of the patriotic republican discourse are found in her novels. The values of liberty, equality, and fraternity of the First Republic are praised and presented as the core values of a rejuvenated post-revolutionary French nation that rejects materialism and selfishness. Love and marriage between characters of different social backgrounds, between rich

---

34 "Dear old friend, I answered you the day before yesterday and my letter took such proportions that I sent it as an article to *Le Temps* [...]." (Sand 1921: 224)

and poor, aristocrats and workers, are envisioned as a means towards greater social equality, towards a more perfect national union. Out of the group of writers examined in this book, Sand is also the most explicit in her definition of secularism as a transfer of faith from religion to the nation.

Patriotism and nationalism are dominant themes in the novels, diary, and letters Sand wrote in the late 1860s and early 70s. In the years leading up to the Franco-Prussian war she did not believe in the possibility of war, contrary to her friend Barbès, who as early as 1866, expressed concerns over France's military weakness and repeatedly shared the strong misgivings he had about Prussia's growing power with his friend. "I note with a tender emotion that you are as chauvinistic as ever [...]," Sand teased him, "still the old warrior and knight, just as I am still the old troubadour who believes in love, art, ideal, and who still sings even when the world hisses and jabbers" (1999: 126). France's military defeat at Sedan in early September 1870 and the Prussian occupation of France thus came as a surprise and led her to reconsider her 'troubadourism.' Both her *Diary of a Traveler during the War* and her letters to Gustave Flaubert during the war confirm what her novels of the period also reveal: her sustained preoccupation with the fate of the nation, her love of the *patrie*. In an 11 October 1870 entry of her *Diary* she noted with some pride that of the two balloons that successfully left Paris during the siege, one of them was named Armand Barbès, the other George Sand (1980c: 101). Mostly forgotten today, this significant homage from her fellow citizens gives a good measure of Sand's reputation as a republican patriot in her lifetime in France.

Sand's and Mérimée's passionately emotional reactions to the defeat prove beyond a doubt that the national habitus shaped the personality structure of members of the higher social strata by the 1870s. On the one hand, the defeat had a determining impact on the policies of the Third Republic with regard to universal suffrage, conscription, and above all education, through the Jules Ferry laws on primary schooling in the early 1880s. On the other hand, these three "pillars of Jacobin democracy" did not only democratize France, they also nationalized it. As Zeev Sternhell (1977: 15 – 32) has shown, liberal democracy and positivism, the dominant belief systems for decades in France, fell into discredit in the "last twenty years" of the century, and nationalist ideas that had been dormant since the early 1800s took on unprecedented influence at that point.

Conclusion

> *For what we call the history of Europe is to this day still written to such a great extent from the viewpoint of the victors that the viewpoint of the defeated seldom enters into the current picture of history; and the polyphony of ways of life, the absorption of typically upper-class patterns by middle and lower classes, the rise of lower- and middle class patterns of behaviour and feeling to the top and the transformation of social structures, the framework within which these changing patterns occur, remain largely unexplored.*
>
> (Elias 1996: 74–75)

At the end of this study, we can conclude to the pertinence of Elias's analysis of the national habitus and to the usefulness of his toolset for examining the genesis of the national habitus in France between 1789 and 1870. The writings of the six French revolutionary and post-revolutionary writers who are the focus of this book provide ample clues on the mental orientation towards future and/or past that informs them; detailed accounts, in some cases, of the conflict between bourgeois and aristocratic values that is constitutive of the makeup of the national habitus; and a great deal of information on the writers' attitudes towards physical violence in general and war in particular. Our examination of their sense of national belonging, of their 'we-feelings,' has allowed to us to see the concept of nation expand over time, to show that the nation was not a static, but an evolving concept in nineteenth-century France and that there were different ways of feeling French prior to the establishment of the Third Republic. We were also able to observe that the more inclusive the concept of nation became, the more the need to proclaim its uniqueness and superiority over foreign nations asserted itself, turning doves into hawks at times of national crisis.

Of the three writers of the revolutionary field examined in this book, Olympe de Gouges and Germaine de Staël represent the progressive pole of the 1789 Revolution. Both writers drew from Enlightenment principles and from the Judeo-Christian tradition to criticize the failings of the aristocracy in power and to justify the middle class's claims for the political power sharing arrangement the *Tiers-Etat* fought for, and obtained in 1789. But the liberty, equality, and fraternity they proclaimed was meant to cement a nation comprised of an elite only,

Royalists like themselves who were enlightened partisans of a Constitutional monarchy and an aristocracy they hoped to reform, to convince to give up its code of honor and adopt their bourgeois values, their beliefs in the common good, reason, virtue, and goodness for the sake of the *patrie*. From their vantage point, Chateaubriand stood in the camp of the accused, as the recalcitrant aristocrat who would not budge and who remained faithful to an aristocratic conception of identity based in honor.

A year before the Revolution, Olympe de Gouges denounced the aristocratic code of conduct as one of "cruelty, fanaticism, and hypocrisy" in *Madame de Valmont's Memoirs*. Too many aristocrats had no moral principles, were "deaf to the cries of nature;" claimed to be Catholics but actually used religion to the benefit of their estate; and last but not least, did not behave fairly and morally with the bourgeois members of high society. As Gouges saw it, however, the initial purpose of the Revolution was not "to touch the sacred antique tree of the Monarchy, just to prune its [...] branches." As her various projects of voluntary taxation in the early phase of the Revolution indicate, her sense of identity as a French woman was already very strong prior to the start of the Revolution. A long tradition of being called upon to bail out the state in time of financial crisis, to sacrifice for the good of the kingdom, undoubtedly accounts for the high bourgeoisie's early sense of patriotism in general and for Gouges's in particular. As David A. Bell reminds us, however, this kind of patriotism was premised on "inseparability of king and *patrie*, and king and nation," but "[o]n the left, the king came to appear not only detachable from both, but positively inimical to both" (Bell 2001: 77). In Gouges's case, patriotism took on a new meaning under the pressure of revolutionary events, and in particular in light of the aristocracy's deafness to her pleas for reform. Already unwilling to make financial sacrifices to save their country from financial ruin, the princes suddenly left it in time of need, showing their preference for members of their aristocratic caste outside the kingdom over their fellow citizens, and, to her unspeakable horror, bearing arms against them. The aristocratic desertion came as a shock to those who, like Gouges, only wanted to expand the definition of the nation so as to be fully included in it. It did not dampen, but it changed the nature of her patriotism since her 'we-feelings' could no longer include aristocrats and a king who had, through their actions, demonstrated that they did not love the *patrie* the way she did.

In Gouges's writings, the new 'we' is constructed both negatively in opposition to a "them" that refers to "foreigners," – Necker, Marat, "Pitt and the King of Prussia," and the *Cromwelliens* – and positively in a personal Pantheon that creates a mixed legacy of memories, at once monarchic through the inclusion of great kings; aristocratic, but only through its female line; and bourgeois, through

the inclusion of French Enlightenment philosophers as well as Greek predecessors. Gouges's patriotic exaltation reached its peak in the last two years of her
life in pamphlets and plays that depict the French Revolution as the outcome
of the struggle for human rights, the *patrie* as a beacon for humanity, and war
against "the tyrants" as evidence of humanity's march toward liberty and progress. But in spite of her willingness and efforts to adjust to the rapid pace of the
Revolution, Gouges could not keep up with the continuous redefinition of the national 'we.' She was always a little too late, as it contracted politically, always a
step behind as it expanded socially. In spite of her inflamed declarations of un-
dying patriotic faith she ended up being viewed as one of "them" and paying for
it with her life.

Bourgeois reformists like Gouges and Staël who wanted aristocrats to abandon their code of conduct and adopt theirs did not realize how difficult it is to
change a person's or a caste's habitus. In Chateaubriand's case, the recent full
re-admission of his family to the aristocratic club represented an additional obstacle. There was simply no incentive to want to be French differently. Aristocrats
like him experienced the Revolution as a traumatic event, as the disintegration
of the world as they knew it. It robbed them of family members, of their country,
of their identity, and of their sense of place and social superiority. As Elias
writes:

> The connection between the group-specific self-denials and frustrations imposed by the
> upper-class code upon each member, and the simultaneous pleasure which they draw as
> a compensation for the frustrating self-constraint [...] is seen more vividly when the
> power of such an establishment begins to crumble. [...] The meaning and value of conven-
> tional self-denials [...] are lost in the disintegration; and with the loss of power, even its
> own members doubt the meaning and value of the group. In such a situation, it is almost
> impossible for the members of the falling group to form or even to borrow another code
> which would enable them to regulate their lives in a way they would find equally meaning-
> ful and valuable. (Elias 1996: 73)

For a young man like Chateaubriand, it meant that all sacrifices consented to belong to this exclusive social group had been in vain, that there was no future in
sight. The melancholic tone of his writings, his Romanticism, stems from this
deep sense of personal loss and mourning. Understandably, Chateaubriand
had neither regard for the Revolution nor affection for the new France it had
given birth to. In a belated response to the bourgeois critique of the aristocratic
code of conduct, the young *émigré* went on the attack and denounced a bourgeois understanding of virtue and morality that had only produced bloodshed
and social chaos. Responding to the accusation of aristocratic irreligion in
pre-revolutionary France, he laid the blame squarely on an immoral court that

had allowed the "philosophical sect's" ascent, particularly during the Regency, and, as a result, the annihilation of morals, the destruction of the family, and thus also the rise of a pernicious, selfish, individualism in France. As far as he was concerned, civility and honor were better foundation blocks for French society.

In spite of Chateaubriand's political conservatism, the discursive strategies used in his *Essay on Revolutions* to void the Revolution's accomplishments show that he had already partly appropriated the new sense of national identity, the modern sense of distinguishing between 'us' and 'them.' The Enlightenment philosophers and their disciples, the Jacobins, whom he held responsible for the disastrous revolution, were not French, he claimed. As they lived in books instead of their country, they loved foreign institutions and tried to transform France into the pastiche of a Greek republic or a copy of England. They had changed the French character by adopting British "cruelty" and killing Louis XVI, as the British had killed Charles I. In England, however, the aristocracy had learned its lesson and was mending its ways in order to avoid a revolution of the kind France had just experienced. It was time to do the same in France, to return the country to its true identity by restoring French institutions, the monarchy and the church, and the country to its Catholic faith so as to improve the people's morality and prevent social upheavals down the road.

In Chateaubriand's case, embracing Catholicism was certainly a way of finding some kind of identity at a time when the France he had known no longer existed. In that regard, *The Genius of Christianity* deserves to be seen as an effort to make Christianity palatable to people who, like him, had lost touch with it. But the book's function is perhaps less to reconnect France to its religious past than to create a new imaginary community, a new French identity. By opposing the universalism of Christianity to the universalism of reason, by arguing that severing the link between politics and religion could only destroy the identity of France, *The Genius of Christianity* proposes a counter-revolutionary model of the nation. As such, it inaugurates the long line of works commonly designated as 'nationalist' due to their grounding of national identity in soil, faith, and ancestry. It marks the beginning of the century and a half long struggle between two competing universalist visions of French identity.

Germaine de Staël had a clear political vision of 1789. A peaceful revolution was to replace the absolute monarchy with a constitutional monarchy; distinctions of any kind would no longer exist in the new nation. From our vantage point, statements of this kind are likely to be interpreted as professions of democratic faith. But the narrow understanding of the nation on which they are based, as the union of aristocratic and bourgeois elite only, casts a different light on them. It provides, in fact, an excellent illustration of Bourdieu's claim that "universalization is the ultimate strategy of dissimulation" (2012: 233). In 1802, sensing that France was headed towards a military dictatorship, Staël published a novel, *Delphine*, that laid bare the reasons for the Revolution's failure to bring about her ideal vision of the nation in 1789. The aristocracy's refusal to support the bourgeoisie's legitimate claims, to renounce the aristocratic code of honor and adopt enlightened principles has led to the Terror and to war. While Staël's claims were clearly one-sided, her exclusive focus on Parisian high society and on the early phase of the Revolution in the novel documents her narrow understanding of the nation as the union of aristocratic and bourgeois elite only. Her account of the ill-fated love affair between aristocratic Léonce and bourgeois Delphine highlights the superiority of enlightened bourgeois values over the aristocratic ethos. Her contrast between Delphine's sensibility, compassion, morality, and sense of religion, and Léonce's insensitivity to religion, stands as a rebuttal of Chateaubriand's central claim in the *Genius of Christianity* that adherence to a rational ethos precludes a sense of religion and breeds immorality. Exposing Chateaubriand's defense of Christianity for what it is, a sudden, tactical conversion on the aristocracy's part, Staël counters that religion has nothing to do with the aristocratic code of conduct. But highlighting the dire consequences of the aristocracy's defection during the early phase of the Revolution, as she does in the novel, is also a way to appeal to "moderate Royalists" like Chateaubriand to side with her camp, to put their political differences aside and prevent Napoleon Bonaparte's further ascent. In her eyes, the stake of this second attempt to create the nation the Revolution was initially meant to bring about was the preservation of the common culture of civility that embodied French identity, *le caractère français*, the social world in which her identity was grounded.

Staël's hopes were once again shattered, however. Bonaparte became Napoleon I and her active opposition to his rule resulted in her last exile from France. Thus bereft of her French identity, she continued to reflect on the nation and on national belonging as she had already done in *On Literature* in 1800, consigning her insights in her 1807 novel *Corinne* and in her 1809 essay *On Germany*. In our analysis of *Corinne*, we have argued that the novel stages the encounter between cosmopolitanism and nationalism but only to conclude to the demise of enlightened supranational aspirations and to the inevitability of having to anchor one's identity in national belonging in the modern age. Although *Corinne* returns to the theme of French aristocratic imperfections, it more importantly contrasts old and new ways of being French, underscoring, through the character of Count Raimond, how the national character could be bettered through the positive influence of rationality and philosophical ideas and the abandonment of aristocratic selfishness. Nonetheless, the focus of Staël's examination of the national habitus is England, the only country in Europe where her dream of aristocratic and bourgeois union had been realized by then, where "the tensions between parts of the nobility and parts of the middle class had already diminished in the course of the 17th century [...] and the code of the 'English gentleman' shaped the British national code" (Elias 1996: 62). Lord Oswald Nelvil exemplifies the modern national whose identity is grounded in national belonging; whose opinions and tastes are shaped by this attachment, a bond perceived as natural, as emanating from the "natural order of things"; whose 'we' feelings fulfill a deep emotional need and are expressed in symbols endowed with an aura of sacredness ('God save the King') and at the same time constructed in opposition to a 'them' coined as foreign and inferior (Italian, French).

The union of aristocratic and bourgeois forces that Staël had tried in vain to bring about eventually occurred through the common opposition of these forces to the "Corsican tyrant." At the fall of the Empire, her works and Chateaubriand's were hailed in England, Restoration France, and elsewhere in Europe as heroic examples of resistance to the Napoleonic "usurpation." The new Restoration regime temporarily fulfilled their wishes: for Chateaubriand, it restored the legitimate monarchy in the person of a Bourbon King, a brother of Louis XVI; and for Staël the establishment of a constitutional monarchy reconnected the Revolution to the point where it should have ended in the first place. But as Stendhal pointed out, the people who governed France in the 1820s were desperately clinging to a past that was gone, pretending that the Republic and the Empire had not occurred and that France had not changed in their absence. For him, by contrast, the revolutionary era had left a significant, indelible mark on the country, brought more changes to France than the monarchy in centuries.

As their common rejection of revolutionary "barbarians" indicates, high society members like Chateaubriand, Staël, and to a lesser extent even Gouges, shared no 'we-feelings' with fellow countrymen below their own station. They could more readily identify with members of the corresponding high society of another kingdom and usually had few difficulties gaining admission to it – as Chateaubriand's and Staël's stays in England in the 1790s illustrate. For the three writers discussed in the second part of the book, by contrast, affinities with their fellow countrymen were on balance stronger than those with people of a corresponding station in other countries. The expanded understanding of the concept of nation we find in their writings reflects the accession of the middle class, and their own, to positions of increased political, social, and cultural power in post-revolutionary France.

The articles on France Stendhal penned for three British magazines between 1822 and 1829, *Chronicles for England*, attest to his wider understanding of the nation, to his forward-looking attitude, and to his political understanding of national identity: "principles, wishes, feelings, and tastes," not borders, determined in his eyes who was a foreigner and who was not. As he explicitly stated, measured with that yardstick, Chateaubriand and Staël were foreigners for him. As the representative of a new kind of Frenchman, Stendhal saw it as his duty to correct the misperceptions about the revolutionary era these two writers had spread abroad and in particular to counter their demonization of the Terror and of Napoleon. He was willing to acknowledge revolutionary errors but also to explain why they had occurred; to criticize the Jacobin leaders but also to celebrate their courage in light of the challenges they had faced; to examine the flaws of the First Empire, but also give credit to Napoleon where it was due. His efforts to excuse the Jacobins' mistakes due to their political inexperience, his praise of the First Empire for rewarding individual talent and merit without consideration of social origin, further testify to a more inclusive understanding of the nation than was the case with the three previous writers.

In *Chronicles for England* and *Memoirs of a Tourist* Stendhal's main concern was to assess and monitor change in France in the 1820s and 1830s, to record progress and setbacks in the implementation of the Revolution's principles among the French population, their impact on the upper-class and *le caractère français* as well as their progress in rural France. Stendhal applauded to "the rise of lower- and middle class patterns of behaviour and feeling to the top" (Elias 1996: 74). Comparing the common people's qualities to the upper-class' defects, he took note of the energy and efficiency of the former, as opposed to the formality and inability to act of the latter; of the high moral standards Napoleon had imposed on his inner-circle, and by contrast, of the permissiveness typical of Old Regime mores at Louis XVIII's court. The 1789 Revolution, he noted, had ushered France into the democratic age by creating secular schools and science-based curricula attuned to the needs and aspirations of the new nation. In concert with the Catholic Church, the Restoration government had done its best to turn the clock back in matters of education by propping up religious institutions that stamped out the love of liberty and equality. But they had failed: their seminaries bred hypocrisy; their religion, immorality.

To the Catholics and Protestants who advocated religion as a cure for modern individualism, Stendhal responded that individualism was not a disease, but the expression of liberty, of the right to pursue happiness according to one's "principles, wishes, feelings, and tastes." In that regard, he thought, "the absorption of typically upper-class patterns by middle and lower classes" (Elias 1996: 74) represented a challenge. As if it was not enough that high society had not learned to free itself from fashion, the 'gift' it had received from absolute kings in exchange for its political freedom, the middle class was now falling into the same trap and willingly giving up liberty for fashion, this "*hochet,*" this toy.

Modern materialism, in the form of an expectation of physical well-being and material comfort, reinforced the tendency to conform to a common norm in matters of tastes and behaviors – as evidenced by the tourist's narrow range of likes and dislikes. Paradoxically, the representative system in democratic or semi-democratic states added limitations to the expression of individual freedom. The fear of displeasing others being the corollary to the tyranny of the majority, it too led to conformism, to a tendency to adopt ready-made thoughts instead of developing one's own, to yet another kind of self-censorship.

The outcome was a phenomenon Stendhal described at length in *Memoirs of a Tourist:* the progressive disappearance of all kinds of characteristics that marked people as different from one another in earlier times, the leveling of identities to a standard norm. Exceptions to the norm could still be found in Southern France and Spain in the 1830s, but it was only a matter of time until they too disappeared. Stendhal labeled this process "Anglicization" because the standardization of behavior he observed in France originated in England and America but the phenomenon was supra-national in his eyes. He was ambivalent about this process. His 'we-feelings' were split between a concrete dislike of contemporary countrymen he perceived as uninteresting clones of each other in looks and tastes, habits and behaviors, beliefs and thoughts, and a theoretical political solidarity with all of them. Stendhal wanted the nation to include everyone and yet he could not bring himself to love the people – the lower classes' manners were too coarse; the culture gap between him and them too wide. But in spite of this honest admission that the happiness democracy promised was not his cup of tea, his outlook remained optimistic, his mind turned towards the future. In a wink to future readers he would never know, he predicted that the dream of democratic happiness would be realized one day, "in 1900 perhaps," he thought. But more importantly, he ruthlessly tracked the obstacles that stood in the way of a real implementation of the French Revolution's principles for their benefit, thereby demonstrating his concern and solidarity with his fellow human beings.

Prosper Mérimée agreed with Stendhal's understanding of the revolutionary era as the dawn of a new age. In his historical novel *A Chronicle of the Reign of Charles IX*, this break is articulated through the contrast between the civilized present in which author and readers are situated and a past described as dominated by the aristocratic ethos of ruthless pursuit of self-interest, the absence of self-restraint in personal behavior, and the prevalence of violence in society. By focusing on this 'foreign' past, the nineteenth-century historical novel underscores the outcome of the civilizing process, i.e., the progress humanity has made by adopting "lower- and middle class patterns of behaviour and feeling." In Mérimée's novel, but more generally in the historical novel and drama of the period, religion is at the root of social division, civil war, and violence. From a nineteenth-century's vantage point, therefore, the degree of civilization of a particular nation is best measured by its ability to free itself from the socio-political influence of church and religion – as Stendhal's constant attention to this topic also attests. The fantastic genre of the Romantic era deals with the same issues but operates in a different mode. In Mérimée's short stories, the narrator demonstrates his immunity to the obscure forces of superstition by creating stories that center on the irruption of the irrational, thereby testing the readers' ability to resist its appeal, and in the end compelling them to acknowledge that the superstitious age is over.

If the narrator's playful mastery of irrational forces foregrounded in the fantastic genre is a sign of the middle class's growing self-assurance, the appropriation of "typically upper-class patterns," in this case the invocation of lineage in support of claims to legitimacy, offers a second illustration of this phenomenon. "Just as aristocratic groups had based their pride and their claim to a special value on their family's ancestry," Elias notes, "so, as their successors, the leading sections of the industrial middle classes [...] increasingly based their pride and their claim to a special value either on their nation's ancestry or on seemingly unchanging national achievements, characteristics and values" (Elias 1996: 135). As Inspector general of historical Monuments, Mérimée played an influential role in this process. As he identified and classified historical monuments dating from all periods of French history, he presided over the construction of the national memory. The operative principles of this bourgeois 'invention of tradition' are twofold: the substitution of meaning and the rule of maximum inclusion. On the one hand, monuments become historical artifacts, castles and churches that had once been impressive symbols of aristocratic and religious power are emptied out of their meaning and become works of art. On the other hand, the competing histories of the savage past and of the recent, revolutionary past are incorporated into a national memory wide enough to allow everyone to read his or her own history in it. By offering an ideal image of the past in which former antagonisms are neutralized, the national patrimony serves national reconciliation and cohesion. When compared to the revolutionary practice of destroying symbols of the past, this soft way of dealing with it offers yet another illustration of the middle class' growing self-confidence.

Mérimée's preoccupation with the past takes yet another form in his short story *Colomba*, that of an investigation of the survival of age-old, local practices in contemporary France. Against the critical tendency to read this text as characteristic of the Romantic fascination with local color and exoticism, we have argued that it centers of the issue of identity, or more specifically on the contrast between on the one hand a disappearing sense of identity grounded in kinship, an ethos of personal vengeance that begets unceasing violence and is derived from the unwillingness to forget past offenses; and on the other hand a modern sense of identity grounded in belief in the individual's autonomy, respect of the nation-state's institutions, and a male honor understood as the willingness to defend and die for the *patrie* but also to forget past offenses and thus to foster peace. In *Colomba* as in the historical novel and the fantastic tales, we concluded, the savage Corsican present is invoked so as to better underscore its demise. In Mérimée's eyes the frequent recurrence of revolutionary violence in nineteenth-century France posed a far more serious danger to national cohesion than the survival of local customs, if indeed they were still alive. Our examination of his 1853 essay on Mormons shows that in spite of his life-long anticlericalism, the fear of revolutions that periodically threatened the stability of the French state, as well as the security and property of middle class citizens in the nineteenth century, led him to reconsider the role of religion as a means of social cohesion and national unity. On the one hand, his focus on the creation of a national patrimony must be seen as an instance of "the increasing tendency to conceptualize processes as if they were unchanging objects" (Elias 1996:123) that is characteristic of nationalism. On the other, his willingness to deprive others situated below him on the social scale of a secular, forward-looking ideal associated with human progress he still claimed for himself testifies to the middle class' abandonment of its enlightened and revolutionary ideals and to its replacement with a nationalist belief system. But as hypocritical as Mérimée's recourse to religion for others as a means of creating national unity may appear, it still underscores his all-inclusive understanding of the nation.

George Sand also felt that 'we' meant the entire nation, "owners and workers, the educated and the peasantry, civil servants and soldiers," not a specific class. But as opposed to Stendhal, who distinguished between a rational and an emotional 'we,' and Mérimée who could bond with imaginary ancestors but found it harder to identify with his revolutionary fellow citizens, Sand sought to overcome these oppositions. If, like Ernest Renan, she viewed the nation as both "rich legacy of memories" and "present-day" she also made it a priority to focus on the issue on which Stendhal and Mérimée had foundered: on the means of eliciting these emotional 'we feelings.' Examining the reasons for the repeated failure to implement the Revolution's principles in *Story of my life*, she came to the conclusion that the absence of a "social religion" had doomed prior efforts to turn the republican ideal into reality. The solution she proposed in May 1848 was to create a "religion, dogma, and cult of France," a new Gospel of liberty, equality and fraternity steeped in revolutionary fervor that would unite all French people in a common faith in the nation. The novels she wrote after 1848 have in common to suggest strategies for implementing this very project. Her characters learn to rise above social prejudices by giving in to the feelings of love they feel for each other; they learn to see the world from the other's point of view, to correct their initial deficiencies, and to become better human beings. By instilling feelings of solidarity with individuals initially perceived as different, and thus as incompatible with each other, this process of sentimental education, she believed, would bring the people together, reduce the gap between social classes and thereby contribute to national unity.

Sand's writings also vividly illustrate the fact that the strengthening of the 'we-feelings' for fellow country men she envisioned as the path to the republican nation has as its counterpart a weakening of the feelings of solidarity with non-nationals. Like many of her republican contemporaries, she adhered to a nationalist ideology that pitted an idealist, moral, altruistic France against an amoral, materialist, and selfish England. As the absence of a critique of colonization in Stendhal, Mérimée, or Sand implies, the notion that France embodied the highest stage of civilization fueled feelings of national superiority towards other nations. When Sand's novels are set in a historical period of international crisis, war is not only presented as a legitimate way of solving conflicts, it is also associated with an ardent patriotism that has as its counterpart feelings of contempt and hatred for enemies of the *patrie*. Conversely, military defeat brings humiliation and shame without, however, extinguishing or diminishing feelings of faith in the nation. These writings exemplify the contradictory nature of the national habitus: its adherence not only to a "moral code [...] that is egalitarian and whose highest values is 'man,'" but also to a "nationalist code descended from the Machiavellian code of princes and ruling aristocracies, inegalitarian in character, and whose highest value is a collectivity–the state, the country, the nation" (Elias 1996: 154–55). More clearly than those of the other writers examined here, Sand's writings bring to light the dual contradictory nature of the national habitus: the benign love of the nation that prevails at times of peace gives way to feelings of chauvinism and xenophobia at times of war. One of the central findings of this study is that patriotism and nationalism are indeed two sides of the same coin. As we saw consistently throughout the book, one of the characteristics of the national habitus is that it is acquired in part through the affirmation of difference, by opposing a foreign 'them' to the national 'we.'

One of the risks involved in dealing with nationalism is to take declarations of national difference at face value and thus to reproduce that discourse instead of analyzing it. Elias's approach makes it easier to disentangle oneself from the web of nationalist rhetoric. His dynamic understanding of cultures as fields of tensions between competing claims makes it possible to observe, within the other national culture, virtually all forms of discourse that are typically used to reduce the other to one of its dominant features. These commonalities appear, for instance, if we consider that prior to the establishment of the First Republic and the execution of Louis XVI, women bourgeois reformers in Europe, Olympe de Gouges in France or Hannah More in England, were denouncing the aristocracy's moral failings and issuing calls for the moral reform of that estate. Although their critique was essentially the same, the fact that these upper-class practices had originated in France allowed a bourgeois reformist like More to present the British aristocracy's flaws "not merely as amoral or non-Christian but also as French" (Mellor 2000: 20). Conversely, the fact that the constitutional monarchy was a British invention, allowed Gouges to attribute the fall of the absolute monarchy to France's adoption of a foreign political model and to make the Anglophile Jacques Necker personally responsible for the revolutionary chaos that ensued. Here again, however, Gouges's bourgeois critique of political change was no more specific to one country than the cultural critique of aristocratic depravity. In England, Angelica Gooden tells us, music historian Charles Burney forbade his daughter Frances to associate with Germaine de Staël in 1793 not only because she had "ran adulterously after Monsieur de Narbonne" (Goodden 2008: 46), but also because he too "believed Necker and the nobles who moved for change to be the begetters of the French Revolution, and held all Frenchmen and – women who wanted to alter the status quo responsible for the violence it had brought with it" (48). Reformers in both countries had thus more in common than their recourse to finger-pointing at foreigners would lead us to believe. In both countries, they were convinced of the superiority of the bourgeois values they held dear and wanted the whole nation to share; in both cases, they presented those they disliked and combatted as foreign. To take the nationalist discourse of these writers at face value makes it impossible to see that "the rise of lower- and middle class patterns of behaviour and feeling to the top" was a process that affected both countries, as Stendhal realized in the 1830s. The fact that the process of nationalization of feelings and thoughts started almost a century and a half earlier in England than in France enabled British critics of the French Revolution to view revolutionary violence as a uniquely French phenomenon, to forget in other words, that the model of liberty embodied by their constitutional monarchy was also the product of revolutionary violence and civil war. Conversely, the history of England allowed French critics of that particular model of liberty, Gouges and Chateaubriand among them, to view revolutionary violence as essentially "British."

As absurd as these claims and counter-claims may seem in retrospect, it is important to remember them because the mode of thinking that inspired them still inhabits us. In the 1990s, it was common practice in French Studies to oppose American pluralism to French universalism as radically different and incompatible models of the nation – a dichotomy inspired by the belief in the superiority of the former over the latter. So well engrained was this dichotomy that Jean-Philippe Mathy (2000) published a book to debunk it. Arguing that "the two countries are more comparable than the current polarized rhetoric of tolerance and exclusion, pluralism and centralization, would lead us to believe," Mathy countered the dominant American vision of a republican, universalist France by emphasizing the neo-liberal grip on a number of prominent French intellectuals at the time; and conversely, he contested the notion of an all-liberal American society by underscoring neo-Jacobin lines of argumentation in the works of contemporary American intellectuals. Earlier on, Le Bras and Todd (1981: 77), who also saw more similarities than difference between between the United States and France, attributed this resemblance to the common challenge the two countries had faced of having to create national unity out of anthropological diversity. Bourdieu (1992b) similarly resisted this neat categorization, arguing that to the extent that both nations embodied "imperialisms of the universal" they were actually more alike than usually thought.

Ironically, so strong is the hold of the national habitus that its imprint can be even found in the work of Bourdieu, a scholar who has devoted much of his work to the analysis of power relations and symbolic violence and who fully appreciates the significance of belonging to a national field. While acknowledging that some blind spots in his work are due to this phenomenon (Bourdieu 2012 : 252), he did not question the validity of the accepted opposition between German 'Kultur' and French 'Zivilisation' prior to 1992, for instance: "The French model is the Enlightenment model: cosmopolitanism, rationalism, abstract, formal universalism; [...] the German one is linked to Romanticism [...]." (Bourdieu 2012: 554) Similarly, one finds statements in his work that rest on the questionable opposition between an alleged British culturalist understanding of the nation and a French universalist model, so for instance when he writes that "English culture is constructed against the French model," or that "Englishness defines itself against France" (249). Because Gouges, Chateaubriand, and Staël lived at a time when the national habitus was still in gestation, these writers could still see what we and Bourdieu no longer can, that "[t]he French declaration of rights in 1789 contained the best part of those of England and America" (Staël 2008: 184), in other words, that the universalist aspirations of the people, the forward-looking attitude that led to the American and to the French Revolutions actually originated in Great Britain. For Staël by constrast, the British constitutional monarchy was the embodiment of these universal principles: "Suddenly Providence permitted England to solve the problem of constitutional monarchies; and America, a century later, that of federal republics." (Staël 2008: 737). Similar observations can be made with regard to colonization, so for instance when Bourdieu, comparing the French and the British models of coloni-

zation, argues that "the French State has the most powerful rhetoric of universalization" (233). Elias, by contrast, disproves this generalization when he provides
evidence of the same universalist rhetoric in England in arguments put forth to
justify British colonization, for instance in this sentence from Matthew Arnold's
Mixed Essays (first published in 1880): "Civilization is the humanization of man
in society." (Arnold, quoted in Elias 1996: 458) The point of my remarks is to underscore how difficult it is to think outside the national box. Knowing that national distinctions we take for granted are the product of nationalism does not
entirely void the efficacy of these stereotypes.

Both Bourdieu's and Elias's approaches are particularly useful when it
comes to challenging deep-seated nationalist assumptions of this kind. Uncover-
ing the historical processes that led to their emergence and, over time, to their
essentialization, tracing national stereotypes back to their field of origin reveals
their contested nature, making it possible to question their validity. Elias does so
himself with regard to the opposition between "French civilization" and "German
culture" when he brings back to memory an instance of German universalism
undistinguishable from the so-called "French" universalism – Schiller's 1789 lecture "What does universal history mean and why do we study it?" Jürgen Habermas similarly shows, in *The Postnational Constellation*, that universalism was
still blossoming in Germany at the time when the culturalist understanding of
the nation was beginning to take root. The claims for political independence
made by German culturalist on the basis of "the spirit of the people," he points
out, were opposed by democrats like Fröbel and Gervinus who grounded theirs
in the competing principle of "the people's desire for democratic self-determination" (Habermas 2001: 9). According to Habermas, even Renan's concept of citizenship as a *plébicite de tous les jours* was already anticipated by Fröbel's "clear-
eyed reflection" [that] "the ethical, free, political moment in the existence of a
people is freely chosen fellowship" (9). Staël's writings similarly remind us
that France had no monopoly on the universal at the time of the Revolution –
since in her eyes, France was simply copying England. As for Chateaubriand's
essays, they show that Germany had no monopoly on the culturalist understanding of the nation in the early nineteenth century. In both cases, in fact, this cultural understanding of the nation emerged in reaction not to French universalism
– Chateaubriand praised the Church's universalism – but to state centrism and
revolutionary violence.

The Bourdieusian "anamnesis of origin" (2000: 115) also makes it possible to
realize that truths we take for self-evident are more complex than we know.
Taken out of their historical context, for instance, Germaine de Staël's impas-
sionate pleas for liberty make her sound like a great democrat; but replaced
in the context of the historical struggles she waged to impose her narrow defini-

tion of the nation, they should mean the opposite to people who have an all-inclusive understanding of this concept. Restituting the meaning the word 'nation' had for her at the time, instead of projecting our own understanding onto it, also clears the way for a better understanding of her political priorities and apparent reversals. It helps us understand how she could be for war in 1791–92 when the realization of her ideal nation depended on its success; and against it during the Empire when it was waged on behalf of a wider conception of the nation; or how she could embrace an Old Regime cosmopolitanism that had ensured French cultural dominance all over Europe as long as it matched her ideal of civility, but reject it when Napoleon tried to link his reign to the same tradition by exporting French law, institutions and culture to other European states. Much of her opposition to this new French imperialism, most clearly evidenced in her claim for the cultural and political specificity of each nation, was derived from the clash between her narrow understanding of the nation and the expanded social definition Napoleon gave to it.

People who are convinced of the great value of their institutions tend to want other countries to adopt them as well and are paradoxically willing to demonstrate the superiority of their national ways by waging war against them. In the first decade of the twenty-first century, for instance, exporting democracy to Iraq was largely seen as a worthy cause by the US and British governments, public opinion, and even some scholars (Schraeder 2002). A decade later, half a million people are dead, bomb attacks still rock the country and democracy is still a shaky experiment at best. Among the voices who predicted early on that the war was a mistake, Eric Hobsbawm argued, in an article published in January 2005 in *The Guardian*, that one cannot "easily effect social change by transferring institutions across borders." Another related insight in this book is that the adoption of democratic institutions does not suffice to implement democracy. Even in a country like France that had a well-established state on the eve of the French Revolution, it took two generations to turn subjects into citizens, and this transformation pertained only to the 'civlized' elite. By 1870, the point at which this book ends, the process of winning the hearts and minds of the entire population was just about to begin in earnest with the establishment of free and compulsory school system, which, as Sternhell (1977: 25) and Bourdieu (2012: 251) point out, is not only a key factor in a nation's democratization, but also in its nationalization.

Understanding that the acquisition of a national habitus takes time, that it cannot be acquired simply through a change of regime is thus an important lesson. Just as significant is the realization that democracy cannot be imposed through violence. In France, revolutionary terror led to dictatorship and Napoleon's attempt to export republican institutions to the rest of Europe through warfare not only failed but cost millions of deaths. The establishment of democracy is not only delayed by internal or external violence, it also necessarily creates a backlash against democracy itself when violence is seen as its product. The great question with which we must conclude therefore is whether it is possible to rid the national habitus of its aristocratic DNA, or as Bourdieu puts it: Can we have a republic without having a nation? Can we have it both ways somehow?

> Can we keep the profits of universalization brought along by the state without suffering the losses, the costs of particularization, nationalization, and nationalism that are historically inseparable from the construction of a *res publica* and of a state? (Bourdieu 2012: 462).

Although this book does not answer this question it was written in the hope that a better understanding of the national habitus, of the historical processes that led to its genesis, would make it possible to solve it some day.

Works cited

Primary texts

Chateaubriand, François René de (1815) *An Historical, Political, and Moral Essay on Revolutions, Ancient and Modern* [1797] (London: Henry Colburn).

Chateaubriand, François René de (1848) *Memoirs from Beyond the Grave*, trans. A.S. Kline, http://wikilivres.ca/wiki/Chateaubriand%27 s_memoirs (accessed 27 August 2013).

Chateaubriand, François René de (1856) *The Genius of Christianity or the Spirit and Beauty of the Christian Religion* [1802], ed. and trans. Charles I. White (Baltimore: John Murphy & Co; Philadelphia, J.B. Lippincott & Co; London: Charles Dolman).

Chateaubriand, François René de (1973) *Mémoires d'Outre-Tombe* [1848], 3 vols (Paris: Livre de Poche).

Chateaubriand, François René de (1978) *Essai sur les révolutions, Génie du Christianisme*, ed. and introd. Maurice Regard (Paris: NRF-Gallimard, La Pléiade).

Chateaubriand, François René de (2004) *On Buonaparte and the Bourbons* [1814], in *Critics of the Enlightenment. Readings in the French Counter-Revolutionary Tradition*, ed. and trans. Christopher Olaf Blum (Wilmington: ISI Books), 3–40.

Gouges, Olympe de (1791) *Les droits de la femme. A la reine.* (Paris: s.n.), http://gallica.bnf. fr/ark:/12148/bpt6k64848397.r=gouges+declaration+des+droits+de+la+femme.langEN (accessed 29 August 2013).

Gouges, Olympe de (1989) *L'Esclavage des Noirs, ou l'heureux naufrage* [1792], ed. and introd. Eléni Varikas (Paris: Côté-femmes).

Gouges, Olympe de (1991) *Théâtre politique* [1790–1793], ed. and introd. Gisela Thiele-Knobloch (Paris: Côté-femmes).

Gouges, Olympe de (1993a) *Théâtre politique* [1790–1793], vol. 2, ed. and introd. Gisela Thiele-Knobloch (Paris: Indigo and Côté-femmes).

Gouges, Olympe de (1993b) *Ecrits Politiques* [1788–1793], ed. and introd. Olivier Blanc, 2 vols (Paris: Côté-femmes).

Gouges, Olympe de (1995) *Mémoire de Madame de Valmont* [1788] (Paris: Indigo and Côté-femmes).

Gouges, Olympe de (2009a) 'Preface to *Black Slavery*', in *Translating Slavery, Gender and Race in French Abolitionist Writing, 1780–1830*, ed. Doris Y. Kadish and Françoise Massardier-Kenney, trans. Maryann De Julio (Kent, OH: Kent State University Press), 93–95.

Gouges, Olympe de (2009b) 'Response to the American Champion', in *Translating Slavery, Gender and Race in French Abolitionist Writing, 1780–1830*, ed. Doris Y. Kadish and Françoise Massardier-Kenney, trans. Maryann De Julio (Kent, OH: Kent State University Press), 125–129.

Mérimée, Prosper (1835) *Notes d'un voyage dans le Midi de la France*, http://archive.org/de tails/notesdunvoyageda00mr (accessed 2 December 2012).

Mérimée, Prosper (1838) *Notes d'un voyage en Auvergne*, http://archive.org/details/note sdunvoyageen00mruoft (accessed 2 December 2012).

Mérimée, Prosper (1840) *Notes d'un voyage en Corse*, http://archive.org/details/note sdunvoyage00mruoft (accessed 2 December 2012).

Mérimée, Prosper (1945) *Correspondance Générale* [1844–1846], ed. Maurice Parturier, vol. 4 (Paris, Le Divan; Toulouse: Edouard Privat).

Mérimée, Prosper (1946) *Correspondance Générale* [1847–1849], ed. Maurice Parturier, vol. 5 (Paris, Le Divan; Toulouse: Edouard Privat).

Mérimée, Prosper (1947) *Correspondance Générale*[1850–1852], ed. Maurice Parturier, vol. 6 (Paris, Le Divan; Toulouse: Edouard Privat).

Mérimée, Prosper (1890) *A Chronicle of the Reign of Charles IX* [1829], trans. Georges Saintsbury (London: Nimmo), https://archive.org/stream/achroniclereign00mrgoog# page/n9/mode/2up (accessed 15 November 2013).

Mérimée, Prosper (1930) *Les Mormons* [1853], in *Oeuvres complètes de Prosper Mérimée*, ed. Georges Connes, vol. 28 (Paris: Honoré Champion).

Mérimée, Prosper (1964) *Colomba* [1840], ed. and introd. Roger Salomon (Paris: Garnier Flammarion).

Mérimée, Prosper (1978) *Théâtre de Clara Gazul, Romans et Nouvelles*, ed. and introd. Jean Maillon and Pierre Salomon (Paris: Gallimard).

Mérimée, Prosper (1978a) *Les Âmes du Purgatoire* [1834], in *Théâtre de Clara Gazul, Romans et Nouvelles*, ed. Roger Salomon (Paris: Garnier Flammarion), 669–720.

Mérimée, Prosper (1978b) *Chronique du règne de Charles IX* [1829], in *Théâtre de Clara Gazul, Romans et nouvelles*, ed. Roger Salomon (Paris: Garnier Flammarion), 251–450.

Mérimée, Prosper (1978c) *Frederigo* [1829], in *Théâtre de Clara Gazul, Romans et Nouvelles*, ed. Roger Salomon (Paris: Garnier Flammarion), 501–511.

Mérimée, Prosper (1987) *Nouvelles*, ed. and introd. Michel Crouzet, 2 vols (Paris: Lettres françaises).

Mérimée, Prosper (1987) *Mateo Falcone* [1829] in *Nouvelles*, vol.1, ed. Michel Crouzet (Paris: Lettres françaises), 75–87.

Mérimée, Prosper (1987) *Colomba* [1840] in *Nouvelles*, vol.2, ed. Michel Crouzet (Paris: Lettres françaises), 9–120.

Mérimée, Prosper (1989) *Notes d'un voyage dans l'Ouest de la France* [1837], introd. Pierre-Marie Auzas (Paris: Adam Biro).

Mérimée, Prosper (1998) *Colomba* [1840], ed. and trans. Nicholas Jotcham, in *Carmen and Other Stories* (Oxford: Oxford University Press), 162–290.

Sand, George (1857) *Le Diable aux champs* [1857] (Paris: Jaccottet &Bourdilliat), https://open library.org/books/OL24819882M/Le_diable_aux_champs (accessed 19 November 2013).

Sand, George (1901) *Nanon* [1872], in *The Masterpieces of George Sand*, vol. 14, trans. G. Burnham Ives (Philadelphia: George Barrie & Son).

Sand, George (1902a) *The Marquis of Villemer* [1861], in *The Masterpieces of George Sand*, vol. 17, trans. G. Burham Ives (Philadelphia: George Barrie & Son).

Sand, George (1902b) *Mauprat* [1837],in *The Masterpieces of George Sand*, vol. 19, trans. Mary W. Artois (Philadelphia: George Barrie & Son).

Sand, George (1921) *The George Sand-Gustave Flaubert Letters*, introd. Stuart P. Sherman, trans. Aimée McKenzie (New York: Boni and Liveright, Inc.).

Sand, George (1970) *Histoire de ma vie* [1854], in *Oeuvres Autobiographiques*, ed. and introd. Georges Lubin, 2 vols (Paris: NRF-Gallimard, La Pléiade).

Sand, George (1975) *Mademoiselle de la Quintinie* [1863], ed. and introd. Simone Balayé (Paris, Genève: Ressources).

Sand, George (1977) *The Country Waif* [1850], ed. Dorothy Wynne Zimmerman, trans. Eirene Collis (Lincoln: University of Nebraska Press)

Sand, George (1979) *Cadio* [1868], in *Oeuvres complètes* vol. 3 (Genève: Slaktine Reprints).

Sand, George (1980a) *Francia* [1872], in *Oeuvres Complètes* vol. 12 (Genève: Slatkine Reprints).

Sand, George (1980b) *François Le Champi* [1850], in *Oeuvres Complètes* vol. 12 (Genève: Slatkine Reprints).

Sand, George (1980c) *Journal d'un voyageur pendant la guerre* [1871], in *Oeuvres complètes* vol. 19, (Genève: Slaktine Reprints).

Sand, George (1981) *Mademoiselle Merquem* [1868], ed. and introd. Raymond Rhéault (Ottawa: Éditions de l'Université d'Ottawa).

Sand, George (1982) *Horace* [1842], ed. and introd. Nicole Courrier (Meylan: Les Éditions de l'Aurore).

Sand, George (1986) *Jeanne* [1844], ed. and introd. Simone Vierne (Meylan: Les Éditions de l'Aurore).

Sand, George (1988) *Le Marquis de Villemer* [1861], ed. and introd. Jean Courrier. (Meylan: Les Éditions de l'Aurore).

Sand, George (1989) *La Ville noire* [1861], ed. and introd. Jean Courrier (Meylan: Les Éditions de l'Aurore).

Sand, George (1991a) *Simon* [1836], ed. and introd. Michèle Hecquet (Grenoble: Les Éditions de l'Aurore).

Sand, George (1991b) *Story of my Life* [1854], trans. Thelma Jurgrau (Albany, NY: State University of New York Press).

Sand, George (1992a) *La Daniella* [1857], ed. and introd. Annarosa Poli, 2 vols (Meylan: Les Éditions de l'Aurore).

Sand, George (1992b) *Malgrétout* [1870], introd. Claude Tricotel, ed. Jean Chalon (Grenoble: Les Éditions de l'Aurore).

Sand, George (1994a) *Les Maîtres Sonneurs* [1853], ed. and introd. Joseph-Marc Bailbé, 2 vols (Paris: Éditions Glénat).

Sand, George (1994b) *The Master Pipers* [1853], trans. by Rosemary Lloyd (Oxford: Oxford University Press).

Sand, George (1995a) *La Mare au diable* [1846], ed. and introd. Marielle Caors (Paris: Livre de Poche).

Sand, George (1995b) *Horace* [1842], trans. Zack Rogow (San Francisco: Mercury House).

Sand, George (1995c) *The Miller of Angibault* [1845], ed. and trans. Donna Dickenson (Oxford: Oxford University Press).

Sand. George (1997a) 'Questions de demain: la religion de la France; le dogme de la France; le culte de la France' [1848], in *George Sand. Politique et Polémiques (1843–1850)*, ed. and introd. Michelle Perrot (Paris: Imprimerie nationale), 451–467.

Sand, George (1997b) *Nanon* [1872], ed. and introd. Nicole Mozet (Meylan: Les Éditions de l'Aurore).

Sand, George (1999) *Sand-Barbès, Correspondance d'une amitié républicaine 1848–1870*, ed. Michelle Perrot (Lectoure: Éditions Le Capucin).

Sand, George (2004a) *The Devil's Pool* [1846], in *The Devil's Pool and Other Stories*, trans. E.H. Blackmore, A.M. Blackmore and Francine Guiguère, (Albany, NY: State University of New York Press), 86–153.

Sand, George (2004b) *The Black City* [1860], trans. Tina A. Kover (New York: Carroll and Graf Publishers).

Sand, George (2008) *Marianne* [1876] (Saint-Malo: Pascal Galodé).

Staël, Germaine de (1798) *A treatise on the influence of the passions upon the happiness of individuals and of nations*, http://galenet.galegroup.com.ezproxy1.library.arizona.edu/servlet/ECCO (accessed 28 October 2013)

Staël, Germaine de (1820–21) *De la littérature considérée dans ses rapports avec les institutions sociales* [1800], in *Oeuvres complètes*, vol. 4 (Paris: Treuttel and Würtz).

Staël, Germaine de (1820–21b) *Corinne ou l'Italie* [1807], in *Oeuvres complètes*, vols. 8–9 (Paris: Treuttel and Würtz).

Staël, Germaine de (1835) *The Influence of Literature upon Society* [1800] (New York: Pearson), http://books.google.com/books?id=eVALAAAAMAAJ&oe=UTF-8 (accessed 28 October 2013)

Staël, Germaine de (1906). *Dix années d'exil* [1821], introd. Madame Necker de Saussure (Paris: Garnier).

Staël, Germaine de (1968) *De l'Allemagne* [1809], ed. and introd. Simone Balayé, 2 vols (Paris: Garnier Flammarion).

Staël, Germaine de (1979) *Des circonstances actuelles qui peuvent terminer la révolution et des principes qui doivent fonder la république en France* [1798], ed. and introd. Lucia Omacini (Genève: Droz).

Staël, Germaine de (1983) *Considérations sur la Révolution française* [1818], ed. and introd. Jacques-Léon Godechot (Paris: Tallandier).

Staël, Germaine de (1987a) *Delphine* [1802], ed. Simone Balayé and Lucia Omacini (Genève: Droz).

Staël, Germaine de (1987b) *Corinne, or Italy* [1807], introd. and trans. Avriel H. Goldberger (New Brunswick: Rutgers University Press).

Staël, Germaine de (1995) *Delphine* [1802], introd. and trans. Avriel H. Goldberger (Dekalb: Northern Illinois University Press).

Staël, Germaine de (2000) *Ten years of Exile* [1821], introd. and trans. Avriel Goldberger (DeKalb: Northern Illinois University Press).

Staël, Germaine de (2008) *Considerations on the Principal Events of the French Revolution* [1818], ed. and introd. Aurelian Craiutu (Indianapolis: Liberty Fund).

Stendhal (1929) *Mémoires d'un touriste* [1838], ed. Henri Martineau. 3 vols (Paris: Le Divan).

Stendhal (1930) *Voyage dans le midi de la France* [1839], ed. Henri Martineau (Paris: Le Divan).

Stendhal (1962) *Memoirs of a Tourist* [1838], trans. Allan Seager (Evanston: Northwestern University Press).

Stendhal (1964a) *La Chartreuse de Parme* [1839], ed. Michel Crouzet (Paris: Garnier Flammarion).

Stendhal (1964b) *Le Rouge et le noir* [1830], ed. Michel Crouzet (Paris: Garnier Flammarion).

Stendhal (1967) *Correspondance*, introd. Victor Del Litto, ed. Henri Martineau and Victor Del Litto, vol. 2 [1821–1834] (Paris: NRF-Gallimard, La Pléiade).

Stendhal (1968a) *Correspondance*, introd. Victor Del Litto, ed. Henri Martineau and Victor Del Litto, vol. 1 [1800–1821] (Paris: NRF-Gallimard, La Pléiade).

Stendhal (1968b) *Correspondance*, introd. Victor Del Litto, ed. Henri Martineau and Victor Del Litto, vol. 3 [1835–1842] (Paris: NRF-Gallimard, La Pléiade).

Stendhal (1970) *Travels in the South of France*, introd. Victor Brombert and trans. Elisabeth Abbott (New York: Orion Press).

Stendhal (1980) *Chroniques pour l'Angleterre. Contributions à la presse britannique* [1822], ed. and introd. K.G. McWatters, trans. Renée Dénier, vol. 1 (Grenoble: Publications de l'Université des langues et lettres).

Stendhal (1982a) *Chroniques pour l'Angleterre. Contributions à la presse britannique* [1822–1824], ed. and introd. K.G. McWatters, trans. Renée Dénier, vol. 2 (Grenoble: Publications de l'Université des langues et lettres).

Stendhal (1982b) *Journal (1818–1842)*, in *Oeuvres Intimes*, ed. Victor Del Litto, vol. 2 (Paris: NRF-Gallimard, La Pléiade), 2–423.

Stendhal (1982c) *Souvenirs d'égotisme* [1832], in *Oeuvres Intimes*, ed. Victor Del Litto, vol. 2 (Paris: NRF-Gallimard, La Pléiade), 425–521.

Stendhal (1982d) *Vie de Henry Brulard* [1835–1836],in *Oeuvres Intimes*, ed. Victor Del Litto, vol. 2 (Paris: NRF-Gallimard, La Pléiade), 523–959.

Stendhal (1983) *Chroniques pour l'Angleterre. Contributions à la presse britannique* [1825–1826], ed. and introd. K.G. McWatters, trans. Renée Dénier, vol. 3 (Grenoble: Publications de l'Université des langues et lettres).

Stendhal (1985) *Chroniques pour l'Angleterre. Contributions à la presse britannique* [1824–1825], ed. and introd. K.G. McWatters, trans. Renée Dénier, vol. 4. (Grenoble: Publications de l'Université des langues et lettres).

Stendhal (1988) *Chroniques pour l'Angleterre. Contributions à la presse britannique* [1824–1826], ed. and introd. K.G. McWatters, trans. Renée Dénier, vol. 5 (Grenoble: Publications de l'Université des langues et lettres).

Stendhal (1991a) *Chroniques pour l'Angleterre. Contributions à la presse britannique* [1826], ed. and introd. K.G. McWatters, trans. Renée Dénier, vol. 6 (Grenoble: Publications de l'Université des langues et lettres).

Stendhal (1991b) *Chroniques pour l'Angleterre. Contributions à la presse britannique* [1827–1829], ed. and introd. K.G. McWatters, trans. Renée Dénier, vol. 7 (Grenoble: Publications de l'Université des langues et lettres).

Stendhal (1995) *Index.Chroniques pour l'Angleterre. Contributions à la presse britannique* ed. and introd. K.G. McWatters, trans. Renée Dénier, vol. 8 (Grenoble: Publications de l'Université des langues et lettres).

Stendhal (1997) *Paris-Londres, Chroniques*, ed. Renée Dénier (Paris: Stock).

Stendhal (2001) *D'un nouveau complot contre les industriels* [1825], ed. Michel Crouzet (Paris: La Chasse au Snark).

Stendhal (2002) *The Life of Henry Brulard* [1835–1836], introd. Linda Davis, trans. John Sturrock (New York: New York Review of Books).

Stendhal (2003) *The Red and the Black* [1830], ed. James Madden, introd. Diane Johnson, trans. Burton Raffer (New York: Random House).

Stendhal (2006) *The Charterhouse of Parma* [1839], ed. and trans. John Sturrock (London: Penguin).

Stendhal (2007) *Lucien Leuwen* [1834–1835], (Paris: Livre de poche).

Secondary sources

Ancelot, Virginie (1858) *Les salons de Paris, foyers éteints* (Paris: Tardieu), http://archive.org/details/lessalonsdeparis00ance (accessed 2 December 2012).

Ansel, Yves (2000) 'Les Provinciales de Stendhal', in *Paris-Province. Topographies littéraires du XIXe siècle*, ed. Ame´lie Djourachkovitch and Yvan Leclerc (Mont Saint-Agnan: Université de Rouen), 131–144.

Ansel, Yves, Philippe Berthier and Michael Nerlich (eds) (2003) *Dictionnaire de Stendhal* (Paris: Honoré Champion).

Ansel, Yves (2003) 'Libéral, Libéralisme', *Dictionnaire de Stendhal*, ed. Yves Ansel, Philippe Berthier and Michael Nerlich (Paris: Honoré Champion), 399–400.

Appel, Sabine (2006) *Madame de Staël. Biografie einer großen Europäerin* (Düsseldorf: Artemis & Winkler Verlag).

Arguelles-Ling, Althea (2007) '*Famille, Révolution, Patrie:* National Imaginings in the Plays of Olympe de Gouges', *Australian Journal of French Studies* 44.3, 244–256.

Augry-Merlino, Muriel (1990) *Le Cosmopolitisme dans les textes courts de Stendhal et de Mérimée* (Genève and Paris: Slatkine).

Aureau, Bertrand (2001) *Chateaubriand, Penseur de la Révolution* (Paris: Honoré Champion).

Autin, Jean (1983) *Prosper Mérimée, écrivain, archéologue, homme politique* (Paris: librairie académique Perrin).

Badinter, Elizabeth (1980) *L'Amour en plus. Histoire de l'amour maternel- XVII-XXe siècle* (Paris: Flammarion).

Balayé, Simone (1968) 'Introduction', Germaine de Staël, *De l'Allemagne*, 2 vols. (Paris: Garnier Flammarion), 17–31.

Balayé, Simone (1979) *Madame de Staël. Lumières et liberté* (Paris: Klincksieck).

Balayé, Simone (1994) *Madame de Staël. Écrire, Lutter, Vivre* (Genève: Droz).

Balayé, Simone (1996) *Madame de Staël et les Français* (Oxford: Clarendon Press).

Behrent, Michael (2004) 'Religion, Republicanism and Depoliticization: two intellectual Itineraries – Régis Debray and Marcel Gauchet', in *After the Deluge: New Perspectives on Postwar French Intellectual and Cultural History*, ed. Julien Bourg (Lanham, Md.: Lexington Books), 325–352.

Bell, David, A. (2001) *The Cult of the Nation in France. Inventing Nationalism, 1680–1800* (Cambridge, MA: Harvard University Press).

Bénéton, Philippe (2004) 'Foreword', in Christopher Olaf Blum, *Critics of the Enlightenment* (Wilmington: ISI Books) vii–li.

Bercé, Françoise (1986) 'Arcisse de Caumont et les sociétés savantes', in *Les Lieux de mémoire II. La Nation*, vol. 2, ed. Pierre Nora (Paris: NRF-Gallimard), 533–567.

Bercé, Françoise (2010) 'Prosper Mérimée et la seconde république', in *Écritures XIX 6, Prosper Mérimée*, ed. Antonia Fonyi (Caen: Lettres modernes Minard), 157–168.

Berger, Guy (2002) 'L'idée de perfectibilité de L'Essai sur les révolutions au Genie du Christianisme', in *Bulletin de la Société Chateaubriand* 45, 93–110.

Bernard, Claudie (2005) 'Families and communities in post-revolutionary France', *The Romanic Review* 96.3–4, 259–274.

Berthier, Philippe et al. (eds) (1983) *Le plus méconnu des romans de Stendhal, Lucien Leuwen* (Paris: SEDES).

Berthier, Philippe (1987) *Stendhal et Chateaubriand. Essai sur les ambiguïties d'une antipathie* (Genève: Droz).

Berthier, Philippe (ed) (1988) *Relire Les Mémoires d'un touriste (1838–1988)* (Grenoble: Presses Universitaires de Grenoble).

Berthier, Philippe and Pierre-Louis Rey (eds) (2001) *Stendhal journaliste anglais* (Paris: Presses de la Sorbonne Nouvelle).

Berthier, Philippe (2010) *Stendhal. Vivre, Écrire, Aimer* (Paris: Éditions de Fallois).

Bertho, Catherine (1980) 'L'invention de la Bretagne. Genèse d'un stéréotype', *Actes de la Recherche en Sciences Sociales* 35, 45–62.

Birnbaum, Pierre (1993) *"La France aux Français!" Histoire des Haines nationalistes* (Paris: Seuil).

Blanc, Olivier (1981) *Olympe de Gouges* (Paris: Syros).

Blanc, Olivier (1993a) 'Itinéraire politique et biographique d'Olympe de Gouges', in Olympe de Gouges, *Ecrits Politiques*, vol. 1 (Paris: Côté-femmes), 7–34.

Blanc, Olivier (1993b) 'Introduction', in Olympe de Gouges, *Ecrits Politiques*, vol. 2 (Paris: Côté-femmes), 7–46.

Blum, Christopher Olaf (ed and trans) (2004) *Critics of the Enlightenment. Readings in the French Counter-Revolutionary Tradition* (Wilmington: ISI Books).

Bonnet, Jean-Claude (2009) 'Chateaubriand, Mercier et Michelet au musée des monuments français', in *Chateaubriand, penser et écrire l'histoire*, ed. Ivanna Rosi and Jean-Marie Roulin (Saint-Etienne: Publications de l'Université de Saint-Etienne), 283–298.

Bourdenet, Xavier (2003) 'Démocratie', in *Dictionnaire de Stendhal*, ed. Yves Ansel, Philippe Berthier and Michael Nerlich (Paris: Honoré Champion), 210.

Bourdieu, Pierre (1979) *Algeria 1960: The Disenchantment of the World: The Sense of Honour: The Kabyle House or the World Reversed: Essays*, trans. Richard Nice (Cambridge: Cambridge University Press).

Bourdieu, Pierre (1980) 'L'identité et la représentation. Éléments pour une réflexion critique sur l'idée de région', in *Actes de la recherche en sciences sociales* 35, 63–72.

Bourdieu, Pierre (1984) *Distinction. A Social Critique of the Judgement of Taste*, trans. Richard Nice (Cambridge, MA: Harvard University Press).

Bourdieu, Pierre (1989) *In Other Words. Essays Towards a Reflexive Sociology*, trans. Matthew Adamson (Stanford: Stanford University Press).

Bourdieu, Pierre (1990) 'A Lecture on the lecture', in *In Other Words. Essays. Towards a Reflexive Sociology*, trans. Matthew Adamson (Stanford: Stanford University Press), 177–190.

Bourdieu, Pierre and Loïc J.D. Wacquant (1992a) *An Invitation to Reflexive Sociology* (Chicago: Chicago University Press).

Bourdieu, Pierre (1992b) 'Deux impérialismes de l'universel', in *L'Amérique des Français*, ed. Christine Fauré and Tom Bishop (Paris: François Bourrin), 149–155.

Bourdieu, Pierre (1996) *The Rules of Art. Genesis and Structure of the Literary Field*, trans. Susan Emmanuel (Stanford: Stanford University Press).

Bourdieu, Pierre (1999) *Language and Symbolic Power*, trans. Gino Raymond and Matthew Adamson (Cambridge, MA: Harvard University Press).

Bourdieu, Pierre (2000) *Pascalian Meditations*, trans. Richard Nice (Stanford: Stanford University Press).

Bourdieu, Pierre (2012) *Sur l'Etat. Cours au Collège de France 1989–1992* (Paris: Raisons d'agir/Seuil).

Boutry, Philippe (1991) 'Le triomphe de la liberté de conscience et la formation du parti laïc', in *Histoire de la France religieuse*, vol. 3, ed. Jacques Le Goff and René Rémond (Paris: Seuil), 156–175.

Burgess, Anthony and Francis Haskell (1967) *The Age of the Grand Tour* (London: Crown Publishers).

Byrnes, Joseph F. (2005) *Catholic and French Forever. Religious and National Identity in Modern France* (University Park: The Pennsylvania State University Press).

Calhoun, Craig (1997) *Nationalism* (Minneapolis: University of Minnesota Press).

Carlson, Marvin (1996) *The Theatre of the French Revolution* (Ithaca: Cornell University Press).

Carpenter, Scott (2009) *Aesthetics of Fraudulence in Nineteenth-Century France. Frauds, Hoaxes, and Conterfeits* (Burlington, VT: Ashgate Publishing Company).

Castex, Pierre-Georges (1951) *Le Conte fantastique en France* (Paris: Corti).

Castillo, Robert (2006) *The Empire of Stereotypes. Germaine de Staël and the Idea of Italy* (New York: Palgrave Macmillan).

Certeau, Michel de, Dominique Julia and Jacques Revel (1993) 'La beauté du mort', in: *La culture au pluriel* (Paris, Seuil), 45–72.

Chaitin, Gilbert (2004) 'Sand and the Politics of the Thesis Novel: *Mademoiselle de la Quintinie*'s Evil Empires', in *George Sand et l'Empire des lettres*, ed. Anne E. McCall-Saint-Saëns (New Orleans: Presses Universitaires du Nouveau Monde), 73–81.

Chantreau, Alain (ed) (1978) *Stendhal et Balzac II. La Province dans le roman* (Nantes: Société Nantaise d'Études littéraires).

Charles, David (1999) '*Mosaïques. Les Orientales* de Mérimée', in *Prosper Mérimée: Écrivain, Archéologue, Historien*, ed. Antonia Fonyi (Genève: Droz), 111–122.

Chartier, Roger (1991) *The Cultural Origins of the French Revolution* (Durham, NC and London, UK: Duke University Press).

Chartier, Roger (1996) 'Do books make revolutions?', in *The French Revolution in Social and Political Perspective*, ed. Peter Jones (London, New York, Sydney, Auckland: Arnold), 166–188.

Chastel, André (1986) 'La notion de patrimoine', in *Les Lieux de mémoire II. La Nation*, vol. 2, ed. Pierre Nora (Paris: NRF-Gallimard), 405–450.

Chelebourg, Christian (2010) 'Le sens de la famille: filiation, transmission, générations chez Prosper Mérimée', in *Écritures XIX 6, Prosper Mérimée,* ed. Antonia Fonyi (Caen: Lettres modernes Minard), 43–52.

Clark, Robert, L.A. (2000) 'South of North: *Carmen* and French Nationalism', in: *East of West. Cross-Cultural Performance and the Staging of Difference*, ed. Claire Sponsler and Xiaomei Chen (New York: Palgrave), 187–216.

Clément, Jean-Paul (2006) 'Chateaubriand Rousseauiste et 'Monarchien'', in *Chateaubriand avant le Génie du Christianisme,* ed. Béatrice Didier and Emmanuelle Tabet (Paris: Honoré Champion), 63–75.

Cohen, Margaret (1999) *The Sentimental Education of the Novel* (Princeton: Princeton University Press).

Contamine, Philippe (1996) 'Mourir pour la patrie', in *Les Lieux de mémoire II. La Nation*, vol. 1, ed. Pierre Nora (Paris: NRF-Gallimard), 11–43.

Cropper, Corry L. (2001) 'Fictional Documentary: the Other as France in Mérimée's *Les Mormons*', *French Literature Series* 28, 51–64.

Cropper, Corry L. (2004) 'Prosper Mérimée and the Subversive 'Historical' Short Story', *Nineteenth-Century French Studies* 33.1–2, 57–74.

Cropper, Corry L. (2008) *Playing at Monarchy. Sport as Metaphor in Nineteenth-Century France* (Lincoln: University of Nebraska Press).

Crouzet, Michel (1978) 'Province et Nation chez Stendhal', in *Stendhal et Balzac II. La Province dans le roman*, ed. Alain Chantreau (Nantes: Société Nantaise d'Etudes Littéraires), 35–60.

Crouzet, Michel (1983) *'Lucien Leuwen* et le 'sens politique'', in *Le plus méconnu des romans de Stendhal, Lucien Leuwen,* ed. Philippe Berthier et al (Paris: SEDES), 99–139.

Crouzet, Michel (1987) 'Introduction. Mérimée, ethnologue et mythologue romantique', in Prosper Mérimée, *Nouvelles,* vol. 1, ed. Michel Crouzet (Paris: Lettres Françaises), 9–60.

Darcos, Xavier (1998) *Prosper Mérimée* (Paris: Flammarion).

Darnton, Robert (1996) 'What was revolutionary about the French revolution?', in *The French Revolution in Social and Political Perspective,* ed. Peter Jones (London, New York, Sydney, Auckland: Arnold), 18–29.

Darriulat, Philippe (2001) *Les Patriotes, La Gauche républicaine et la nation, 1830–1870* (Paris: Seuil).

Déchaux, Jean-Hughes (1993) 'N. Elias and P. Bourdieu. Analyse conceptuelle comparée', *Archives Européennes de sociologie* 34.2, 364–385.

Dédéyan, Charles (1973) *Chateaubriand et Rousseau* (Paris: SEDES).

Del Litto, Victor (1978) 'La province dans l'oeuvre romanesque de Stendhal', in *Stendhal et Balzac II. La Province dans le roman,* ed. Alain Chantreau (Nantes: Société Nantaise d'Études littéraires), 21–34.

Dickenson, Donna (1995) 'A Chronology of George Sand', in *The Miller of Angibault,* ed. and trans. Donna Dickenson (Oxford: Oxford University Press), xxi-xxv.

Didier, Béatrice (1968) 'La Querelle du *Génie du Christianisme* ou l'imaginaire mis en question', *Revue d'Histoire Littéraire de la France,* 942–952.

Didier, Béatrice (1975) 'Le Moi et l'histoire chez Chateaubriand et Stendhal', *Revue d'Histoire Littéraire de la France,*1004–1017.

Didier, Béatrice (1988) 'Journal et autobiographie dans *Les Mémoires d'un touriste',* in *Relire Les Mémoires d'un touriste (1838–1988),* ed. Philippe Berthier (Grenoble: Presses Universitaires de Grenoble), 85–95.

Didier, Béatrice and Emmanuelle Tabet (eds) (2006) *Chateaubriand avant le Génie du Christianisme* (Paris: Honoré Champion).

Dubé, Pierre H. (1997) *Bibliographie de la critique sur Prosper Mérimée, 1825–1993* (Genève: Droz).

Duerr, Hans Peter (1988–2002) *Der Mythos vom Zivilisationsprozeß* (Frankfurt am Main: Suhrkamp).

Elias, Norbert (1996) *The Germans. Power Struggles and the Development of Habitus in the Nineteenth and Twentieth Centuries,* ed. Michael Schröter, trans. and introd. Eric Dunning and Stephen Mennell (Cambridge: Polity Press).

Elias, Norbert (2000) *The Civilizing Process. Sociogenetic and Psychogenetic Investigations,* ed. Eric Dunning, Johan Goudsblom and Stephen Mennel (Malden, MA and Oxford, UK: Blackwell).

Fauré, Christine and Tom Bishop (eds) (1992) *L'Amérique des Français* (Paris: François Bourrin).

Félix-Faure, Jacques (1974) *Stendhal, Lecteur de Mme de Staël. Marginalia inédits sur un exemplaire des Considérations sur les principaux événements de la Révolution française* (Aran, Switzerland: Editions du Grand Chêne).

Fermigier, André (1986) 'Mérimée et l'Inspection des monuments historiques', in *Les Lieux de mémoire II. La Nation,* vol. 2, ed. Pierre Nora (Paris: NRF-Gallimard), 593–611.

Fonyi, Antonia (ed) (1999) *Prosper Mérimée: Écrivain, Archéologue, Historien* (Genève: Droz).

Fonyi, Antonia (1999) 'La Passion pour l'Archè', in *Prosper Mérimée: Écrivain, Archéologue, Historien,* ed. Antonia Fonyi (Genève: Droz), 197–207.

Fonyi, Antonia (2008) 'Le Récit de Mérimée comme trajet épistémologique', in *Mérimée et le Bon usage du savoir,* ed. Pierre Glaudes (Toulouse: Presses Universitaires du Mirail), 77–92.

Fonyi, Antonia (ed) (2010) *Écritures XIX 6, Prosper Mérimée* (Caen: Lettres modernes Minard).

Frappier-Mazur, Lucienne (1992) 'Histoire et mémoire dans *Le Marquis de Villemer*', *Revue des Sciences Humaines* 276, 161–174.

Fritzsche, Peter (1998) 'Chateaubriand's Ruins. History and Memory after the French Revolution', *History and Memory* 10.2, 102–117.

Fumaroli, Marc (2003) *Chateaubriand. Poésie et Terreur* (Paris: Éditions de Fallois).

Gamboni, Dario (2007) The Destruction of Art: Iconoclasm and Vandalism since the French Revolution (London: Reaktion Books).

Garrigou, Alain (1998) 'Le suffrage universel, 'invention' française'', *Le Monde diplomatique,* http://www.monde-diplomatique.fr/1998/04/GARRIGOU/10288 (accessed 12 December 2012).

Garrigou, Alain (2002) *Histoire sociale du suffrage universel en France, 1848–2000* (Paris, Seuil).

Garval, Michael (2004) 'George Sand. Visions of the Great Women Writer', in Michael Garval, *'A Dream of Stone'. Fame, Vision, and Monumentality in Nineteenth-Century French Literary Culture* (Newark: University of Delaware Press), 112–157.

Gautier, Paul (1921) *Madame de Staël et Napoléon* (Paris: Plon-Nourrit).

Gengembre, Gérard (1989) *La contre-révolution ou l'histoire désespérante: histoire des idées politiques* (Paris: Imago).

Gerson, Stéphane (2003) *The Pride of Place. Local Memories and Political Culture in Nineteenth-Century France* (Ithaca: Cornell University Press).

Glaudes, Pierre (ed) (2008) *Mérimée et le Bon usage du savoir. La Création à l'épreuve de la connaissance* (Toulouse: Presses Universitaires du Mirail).

Glaudes, Pierre (2008a) 'Ce qui fait obstacle au savoir. La dialectique de la raison chez Mérimée', in *Mérimée et le Bon usage du savoir,* ed. Pierre Glaudes (Toulouse: Presses Universitaires du Mirail), 103–134.

Godechot, Jacques-Léon (1983) 'Introduction', in Germaine de Staël, *Considérations sur la Révolution française* (Paris: Tallendier).

Goldberger, Avriel H. (1987) 'Introduction', in Germaine de Staël, *Corinne, or Italy,* (New Brunswick, N.J.: Rutgers University Press), xv-liv.

Goldstein, Jan (2005) *The Post-Revolutionary Self. Politics and Psyche in France, 1750–1850* (Cambridge, MA: Harvard University Press).

Goodden, Angelica (2008) *Madame de Staël, the Dangerous Exile* (Oxford: Oxford University Press).

Gordon, Daniel (2002) 'The Canonization of Norbert Elias in France', *French Politics, Culture & Society* 20.1, 68–94.

Gouin, Thierry (1999) 'Eloge de la dupe. Étude d'un corps étranger dans le *Journal d'un voyage dans le Midi de la France*', *L'année Stendhalienne*, 29–46.

Guerlac, Suzanne (2005) 'Writing the Nation (Madame de Staël)', *French Forum* 30.3, 43–56.

Groen, Roy (2013) 'Feuilles mortes, Mémoires vivants – Chateaubriand et ses arbres', in *Chateaubriand et les choses,* ed. Franc Schuerewegen (Amsterdam : Rodopi), 119–135.

Gutwirth, Madelyn, Avriel Goldberger and Karyna Szmurlo (eds) (1991) *Germaine de Staël: Crossing the Borders* (New Brunswick: Rutgers University Press).

Habermas, Jürgen (2001) *The Postnational Constellation. Political Essays* (Cambridge: Polity Press).

Hamon, Bernard (2001) *George Sand et la politique,"Cette vilaine chose… "*, introd. Michelle Perrot (Paris: L'Harmattan).

Hamon, Bernard (2005) *George Sand face aux églises* (Paris: L'Harmattan).

Harlan, Elizabeth (2004) *George Sand* (New Haven: Yale University Press).

Hartiang, Shannon, Read McKay and Marie-Thérèse Seguin (eds) (1995) *Femmes et pouvoir: Réflexions autour d'Olympe de Gouges* (Moncton: Éditions d'Acadie).

Higonnet, Patrice (1998) *Goodness beyond Virtue. Jacobins during the French Revolution* (Cambridge, MA: Harvard University Press).

Hobsbawm, Eric (2005) 'The Dangers of Exporting Democracy. Bush's Crusade is based on a Dangerous Illusion and Will Fail', *The Guardian*, 22 January 2005 (accessed December 14 2012).

Huet-Brichard, Marie-Catherine (2008) 'Le barbare et le civilisé: Mérimée ethnologue dans *La Guzla*', in *Mérimée et le Bon usage du savoir*, ed. Pierre Glaudes (Toulouse: Presses Universitaires du Mirail), 55–73.

Isbell, John Claiborne (1994) *The Birth of European Romanticism: Truth and Propaganda in Staël's De l'Allemagne, 1810–1813* (Cambridge: Cambridge University Press).

Isbell, John Claiborne (1997) 'Narbonne, Mme de Staël et le programme 'anglais' de Coppet sous l'Assemblée législative', *Studies on Voltaire and the Eighteenth-Century* 358, 203–215.

Israel, Benjamin (2001) *Radical Enlightenment: Philosophy and the Making of Modernity, 1650–1750* (Oxford: Oxford University Press).

Israel, Benjamin (2006) *Enlightenment Contested: Philosophy, Modernity, and the Emancipation of man, 1670–1752* (Oxford: Oxford University Press).

Izemberg, Gerald N. (1992) *Impossible Individuality. Romanticism, Revolution, and the Origins of Modern Selfhood, 1787–1802* (Princeton: Princeton University Press).

Jaume, Lucien (1997) *L'individu effacé ou le paradoxe du libéralisme français* (Paris: Fayard).

Jeoffroy-Faggianelli, Pierrette (1979) *L'Image de la Corse dans la littérature romantique française: le mythe corse* (Paris: Presses Universitaires de France).

Jones, Peter (ed) (1996) *The French Revolution in Social and Political Perspective* (London, New York, Sydney, Auckland: Arnold).

Kadish, Doris Y. and Françoise Massardier-Kenney (eds) (2009) *Translating Slavery, Gender and Race in French Abolitionist Writing, 1780–1830* (Kent, OH: Kent State University Press).

Kete, Kathleen (2012) *Making Way for Genius. The Aspiring Self in France from the Old to the New Regime* (New Haven: Yale University Press).

Knee, Philip (2010) 'Mémoire et autorité: Chateaubriand ironiste', *Nineteenth-Century French Studies* 38.3–4, 147–158.

Kroen, Sheryl (2000) *Politics and Theater. The Crisis of Legitimacy in Restoration France, 1815–1830* (Berkeley and Los Angeles: University of California Press).

Le Bras, Hervé and Emmanuel Todd (1981) *L'invention de la France. Atlas anthropologique et politique* (Paris: Livre de Poche).

Le Goff, Jacques and René Rémond (eds) (1991) *Histoire de la France religieuse*, 3 vols (Paris: Seuil).

Le Hir, Marie-Pierre (1992) *Le Romantisme aux Enchères: Ducange, Pixerécourt, Hugo* (Amsterdam: John Benjamins).

Le Hir, Marie-Pierre (2007) 'Stendhal et l'invention de l'intellectuel', *Nineteenth-Century French Studies* 36.1–2, 21–44.

Le Hir, Marie-Pierre (2008) 'Le sentiment d'appartenance nationale dans l'oeuvre de George Sand', *Romantisme* 142.4, 91–104.

Le Hir, Marie-Pierre (2009) 'Olympe de Gouges, Feminism, Theater, Race', in *Translating Slavery, Gender and Race in French Abolitionist Writing, 1780–1830*, ed. Doris Y. Kadish and Françoise Massardier-Kenney (Kent, OH: Kent State University Press), 65–88.

Levy, Darline Gay, Harriet Branson Applewhite, Mary Durham Johnson (eds) (1979) 'The Trial of a Feminist Revolutionary, Olympe de Gouges', *Women in Revolutionary Paris 1789–1795* (Urbana & Chicago: University Press of Illinois), 254–59.

Lubin, Georges (1970) 'Introduction à l'*Histoire de ma vie*', in George Sand, *Oeuvres autobiographiques*, vol.1, ed. and introd. Georges Lubin (Paris: NRF-Gallimard, La Pléiade), xiii-xxviii.

Maillon, Jean and Pierre Salomon (1978) 'Approche de Mérimée', in Prosper Mérimée, *Théâtre de Clara Gazul, Romans et nouvelles* (Paris: NRF-Gallimard, La Pléiade), ix-lvi.

Maire, Catherine-Laurence (1998) *De la cause de Dieu à la cause de la Nation. Le Jansénisme au XVIIIe siècle* (Paris: Gallimard).

Maistre, Joseph de (1970) 'Extract from the Seventh of the St Petersburg Dialogues', in *The French Right (from de Maistre to Maurras)* ed. and introd. J.S. McClelland (London: Cape), 48–59.

Mathy, Jean-Philippe (2000) *French Resistance. The French-American Culture Wars* (Minneapolis: University of Minnesota Press).

McCall-Saint-Saëns, Anne E. (ed) (2004) *George Sand et l'Empire des lettres* (New Orleans: Presses Universitaires du Nouveau Monde).

McClelland, J.S. (1970) 'Introduction', *The French Right (from de Maistre to Maurras)* ed. and introd. J.S. McClelland (London: Cape), 13–36.

McClelland, J.S. (1970) 'Joseph de Maistre', *The French Right (from de Maistre to Maurras)* ed. and introd. J.S. McClelland (London: Cape), 37–38.

McClelland, J.S. (1970) *The French Right (from de Maistre to Maurras)* ed. and introd. J.S. McClelland (London: Cape).

McMahon, Darrin (2001) *Enemies of the Enlightenment: the French counter-Enlightenment and the Making of Modernity* (Oxford: Oxford University Press).

Mellor, Anne K. (2000) *Mothers of the Nation. Women's Political Writing in England, 1780–1830* (Bloomington: Indiana University Press).

Meynard, Cécile (2005) *Stendhal et la Province* (Paris: Honoré Champion).

Millet, Claude (1999) 'Le légendaire de Mérimée. Le mémorial de la barbarie', in *Prosper Mérimée: Écrivain, Archéologue, Historien*, ed. Antonia Fonyi (Genève: Droz), 89–97.

Minart, Gérard (2003) *Les opposants à Napoléon, 1800–1815: l'élimination des royalistes et des républicains* (Toulouse: Privat).

Mueller-Vollmer, Kurt (1991) 'Staël's *Germany* and the Beginnings of an American National Literature', in: *Germaine de Staël: Crossing the Borders*, ed. Madelyn Gutwirth, Avriel Goldberger and Karyna Szmurlo (New Brunswick: Rutgers University Press), 141–158.

Naginski, Isabelle Hoog (1991) *George Sand, Writing for her Life* (New Brunswick: Rutgers University Press).

Naginski, Isabelle Hoog (2000) 'Préhistoire et filiation: le mythe des origines dans *Jeanne*', *Romantisme* 110, 63–71.

Naginski, Isabelle Hoog (2003–2004) 'George Sand: ni maîtres, ni disciples', *Romantisme* 122, 44–53.

Nemoianu, Virgil (2006) *The Triumph of Imperfection. The Silver Age of Sociocultural Moderation in Europe, 1815–1848* (Columbia: University of South Carolina Press).

Nerozzi, Patrizia (2006) 'Sept ans de séjour en Angleterre', in *Chateaubriand avant le Génie du Christianisme*, ed. Béatrice Didier and Emmanuelle Tabet (Paris: Honoré Champion), 11–27.

Nesci, Catherine, Gretchen Van Slyke and Gerald Prince (eds) (1999) *Corps/décors: Femmes, orgie, parodie* (Amsterdam: Rodopi).

Nesci, Catherine (1999) 'La Passion de l'impropre: lien conjugal et lien colonial chez Olympe de Gouges', in *Corps/décors: Femmes, orgie, parodie*, ed. Catherine Nesci, Gretchen Van Slyke and Gerald Prince (Amsterdam: Rodopi), 45–56.

Nora, Pierre (ed) (1984) *Les Lieux de mémoires, I. La République* (Paris: NRF-Gallimard).

Nora, Pierre (ed) (1986) *Les Lieux de mémoires, II. La nation*, 3 vols. (Paris: NRF-Gallimard).

Ousselin, Edward (2007–2008) 'Mme de Staël et Victor Hugo face à la réalité et à la légende de Napoléon', *Nineteenth-Century French Studies* 36.1–2, 9–20.

Ozouf, Mona (1963) *L'Ecole, l'Église et la République, 1871–1914* (Paris: Armand Colin).

Ozouf, Mona (1984) 'Le Panthéon. L'École normale des morts', in *Les Lieux de mémoires*, vol.1, ed. Pierre Nora (Paris: NRF-Gallimard), 140–166.

Perrot, Michelle (1997) 'Sand, une femme en politique', in *George Sand. Politique et polémiques (1843–1850)*, ed. Michelle Perrot (Paris: Imprimerie nationale), 7–57.

Perrot, Michelle (1999) 'Preface', in *Sand-Barbès, Correspondance d'une amitié républicaine 1848–1870*, ed. Michelle Perrot (Lectoure: Editions Le Capucin), 5–16.

Poisson, Olivier (1999) '*La Vénus d'Ille*. Entre archéologie et littérature en 1834', in *Prosper Mérimée: Écrivain, Archéologue, Historien*, ed. Antonia Fonyi (Genève: Droz), 27–38.

Polowetzky, Michael (1993) *A Bond Never Broken: The Relations between Napoleon and the Authors of France* (London and Toronto: Associated University Presses).

Poulot, Dominique (1986) 'Alexandre Lenoir et les musées des Monuments français', in *Les Lieux de mémoire II. La Nation*, vol. 2, ed. Pierre Nora (Paris: NRF-Gallimard), 497–531.

Prickett, Stephen (2009) *Modernity and the Reinvention of Tradition* (Cambridge: Cambridge University Press).

Rebardy, Emmanuelle (1997) 'La révolution contraire: Chateaubriand et le *Génie du Christianisme*. 1802: Genèse d'une pensée réactionnaire', *Annales de la Révolution française*, 499–501.

Reddy, William M. (1997) *The Invisible Code. Honor and Sentiment in Post-revolutionary France, 1814–1848* (Berkeley and Los Angeles: University of California Press).

Regard, Maurice (1978a) 'Notice *sur L'Essai sur les révolutions*', in Chateaubriand, *Essai sur les révolutions, Génie du Christianisme* (Paris: NRF-Gallimard, La Pléiade), 1377–1580.

Regard, Maurice (1978b) 'Notice sur le *Génie du christianisme*,' in Chateaubriand, *Essai sur les révolutions, Génie du Christianisme*, (Paris: NRF-Gallimard, La Pléiade), 1580–1967.

Régnier, Philippe (2004) 'Théories et pratiques sandiennes de l'indépendance: entre champ littéraire et champ politique', in *George Sand et l'Empire des lettres*, ed. Anne McCall-Saint-Saëns (New Orleans: Presses Universitaires du Nouveau Monde), 129–147.

Reid, Martine (2010) *Des femmes en littérature* (Paris: Belin).

Rémond, René (1962) *Les Etats-Unis devant l'opinion française. 1815–1852*. 2 vols (Paris: Armand Colin).

Renan, Ernest (1882) *Qu'est-ce qu'une nation?* (Paris: Calmann-Levy).

Renan, Ernest (1882) *What is a Nation?*, www.nationalismproject.org/what/renan.htm (accessed 28 August 2013).

Rincé, Dominique (1977) 'Les premières oeuvres de Chateaubriand: la génèse d'un projet autobiographique', *Revue d'Histoire littéraire de la France*, 30–47.

Ringer, Fritz K. (1992) *Fields of Knowledge. French Academic Culture in Comparative Perspective 1890–1920* (Cambridge: Cambridge University Press).

Rouff, Marcel (1929) *La Vie de Chateaubriand* (Paris: Gallimard).

Roulin, Jean-Marie (1994) *Chateaubriand, l'exil et la gloire. Du roman familial à l'identité littéraire dans l'œuvre de Chateaubriand* (Paris: Honoré Champion).

Rosi, Ivanna and Jean-Marie-Roulin (eds) (2009) *Chateaubriand, penser et écrire l'histoire.* (Saint-Etienne: Publications de l'Université de Saint-Etienne).

Rubat du Mérac, M.-A (1994) 'La correspondance entre Sand et Lamennais', in *George Sand et son temps: hommage à Annarosa Poli*, ed. Elio Mosele (Genève: Slatkine), 410–417.

Rumph, Stephen C. (2004) *Beethoven after Napoleon. Political Romanticism in the late Works* (Berkeley and Los Angeles: University of California Press).

Sacquin, Michèle (1998) *Entre Bossuet et Maurras. L'Antiprotestantisme en France de 1814 à 1870* (Paris: École des Chartes).

Schmitt, Alain (2010) 'Mérimée libéral', in *Écritures XIX 6, Prosper Mérimée*, ed. Antonia Fonyi (Caen: Lettres modernes Minard), 105–115.

Schor, Naomi (1993) *George Sand and Idealism* (New York: Columbia University Press).

Schraeder, Peter J. (ed.) (2002) *Exporting Democracy: Rhetoric vs. Reality* (Boulder: Lynne Rienner Publishers).

Schuerewegen, Franc (ed.) (2013) *Chateaubriand et les choses* (Amsterdam: Rodopi).

Schraeder, Peter J. (2002) 'Promoting an International Community of Democracies', in *Exporting Democracy*, ed. Peter Schrader (Boulder: Lynne Rienner Publishers), 1–14.

Schwerhoff, Gerd (1998) 'Zivilisationsprozeß und Geschichtswissenschaft: Norbert Elias' Forschungsparadigma in historischer Sicht', *Historische Zeitschrift* 266.3, 561–605.

Scott, Joan Wallach (1996) *Only Paradoxes to Offer. French Feminists and the Rights of Man* (Cambridge, MA: Harvard University Press).

Scott, Joan Wallach (2005) *Parité: sexual equality and the crisis of French universalism* (Chicago: Chicago University Press).

Sepinwall, Alyssa Goldstein (2005) *The Abbé Grégoire and the French Revolution. The making of modern universalism* (Berkeley: University of California Press).

Sewell, William H. (1994) *A Rhetoric of Bourgeois Revolution. The Abbé Sieyès and What Is the Third Estate?* (Durham, NC and London, UK: Duke University Press).

Sluga, Glenda (2003) 'Gender and the Nation: Madame de Staël or Italy', *Women's Writing* 10.2, 241–251.

Smethurst, Colin (2009) 'L'histoire au service du discours politique', in *Chateaubriand, penser et écrire l'histoire*, ed. Ivanna Rosi and Jean-Marie Roulin (Saint-Etienne: Publications de l'Université de Saint-Etienne),147–157.

Spitzer, Alan B. (1987) *The French Generation of 1820* (Princeton: Princeton University Press).

Sternhell, Zeev (1978) *La Droite révolutionnaire 1885–1914. Les origines françaises du fascisme* (Paris: Seuil).

Sutherland, D.M. G. (2003) *The French Revolution and Empire: The Quest for a Civic Order* (Oxford: Blackwell).

Tackett, Timothy (1996) 'Nobles and the Third Estate in the revolutionary dynamic of the National Assembly, 1789–1790', in *The French Revolution in Social and Political Perspective*, ed. Peter Jones (London, New York, Sydney, Auckland: Arnold), 314–338.

Thiele-Knobloch, Gisela (1991) 'Preface', in Olympe de Gouges, *Théâtre politique* (Paris: Côté-femmes), 7–32.

Thiesse, Anne-Marie (1999) *La Création des identités nationales. Europe XVIIIᵉ-XXᵉ siècle.* (Paris: Seuil).

Tocqueville, Alexis de (2000) *Democracy in America* [1835,1840], ed. Harvey C Mansfield and Delba Winthrop (Chicago: University of Chicago Press).

Trahard, Pierre (1928) *La Jeunesse de Prosper Mérimée. Prosper Mérimée de 1834 à 1854.* (Paris: Honoré Champion).

Trahard, Pierre (1930) *La Vieillesse de Prosper Mérimée de 1854 à 1870* (Paris: Honoré Champion).

Vallois, Marie-Claire (2001) 'Gendering the Revolution: Language, Politics, and the Birth of the Nation', *The South-Atlantic Quarterly* 100.2, 423–445.

Vanpée, Janie (1999) 'Performing Justice: The trials of Olympe de Gouges', *Theater Journal* 51, 45–65.

Venayre, Sylvain (2013) Les *Origines de la France. Quand les historiens racontaient la nation* (Paris: Seuil).

Walsh, Henry. H. (1967) *The Concordat of 1801. A Study of the Problem of Nationalism in the Relations of Church and State* (New York: AMS Press).

Weber, Eugen (1976) *Peasants to Frenchmen. The Modernization of Rural France, 1870–1914* (Stanford: Stanford University Press).

Weil, Patrick (2004) *Qu'est-ce qu'un Français? Histoire de la nationalité française depuis la Révolution* (Paris: Gallimard).

White, Charles I. (1856) 'Notice of the Viscount de Chateaubriand', in François René de Chateaubriand, *The Genius of Christianity* (Baltimore: John Murphy & Co; Philadelphia, J.B. Lippincott & Co; London: Charles Dolman), 23–42.

Wick, Daniel (1996) 'The court nobility and the French Revolution: the example of the Society of Thirty', in *The French Revolution in Social and Political Perspective*, ed. Peter Jones (London, New York, Sydney, Auckland: Arnold), 214–230.

Witkin, Sylvie Charron (1995) 'Les Nouvelles de George Sand: fictions de l'étrangère', *Nineteenth-Century French Studies* 23.3–4, 365–372.

Zielonka, Anthony (1983) ''La Province' et 'le provincial' dans *Lucien Leuwen*', in *Le plus méconnu des romans de Stendhal* Lucien Leuwen, ed. Philippe Berthier (Paris: SEDES), 37–56.

Index of names

Index of subjects

.

www.ingramcontent.com/pod-product-compliance
Lightning Source LLC
Chambersburg PA
CBHW050451270326
41927CB00009B/1696